Collection and Recollections

Collection and Recollections

Economic Papers and their Provenance

I. M. D. Little

CLARENDON PRESS · OXFORD
1999

Oxford University Press, Great Clarendon Street, Oxford OX2 6DP
Oxford New York
Athens Auckland Bangkok Bogotá Buenos Aires Calcutta
Cape Town Chennai Dar es Salaam Delhi Florence Hong Kong Istanbul
Karachi Kuala Lumpur Madrid Melbourne Mexico City Mumbai
Nairobi Paris São Paulo Singapore Taipei Tokyo Toronto Warsaw
and associated companies in
Berlin Ibadan

Oxford is a registered trade mark of Oxford University Press

Published in the United States
by Oxford University Press Inc., New York

First published 1999

British Library Cataloguing in Publication Data
Data available

Library of Congress Cataloging in Publication Data
Little, Ian Malcolm David.
Selected papers / I.M.D. Little.
p. cm.
Includes bibliographical references.
1. Economics. I. Title.
HB103.A2L58 1999 330—dc21 98-40743
ISBN 0-19-829524-3

1 3 5 7 9 10 8 6 4 2

Typeset by Hope Services (Abingdon) Ltd.
Printed in Great Britain
on acid-free paper by
Bookcraft Ltd.
Midsomer Norton, Somerset

Acknowledgements

Jean Floud and my wife, Lydia Segrave, have read and commented on all the autobiographical chapters. Maurice Scott advised me on the selection of papers, and commented on, and provided figures for, the section on fund management in Part III. I am grateful for their help. I am also grateful to Elaine Herman for secretarial assistance.

Contents

PART I: HOW I BECAME AN ECONOMIST

PART II: MOSTLY WELFARE ECONOMICS

PART III: DEVELOPMENT ECONOMICS

PART IV. LOOSE ENDS

PART I

How I Became an Economist

This historical snippet is written entirely from memory. I was born on 18 December 1918. I have never kept a diary, and have no records other than my RAF log book. I do not think that anyone who knew me as a child is alive. All my siblings are dead, and probably all the cousins who knew me. Some school fellows may survive, but they would not remember anything of interest about me. A very few who knew me as an undergraduate before the Second World War are alive, and rather more who knew me in the period 1945–7 when I was again an undergraduate. But I have consulted none of them.

Ancestry and Education, 1918–1948

NATURE

My lineage on both my father's and my mother's side is devoid of any intellectual or artistic distinction. It so happens that my Little forebears have been traced back at least to the fourteenth century, but not because of high distinction. My Little grandfather, born in 1810, became a full general and was knighted. One earlier Little. a doctor, was also knighted: him apart, there were no professionals—no clergymen, lawyers, bankers, or civil servants. They seem to have been mostly merchants, farmers, and land agents. None before my generation went to a university, but one did win the Grand National. My father, who, like his father, commanded the Ninth Lancers, went to Sandhurst.

On my mother's side, there was one forebear of immense but not intellectual distinction: Mr Thomas Brassey, who at the time of his death in 1870 had I believe built about five per cent of the world's railways, operating in North and South America, Europe, Russia, India, and Australia.

Brassey's three sons accomplished less. The eldest, who eventually became Earl Brassey, was a junior minister, and a governor of Victoria. He wrote a book on wages.[1] This is the only incursion into the realm of economics made by anyone before myself of known Little or Brassey descent. It was a worthy pedestrian work, full of facts and anecdotes, but with little or no analysis. The most notable passage is:

> On my father's extensive contracts, carried on in almost every country of the civilised world and in every quarter of the globe, the daily wage of the labourer was fixed at widely different rates; but it was found to be the almost invariant rule that the cost of labour was the same—that for the same sum of money, the same amount of work was everywhere performed. (p. 75)

The reality of the conclusion of Paul Samuelson's famous 'factor price equalization' theory was thus established three-quarters of a century before he advanced it. But I do not think that Samuelson was inspired by the need to explain an interesting phenomenon.

Earl Brassey was distinguished more as a yachtsman than as a politician. Assisted by his wife and a crew of about thirty, as plain Mr Brassey he sailed his

[1] Brassey, *On Work and Wages.*

yacht, the 'Sunbeam', around the world in 1876/7. I believe this was the first circumnavigation of the globe by a private yacht. His wife wrote an enduring account of the voyage.[2] Later Brassey took Mr Gladstone on a three-week holiday trip to Norway in 1885. He was made a baron in the following year.

My grandfather Mr Albert Brassey, the youngest of Thomas Brassey's three sons, was neither ennobled nor knighted. He was master of the Heythrop hounds for forty-five years. He was also an MP for nine years. A tribute paid to him states: 'He never caught the Speaker's eye, but was beloved by the Whips for his regular attendance.'[3] Such regularity must have interfered with hunting, and he resigned declaring that he preferred the appellation MFH to MP.

NURTURE

Thanks to Thomas Brassey, I was brought up in a wealthy household. The interests of my parents and my four elder brothers centred on the horse. They hunted, played polo, and went racing. My father, who was 60 when I was born, also bred thoroughbreds in a minor way. All my brothers rode well. I, like my elder sister, was an exception and was never very happy on a horse.

The house was almost wholly devoid of any intellectual or artistic content. The few books I remember included several of John Buchan's novels, and one or two volumes of the campaigns of Stonewall Jackson. (Presumably my father must have attended some campaign course during his military career.) There was also a volume of the verse of the Australian national poet J. B. (Banjo) Patterson. I was much moved by 'Old Pardon, the Son of Reprieve', showing that I was not wholly detached from horse sentimentality. This was there because Patterson, who was a reporter during the Boer War, presented it to my father, who was then commanding the regiment to which Patterson was attached. Unfortunately, this inscribed volume was lost in one of many subsequent moves.

The daily papers taken were the *Morning Post*, the *Daily Mail*, and the *Sporting Life*. When the *Morning Post* ceased to exist, it was replaced by *The Times*. The *Daily Mail* was cancelled after my father's death. The weeklies were the *Horse and Hound*, the *Field*, and the *Illustrated London News*; there may have been *Punch*, but I am not sure.

There was virtually no music in the house. There was a gramophone, but I can recall only three records, of which only one was music. I think it was *Cavalleria Rusticana*. I do not think that my lack of musical ability can be fully accounted for by this absence of music. It is quite extraordinary. I cannot reproduce a note, though I can hear the difference between notes. I have no musical memory at all, so that I do not recognize any tunes, not even 'God Save the Queen', for sure. I

[2] Lady Brassey, *A Voyage in the Sunbeam*. [3] *Vanity Fair*, 15 March 1906.

also have no sense of rhythm, so that I cannot dance competently. But now I am straying beyond the boundaries of purely intellectual history.

SCHOOL

I shared my sister's governess (my sister, like her mother, did not go to school) until the age of 9 when I went to a small boarding school. The teaching and my brains were good enough to get me into Eton. I think it would have been very unusual indeed to fail. My father died while I was still at prep school.

At Eton I was usually near the bottom of the top forms in my year. In exams ('trials') I did better, and was usually third in the overall marking. This was because I worked very hard preparing for them. I suppose I was quite competitive, and needed to shine in the exam placings, as I was no good at games. However, I showed no flair. I have lost my school reports, but recall one from Mr Wilkes, later headmaster of Radley: he reported that I would never be a scholar. One deficiency that I remember very clearly was an inability to learn by heart. Those like myself who opted not to join the Officers Training Corps (OTC) were committed to a period of 'saying lessons', whence I discovered this incapacity. I knew then that I could never be an actor, or pursue any career that involved public speaking. It also made me desperate to leave Eton as soon as my entry to New College, Oxford, was assured. Staying on would have propelled me into the sixth form. Members of the sixth form were required to accept the honour of making a 'speech' (saying lesson!) to an audience of parents on the fourth of June—Eton's great day. This was an ordeal the prospect of which terrified me. I badgered my mother tirelessly, thanked God for success, and departed abroad, supposedly to learn German, in January 1937, thus enjoying a 'gap year' before going up to Oxford in October. I chose German because trying to learn French at school had put me off that language. French would have been very useful later; German never was.

Eton did nothing to arouse any lasting interest in any subject, and so compensate for the lack of culture at home. After taking School Certificate, I specialized in history. I do not now remember even what periods I studied. I had been above average in mathematics, but one could continue with it, after taking School Certificate, only if one was of scholarship material. This was a fault of the system. It would have been a great advantage to have been able to continue with some mathematics after the age of 16.

The travel of the gap year in Switzerland and Austria gave me some small measure of self-confidence which had been woefully lacking. My horizons, if not my mind, were broadened by making friends who were not horse-bound; and I learned to ski and did some mountaineering. But there was no intellectual breakthrough.

OXFORD

Back in England, in my first year at Oxford. I was a lost soul. I suppose my state of mind might now be described as undergoing an identity crisis. What would I become? Where was I going? Long circular walks produced no answer. None of the possibilities apparently open to the youngest son of a Shires family attracted me at all. Nothing did. There was no enthusiasm. I had chosen to read politics, philosophy, and economics (PPE), largely because these subjects were not taught at school, but the prelude of 'Pass Mods' seemed a bleak beginning. I went back to hunting and racing. I took up drinking and gambling, and did very little work. The gathering threat of war did not help. As I had not joined the OTC at school, I thought I was in danger of becoming a mere private in the army when war broke out. An RAF officer seemed a more comfortable option, so I joined the OU Air Squadron, and the RAF Volunteer Reserve. I learned to fly competently, without any problems.

My state of mind improved greatly in my second year. I began philosophy, with Isaiah Berlin as my tutor. I had never met anyone remotely like him. This was not surprising, since there never has been anyone remotely like him. He could not help being a stimulus. I remember the first tutorial vividly. He said, you must write an essay on 'Cogito ergo Sum'. My Latin was just about good enough to translate. I feebly enquired what I should read. He said 'There is nothing worth reading. Well, I suppose you should look at Descartes himself.' Rather similarly, he could not recommend any lectures; the lecturers were either charlatans or very boring.

A fellow undergraduate, C. M. Woodhouse, was even more instrumental in awakening my latent abilities. He was held in high regard as a first-class classical scholar, who won university prizes. The fact that he enjoyed talking to me, about philosophy and life in general, was very reassuring. He convinced me that I had a good mind, and that I had the makings of an intellectual, a concept new to me. During the war, when he was not incommunicado in the mountains of Greece, he continued our friendship by correspondence. I owe him a lot.

An interest in philosophy had certainly been aroused, though it was somewhat narrowly based on Descartes, Locke, Berkeley, and Hume, with a whiff of Kant. Apart from these classics, Ayer's *Language, Truth, and Logic* was highly influential, and seemed to make it quite unnecessary to read many volumes of tedious stuff. I must also have read some economics, though I cannot recall what. I did buy Keynes's *How to Pay for the War* when it came out in March 1940. I think I understood it. My intellectual arousal had come too late for there to have been any possibility of my doing well in Schools. If it had not been for the war I would not have got a first, perhaps not even a second.

THE WAR

I was called up only a few days after war was declared on 3 September 1939. The next six years as a pilot in the RAF were intellectually uneventful. A very few strong-willed determined persons used the many hours of professional idleness to further their education. I was not one of them, and spent a lot of time playing cards, smoking, and drinking beer—like most of my companions. I had in my second year at Oxford agreed unenthusiastically that I might try to become a barrister, and had therefore eaten a few dinners at Grays Inn. I started a correspondence course in Contract Law, but did not get very far with it. I think I read Ayer's *Foundations of Empirical Knowledge* soon after it was published in 1940. I recall giving my wife-to-be some instruction in philosophy a few years later; happily, this did not put her off marrying me. From this, and from annotations in a few books bought in the war years, it appears that I continued to read a little in the British empirical tradition. The seed had been sown, and as the end of the war came into sight I had determined to return to Oxford, take my degree, and if possible become a don. I was not officially released from the RAF until February 1946, but I managed to wangle special leave which permitted me to go back to Oxford in October 1945.

If one admits to having been an RAF pilot, one is almost always asked 'In fighter or bomber command?' I was never in either, spending the greater part of the war in a unit called the Airborne Forces Experimental Establishment. There I flew some rather strange machines, including a Willys Jeep converted into a rotary wing glider. I was awarded an AFC.

AN UNDERGRADUATE AGAIN, 1945–1947

Those returning after the war were allowed to take Schools in two of the three subjects of PPE. I had no difficulty in dropping politics; as taught to me before the war, it had seemed a very uninspiring non-analytic subject. This meant that I took six papers, three in philosophy and three in economics.

In philosophy I began again with Isaiah Berlin, sharing tutorials with Geoffrey Warnock. I think I seldom got beyond the third sentence of the essay I had written. But it was fun. 'That was Averell Harriman', he gave as an explanation of one rather lengthy interruption on the telephone. We both moved to Herbert Hart, who was very new to teaching philosophy. He said I was his last client as a barrister (there was some rearrangement of a family trust of which I was unaware) and his first pupil. According to Jenifer, his widow, he arranged to have Geoffrey and myself at the beginning of the week so that he would have a good idea of the questions that might come later from other undergraduates. Herbert once told me that a pupil had fallen asleep in a tutorial. I asked him what he did;

he said, 'I lowered my voice.' I went to a few lectures and seminars—those of John Austin, who destroyed my faith in Freddie Ayer; Waismann, who was believed to be conveying a taste of Wittgenstein; and Gilbert Ryle, whom I got to know.

In economics I was sent to Philip Andrews. Henry Phelps Brown, the economics tutor at New College, did not, I think, come back from the army in time to teach for the Michaelmas term. When he did he probably felt rusty, and anyway did not wish to break the Andrews connection. Philip Andrews soon became a very controversial figure with his book *Manufacturing Business*, which challenged orthodox imperfect competition theory. He was a very competent tutor for Statistics and Organization (the more applied policy-oriented paper). He was not much good for principles, apart from his own special corner. I do not think he understood much of macroeconomics. There was no good macroeconomic textbook available in 1946, and the recent journal articles I was recommended to read seemed to implode into a maelstrom of confusion. This had the great advantage of making me think that there was room for me in the subject.

A GRADUATE STUDENT: NUFFIELD AND ALL SOULS, 1947–1949

I got an un-vivaed First in Schools in 1947. One had a viva voce examination only if one was near a border line, to give one a chance of pushing oneself up a class. I soon had to choose between philosophy and economics. I chose economics although I thought I was better at philosophy. The main reason was that in philosophy one could only teach philosophy. Although I wanted to be a don, the fact that economics offered wider possibilities was an attraction in case I got tired of academic life. Also, although I was more confident in philosophy than economics, it seemed to me that philosophers were cleverer than economists and so the competition would be more severe.

I applied for and obtained a graduate studentship at Nuffield College. In effect, I had done less than a year's economics. I did not know what I wanted to do (for a B.Litt. or D.Phil.) and suggested some study of J. S. Mill's economics and philosophy. There was no graduate programme. John Hicks became my supervisor. Possibly for this reason, I read some welfare economics. This acted as an irritant, and I began thinking about, and very soon writing about, welfare economics. Mill was forgotten. The gist of this writing is in the first selection from my work contained in this book. It is clearly critical of Hicks. He was affronted, and tried to divert me from theory, or any critique of theory, to some empirical study. I was not amenable. He threatened to get my studentship discontinued. I called in philosophers to redress the balance of economic power. Gilbert Ryle (and, I think, Isaiah Berlin) interceded with the warden, Sir Henry Clay. My studentship was saved.

Hicks and I parted company. David Champernowne became my new supervisor, and my studentship continued. This turned out to be unimportant, for I took the All Souls Prize Fellowship Examination, and was elected a Fellow in November 1948. Isaiah Berlin has remarked that I was the most ignorant person ever to have been elected a Fellow of All Souls. He was certainly right then, and almost certainly remains right.

In 1948 and 1949 I produced a flurry of articles on the theory of economic behaviour and welfare. These were mostly incorporated in *A Critique of Welfare Economics*, which was my doctoral thesis submitted in the spring of 1949, just two years after taking Schools. In the preface of the book (dated August 1949) I thanked Professor D. G. Champernowne, Mr G. D. N. Worswick, Mr T. Wilson and Mr P. W. S. Andrews for reading some or all of an earlier draft, and for making various helpful criticisms. I was also indebted to Mr C. A. R. Crosland, at whose insistence 'many improvements of style and exposition have been made'.

Probably of even greater influence than these were three graduate students working, respectively, in Oxford, Cambridge, and London. They were L. W. Mackenzie, J. de V. Graaff, and W. J. Baumol. Lionel Mackenzie submitted a doctoral thesis on welfare economics, which was rejected. Roy Harrod was one of the examiners. Lionel has since told me that Harrod was right, and that his thesis was too poetical. He was not then a high-powered mathematician. He knew more than I, but that was not difficult. Perhaps it was this rejection that stimulated him to become one of the half-dozen leading mathematical economists in the world.

Jan Graaff's definitive *Theoretical Welfare Economics* was not published until 1956. But his work was contemporaneous with mine, and we had many conversations. He was the most brilliant theorist of his generation studying in England. But he did not always convince me that I was wrong where we differed. I was astonished to discover that he did not regard himself as an economist, and had no intention of becoming one—to which he adhered, despite occasional re-incursions into British academe. I knew, but was not quite so well acquainted with, Bill Baumol at the time. His thesis, which became that excellent book *Welfare Economics and the Theory of the State*, was exactly contemporaneous with mine; however, I was quicker off the mark and managed to publish a year earlier. Both Jan Graaff and Bill Baumol became and have remained good friends, despite being quite forceful critics.

My thesis was examined by Arthur Lewis and David Worswick. There was a routine question, followed by the traditional glass of sherry. After a few changes it was submitted to Macmillan, and was rejected. I was shown the anonymous referee's report. This said that I seemed incapable of grasping the elementary distinction between the size of the cake and the way it is sliced. As it was a very central and closely argued message of the thesis that no such distinction can be drawn because one does not know the size of the cake until one knows how it is sliced, this was a frustrating comment. I do not know for certain who the referee was, but I think it was Pigou. I then submitted the typescript to the Oxford University Press. Hubert Henderson was the referee, and told me so. He very quickly advised the Delegates of the Press to publish it.

Not long after, I was at a party in Strasbourg where Tony Crosland was attending the Council of Europe. He introduced me to Harold Macmillan saying, 'This is Ian Little whose brilliant book you refused to publish.' I received a very limp handshake, and never met him again. I did not then know that he could shake hands only limply. In any case the decision was wrong. *A Critique* sold about 70,000 copies.

This completes the account of my intellectual development up to about 1949, when my economic career may be said to have begun.

1949–1953: ALL SOULS, TRINITY, AND NUFFIELD

I had begun to teach in my studentship year at Nuffield College, when I taught general philosophy for New College. I hazily remember Lord Montague as a pupil. I do not suppose that Berkeley and Hume inspired the foundation of his famous motorcar museum. While at All Souls I was also a lecturer in economics at Merton and University Colleges. This was when I first got to know Tony Crosland, who became a close friend. I succeeded him as Economics Tutor and Fellow of Trinity College in 1950. In my two years at Trinity I wrote two articles included in this volume, 'Direct versus Indirect Taxes' and 'Social Choice and Individual Values'.

I was elected an Official Fellow of Nuffield College in 1952. Although Trinity common room was a friendly and amusing place, I accepted Nuffield in order to escape undergraduate teaching. I spent one year at Nuffield before getting leave to become Deputy Director of the Economic Section of the Treasury in 1953. I spent this year writing *The Price of Fuel*, an essay in applied welfare economics. Some wondered that I could apply welfare economics after (supposedly) demolishing the theory. I tried to justify this in the preface to *The Price of Fuel*. I have mostly been doing applied welfare economics ever since.

All my work in welfare theory was done before I joined the Treasury. The next chapter discusses this work, and what I believe to be its value. The first four papers in Part II illustrate it.

PART II

Mostly Welfare Economics

The best introduction to this part is to review sympathetically A Critique of Welfare Economics, *for this book incorporates all my work on welfare theory, excepting only 'Social Choice and Individual Values', an article which is reprinted in this volume. I am sorry that it is a posthumous review, in that the book went out of print about twenty years ago. It had sold about 70,000 copies, despite being rather unfavourably reviewed, or not reviewed at all, in the learned journals.*[1]

[1] The number sold is an estimate, as the records have gone astray. I think the paperback edition was selling over 500 copies a year in the early 1970s, but this was not considered enough to justify reprinting a paperback.

Welfare Theory

I think *A Critique* advanced four ideas of some importance. First, it grounded welfare economics on individual choice. Using Occam's razor, it showed that the theory was based on the value judgement that a person was better off in one situation than in another if the former could be said to have been chosen rather than the latter. This was not, perhaps, a very important contribution. But it was a shade more austere than Paul Samuelson's concept of 'revealed preference'. One did not have to suppose that choice revealed preference. A person might choose B rather than A although he or she preferred A. One could jump straight to the value judgement that welfare was increased if someone should reach a chosen position, and be better off in this sense. One did not need to claim that he or she was more satisfied. One did not have to be a utilitarian.

If 'in a chosen position' were to be judged objectively from market information, then there would be no room for the concept of indifference. I therefore labelled the traditional 'iso-utility' or 'indifference' curve a 'behaviour line', the points on which could be thought of as ordered. This did not catch on. However, emphasizing the choice criterion of being better off was useful. It is more transparent to discuss whether 'in a chosen position' is an acceptable criterion of being better off, than it is to discuss whether greater utility is a good criterion. The budding economist need no longer write an essay about the meaning of utility. Chapter 2 of *A Critique* explained all this. It concluded that traditional welfare economics could be based on an ordinal utility system interpreted in terms of choice. Cardinal utility was not required. But this did not imply that I thought that interpersonal comparisons of satisfaction or happiness could not be made, or were value judgements. I revert to this matter when discussing distribution.

The second advance I attribute to *A Critique* is, I think, more important. It was argued that welfare economics is essentially an ethical subject. Its conclusions concern the welfare of societies—whether or not, for instance, some change of economic policy would make people better off. Put like this, it seems that no one could deny the need for some value premisses. But then, economists did not put matters so starkly. They considered that concepts such as wealth, real income, economic efficiency—even economic welfare—could be given 'objective' definitions. Some probably still do. *A Critique* maintained that, if welfare economics was to be more than a classroom exercise, then all such expressions must be interpreted in terms of the welfare of communities, that is of collections of persons.[2] Economics is not so pure a subject that the ordinary language implications of the words it uses should be neglected. This is fully argued in 'The Foundations of Welfare Economics', Paper 1 in this collection, which was published before *A Critique* in 1949. Paper 2 is the concluding chapter of *A Critique*. It is not only a good summary of my thinking at the time, but is also a statement that I can still endorse.

I can claim some success for my insistence on the importance of attending to the ordinary language implications of economic concepts. Before *A Critique*, reference was often made to 'the optimum' in economic articles and books. In *A Critique* the word 'optimum' was always put in inverted commas, or else the phrase 'Pareto optimum' was used. This has caught on among economists. The 'optimum' is successfully neutered by the sobriquet 'Pareto'. Who or what is Pareto?! However, this success is limited, for 'economic efficiency' and similar expressions are still often used to persuade people that some policy would be good without those persuaded having any idea as to the connection between so-called economic efficiency and anything they would see as an improvement in the state of society. (I sometimes do it myself.)

The third important feature of *A Critique* was the insistence that one should not ignore the distribution of gains and losses when claiming that some change would increase or decrease the welfare of society (or real income, or economic efficiency). The so-called 'new welfare economics' associated with the names of Hicks and Kaldor, against which I was tilting, advanced the idea that one could speak of an increase in welfare if the gainers from a change could more than compensate the losers, thereby, it was thought, bypassing the problem of interpersonal comparisons of utility. (The new welfare economists were not full-blooded utilitarians, for they did not believe that utility was a cardinal magnitude that could be summed over individuals.) I was not the first to attack the criterion of hypothetical over-compensation,[3] but I did so with notable force. The need to consider distribution led to the formulation of a sufficient criterion for an increase in welfare that included a judgement concerning the desirability of any redistribution that was involved, of which more anon.

Another variant of the new welfare economics, which also seemed to side-step interpersonal comparison of utility, was based on the concept of a social welfare function (SWF). A SWF implies that all configurations of society—all social states—are somehow consistently valued, in the same way as a rational individ-

[2] Productive efficiency may be seen as an exception. The adjective 'productive' suggests that this sort of efficiency may have its limitations regarded as something necessarily desirable. Moreover, a clear meaning can be and is assigned that is independent of the wealth or welfare of persons. Productive efficiency is thus taken to mean that no more of anything can be produced without there being less of something else.

[3] Baumol, 'Community Indifference'.

ual values all the possibilities open to himself. This made it possible to derive the economic requirements, or necessary conditions, for what has come to be called a Pareto optimum, that is a state of society such that it is impossible to make one person better off without making another worse off. I complained that this approach tended to concentrate on such necessary conditions for an 'optimum' to the neglect of sufficient conditions for an improvement, and was in this respect utopian. Moreover, even if a Pareto optimum state were achieved, there was still the problem that it might well be worse than a great many sub-optimal states. One might decrease welfare in moving to a Pareto optimum. It was the combination of the need, for any application of welfare theory, to compare sub-optimal states, and to consider who gained and lost from a move from one to the other, that resulted in the Little criterion (see below).

The fourth feather of *A Critique* that stands out is the intuitive recognition of what is known as second best theory. An important conclusion of this theory is that satisfying one of the necessary conditions for a Pareto optimum when others are not satisfied does not entail that the gainers thereby could compensate the losers. Anyone who wades through Chapters VIII and IX of *A Critique*, in which I elaborated the 'optimum' conditions of production and exchange, will find this point stressed time and again. The article 'Direct versus Indirect Taxes', reproduced here as Paper 3, is also an early example of the application of second best theory. The usual case against indirect taxation was that it drove a wedge between the rates of production transformation and of consumer substitution of goods. But this ignored another 'optimum' condition, that of the equality of the rates of substitution and transformation of leisure and goods. This equality, previously satisfied for leisure and the untaxed good, would be destroyed by a move from indirect to direct taxation. It followed that direct taxation was not necessarily superior.

Unfortunately for me, I did not name the theory! This was later done by James Meade, whose Chapter VII of *Trade and Welfare* is entitled (somewhat misleadingly, for there are no general marginal conditions for the second best) 'The Marginal Conditions for the Second Best'. Meade correctly wrote: 'if there are a number of existing divergences between marginal values and costs, then the reduction of one of these divergences—the others all remaining unchanged—will not necessarily lead to an increase in economic welfare'. He then worked out a number of arithmetic examples of this, using distributional weights. However, the theory is usually and rightly associated with Lipsey and Lancaster, who generalized it in an enlightening manner (with extensive references to *A Critique*).[4]

THE LITTLE CRITERION

For the reasons given above, and in Paper 2, a sufficient condition for an economic change to be said to increase economic welfare was that (*a*) it would

[4] Lipsey and Lancaster, 'The General Theory of Second Best'.

produce a not-unfavourable redistribution of income, and (*b*) the losers by the change could not bribe the gainers to vote against it without losing more than they would if the change were carried. The distributional judgement must be made, or at least accepted, by whoever decides whether or not to make the change. The proviso (*b*) was called the Scitovsky criterion. The dual criterion is the Little criterion.

A fuller analysis of when a change should be made involves also a consideration of the Kaldor–Hicks criterion (which is satisfied if the gainers could compensate the losers) and of whether compensation can actually be paid. This was laid out somewhat incorrectly in the first edition of *A Critique*, and correctly in the second edition (Chapter VI). But the narrower version of the Little criterion suffices for the discussion here.

The criterion evoked strong attacks, principally by K. J. Arrow, in his generally rather unfavourable review of the first edition,[5] and C. M. Kennedy.[6] I corrected an error pointed out by Arrow in the second edition (1956), and he has not, so far as I am aware, commented since. But an explosion of comment erupted in the *Economic Journal* in 1962 and 1963 following a review of the book by James Meade in 1959. This review extravagantly praised the book, apart from the criterion, which Meade mistakenly claimed to be contradictory. In the subsequent exchanges, Meade admitted his mistake but continued to maintain that the Little criterion was redundant, and that distributional considerations should enter in by attaching weights to individuals' consumption, as in his Chapter VII of *Trade and Welfare*. I do not know whether it is the nature of the subject or my own style that creates misunderstanding. But misunderstanding was certainly rife in these exchanges, which include contributions by Sir Dennis Robertson, J. E. Meade, E. J. Mishan, Maurice Dobb, Amartya Sen, and Charles Kennedy (and, of course, myself). Sen brilliantly clarified the issues, and buried the corpse for many years. He and Sir Dennis tentatively found some use for the criterion. Meade doubted this and Kennedy, as before, lampooned it. Dobb and Mishan misinterpreted what I was trying to do, Dobb in particular being unable to escape from the notion that there is something out there like a cake, which can have both a size and a distribution. Some fifteen years later the corpse was resurrected, and 'rehabilitated', by Y.-K. Ng.[7] This rehabilitation was supported by Kotaro Suzumura.[8] Only Asians understand and sympathize with my views! My own last word is Paper 4 (1979) in this volume, in which I claim that the criterion is active and well. I continue to maintain this claim.

Before leaving the subject, I should emphasize that I am not against using distributional or 'social' weights, and that Little and Mirrlees (*Project Appraisal and Planning for Developing Countries*, 1974), showed how a decision-maker might do

[5] Arrow, 'Little's Critique of Welfare Economics'.

[6] Kennedy, 'The Economic Welfare Function and Dr Little's Criterion'.

[7] Ng, *Welfare Economics*.

[8] Suzumura, 'On Distributional Value Judgements and Piecemeal Welfare Criteria'.

so. This was in contrast to the *Manual of Industrial Project Analysis in Developing Countries* by Little and Mirrlees (1969), where distribution was accorded a less formal treatment. The World Bank manual of cost–benefit analysis[9] used the same system of weighting as Little and Mirrlees (1974)—and the term 'social analysis' was used. If weights were not applied, the term 'economic analysis' was used. There was quite strong opposition within the Bank to using distributional weights, and I am not aware that they were ever used in operational project appraisal. Opposition came from such influential economists as Al Harberger and Bela Balassa, and in general from members of the Chicago School. Since they surely could not argue that distribution was irrelevant, it would seem that they implicitly preferred the Little criterion.

Much interesting work, especially on optimal taxation, implies interpersonal comparability and uses a cardinal utility framework. This does not commit the author to a Benthamite conception of utilitarianism whereby marginal utility means some amount of pleasure or satisfaction. The distributional weights or marginal utilities can be interpreted as the value judgements of the decision-maker, who consults his Paretian social welfare function.[10] That, however, puts an end to any discussion.

It now seems to me that the 'new welfare economics' based on ordinal utility or choice theory, as expounded in *A Critique*, usefully demonstrated the minimal behaviouristic basis needed for deriving most of the widely accepted propositions of welfare economics; but it also inhibited the analysis of social and ethical problems that can be usefully discussed only by appeal to interpersonal comparisons of pleasure, satisfaction, and happiness, as well as other factual or ethical considerations.

Paper 5, 'Social Choice and Individual Values', has an interesting genesis. I was at the time (probably late 1951) a Fellow of Trinity College, Oxford. Like other colleges, Trinity did not provide its fellows with any secretarial assistance, although I doubt whether any of them could type. I obviously felt that it was a very urgent matter to set Arrow's theory in proper context, and did not want to waste time (or money). So I sent the article to the *Journal of Political Economy* in manuscript. The editor or his assistant was no doubt perplexed. It was thought that the reason for the archaic form of my submission was that there was still a shortage of paper in England. I received back across the Atlantic a thick parcel of paper. So I found a typist, and the article was resubmitted and accepted straightaway without comment. Fortunately, the concept of a referred journal did not yet exist.

The article is included in Part II although one of the main points made was that Arrow's famous book of the same title had no bearing on traditional welfare economics. One of the reasons given was that the conditions required of a

[9] Squire and Van der Tak, *Economic Analysis of Projects*.

[10] See Sugden and Weale, 'A Contractarian Reformulation of Certain Aspects of Welfare Economics'.

satisfactory 'social welfare function' (SWF) were stated in terms of changes in individual ordering, whereas the *locus classicus* of a SWF[11] stated it for a given set of orderings.[12] It seems that too much was made of this, in that it has been subsequently shown that a very similar impossibility theorem can be proved for a given set of orderings.[13]

More important is the article's attack on the very idea that an ordering produced by rule from a set of individual orderings should be considered as a moral order to which I might be obliged to defer. So I objected strongly (and still do) to the phrase 'social welfare function'. This objection was not on the grounds that the strength of preferences should be taken into consideration in making social decisions, though I agree that sometimes it should be. It is rather that no general will exists: and I did not need Professor Arrow to prove it.

I do not differ from Professor Bergson's latest (so far as I know) interpretation of his famous 1938 article which set the SWF in motion.[14] Applied welfare economics is a form of counselling for some decision-maker. Provided the decision-maker accepts the standard Pareto criteria, the economic adviser can do business. But he can refuse to counsel if he disapproves of the decision-maker's values, or even if he disapproves of the way in which the decision-maker came to be in that position.

This fits in perfectly with the Little criterion. How, then, does a so-called social welfare function come in? When the counsellor asks the decision-maker whether he approves or disapproves of some movement along a utility possibility curve, it has to be presumed that the latter has a consistent ordering of points in utility space in mind, to avoid all possibility of contradiction if he is repeatedly asked for a ruling. This supposed ordering is called the social welfare ordering, and the decision-maker's answers are deemed to be a function of that ordering. Of course, in practice no decision-maker will have more than a very partial ordering in mind, and he may not be asked for many rulings. So progress can perhaps be made, and decisions taken.

Finally, I note that Professor Bergson concluded 'there is, I think, further reason to conclude, as I have concluded before, and others, chiefly Little (1952) and Samuelson (1967a, b)[15] have also concluded: that the Impossibility Theorem is at most only tenuously related to welfare economics. Continued affirmation otherwise can only be at the expense of confusion regarding both Arrow's real contribution and welfare economics.'

[11] Bergson, *Foundations of Economic Analysis*.

[12] But Bergson himself used the phrase 'economic welfare function'.

[13] Kemp and Ng, 'On the Existence of Social Welfare Functions, Social Orderings and Social Decision Functions'.

[14] Bergson, 'Social Choice and Welfare Economics under Representative Government'.

[15] The references to Samuelson are (*a*) Foreword in Graaff, *Theoretical Welfare Economics*, and (*b*) 'Arrow's Mathematical Politics', in Hook, *Human Values and Economic Policy*.

The Treasury (1953–1955) and the years 1955–1958

The economy was peaceful during my time at the Treasury, 1953–5. I saw the Chancellor, R. A. Butler, only once, when my boss, Sir Robert Hall, was away. I was supposed to lead the Economic Section on foreign economic policy, a subject to which I had paid no more attention than was required for undergraduate teaching.

The main non-event I remember was a second attempt by the Bank of England and the Overseas Finance Division of the Treasury to make the pound convertible on current account for non-residents. The first attempt had been made in 1952, and is well known as Robot. It was defeated by Sir Donald MacDougall and Lord Cherwell.[1] This second attempt, called 'the collective approach', is not so well known. I wrote a long internal document in 1954 rejecting the collective approach as too dangerous, while advocating a gradual approach to convertibility; this latter was not easy, given the existing European Payments Union and our sterling area liabilities. It may have played some part in consolidating views within the Economic Section, and even in securing the rejection of the collective approach.[2] Convertibility was finally achieved only in 1958, following a German initiative.

My personal life was not peaceful at this time, which may or may not have reduced my effectiveness. However, although there does not seem to have been anything clearly wrong with my economic work,[3] the 'establishment' must have decided that I was not suited to be a member. Unlike many economists who became temporary civil servants, I was never again offered an appointment, or supported by the government for one, except when my close friend Tony Crosland was a minister (see below). Maybe I sometimes gave a false impression of being frivolous, insouciant, and unreliable. An article I wrote on the role of economic advice, which was critical of the economic reasoning of Treasury officials, may not have helped.[4]

[1] MacDougall, *Don and Mandarin*.

[2] I have a copy of this document which may be of historical interest, but I thought it too long and too dated for inclusion here. It is mentioned in Cairncross and Watts, *The Economic Section 1939–1961*, p. 153. This work gives an account of the collective approach and the part played by the Economic Section.

[3] Witness Cairncross and Watts, *Economic Section*, and Lord Roberthall's diaries (Cairncross 1991).

[4] Little, 'The Economist in Whitehall'.

Between leaving the Treasury in 1955 and 1958, when I went to India and became a 'development economist', I did some miscellaneous research, in addition to a little supervision of graduate students. The most important work was preparing the second edition of *A Critique*. I also spent the best part of two delightful summer vacations in Italy working at the Cassa di Mezzogiorno (Svimez) with Paul Rosenstein Rodan, the founder of development economics. This resulted in a life-long friendship and a pamphlet on the need for nuclear energy in Italy.[5] I supervised and co-authored a worthy but very boring book on concentration in British industry on behalf of the National Institute for Economic and Social Research.[6] I wrote an article on capital theory,[7] which arose from giving a seminar (with my old antagonist Charles Kennedy) on Joan Robinson's fleetingly famous book.[8] I think this convinced me that my minimal mathematics precluded me from making any contribution to economic theory. I have included none of this in the present volume.

Together with Professor R. R. Neild and the late C. R. Ross, I wrote in 1957 a long Memorandum of Evidence for the Radcliffe Committee.[9] This downplayed the use of monetary policy to influence aggregate demand, or inflation. I believe it echoed the views of the Economic Section of the Treasury (of which we had all been members), which viewed with alarm a new faith in the efficacy of regulating the quantity of money, which was becoming apparent in the mid-1950s. I have not included the memorandum in this volume because full capital convertibility and vast increases in the volume of capital flows has made some of the discussion too dated. However, some of what seems to me to remain valid concerning the use of monetary versus fiscal policy was repeated in 1963 in my chapter on 'Fiscal Policy' in G. D. N. Worswick and P. H. Ady (eds.), *The British Economy in the 1950s*. Excerpts from this chapter are included as Paper 16 in part IV, and discussed in the chapter on 'Miscellaneous Activities'.

[5] Little and Rosenstein Rodan, 'Nuclear Power and Italy's Energy Position'.

[6] Evely and Little, *Concentration in British Industry*.

[7] Little, 'Classical Growth'.

[8] Robinson, *The Accumulation of Capital*.

[9] Committee on the Working of the Monetary System, Principal Memoranda of Evidence, vol. 3, no. 23.

I

The Foundations of Welfare Economics (1949)

1. THE CRITERION FOR AN INCREASE IN WELFARE

The formulation of the theory of economic welfare, which appears to be accepted by many economists today, consists of a number of elegant deductions from unacceptable premisses. This paradoxical state of affairs is the result of some logical and philosophical confusions. It is proposed, in this article, to discuss the criteria for an increase in the economic welfare of individuals and of society, and other related questions.

The criterion for an increase in the economic welfare of an individual over some earlier situation is that the goods of the earlier situation are in the later situation rejected in favour of those actually bought; i.e., the earlier set of goods could again have been bought, but was not. This criterion may be written for short $\Sigma p_2q_2 \geqslant \Sigma p_2q_1$. It seems that most people would probably be willing to accept this criterion. But, as thus stated, it is not adequate for the purposes of welfare theory. It must also be assumed that there are individuals who are perfectly consistent;[1] that is, roughly speaking, the pattern of their economic behaviour must remain unchanged so long as all prices remain unchanged. It is possible that eagerness to apply the theorems of welfare economics may have led economists to overestimate the consistency of individuals, and perhaps also to overestimate the extent to which the choice criterion of an increase in economic welfare is acceptable. But with these matters we shall not here concern ourselves. We shall assume that if 'on a higher behaviour line or indifference curve' can be taken to mean anything, then it is a good criterion for an increase in the economic welfare of the individual, so long as he is independent of the welfare levels of other individuals. That is all that welfare theory requires.

Welfare economics is primarily concerned with the welfare of the community, and not the individual. The latter is only important in so far as it is thought that changes in the welfare of a group must be defined in terms of changes in the welfare of individuals. Since 1939 writers on welfare economics have relied largely

This paper first appeared in *Oxford Economic Papers*, NS1 (June 1949). Permission to reproduce is gratefully acknowledged.

[1] I have sought to explain more exactly the meaning of consistency in a previous article: 'A Reformulation of the Theory of Consumer's Behaviour', *OEP*, NS1, Jan. 1949.

on the criterion for an increase in social welfare proposed by Mr Kaldor.[2] This criterion is to the effect that social welfare has increased if a certain change has benefited at least one person and harmed no one; or, if some are harmed, then the beneficiaries must be able to compensate the losers without any of them themselves becoming losers, and at least one of them remaining a beneficiary.[3]

The salient feature of the new welfare economics is that it does not require the assumption that satisfactions are quantities which can, therefore, be added. In fact, different individuals' satisfactions are regarded as incommensurable, and the class, each member of which is the satisfaction of a different individual, is a heterogeneous collection. Now one such collection can only be said to be larger than another if some one item is larger and no item is smaller. This is the *only* meaning which can be attached to 'larger than' when one is dealing with incommensurable items. Therefore, if 'general welfare' refers to a collection of satisfactions, then one cannot, as a matter of logic, say that the general welfare has increased if anyone is harmed. Yet clearly there is nothing absurd about saying that the general welfare has increased when some people are harmed. It is frequently said, and there is nothing wrong with saying it.

From the above argument it follows either (1) that everyone who regards such a statement as 'the general welfare has increased' as meaningful is a utilitarian, in that he believes it makes sense to speak of adding different people's satisfaction, or (2) that 'the general welfare' does *not* refer precisely to a collection of satisfactions. Of these alternatives, the first is false, and therefore the second must be accepted. Also, since the criterion under consideration only provides *hypothetical* compensation for the losers, it follows that anyone who accepts it must either make interpersonal comparisons and decide that money has the same utility for everyone, or must abandon the view that 'the happiness of the group' is a name for a collection of individual satisfactions. Of these alternatives, the first again must be abandoned, because the new welfare economics prides itself on having got rid of the necessity of comparing different individuals' satisfactions.

Since, therefore, the happiness (or well-being) of the group is not the name of a collection of satisfactions, it must be otherwise defined; or, rather, some instructions about the usage of the phrase 'increase in the happiness (or well-being) of the group' must be given. Now it may be claimed that this is just what the criterion under consideration does. An 'increase in general welfare' is to be regarded as a technical term, and the criterion instructs us how to use it.

[2] N. Kaldor, 'Welfare Propositions in Economics and Interpersonal Comparisons of Utility', *EJ*, Sept. 1939.

[3] A. Bergson, in his important article 'A Reformulation of Certain Aspects of Welfare Economics' (*Quarterly Journal of Economics*, 1938), does not propose a sufficient criterion for an increase in economic welfare. He deduces the 'optimum' conditions from explicit value premisses as necessary conditions for a formal economic Utopia. On this formulation, the only sufficient condition for an increase in economic welfare, which is implied, is that all the 'optimum' conditions, together with an 'optimum' real income distribution, be put into operation together. It is Utopia or nothing.

Since the new welfare economists are not utilitarians, the above position seems to be the only possible one which they can take up. Is there anything wrong with this position? The answer would be 'no' if the phrase under discussion were of the same type as, for instance, the word 'gravity' or the word 'force'. But it is not of the same type, and it is indefensible to claim that this is a perfectly objective scientific procedure. Such phrases as 'an increase in general welfare' and 'an increase in the happiness of society' and 'socially advantageous' are persuasive, influential, quasi-ethical terms. Any definition which one proposes for a phrase of this kind conceals an ethical judgement. There is no doubt that, if one states that a certain change would increase the general welfare, or would benefit society, then one's statement implies that that change is *good*, and that it ought, other things being equal, to be made. By 'other things being equal' is meant 'assuming that no other ethical considerations are involved'. Thus, it follows from the nature and usage of welfare language that welfare judgements are, partly at least, value judgements. It should be noted that this does not exclude the possibility that they may also be descriptive. One can, of course, both describe some change and imply that it is good. This is exactly what one is doing if one lays down a definition of 'an increase in welfare', and then uses the phrase in accordance with the definition. Thus, when a new welfare economist states that a certain change has increased welfare, he is stating that either someone has benefited and no one has lost; or that, if there are losers, the beneficiaries could compensate them, and at least one person end up as a beneficiary. What is not generally realized is that he is also saying that this is a good thing to have occurred. To put the matter shortly, one may say that any definition (or criterion) of an increase in the general welfare is bound to be a persuasive definition, or criterion, in just the same way as any definition of 'a gentleman' is a persuasive definition.[4]

There is, of course, no reason why we should not make persuasive definitions if we want to, but we should realize what we are doing. It has been claimed that the new welfare economics is objective and scientific, because it was thought that by rendering interpersonal comparisons unnecessary value judgements had been eliminated. As will be argued later, it is not only false that interpersonal comparisons are not required, but it is also false that interpersonal comparisons are primarily value judgements. They are quite certainly more scientific and more objective than judgements about 'the welfare of society'.

We may now examine the question whether the criterion under consideration is acceptable or not. I think it could be regarded as acceptable if a large majority of people would be likely to accept it. (The mere fact that people might refuse to accept it is sufficient proof that it is a persuasive criterion.) Now it seems unlikely that many people would accept the proposed criterion, largely because it only makes compensation hypothetical. Thus, if a certain change makes the poor poorer, but the rich so much richer that they could compensate them, we

[4] Persuasive definitions were brought to light by Professor Stevenson, in an article of that title in *Mind*, March 1938.

must, by this criterion, say that the welfare of the community has increased, even if the poor are not, in fact, compensated. It is suggested that, in the prevailing climate of opinion, comparatively few people would be prepared to recommend such a change; yet to say that such a change would increase the welfare of society is to recommend it. The trouble is not that people would never say that welfare had increased when some people were harmed, but that they would want to know which individuals, or what class of individuals, was to suffer. The criterion proposed in no way identifies the individuals to be harmed. Everyone, except one person, might be harmed, and it would still be an increase in welfare.

Some objections may now be considered. The first objection is that the new welfare economics is about changes in *economic* welfare, not welfare in general. But to say that the economic welfare of society has increased can only mean that economic causes have increased the welfare of society. It may happen that some change, which would be called an economic change, would have both economic and political effects. These effects may be held respectively to cause an increase and a decrease in welfare—in which case one might say that economic welfare had increased and political welfare decreased. To say then that economic welfare has increased is, in effect, to say that the consumption of goods (in a very wide sense) and the work done have changed in a favourable manner. Thus, if a person argues that a certain change would increase economic welfare, it is open to anyone to argue that it would decrease spiritual or political welfare. Therefore, if the word 'economic' is inserted before the word 'welfare', the persuasive and influential effect of the statement is diminished. It is diminished, but not eliminated; after all, people still feel strongly even about economic welfare. Moreover, and this is important, while economists may begin by writing about changes in *economic* welfare—or, weaker still, changes in real income—the phraseology often gets changed after a few pages into the more forceful mode of expression. The frequent omission of the word 'economic' is not insignificant.[5]

The second objection is that, even if what is here maintained is true, still a choice of colourless language can be made and, once again, the new 'welfare' economics would be respectable and scientific. This objection is valid, but it misses the fact that it is welfare that people are interested in. Some people, on the one hand, want to make recommendations, and others want to be told, without the

[5] It should be noted that, in the article cited, Mr Kaldor did not explicitly propose the hypothetical compensation formula as a criterion for an 'increase in welfare'. He actually proposed it as a criterion for (*a*) 'an increase in physical productivity', (*b*) 'an increase in aggregate real income', and (*c*) 'an increase in the sum total of wealth'. Later, in reply to an article by W. J. Baumol, attacking the hypothetical compensation formula ('Community Indifference', *RES*, 1946–7), Mr Kaldor wrote: 'The important point surely is that when the production of wealth goes up, some income distribution could be found which makes some people better off, and no one worse off than before.' This is not an important point, but an important definition of the phrase 'increase in the production of wealth'. All these four phrases are emotive and suggest, more or less strongly, that a change, such that the gainers by it could compensate the losers, would be a good thing. Why can't we just say that the change would benefit some people enough to compensate those who lost? Why must we go on to describe such a change as increasing the sum total of wealth, etc.?

responsibility of deciding for themselves, what is the best thing to do. If they are told without its becoming too obvious that they are being told, so much the better. It is, in fact, attractive to some people to have a theory which tells them what is the best thing to do. If the emotive and influential elements of welfare theory were removed, it would lose a great deal of its appeal, for people would then have to think how far the changes described really were relevant to their welfare judgements. A colourless transcription of 'this change would increase the welfare of society' would be: 'If this change were made, then we should have a situation in which it would theoretically be possible to put everyone (if everyone was like the perfectly constant and consistent "individual" of economic theory) in such a position that they could choose at least what they had now. Practically, of course, it could not be done; some would gain and some would lose.' Most people would surely want to know more before they were prepared to say 'Yes, it would increase the welfare of society.' The theory of 'welfare economics' could certainly be stated in colourless language, just as Euclidian 'geometry' need not employ spatial words. But, if the theory is to be applied, a normative interpretation is essential. Indeed, applying 'welfare economics' (that is, removing the inverted commas) is nothing other than giving it a normative interpretation. And if the theory is to be interesting in any other way than as a purely logistical exercise, it must be interpreted. The choice is not between an uninterpreted abstract system, which employs colourless concepts so as not to suggest an interpretation, and a normative system, but rather between an acceptable and an unacceptable normative system.

We must now examine a defence of the Kaldor criterion which has been put forward by Mr Hicks.[6] Mr Hicks writes:

> In fact, there is . . . a perfectly objective test which enables us to discriminate between those reorganizations which improve productive efficiency and those which do not. If A is made so much better off by the change that he could compensate B for his loss, and still have something left over, then the reorganization is an unequivocal improvement. . . . If the economic activities of a community were organized on the principle of making no alterations in the organization of production which were not improvements in this sense, and making all alterations that were improvements that it could possibly find, although we could not say that all the inhabitants of that community would be necessarily better off than they would have been if the community had been organized on some different principle, nevertheless, there would be a strong probability that almost all of them would be better off after the lapse of a sufficient length of time.

It may be noticed that Mr Hicks does seek to justify the criterion and that he is thereby, in effect, agreeing that one cannot simply define changes in welfare as one will. It may also be noted that he begins by giving a criterion for an improvement in productive efficiency, but ends up by saying that a reorganization which effects this is an '*unequivocal improvement*' (my italics). The justification for

[6] J. R. Hicks, 'The Rehabilitation of Consumer's Surplus', *RES*, Feb. 1941, p. 111.

saying this is that, if all such 'improvements' were made, then, after a long time, almost everyone would be better off than he would have been otherwise. If this were true, it might be considered to be a good justification for saying that such a policy would, in the end, probably lead to an improved state of affairs, though not for saying that every change made under that policy was itself an improvement. But is it true? It is very dangerous to appeal to a long period of time, because over a long period tastes change, and the criterion for an individual's change in welfare becomes very shaky (or, if one insists too much on its rigorous interpretation in terms of indifference curves, it becomes meaningless). For the same reason, changes that would otherwise have been correct by the criterion may cease to be correct. Also, over a long period of time many people die, and, for this reason, the contention that almost everyone would be better off becomes rather absurd. Again, Mr Hicks appeals to a whole series of such changes. But a whole series of the kind of changes envisaged would require political adjustments; so, when appealing to such a series of changes, it becomes important to insert the word 'economic' before the word 'improvement'. Finally, even if it could be said that there was a high probability that almost everyone would be economically better off in the end, it would not follow that everyone would agree that the result could be said to be an unequivocal improvement.

Nevertheless, there is clearly something in this justification. Whether it would be held to justify a series of changes or not would clearly depend on the magnitude of the expected potential 'gains'. It might, for instance, justify us in introducing important labour-saving inventions. Then, especially if the large losers were actually compensated, distributional effects might more or less cancel out. Admittedly, in some cases the compensation of large losers might be thought wrong in that they might be held to be the sort of people who ought to be made poorer. Prevailing ethical opinion would, on the other hand, probably think it better to make a redistribution of income in a less arbitrary manner.[7] Perhaps it might also be applied to a series of changes, such as making price equal to marginal cost in a large number of firms. It should be noted, however, that it only follows from 'welfare' theory that price ought to equal marginal cost if *all* other 'optimum' conditions of production and exchange are fulfilled. It is quite wrong to suppose that the theory implies that price ought to equal marginal cost in a few public utilities in an economy in which the other 'optimum' conditions are certainly not fulfilled, and where price is not equal to marginal cost elsewhere. It is indeed exceedingly difficult to imagine a *real* economy in which one could say with any reasonable degree of confidence that if price were made equal to marginal cost then the gainers could compensate the losers. Although, then, there

[7] It should be noted that the advocacy of actual compensation does not (as has been stated) necessarily 'betray' a conservative bias. It may rather 'betray' a bias towards equity. It is quite consistent to hold that the rich ought to be made poorer, and that those rich people who lose as a result of a certain change ought to be compensated. Indeed, this attitude appears to prevail in England at present.

seems to be something in Mr Hicks's justification, we must conclude that there is certainly not enough in it to justify the extraordinary emphasis which, in recent economic literature, has been laid on the fulfilment of the 'optimum' conditions of production and distribution.

Whatever the merits of the justification discussed above, in relation to certain kinds of change, there are other kinds of change to which it could not be reasonably applied. For instance, the institution or removal of a general tariff would be a change which could not reasonably be said to form part of a series of changes, the distributional effects of which would cancel out. Taking, then, a change which has to be decided alone on its own merits or demerits, we find ourselves back at the difficulty that such a change cannot properly be said by the new welfare economists to increase economic welfare unless full compensation is paid to everyone, which is impossible and might be undesirable.

Unless we admit the discussion of changes which alter the distribution of real income, and set a valuation on the alteration, we remain within the realm of what Professor Samuelson has called ''twere better' statements. 'Twere better to make the change and compensate all losers, rather than do nothing. The Hicksian justification we discussed above is, in fact, an appeal to the conservative forces of nature to make our compensations for us.

Professor Samuelson seeks to emerge from this realm of useless statements by introducing some mythical personage, who arranges all conceivable configurations of the economic system in order of value. He lays down an economic welfare function. A position of increased welfare is a position which is higher up on the perfectly ordered scale of values belonging to this personage. What this really boils down to is that welfare conclusions cannot be reached without value premisses. The introduction of such a 'policy-maker' is, of course, only an expositional device. It must not be taken to mean that the welfare economist has to wait for someone to lay down value judgements so that he can get on with the job of making deductions. There is no reason why we should not reach welfare conclusions so long as we make clear what our premisses are. Our chief point is that among our premisses there must be some value judgement about the distribution of real income. This remains the case even when we think that distribution can be left to take care of itself. Mr Hicks, in effect, argued that distributional effects can be neglected. This outburst of classical optimism seems to involve (*a*) the factual statement that such effects will be small, and (*b*) the value judgement that, being small, they ought to be neglected.

Why are some economists so keen on avoiding obvious value judgements? Presumably because they want to be scientific and objective. If this is their wish, then they must not become welfare economists. They may, of course, confine themselves to the formal logical system which has recently called itself welfare economics, so long as they take care not to give their system a suggestive interpretation. There is little objection to such conclusions as '*x* will extend the possibility-locus to the north-east', if it is made clear that this form of words must not be interpreted as 'x will increase welfare'. However, if economists do so confine themselves they are not, of course, being scientific or objective; as pure mathematicians or logicians, they live only in the realm of symbols and words.

We have already introduced the value judgement that it is a good thing that an individual be in a chosen position. We now propose that every welfare conclusion must be premissed by a judgement to the effect that the change in question will at least not lead to an unfavourable distribution of income. As an alternative, we could use the premiss that a man is happier if in a chosen position, in which case our conclusions about the happiness of the community would require the premiss that the change will not cause a redistribution which would tend to decrease the happiness of the community. We propose to use the former set of premisses, because we are discussing welfare economics, and not happiness economics. The two are not the same thing. The word 'welfare' is at once less descriptive and more recommendatory than the word 'happiness'. It would perhaps have been better if happiness economics had not given place to welfare economics. People would have been more inclined to suspect such a conclusion as 'the happiness of the community would be increased if price were made everywhere equal to marginal cost' than they do the conclusion 'welfare would be increased if. . . . ' The difference is terminological, but not *merely* terminological. Terminological differences can be of enormous importance. Happiness conclusions require happiness premisses, and welfare conclusions, value premisses.

Having decided to introduce the distribution of real income as a variable, we now have three different kinds of change.[8] First there will be changes which would lead to an unfavourable redistribution.[9] These we can dismiss fairly briefly. They do not satisfy our most important premiss, so it does not matter to us whether the Kaldor–Hicks criterion is satisfied or not. This is not to say that there is anything fundamentally indeterminate about these cases. It might, for instance, happen that a rich person was made so very much better off that someone, who considered that distribution ought to be more equal, would nevertheless judge the change to be good, although a poor man was harmed. Our system cannot, however, say anything about such cases. If the change in distribution is unfavourable, nothing follows. It may, however, be noted that it might be possible in such cases to pay compensation in such a way that there would be no unfavourable distribution effects. In that event, compensation ought to be paid, and the case then comes under one of the following two classes.

The second class comprises those changes in the distributional effects of which would be thought to be small, such that it is therefore thought that these effects would not be unfavourable. Of such changes as these, we can say that they

[8] A more formal presentation of some of the argument of the following two pages has been given in my article 'Welfare and Tariffs', *RES*, 16/2 (1949).

[9] It should be noticed that we can lump together questions of justice and welfare, and simply ask whether a certain change in distribution would be a good thing. A change in distribution could be said to increase welfare but be undesirable on grounds of equity. We require as a premiss the judgement that the redistribution would not be bad, taking everything into consideration.

increase welfare if they also satisfy the Kaldor–Hicks criterion. The ground for saying this is not that everyone would be better off (even if every man were an economic man). It is rather that a similar but 'neutral' redistribution of income (e.g. by lump-sum payments) could not make everyone as well off as they would be if the change were carried out. The redistribution by itself would not decrease welfare. Therefore the same redistribution carried out in such a way that the gainers could over-compensate the losers would increase welfare.

Our third class consists of changes which would have a considerable but favourable effect on real income distribution. This class is more complicated than the other two. We can, indeed, say that such changes would increase welfare if they also passed the Kaldor–Hicks criterion. But that is not to say that the change ought to be made, because it might conceivably be possible to increase welfare more by carrying out the real income distribution which the change would cause in a 'neutral' manner, and without making the change. The explanation of this possibility requires a discussion of Professor de Scitovszky's objection to the Kaldor–Hicks criterion.

Scitovszky pointed out that the Kaldor–Hicks criterion for an increase in welfare might give rise to a contradiction.[10] Suppose that a change passed by this criterion is made, no compensation being paid. We may then have a distribution of real income which might differ considerably from the initial distribution. It would then be possible that the reverse change (back to the initial situation) would also be sanctioned by the criterion. In order to get over this difficulty, Scitovszky suggested a double criterion for an increase in welfare. Welfare is increased if (*a*) the gainers could over-compensate the losers, and if (*b*) 'the people who are against the change would be incapable of bribing those in favour to vote against it, without thereby losing more than they would if the change were carried'.[11] The second part of this criterion is the Kaldor–Hicks criterion in reverse. It asks whether, given that every individual were actually in the position he would be in after the change, the gainers by the reverse change could compensate those who would lose by it. If they could do so, then the Scitovszky criterion (as we will call the criterion (*b*) above) is not satisfied.

The double criterion is, formally speaking, an improvement. But we cannot accept it as a criterion of an increase in welfare. If compensation is not paid, nothing alters the fact that there would, as a result of the change, be some actual gainers and some actual losers. If compensation is paid, the 'contradiction' cannot arise. Nevertheless, the Scitovszky amendment is important. We can use it to tell us whether a favourable redistribution of real income, which a certain change would cause, would be better brought about by making the change, or by redistributing money in a 'neutral' manner.

Let us return to our case, where a change passed the Kaldor–Hicks criterion and caused a favourable redistribution. Given the situation after the change, it

[10] T. Scitovszky, 'A Note on Welfare Propositions in Economics', *RES*, 9/1 (1941).

[11] T. Scitovszky, 'A Reconsideration of the Theory of Tariffs', *RES*, 9/2 (1941).

would be possible, if the Scitovszky criterion is not satisfied, further to increase welfare by making the reverse change and compensating the losers. It clearly follows that it would have been better not to have made the change, and instead to have simply redistributed money. If, on the other hand, the Scitovszky criterion were satisfied, it would not matter whether the Kaldor–Hicks criterion were satisfied or not. Redistributing money alone would increase welfare, and if we actually did this, and if the Scitovszky criterion then proved to have been satisfied, it would follow that we could further increase welfare by making the change and compensating (because, given the new distribution of income, the gainers could over-compensate the losers if the change were made). It would, in fact, have been better to have made the change. It follows that changes of this third class ought to be made if income redistribution is favourable, and if the Scitovszky criterion is satisfied. In the second class of cases, the two criteria coincide; the Kaldor–Hicks criterion is therefore formally redundant in all cases.

Let us sum up the above arguments. First, two general value premisses are required; (*a*) that an 'individual' is better off in a chosen position, (*b*) that it is a good thing that one 'individual' should be better off if none are worse off. Secondly, for every particular change, we require a judgement as to whether the resultant redistribution of real income would be a good thing or not. If it would be a good thing, or at least not bad, we can say whether the change ought to be made or not. It ought to be made if it would be impossible to make everyone as well off as they would be after the change, by a policy of redistributing money by lump-sum payments.[12]

I must add that the above arguments are formal. I do not want to maintain that the scheme proposed for the foundations of welfare economics is of any use. That depends on how realistic the factual assumptions are which we have to make (e.g. consistency of choice on the part of eternal individuals, absence of dynamic elements, applicability of a marginal analysis). These we have not the space to discuss here. The question whether our static welfare model is sufficiently realistic to be useful is a very difficult one to decide. It could in principle, but not in practice, be tested. In principle, we could find some consistent person who would make the required value judgements, and then we could make the changes which we deduced to be good. If these were the only changes, and if our guinea-pig judged that welfare had indeed increased, then the theory would have worked. In the absence of such verification, we can only make untestable guesses as to whether or not the obvious unreality of the axioms is so great that the conclusions are worthless.

Finally, I will briefly give reasons why the present approach is preferred to the 'economic welfare function'[13] approach, from which practical welfare conclusions

[12] When I say 'ought to be made', I mean, of course, 'ought to be made from the point of view of economic welfare'. By definition, economic welfare can only vary with the amount of economic goods which individuals have.

[13] Bergson, op. cit.

can only be deduced if an 'ideal' distribution of real income is given. If an 'ideal' real income distribution has to be presupposed, then there are three possibilities:

(*a*) In a democratic society economists assume that, whatever the distribution of real income is, it is ideal. This is absurd. It is based on the undemocratic Hegelian view that the government is always right, and on the false idea that distribution is always what the government wants it to be, because if it were not as it wanted it to be, then it would have changed it. This is like saying that I must always want to be in the town in which I am, even if I happen to be motoring rapidly through it.

(*b*) In an absolutist state the economist must assume that whatever is, is right. Welfare economics is the servant of the State, and is denied to those who happen to disagree with the prevailing distribution of wealth. Even given this, it still need not be true that the government always wants exactly what it has in the way of real income distribution.

(*c*) There is the possibility that the ideal distribution can be determined in an objective scientific manner. This fallacious notion is dealt with in Section 2 below. Thus, rejecting this possibility, it appears that a welfare economics based on an 'ideal' distribution of real income is applicable at best only in a totalitarian state, and not very well even there. We therefore leave open the question whether a change would cause a favourable, unfavourable, or a neutral change in distribution. Welfare economics can then be of some use to those who do not happen to believe that the prevailing distribution is ideal.

We may now draw some conclusions:

1. Welfare economics cannot be objective or scientific. The phrases 'the welfare of society' and 'the happiness of society' are very vague phrases which can find no place in the statement of any general empirical laws.

2. The new welfare economics is not, as usually formulated, a deductive system which draws out conclusions from generally accepted premisses. Either it reaches no conclusions, or it deduces them from unacceptable premisses.

3. As usually formulated, the new welfare economics is liable by its use of suggestive emotive language to beg the question of its applicability, and to induce people to accept conclusions about the real world which they might not accept if they understood clearly how they were arrived at.

4. Welfare economics is a logical calculus of doubtful applicability formulated in quasi-ethical terms. The fact that it is a value system is, however, by no means a fundamental objection to it. It might still be useful to anyone who accepts its premisses, and who is prepared to give an answer to the open question concerning real income distribution. If it is useless, that is because its factual assumptions are insufficiently realistic. If they are very unrealistic, then we could only be confident that our criteria would be satisfied in the real world if the theoretical gains (in terms of an ideal system of economic men, firms, etc.) were very large, that is if the divergences from so-called optimum conditions were very

great. But if these divergences must be very great, it is likely that welfare economics can tell us no more than common sense. I am inclined to believe that welfare economics is of little use. Whether I am right or not is anyone's guess.

2. THE DISTRIBUTION OF REAL INCOME, AND INTERPERSONAL COMPARISONS

In the first part of this article the concept 'the distribution of real income' has been freely used. But obviously, its use implies the validity of interpersonal comparisons. Those who 'deny' interpersonal comparisons thus have to claim that 'the distribution of real income' is a value concept, and that one can only speak of the distribution of money income in an empirical manner. This position is taken up by Professor Lerner in the following passage:[14]

> This does not mean that the prices will not change and that such changes will not make some people better off and others worse off, even though their money incomes remain the same. It does mean, however, *that we must disregard such changes* when they are the result of changes in demand for the various goods or changes in the supply while the optimum allocation of goods is maintained. If we could say that in the old situation the actual relative well-being of consumers was just what we wanted it to be, then, when prices changed, we would want to make some adjustment in the money incomes, to offset the change in prices, and leave the consumers in the same relative position as before. But we have no way of directly comparing the well-being of different consumers. Our only objective general indication is their money income, and this has not changed. We may have good reason for believing that one consumer is better off than he was before and that another is not so well off as he was before, but we have no more reason for supposing that the old situation is better than the new one (that is, more like the situation we wish to bring about) then for supposing that the new one is better than the old one. (my italics)

This passage clearly shows that indifference-curve analysis cannot tell us in what direction the distribution of real income has changed. As a result, the passage is highly paradoxical. Either it is assumed that we cannot ever know when the distribution of real income (or actual well-being) is what we want it to be, or it is assumed that we can know when it is what we want it to be, *although* we cannot tell whether it is becoming more or less like what we want it to be when it is seen to be changing. The latter alternative is absurd, and so it must be supposed that Professor Lerner is denying that one person can ever be said to be richer, economically, than another in any (objective) sense other than that he has a greater money income. This is, as we have said above, the only possible position to take up, if one insists on denying the validity of interpersonal comparisons of utility. But it is a most unconvincing position. It amounts to telling

[14] A. P. Lerner, *The Economics of Control*, p. 24.

people that they ought to ignore everything but money income (though perhaps capital would be admitted, in so far as it can be reduced to money terms) when they decide what they think the distribution of income ought to be.

Professor Lerner suggests that our only objective criterion of the distribution of relative well-being is money income. The word 'objective' may mean many things, but since Professor Lerner holds that one *cannot ever say* whether one person has more or less satisfaction than another, it appears that he is using 'objective' to mean 'empirical'. Therefore, unless it is held that one has some metaphysical test of relative well-being, it follows that relative well-being cannot mean anything other than relative money income, which cannot, therefore, be said to be a test of relative well-being. What Professor Lerner evidently means, however, is that money income is all we need to be interested in, because it can be proved that an egalitarian distribution of money income is more likely than any other to maximize the aggregate amount of satisfaction in the community. It is worth examining how this conclusion is arrived at.

The general position, Professor Lerner maintains, is that, although we can compare individuals to the extent that we can say that their satisfactions are of the same kind, we cannot say how much satisfaction any one individual has; nor can we say whether a small addition to his income will increase his happiness or satisfaction more or less than a similar addition would increase that of another individual. By assuming that satisfactions are of the same kind, Professor Lerner means, evidently, that they may be added. Now most people think that it makes perfectly good sense to say that A is more satisfied than B, and very little sense to say 'Let us add A's and B's satisfactions.' But there is no need to press this point, because the method by which Professor Lerner gets from this position to his conclusion is invalid. He assumes that, because one never has, he believes, any reason whatever to suppose that A has more or less capacity for satisfaction than B, it is equally probable that a shift of money from A to B, when they have equal money incomes, would increase or decrease total satisfaction. From this assumption it would follow that, out of a large number of such shifts, 50 per cent would increase and 50 per cent would decrease total satisfaction. But from complete ignorance nothing whatever can follow, except complete ignorance. The assumption of equiprobability as a working hypothesis would be legitimate only if there were some conceivable way of testing the conclusion. But, on Professor Lerner's principles, there is no conceivable way of discovering whether the assumption of equiprobability is justified. This step in the argument is, therefore, illegitimate. Professor Lerner's next step is as follows. Out of a large number of such shifts, 50 per cent would probably increase satisfaction and 50 per cent would probably decrease it; but, from the assumption of diminishing marginal utility of money to each individual, each loss would be larger than each gain, and, therefore total satisfaction would probably decrease.

This conclusion does not seem to follow, because each positive shift might represent a large increase in satisfaction, while each negative shift might represent only a small decrease in satisfaction. Thus, the conclusion does not follow, because each positive shift might be from a person with a very low capacity to one with a very high capacity for satisfaction, while each negative shift might be from a person with a capacity for satisfaction very little lower than the person in whose favour the shift was made. Evidently the argument from total methodological ignorance to equiprobability must be invoked again. We can conclude that any argument which 'denies' interpersonal comparisons, and at the same time asserts that an equalitarian division of money income would probably increase satisfaction, must be wrong.

Thus, the contention that we need not worry about anything except money income, because an equalitarian distribution is most likely to produce the maximum amount of happiness, breaks down. Is the contention at all plausible without this support? Assuming an equal distribution of money income, changes in prices would alter relative well-being only in so far as tastes differed. There is some plausibility in assuming that tastes would not differ very much if money incomes were equal, and, therefore, in saying that money incomes (or rather total resources) would be an adequate guide to distribution. But it would still not be very plausible unless tastes were also assumed to be adaptable and price changes small. Moreover, it would still be true that relative money incomes would be taken only as a *guide* to relative real incomes. One would always be ready to abandon the money income criterion if it were observed that some price change made a great difference to some individual. Moreover, as soon as we come to consider an inegalitarian society, the view that only money incomes are important loses all plausibility. No one believes that one must ignore a large change in the price ratio of necessities and luxuries. One would certainly say that the poor had become really better off, or really worse off, in relation to the rich.

The interest that attaches to the study of the distribution of money income is derived from a belief in a correlation between money incomes and real incomes. No interest whatever would attach to comparative money incomes if it was not believed that this correlation existed. It has been shown that no practical welfare judgement can be made without considering the distribution of income. It has also been shown that the distribution of income in which we are interested is the distribution of real income. Since the heterogeneous collection of goods which different people buy may offer no basis for comparison, it is clear that consideration of the distribution of real income involves comparing different people's states of mind or changes in them.

The 'denial' of the possibility of such comparisons is only made by economists. It is not always apparent in what sense they are 'denied'. It is said that they are not objective or scientific. But these words mean very different things. It has also been said that they are value judgements or ethical judgements. But sometimes economists seem to say that a judgement is a value judgement if it is not 'objective'; and, again, it is not clear what the word 'objective' means. In any case, the 'denial' , in some sense, of such judgements has resulted in extraordinary confusions in economic theory. It therefore seems worth while to examine the question systematically.

The first position for those who 'deny' interpersonal comparisons must be that other minds are not analysable in behaviouristic terms, and that behaviour is not evidence in favour of the existence of other minds. It must be noted that, if behaviour is accepted as evidence, then we can certainly compare other minds on the basis of such evidence; for, if we have any evidence for other minds, we have overwhelming evidence. Such a procedure would not be in the least non-empirical, and would be, in that sense, objective and scientific. Therefore, on this view, to deny the comparability of other minds is to deny their existence. The only possible alternative suggestion is that we can, by some kind of metaphysical intuition, get to know that other minds exist, but cannot get to know anything else about them, other than the bare fact that they do exist (for if we could get to know anything else about them, we could compare them). How one can know that something exists, without knowing anything else about it, is impossible to imagine. Anyone who holds this view must, nevertheless, admit that people do make interpersonal comparisons; he therefore has to maintain that they are not true or false, because they are not about matters of fact. They are only significant in that they are ethical (value) judgements. This seems to be the position Professor Robbins maintains, as may be seen from the two following quotations: 'I still cannot believe that it is helpful to speak as if interpersonal comparisons of utility rest on scientific foundations—that is, upon observation or introspection',[15] and 'But I still think, when I make interpersonal comparisons, that my judgments are more like judgments of value than judgments of verifiable fact'.[16]

Thus it is held that, when I say 'A is happier than B', I am making a value judgement. We may ask 'What sort of a value judgement?'—perhaps something like 'B ought to be helped rather than A'? In which case, the statement 'You ought to help B rather than A, because A is happier' becomes a tautology. One can only say that it obviously is not a tautology. Also, 'A is happier than B' cannot be analysed in the same way as 'A is a better man than B.' By the latter statement, a person may intend to convey some fairly definite empirical information. He may himself use such words as 'good' to describe recognizable states of affairs. But there is no generally accepted descriptive usage for such words; that is, they have no general descriptive meaning. On the other hand, words like 'happy' and 'satisfaction' do have more or less definite descriptive meanings. If a person uses the word 'happy' to describe a recognized melancholic, then it would be correct to maintain that he was misusing the word. If, on the other hand, a person says that a man, generally admitted to be bad, is good, then it is incorrect to say that he is literally misusing the word. We might in practice say this, but we should not then be speaking literally; we should rather be saying that we disagreed strongly with his ethical views. We may also notice that Professor Robbins, to be

[15] L. Robbins, *EJ* (1938), p. 640. [16] Ibid., p. 641.

consistent, must maintain that interpersonal comparisons not only of utility, but also of anger, sympathy, kindness, intelligence, and so on, are one and all value judgements, to which no facts have any relevance. We conclude that interpersonal comparisons are not value judgements.

Nevertheless, many people quite rightly feel that there is something in what Professor Robbins says. This is because it is true that interpersonal comparisons are not objective and scientific, in other senses of the words. If a number of people have to read a pointer which, it is agreed by all of them, indicates the true weight of an object, then it is not likely that they will arrive at very different results (although they may differ slightly). If a number of people have to decide whether 'A is happier than B', each uses his own tests, giving his own weights to them, and they may reach quite different conclusions. The extent to which they will do so can, however, be exaggerated. There would be some cases in which almost everyone would say that A was happier than B, but there would be many cases where there would be some disagreement, and where many observers would simply say that they could not tell. In this sense, then, interpersonal comparisons are less scientific and less objective than measuring weights, but it may be noted that it is only a matter of degree.

The fact that interpersonal comparisons are not very objective in this sense is not, however, a ground for 'denying' them. If a person says 'the poor ought to be helped rather than the rich', his statement is quite insignificant unless he can at least sometimes judge 'this man is poorer than that man'. Therefore, a denial of interpersonal comparisons makes complete nonsense of all factual and all general value judgements about income distribution, and consequently makes nonsense of the whole of welfare economics, and much else besides. It must be noted that the statement 'the poor ought to be helped rather than the rich' does not lose significance, because everyone would not agree as to who was poor and who rich.

The bogy of 'interpersonal comparisons' has surely tortured economic theory for long enough. Professor Robbins was right in thinking that welfare economics involved ethics, but wrong in thinking that ethics crept in via interpersonal comparisons. The ethics is there because the welfare terminology is an ethical terminology.

It has been shown that interpersonal comparisons of mental states, or mental characteristics, are essential to judgements of relative economic well-being (for short, in what follows, the word 'wealth' will be used for 'economic well-being') and, therefore, to judgements about the welfare of society. It is apparent, however, that judgements of relative wealth are not direct comparisons of mental states. What, then, are they comparisons of? It might be suggested that they are comparisons of differences in mental states resulting from small changes in money income. Of course, people do not arrive at such judgements by actually going about and offering people small presents to see what difference it makes to them. Nevertheless, whatever evidence is taken into account might be used for estimating the marginal utility of money for different people. A lower marginal utility of money might then be taken as a definition of greater wealth.

The above suggestion is plausible for most cases. People often do make such remarks as 'five shillings a week makes more difference to me than it does to you'. This shows that the idea of comparing marginal utilities of money is a familiar one, which may play a considerable part in judgements of relative wealth. In most cases, it would be paradoxical to say 'A is wealthier than B, but money means more to him'; but not in all cases. A melancholic with hardly any money might, nevertheless, take less delight in a little extra than a man whom most people would want to say was really wealthier.

We may conclude that comparisons of wealth are neither comparisons of money wealth alone, nor are they simply comparisons of states of mind, or of differences in states of mind (although the latter probably play a part). This does not mean that they are non-empirical or meaningless. If I am asked what I mean when I say 'A is really wealthier than B', I can give an account of the evidence which I have considered. This is quite sufficient to make the judgement significant. This evidence would normally include such things as capital, income, prices, and conditions of work, and so on; but it would also include the tastes of the individuals concerned. It is the difference of tastes which makes a comparison of the more objective factors inadequate.

It may be added that people do not claim to make more than very rough comparisons of real wealth or real income. Someone might judge that two people, one a smoker and the other a non-smoker, were economically equal. Then the price of tobacco might double. Even if he knew this, he might still judge that they were economically equal, although he would admit that one was worse off than before, and the other no better off and no worse off. There is no contradiction in this, because 'economically equal' does not mean anything exact, any more than 'politically equal' or 'socially equal' means anything exact. If the so-called contradiction was pointed out, the person would say 'Oh, by equal I mean more or less equal'. 'Equality' in such a context never means more than 'rough equality'. But if 'economic equality' meant 'having the same money income', a contradiction would arise. For this reason the distribution of income, in so far as it has welfare significance, cannot mean anything very precise.

The fact that the 'distribution of real income' is an imprecise concept is a reason for preferring the type of analysis adopted in the first part of this article. We can inform our 'policy-maker' that the shift in real income distribution would be towards certain social classes and away from others; on the basis of such information, he may be prepared to say whether he considers such a change good or bad. We cannot explain exactly what the distribution of real income would be, because we have no language for making such statements. For these reasons, a partial analysis which seeks to ask whether one situation is better than another is preferred to the general approach which seems the optimum by way of an 'economic welfare function', in which all configurations of the economic system are given an ethical valuation. No 'policy-maker' would ever be willing or able to lay down an 'economic welfare function', but he may be willing and able to state in what direction he thinks purchasing power should be shifted. The 'economic welfare function' is a brilliant device which completes the formal mathematical system of 'welfare' economics, but it does not appear to lend itself to interpretation, even in a state with an absolutist government. For instance, the only way a dictator could lay down the ideal real income distribution would be by ostensive definition. He might say, after certain adjustments had been made, 'Now the present distribution of money represents the ideal real income distribution.' His economic advisers would then have the task of keeping those 'optimum' conditions of production and exchange, which could be deduced from his value judgements, in operation without altering the ideal real income distribution. But prices would change, and then how would they know whether the ideal was preserved or not? Evidently it would still be necessary to ask the dictator whether the real income distribution effects of each change would be neutral or not. And if they were not neutral, all the difficulties involved in paying compensation would crop up again.

The general conclusion which emerges most clearly from the above discussion is that little can be gained by attempts to be objective and precise about a subject in which people have an ethical interest, and about which they speak in terms which, in so far as they have any descriptive meaning, are essentially vague. In particular, it may be added that our discussion is not meant to imply that the new welfare economics, or any other welfare economics, is *complete* rubbish. It only becomes absurd if it is pushed too hard in the attempt to precisify what cannot be precise, and if perfect scientific objectivity is claimed. Interpreted in a sufficiently vague manner, there may well be something in it. It is silly to suppose that a discipline is valueless because it is not scientific. How valuable welfare economics can be as a guide to policy is a question which each individual must decide for himself; but too little has been written which might help one to decide, and too much which serves to impress a decision on one.

2

Conclusions to A Critique of Welfare Economics (1957)

This book might, in part, be described as a study of the usage of influential and persuasive language in economics. Wherever it has been found that the terminology of economics is, in this sense, normative, we have suggested that the ethical issues involved should be brought right into the open. Unless this is done, it is often not at all clear whether a dispute is one of fact, or one of value. A discussion which is superficially objective and factual (because frankly ethical expressions are not used), but which is really about values, though the contestants may not realize it, is usually unhelpful, and may tend to create ill feeling.

I am far from suggesting that economists must try to be neutral on ethical issues. (The fact that, for instance, I have chosen to give an exposition of the traditional welfare economics implies an acceptance of certain liberal values.) As I have said, the distinction between economist *qua* economist, and economist *qua* ordinary mortal, is one that cannot be very easily maintained. Bringing ethical questions into the limelight does not imply any kind of neutrality. There is, admittedly, a tendency to think that, once it has been shown that people differ on questions of value, then nothing more remains to be said. But this is a mistake. One can often convince someone, by reasoning with him, that one's own ethical beliefs are better than his. This is, however, different from trying to get one's opinions accepted by means of a propaganda use of language—different, that is, from trying to put something over by means of implicit persuasive definitions.

Thus, I am not crusading against the use of all influential language in economics—that would be to oppose the use of all ethical judgements in the subject. I only want it to be recognized that many of our economic phrases are emotive. If this is not recognized, then many real, though apparently sham (because terminological), battles will continue to be fought. If, however, it is recognized that such battles may be real ones—of values—then they could be better waged, with more enlightenment for the spectators, if the decks were cleared of any encumbering pseudo-objective terminology. I am, in fact,

This is the final chapter from *A Critique of Welfare Economics*, 2nd edn. (Clarendon Press, Oxford, 1957). Permission to reproduce is gratefully acknowledged.

suggesting a better separation, in economics, of different levels of discourse. This cannot be achieved if it is not recognized that many economic statements, which appear at first sight to be merely descriptive, have value implications. Among the most important of such phrases are 'increase of welfare' and 'increase of real income'.

I have rejected the utilitarian view that the logical calculus of 'welfare' economics should be interpreted in terms of satisfaction or happiness, on the ground that it is misleading to describe welfare economics as the science which studies the economic causes of the happiness of communities. So to describe it suggests a degree of objectivity and precision which is lacking. It is, for instance, very much a matter of opinion whether some given redistribution of money would increase or decrease happiness. I also claimed that there is an element of prescription in judgements about the happiness of communities. But even if I am wrong about this, it is, in any case, certain that people will slip into using prescriptive terminology—will slip from statements about happiness to statements about welfare, and thence to the use of words such as 'improvement' and 'benefit'—without paying much attention to the change. I have taken the view that the essential purpose of welfare economics is to prescribe, and that therefore certain questions of value are begged unless it is explicitly based on value judgements.

Thus, my rejection of the utilitarian scheme of things has not been based on the perhaps rather dogmatic objection that satisfactions cannot be added, and certainly not on a 'denial' or interpersonal comparisons. As a matter of fact, I think that many people, in deciding what ought to be done, often employ some sort of hedonistic calculation. But such calculation is not *logically* essential to prescriptive economics. What we require are judgements about the sort of thing that ought to be done; and it does not matter to us what imaginative processes people employ to help them arrive at such judgements.

Accordingly, I have proposed that welfare economics be based on the following sufficient criterion for a desirable economic change: an economic change is desirable if (*a*) it would result in a good redistribution of wealth, and if (*b*) the potential losers could not profitably bribe the potential gainers to oppose the change.[1] Two value judgements are presupposed by this criterion. The first is that an individual becomes better off if he is enabled to reach a position higher up on his order of choice. The second is that the community is better off if one individual becomes better off, and none worse off. It is thought that both of these judgements would be widely acceptable. It has further been shown that the above criterion is sufficient, given enough *factual* assumptions, to deduce that a realization of the 'optimum' conditions of exchange and production would be a good thing, so long as a worse distribution of wealth would not result, or could be avoided by compensation.[2]

[1] This is subject to certain qualifications as to the sense of the word 'desirable' which it would be tedious to repeat at this point.

[2] We also, of course, have to assume that any induced non-economic changes are neutral or good.

I have claimed that the above foundations are firm. Anyone may accept welfare economics on such a basis, or reject it. But the important thing is that it is clear what has to be accepted or rejected. If the conclusions follow from the axioms, and the meaning of the axioms is clear, then a system can be said, I think, to have firm foundations.

The suggested criterion is not, of course, objective. Whether a given economic change would be good or bad remains a matter of personal opinion. For it is a matter of opinion whether or not the change would cause a good, bad, or neutral redistribution of wealth or welfare. It must be emphasized that this does not imply that welfare economics is useless. Most people would accept the two fundamental value judgements. The theory, *if the required factual assumptions are deemed realistic enough*, in any particular case, enables such people to agree on the goodness or otherwise of the change, given that they give the same answer to the question about distribution. And even when there is no agreement about income distribution, useful conclusions may be reached, of the form 'This redistribution would be attained better by change A, than change B'.

Thus, I think that welfare economics may best be considered as the study of whether or not one configuration of the economic system is better or worse than another and whether a change from one to the other should be made. Whenever these questions arise, whether explicitly or by implication, then I suggest that the answer be based on the above criterion. This means that welfare economics is not solely concerned with the prospective changes, but also with the results of actual changes which have occurred. It is obvious that the question whether economic welfare increased over some past period is a question in welfare economics. It is not quite so obvious that the same question, whether posed with reference to real income, wealth, production, real wages, consumption, or standards of living, is also a question in welfare economics. But all these words or phrases belong to the pseudo-objective terminology of economics. They are substantial words which look as though they refer to something, changes in the magnitude of which may be measured; but this appearance is misleading. The size of a collection of incommensurable kinds is a concept which requires the assignment of weights, which determine the relative importance, *for some given purpose*, of the different kinds. One cannot, strictly speaking, discuss the question of changes in the size of such collections at all. The size of a thing *is* something objective, which is independent of the purpose of the measurement. But the 'size' of, say, the national real income has no such independence. Nevertheless, there is a correct answer (or rather, the form of a correct answer) to such a question as 'has real income increased?' This is because the purpose, which determines the weighting, is suggested by the value implications of the sentence 'the real income of society has increased'. In other words, the purpose is to discover whether or not there has been an improvement. Consequently our 'welfare' theory tells us that the weights must be market prices, and that the answer to the question must then be determined by reference to our fundamental criterion.

Welfare economics is, then, likely to be useful if its factual assumptions are realistic enough. We saw that the question whether they are realistic enough is very difficult to answer, because the conclusions of the theory cannot, in practice, be tested. Whether its conclusions, in any particular case, are to be accepted or rejected is thus, even given agreement on all questions of value, a matter of judgement and opinion. There is no question of proof.

The first difficulty is that our criterion often, in practice, rests on the assumption that money may be redistributed without offending against any of the theoretical 'optimum' conditions. Such redistribution would frequently be an administrative or political impossibility.[3] Therefore many changes may have to be admitted to be desirable although they do not satisfy the criterion. Thus, a change may be held to be good if it effects a good redistribution, although, in theory, this redistribution could have been better carried out by 'neutral' money transfers. Therefore our criterion must be regarded only as a sufficient criterion for a desirable economic change, and not as a definition of 'an increase in economic welfare'. Its applicability, in opposing a particular change which would result in a good redistribution of real income, is limited by the practical possibility of carrying out the required redistribution in some better way.

But, in every case, the exact application of the theory would require the existence of eternal and perfectly consistent individuals, who choose between infinitely divisible goods of unchanging quality. In my opinion, this unreality does not in itself suffice to make the conclusions of the theory worthless, but does make it silly to treat them as anything but rough guides to practice. It was argued that any divergence from 'optimum' conditions must be large before one could have any reasonable degree of confidence that an improvement would result from trying to satisfy them.

The above assumptions suffice only for the derivation of the 'optimum' exchange conditions, and, given perfect statistics, for the use of index-numbers in judging whether real income, consumption, etc., has changed. The 'optimum' conditions of production require many further unrealistic assumptions, and are, accordingly, less trustworthy. In particular, we found that the theorem that output ought to be adjusted until price equals marginal cost is extremely shaky, and we did not feel justified in taking much notice of it except in a few special cases. This theorem is the most important and the most controversial conclusion of welfare theory. It lies behind many of the widely accepted practical implications of economic theory. It is highly controversial because it is the only one of the 'opti-

[3] Or it may be impossible because the potential losers have no 'lump-sums' which can be used to bribe the potential gainers. However, if there were no property, then a good redistribution of earned income by direct taxation would satisfy our criterion. The potential losers could not profitably bribe the potential gainers to oppose the change, because the bribes required would be the exact equivalent of the proposed taxation. This would not be the case only if the bribe could be capitalized, and property transferred. Thus, the fact that there might be no 'lump-sums' to transfer does not necessarily render the criterion inapplicable, although it does imply that it might not be a good thing to put the optimum labour-supply condition into operation, or make marginal cost equal to price.

mum' conditions which also has serious political implications. The fact that I cannot bring myself to believe that the distinction between average and marginal cost is, more than very seldom, of the slightest importance to the welfare of society, has led me to the view that this branch of economics—pure static welfare theory—is, or rather should be, of little or no political import.

We can, on the other hand, scarcely doubt that welfare theory is sufficiently realistic to tell us that relative costs of production should not be allowed to get too far out of line with relative market-prices. As a *rough* guide to what ought to be done, it is undoubtedly useful. If one says that welfare economics is useless, one means that its precise conclusions cannot be taken seriously. The common-sense argument that, if the market value of one thing is twice that of another, then it is usually worth producing if it does not cost more than twice as much—ambiguous though it is—is probably just as valuable, and is certainly less misleading than such conclusions as 'price ought to equal marginal cost'.

Common sense is sometimes bad theory, and then it may mislead. But it is often good, but crude, theory. Economic welfare is a subject in which rigour and refinement are probably worse than useless. Rough theory, or good common sense, is, in practice, what we require. It is satisfying, and impressive, that a rigorous logical system, with some apparent reality, should have been set up in the field of the social sciences: but we must not let ourselves be so impressed that we forget that its reality is obviously limited; and that the degree of such reality is a matter of judgement and opinion.

3

Direct versus Indirect Taxes (1951)

The first part of this article is designed to show that the usual theoretical treatment of the problem of direct and indirect taxation is based on extraordinary assumptions, and liable to be misleading. An alternative mode of analysis is suggested. In the second part, I try to show that no case against indirect taxation can be proved from the ordinary, general, purely competitive assumptions of economic theory; and, further, that the special assumption, necessary to prove the case, involves an unplausible conclusion concerning incentives.

I

The usual analysis of direct versus indirect taxation (or subsidization) runs typically as follows.[1]

A single 'economic man' who spends his income on two goods (one of which may be 'money') is assumed. In Figure 1, Q_0 is the equilibrium tax-free position. When an income tax equal to AB of X is imposed, Q_1 is reached. The same sum could be raised by an indirect tax on Y, which would result in a position such as Q_2. From the usual convexity assumption, it follows that Q_2 is worse than Q_1. Q.E.D.

At first sight this result always looks like a conjuring trick. There is no overt reference to marginal costs. Yet it is well known that nothing can be proved without some such reference.[2] The covert reference is as follows. For the proof to be valid, the government must be able to buy the same collection of goods whether the individual is at position Q_2 or at position Q_1. This it can do only if Q_2Q_1

This paper first appeared in the *Economic Journal*, No. 243 (Sept. 1951). Permission to reproduce is gratefully acknowledged.

[1] Cf. M. F. W. Joseph, 'The Excess Burden of Indirect Taxation', *Review of Economic Studies* (June 1939); H. P. Wald, 'The Classical Indictment of Indirect Taxation', *Quarterly Journal of Economics* (Aug. 1945); A. M. Henderson, 'The Case for Indirect Taxation', *Economic Journal* (Dec. 1948); A. T. Peacock and D. Berry, 'A Note on the Theory of Income Redistribution', *Economica* (Feb. 1951).

[2] Cf. the original Frisch–Hotelling controversy—*Econometrica* (1939), pp. 145–60; in particular Professor Hotelling's final note, pp. 158–60.

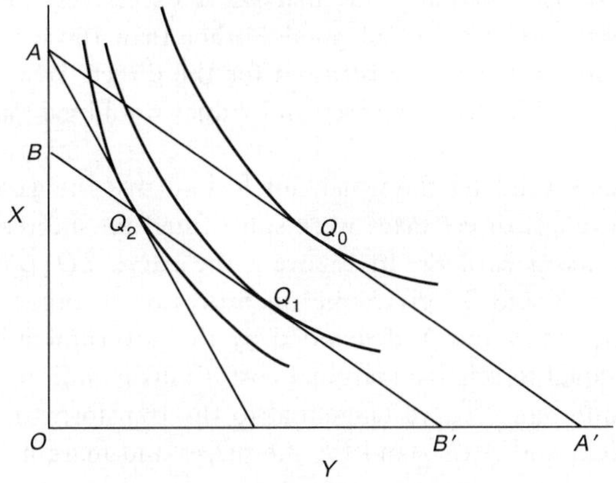

FIGURE 1

has the same slope as the transformation curve of X and Y (the curve showing the maximum amounts of X which could be produced given varying quantities of Y, and fixed amounts of all other goods). From this, it follows that the slope of BB' must equal the relative marginal costs of the two goods. Thus, in Figure 2, relative marginal costs are assumed to be the same at both Q_2 and Q_1.

Although this diagram is drawn with reference to a single individual, it may be presumed that it is designed to illustrate the relative effects, on each of many individuals, of two different tax systems of equal monetary incidence. Therefore, a considerable shift of production must be allowed for. This being the case, the assumption that relative marginal costs are the same at both Q_2 and Q_1 is in conflict with the normal assumption used in this connection, that of a diminishing

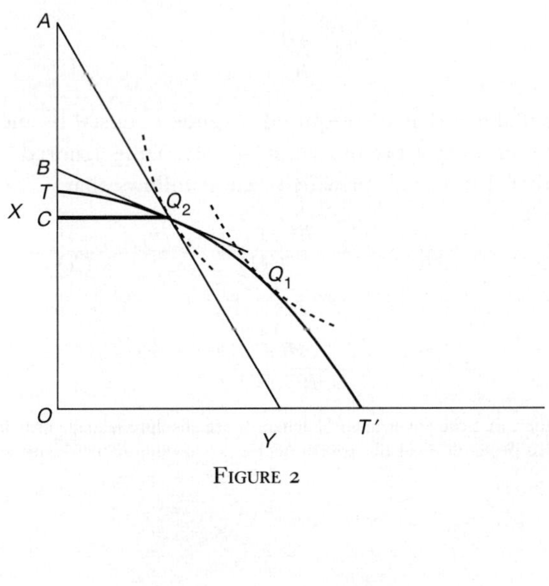

FIGURE 2

marginal rate of transformation. The analysis is excessively and unnecessarily partial in other ways. The prices of goods, other than those represented, may change when the indirect tax is substituted for the direct. When this is allowed for, it is even conceivable that any given individual would gain as a result of the change.

But none of this invalidates the usual conclusion (that the gainers could over-compensate the losers if direct taxes were substituted for indirect) *given that the supply of labour is not a variable*. In Figure 2 the curve TQ_2Q_1T' is the transformation curve of X and Y, given the quantities of all other goods, and also given the quantities of X and Y demanded by the government.[3] At Q_1 relative price is assumed equal to relative marginal cost. (This is indicated by drawing in a 'community indifference' curve tangential to the transformation curve at Q_1.) Letting p_x, p_y, MC_x, and MC_y stand for the prices and marginal costs of X and Y, we have at Q_2,

$$\frac{p_y}{p_x} = \frac{AC}{CQ_2} \tag{1}$$

and

$$\begin{aligned}\frac{MC_y}{MC_x} &= \frac{BC}{CQ_2} \\ &= \text{marginal rate of transformation of } Y \text{ into } X.\end{aligned} \tag{2}$$

Supposing X to be subsidized, otherwise perfect competition, and letting s and t stand for the rate of subsidy and tax respectively, it follows from (1) and (2) that

$$\frac{MC_y}{MC_x(1-s)} = \frac{BC}{CQ_2(1-s)} = \frac{p_y}{p_x} = \frac{AC}{CQ_2},$$

whence

$$s = \frac{AB}{AC}.$$

It is assumed above that the required revenue is raised by means of an income tax, the effects of such a tax on factor supply being ignored. Alternatively, we can suppose that Y is taxed, in which case it follows that

$$\frac{MC_y(1+t)}{MC_x} = \frac{BC(1+t)}{CQ_2} = \frac{p_y}{p_x} = \frac{AC}{CQ_2},$$

whence

$$t = \frac{AB}{BC}.$$

[3] The assumption that the government's demands are absolute is made only for simplicity of exposition. We could in principle treat the government as an 'economic man' with a consistent set of utility curves.

That the position Q_2 is not 'optimum' follows simply from the divergence of relative prices and relative marginal costs. No other proof is required or possible. A 'community indifference' curve can, of course, be drawn tangential to AQ_2 at Q_2. This curve must pass below Q_1 on the given assumptions. This follows from the fact that Q_1 is an 'optimum' position, while Q_2 is not.[4] So nothing is really added by drawing in the indifference curves. What matters is that at Q_2 the individual rates of substitution of X for Y are not equal to the transformation rate. This analysis is more general and requires fewer restrictive assumptions than those usually made. It also has the advantage that it shows quite clearly, for both subsidies and taxes, that the 'case against indirect taxation' is merely a special case of conflict with one of the necessary conditions for the achievement of a Pareto 'optimum', i.e. that relative marginal costs be equal to relative prices. At the purely theoretical level, nothing more can be said; and nothing less is valid without special 'partial' assumptions.

II

In Section I it was arbitrarily assumed that the supply of labour was constant; or, to put it another way, that the consumption of one good, leisure, was unaffected by changes in its own or other prices. This is clearly an indefensible assumption which must be removed. But, for the sake of simplicity, we will continue to ignore savings. The conclusion which we shall reach—that the case against indirect taxation is invalid—can only be reinforced if savings are considered, since an income tax is an indirect tax on savings, as well as on work.

It has been argued by Professor A. M. Henderson that the fact that all marginal taxation is a tax on work (it can also be regarded as a subsidy on leisure, as far as substitution effects are concerned) does not destroy the case against indirect taxation.[5] The argument is that both indirect and direct taxes sin against the necessary 'optimum' condition that the rate of substitution of leisure for any other good must equal the rate of transformation between leisure and that good. But, it is argued, indirect taxes *also* prevent the rates of substitution between pairs of goods, excluding leisure, being equal to their respective rates of transformation. Thus, Professor Henderson writes:

> If a given revenue is required then the resources available to the consumer must be limited to the same extent by either method [i.e. direct or indirect taxation]. But the method of indirect taxation has the further disadvantage of reducing the efficiency with which these resources are used, and therefore imposes an added burden.[6]

[4] Cf. J. de V. Graaff, 'On Optimum Tariff Structures', *Review of Economic Studies* (1949–50), p. 57, n. 3.

[5] Henderson, op. cit.

[6] Ibid., p. 545.

I have previously accepted this argument.[7] But I now think I was wrong to do so. The argument is unsatisfactory because it assumes that the resources used are identical in both cases. In other words, it has to be assumed that the supply of labour is the same whether the taxation is direct or indirect. This amounts to saying that, for every individual, the cross-elasticity of demand for leisure with respect to all other prices is zero; i.e., leisure is not substitutible for any other good. To all intents and purposes, the assumption that the amount of labour does not vary has crept into an argument designed to show that direct taxation is better than indirect taxation, even when the supply of labour is admitted as a variable. This might not matter if it were really plausible to suppose that it would, under no conditions, vary much. I shall suggest below that this is not a plausible supposition.

Consider a perfectly competitive economy with three goods, one being leisure. Designate leisure by Z and the other two goods by X and Y. Let S and T stand respectively for the marginal rate of substitution and the marginal rate of transformation. We can now distinguish three cases as follows:

I. Direct taxation. Here we have

$$S = T \text{ for the pair } (X, Y)$$
$$S \neq T \text{ for the pair } (X, Z)$$
$$S \neq T \text{ for the pair } (Y, Z)$$

II. Indirect taxation on one good other than leisure. Letting the taxed good be X, we have

$$S = T \text{ for the pair } (Y, Z)$$
$$S \neq T \text{ for the pair } (X, Y)$$
$$S \neq T \text{ for the pair } (X, Z)$$

III. Unequal indirect taxation on both goods other than leisure. Here we have

$$S \neq T \text{ for all three pairs.}$$

A comparison of cases I and II makes it sufficiently obvious that no argument against indirect taxation can be perfectly general. The two cases are quite symmetrical. Unless special assumptions are made, whatever can be said about one can be said about the other. But even if case III is considered to be what is normally meant by indirect taxation, nothing appears to follow.

Let us illustrate this. In Figure 3, ABC is the production surface after subtraction of the government's fixed demands. It is assumed that the government succeeds in manipulating the budget surface so that the community's chosen point on that surface is also a point on the production surface ABC. If the chosen point were above the surface, the government would not be getting the goods it required; if below, it would be getting more than it required.

[7] E.g. in the appendix to Chapter IX of *A Critique of Welfare Economics*.

The points Q_0, Q_1, Q_2, and Q_4 are points on the surface. AA', BB', and CC' are surface lines along which one of the three 'optimum' conditions is satisfied. Thus, at any point on the line CC', the partial rate of substitution (leisure constant) of Y for X equals the partial rate of transformation (leisure constant). These contract lines, if projected on to the planes BOC, AOC, and AOB respectively, would be analogous to ordinary contract curves. The point Q_0 is the only point at which all the optimum conditions are satisfied. Case I lands us on the line CC' between C and Q_0. Case II lands us either on AA', between A' and Q_0, or on BB' between B' and Q_0. Case III brings us to some point which lies on none of the contract lines. Part of Figure 2 is embedded in Figure 3. The plane surface $TQ_2Q_1T'O'$ appears in both diagrams

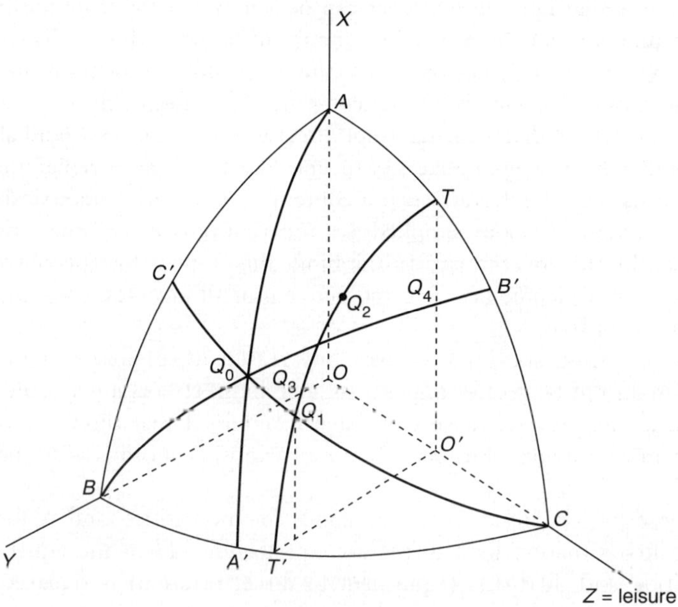

FIGURE 3

The advocates of direct taxation or subsidization have to claim that every point on CC' is better than any other point on the production surface. It is intuitively obvious that there is no reason whatever for claiming that points on the line CC' are superior to those on the lines AA' and BB'. The lesser claim might, however, be made that points on a contract line are superior to points not on a contract line.

What, then, can be said about the relative superiority of points such as Q_0, Q_1, Q_2, Q_3, or Q_4? First Q_0 is 'superior' to any other point because all the 'optimum' conditions are satisfied. In other words, a 'community indifference' surface is tangential to the production surface at Q_0, and cannot lie below the production surface at any other point. Secondly, the 'community indifference' surface appropriate to Q_1 cannot lie below the production surface in the neighbourhood of the point Q_2. This is because it is tangential to the line $T'Q_1Q_2T$ at Q_1. Thirdly, it is quite consistent, both that these two conditions should be fulfilled and that the same indifference surface should or should not lie below the production surface in the neighbourhood of a point such as Q_3. There therefore appears to be no reason whatever to support any claim that Q_1 must be 'superior' to Q_3.[8] A movement from Q_1 to Q_3 would reduce the amount of leisure. But it is also conceivable, given suitable production and indifference surfaces, that the indifference surface of Q_1 should lie below the production surface in the neighbourhood of a point like Q_4, where the amount of leisure is increased. The conclusion is that nothing whatever can be said about the 'superiority' of direct taxation unless it is certain that the amount of leisure will not change.

We have seen that Professor Henderson based his argument on the contention that the supply of labour would be constant. This means, in terms of Figure 3, that it is presumed that a change from direct to indirect taxes would always cause a movement from a point like Q_1 to one like Q_2, leisure remaining constant. Taken to its logical extreme, such a contention is highly paradoxical. It implies that the amount of labour supplied is a function only of the quantities of goods consumed by the government. In the limit, this implies that people would work as much even if income tax were 100 per cent of all incomes, consumption goods being supplied free!

But, apart from subsidies, is there any reason to suppose that the supply of labour might not be greater under a suitable indirect taxation system than under direct taxation? Surely, those who have maintained that direct taxation—quite apart from any 'money illusion'—is more harmful to incentives are not necessarily wrong?

Suppose that Y, in our diagram, stands for 'necessities' and X for 'luxuries'. Let the first situation be a direct tax equilibrium. Then the equal taxation of 'necessities' and 'luxuries' (equivalent to direct taxation) is replaced by a relatively large tax on 'necessities' and a relatively small one on 'luxuries' (case III). Is it not then plausible to suppose that the individual, while keeping his consumption of 'necessities' more or less constant, might increase his consumption of 'luxuries' at the expense of leisure, i.e. move to a point like Q_3, which *may* be 'superior' to Q_1? In case II, where only 'necessities' are taxed, the individual *must* move to a point on BB' between Q_0 and B'. Since the consumption of 'necessities' is not much reduced, this may (given sets of preferences consistent with out

[8] By saying one point is 'superior' to another, we mean that its 'community indifference' surface passes inside (further from the origin than) the other point in the neighbourhood of that point; which implies that the potential losers by a move from the latter to the former would be unable profitably to bribe the potential gainers to oppose the change. Therefore no point x can be 'superior' to any other chosen point y if the indifference surface of x is below the production surface in the neighbourhood of y.

contract lines) entail a reduction in leisure. In the extreme case, when the price elasticity of demand for some necessity is zero, the change from an income tax to an indirect tax on the necessity would result in a movement from Q_1 to Q_0. The reason is as follows. Q_0 is the poll-tax position. But with no poll tax, and the price of Y raised to keep on the same production surface, Q_0 would still be the equilibrium position, since it is consistent with (*a*) zero price elasticity of demand for Y, real income given, and (*b*) unchanged real income. It has often been held that a tax on such a good is the equivalent of an income tax. This is wrong: it is the equivalent of a poll tax; while an income tax is itself the equivalent of a poll tax only if the supply of labour is perfectly inelastic. If, in such a case, we were interested more in incentives than 'welfare', we could increase the tax on 'necessities' in order to pay a subsidy on 'luxuries'. This would amount to a tax on leisure. Leisure would be subsidized in relation to 'necessities', but this would have no substitution effect. It would also be taxed in relation to 'luxuries' which would have an incentive effect.

If any general conclusion can be risked, it is simply that the best taxes are those on goods for which the demand is least elastic. The same holds true for subsidies. Income tax, which is a subsidy on leisure, is not exceptional. Only in so far as the demand for leisure is highly inelastic is it a good tax. The purely theoretical 'case against indirect taxation' is an illusion.

4

Welfare Criteria, Distribution, and Cost–Benefit Analysis (1979)*

Tibor Scitovsky's name is unbreakably linked by 'welfare criteria' with those of Kaldor, Hicks, and myself. For this I am partly to blame. He may not therefore agree that this is a very appropriate subject for an essay in his festschrift. But welfare criteria are surely part of welfare economics, and there can be no doubt that this latter is one of the subjects which have been graced by his writing.

Scitovsky (1941) quickly introduced the concept of distribution into the subject of how one determined whether there was a change in welfare—the national product, real income, or what-have-you. If the Kaldor–Hicks hypothetical compensation criterion declared Q_2 to be bigger than Q_1, it might also proclaim Q_1 to be bigger than Q_2—and most people seem to agree that good criteria should not have such unlimited discretion. The essential reason why this apparent contradiction arose was that there might be a significantly different distribution of wealth or utility before and after the change, and that the potential gain or loss from a change or its reversal was dependent on the distribution from which one started.

It seemed to me to be an obvious step to combine a judgement about the merits of a change in the distribution of utility with an estimate of the sign of the potential net monetary benefits—both for the change from Q_1 to Q_2 and for the reverse change from Q_2 to Q_1. This would not only avoid contradiction, but would also—which is more important—provide an acceptable criterion for a beneficial change. However, this seemingly obvious step has been the subject of a debate which has lasted for a quarter of a century (even longer than the Cambridge–Cambridge argument, despite the far greater simplicity of the issue).

The step has been condemned or criticized by most writers on theoretical welfare economics, and by some of them very often in many articles. It has received explicit support only from Sen (1963) and Ng.[1] As the debate smoul-

This was originally a contribution to *Economics and Human Welfare: Essays in Honour of Tibor Scitovsky*, ed. M. J. Boskin (Academic Press, New York, 1979). Permission to reproduce is gratefully acknowledged.

* I am indebted to Mr Kevin Roberts of Nuffield College for comments.

[1] Y.-K. Ng, 'Little's Welfare Criterion: A Proposed Rehabilitation', mimeographed.

ders mainly in the *Economic Journal* and *Oxford Economic Papers*, the antis appear to have it. Since the *Economic Journal* debate of December 1963, I have not written on the subject. Once a decade is enough. But explicit criticism continues (e.g. Mishan, 1965; Nath, 1969), and so some further comment seems justified, especially as it can be argued that the Little criterion is, in fact, the basis of much—even most—applied welfare economics.

I advanced as a sufficient condition for an improvement (assuming that everyone could not benefit from the change) that both the redistribution should be good (strictly, not bad) and either the gainers could compensate the losers, or the losers be unable profitably to bribe the gainers to oppose the change.

Unfortunately, I cannot avoid including yet again one of the diagrams from *A Critique of Welfare Economics* (Figure 1). The diagram is in ordinal utility space, and curves are loci of points traced out by making lump-sum transfers from Q_1 and Q_2, respectively. The curves are called utility possibility curves (UPCs), but might also be called compensation curves or redistribution curves. Assuming Pareto preferences, a move from Q_1 to Q_2 is indicated if H is preferred to Q_1, and from Q_2 to Q_1 if J is preferred to Q_2.

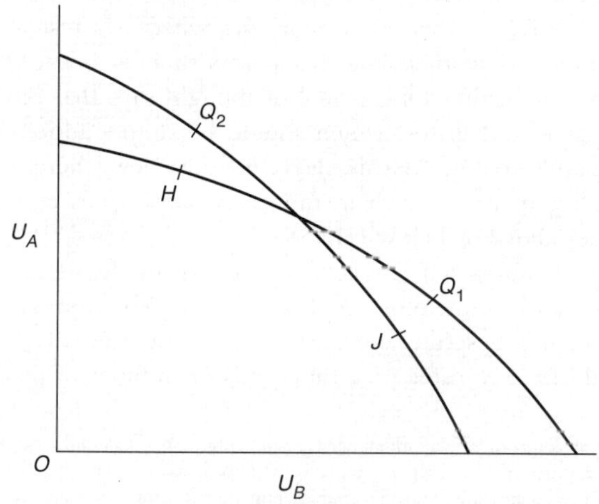

FIGURE 1
Source: Little (1957).

I defined the statement 'Q_2 is a better distribution (of utility) than Q_1' as equivalent to 'there is a point H, attainable by lump-sum transfers from Q_1, which lies to the south-west of Q_2 and is preferred to Q_1.' (Preferred by whom? By whomever makes the judgement!) I attached no meaning to any comparison of rays through the origin; e.g., no sense was attached to such a statement as 'any point on OHQ_2 is *distributionally* better than any point on OJQ_1.'

The main objections to this analysis have been twofold; first, that it leads to contradictions, and second, that it is futile. The first of these can be summarily dismissed. If Smith's preferences are Paretian, and JpQ_2, and HpQ_1, then $Q_2pHpQ_1pJpQ_2$, whence transitivity (and my criterion) *disclose* Q_2pQ_1 and Q_1pQ_2. There is something wrong with Smith, not me![2,3]

This brings me to the objection that the analysis is futile, because, if one can rank points on the same utility possibility curve, one can also rank points such as Q_1 and Q_2 directly (Kennedy, 1952–3). This is harder to deal with, and my previous defence has been called lame.

Perhaps some clue as to whether or not it is futile is to see whether it is used. The application of welfare economics in a piecemeal manner—that is, the application of welfare economics—has come to be called social cost–benefit (SCB) analysis. (That SCB analysis has been mainly applied to investments is neither here nor there; there is in principle no difference between a SCB analysis of an investment project, a tax change, a change in the output of some commodity, etc.) What do SCB analysts do? What do they advocate?

That which seems to be common to all SCB analyses is the use of the Kaldor–Hicks criterion. The Scitovsky double criterion may be employed, but this is rare. (It is implicitly assumed that the curves do not cut.) Analysts answer the question whether the utility possibility curve after the change passes south-west or north-east of Q_1—this often being described as a test of economic efficiency. This is tantamount to saying that points such as H and J are relevant.

Disagreement now begins. One school of thought says that economists should not weight the gains and losses, which should be simply added to establish the position of J relative to Q_1. At this stage, on this view, there is no attempt to locate Q_2 in utility space, or even in monetary space. It is enough to establish that its UPC goes above or below Q_1.

If distribution is to be taken into account, at least by the decision-maker, if not the economist, it can be done more or less precisely. My impression is that actual SCB analyses seldom describe the gainers and losers at all precisely (such a description would have to categorize thousands or millions of people into groups

[2] Contradictions arising out of a conflict between more equality somehow defined and a Paretian improvement have nothing to do with my analysis, although Mishan and Nath associate them with my name: all these demonstrations show is that certain distributional preferences cannot be consistently held together with Pareto preferences. Nath also manufactures contradictions by assuming that the preference-holder has consistent but non-Paretian preferences, while I assumed Paretian preferences. It does not seem to be playing the logical game to remove someone's assumption, and then cry 'How's that!'

[3] Kennedy (1963) suggested that an examiner who compares candidates in a roundabout way using two different principles—by analogy to a Pareto and a distributional judgement—should be dismissed as unreliable. I do not see the appositeness of this analogy. I do not think that north-easterly moves in utility space are all that fundamentally different from north-westerly moves. He also seemed to suggest that having to use a third point might muddle him up—i.e., genuinely *lead to* contradictions. Yet one of the most common forms of ethical discourse is as follows. Someone says he prefers A to B. His discussant says—but I am sure you prefer B to B' (for that is an example of a principle which I cannot believe you do not accept). Now, are you really sure you prefer A to B'? The discussant suspects his friend of being muddled, and hopes B' will disclose this, and make him rethink and perhaps revise his position. The intermediate point is introduced to remove contradictions, not lead to them.

which are of interest to the decision-maker—such groups might or might not be mainly income or wealth groupings), and seldom ascribe a monetary value to their gains or losses. If the compensation test is passed, the decision-maker may decide, with very limited information, that any redistribution would not be bad. If so, he sanctions the change, implicitly deciding that economic welfare would be increased.

If seems to me that this sort of application of welfare economics can be tolerably well described as an application of the Little criterion. If the decision-maker was comparing Q_2 and Q_1 directly, he would surely want a better description of Q_2 than he is usually given; moreover, if his distributional judgement was a direct comparison of the merits of Q_2 and Q_1, he should not have required the economist to assure him about 'efficiency'. The economist in turn should not expect a distributional judgement from the decision-maker, but a direct welfare judgement, based on as precise a description of Q_2 as possible. In fact, the 'efficiency' and 'distributional' elements are usually regarded as separable. I rationalized the separation by taking redistribution to *mean* a movement along a UPC. If we assume that the preference-holder is Paretian and consistent, this is, I believe, the only way of separating (and then combining into a dual criterion) efficiency and distributional judgements. And such dual criteria are undoubtedly used.

However, Mishan (1973) has recently shown that two points such as Q_1 and Q_2, lying on *different* and intersecting 'point' UPCs (i.e., the maximum utility loci of sets of goods), have nevertheless a common point UPC because it is always possible to find some set of goods such that both Q_1 and Q_2 would lie on the UPC of that third set. Given his own definitions, this means that a 'distributional comparison' can be made between Q_1 and Q_2—a comparison not involving a point such as H or J.

This would seem to imply that, if one has to ask for a distributional comparison anyway, then nothing more is required. Dual criteria again become redundant, together with compensation tests and SCB analysis as generally practised.

It seems to me that this ingenious analysis, so far from resolving any paradox, is a red herring which further confuses the issue. It is unreasonable to interpret a distributional comparison of two points as a welfare comparison of them regarded as lying on the UPC of some arbitrary and hypothetical set of goods, chosen on purely theoretical grounds. The importance of a point such as H is that it would actually be reached from Q_1 by lump-sum transfers—it is a point that would be attained by redistribution. Q_2 cannot be reached from Q_1 by redistribution, except in fairyland. Welfare criteria are attempts to reconcile real-world judgements with theoretical analysis; this purpose is not helped by imaginary and unidentified sets of goods.

Mishan seems to have an obsession with sets of goods.[4] I have repeatedly

[4] Mishan also seems to possess two hats—a welfare criterion hat and a SCB hat. Wearing the latter, he writes about compensation, and bases 'pure' SCB analysis entirely on the Kaldor–Hicks criterion without making the strange claim that the gainers must be able to overcompensate the losers with the actual set of goods that would be produced at Q_2. It is also difficult to reconcile his 'resolution of a paradox' with compensation tests at all.

emphasized that the appropriate way to define a UPC for the purpose of a contemplated economic change is with reference to a set of factors of production in an environment which is given (apart from the contemplated change) and not with reference to a set of goods—because *H* must be a point that would *actually* be reached by redistribution. However, it is probable that Mishan's new theorem could be proved for a set of factors of production. But this would not make things any better, for the set of factors of production which would bring Q_1 and Q_2 on to a common UPC would still be imaginary and unidentified.

A more pertinent case can perhaps be made for saying that dual criteria are, or should be, irrelevant. With much more research than is usual, and the proper presentation of information on the distribution of gains and losses, the decision-maker could locate Q_2 in monetary space, and hence in his own mind in utility space. He can then make a direct comparison. The question which then arises is whether he would add up the individual gains and losses. If he adds them up, he regards *H* or *J* as relevant. I suspect he would usually add them up, or complain if the analyst had not done this for him.

The decision-maker surveying the vector of gains and losses might also think it would help him to multiply by a vector of weights. Supposing he does, the question still arises whether he would not also want to know the unweighted total. Again, I would suspect (and hope) that he usually would.

In either of the preceding cases, he may make a direct comparison of Q_1 and Q_2. If so, there is no call to ask what is meant by a distributional judgement, and the Little criterion is not required. But, if I am right, points such as *H* and *J* remain relevant. Why should they be relevant? Suppose Q_2 is judged to be better than Q_1, but the UPCs are as shown in Figure 2. A Paretian would not want to move to Q_2 if *H* is attainable. If one could make lump-sum redistributions, *H* *would* be attainable. One cannot—but altering the tax system in a feasible way might still get one north-east of Q_2. A sketch such as Figure 2 may show up the

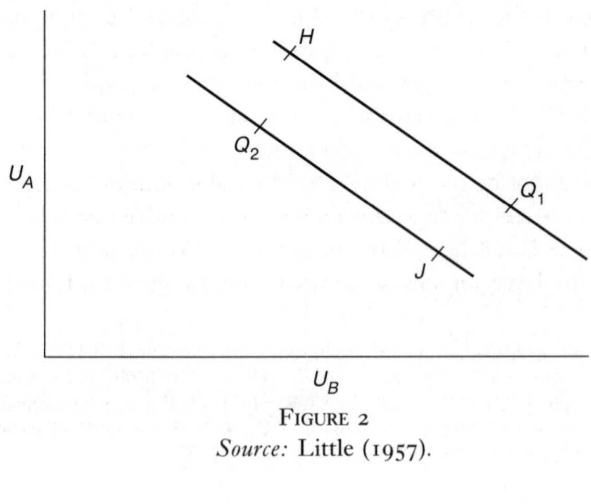

FIGURE 2
Source: Little (1957).

fact that Q_2 is better than Q_1—say, locating an industrial estate in a poor remote region rather than in a richer accessible region—mainly for distributional reasons, in which case it might be a good idea to look at alternatives. Points such as *H* and *J* are now relevant, not so much because they give meaning to the use of a dual criterion, but because they point up the need to consider alternatives which may be better than the change proposed.

I am not against producing a distribution of the gains and losses. Nor am I against applying weights. These direct comparisons (as, e.g. advocated by Kennedy (1952–3) and Meade (1959)) are also advocated by Little and Mirrlees (1974). But it should always be remembered that an increase in welfare as determined by such a direct comparison is not a sufficient reason for doing something. A negative unweighted expected present value may suggest that there could be better alternatives—in other words, compensation tests are not redundant, even when direct welfare comparisons are made.

But the dual criterion of a compensation test plus a distributional judgement—the Little criterion—will continue to be employed. It uses less information, and in practice that is important. On a more theoretical level, what I showed was that one can find an interpretation of the distributional judgement which is logically watertight. Welfare criteria, including those which use weighting systems, are concerned with creating and analysing dialogues between facts and values. One therefore must concern oneself with meanings to be attached to various kinds of value judgement, including distributional judgements. The meaning I attached to a distributional judgement concerning a change from Q_1 to Q_2 may seem a little bizarre to some, but it did not in my opinion do great violence to what any non-economist might mean. Therefore I think I was justified in claiming that a satisfactory basis for applying welfare economics had been provided—in those ordinal days of long ago.

References

Kennedy, C. M. (1952–3), 'The Economic Welfare Function and Dr Little's Criterion', *Review of Economic Studies*.

——(1963), 'Two Comments', *Economic Journal* (Dec.).

Little, I. M. D. (1957), *A Critique of Welfare Economics*. London and New York: Clarendon Press and Oxford University Press.

——and Mirrlees, J. A. (1974), *Project Appraisal and Planning for Developing Countries*. London: Heinemann.

Meade, J. E. (1959), 'Review of *A Critique of Welfare Economics*', *Economic Journal* (March).

Mishan, E. J. (1965), 'The Recent Debate on Welfare Criteria', *Oxford Economic Papers* (July).

——(1973), 'Welfare Criteria: Resolution of a Paradox', *Economic Journal* (Sept.).

Nath, S. K. (1969), *A Reappraisal of Welfare Economics*. London: Routledge & Kegan Paul.

Scitovsky, T. (1941), 'A Note on Welfare Propositions in Economics', *Review of Economic Studies* (Nov.).

Sen, A. (1963), 'Distribution, Transitivity and Little's Welfare Criteria', *Economic Journal* (Dec.).

5

Social Choice and Individual Values (1952)

The purpose of this article is to discuss the implications of Professor Arrow's conclusion that, 'if we exclude the possibility of interpersonal comparisons of utility, then the only methods of passing from individual tastes to social preferences which will be satisfactory and which will be defined for a wide range of sets of individual orderings are either imposed or dictatorial.'[1]

Since Arrow's work may not be generally familiar, I will first give a brief summary of the central theorem.

I. THE ARROW THEOREM

Imagine that there are n possibilities ($n>2$) and m choosers ($m>1$). Each chooser is deemed to have a self-consistent set of preferences ranging over all the possibilities and is assumed to choose or vote accordingly. Coalitions and bluffs are out of court; no one tries to be clever, everyone doggedly consults his own unswerving faith.

The problem is to find whether a self-consistent collective order of the possibilities, which obeys certain 'conditions of correspondence' with the individual orders, is conceivable. So that the problem will be reasonably difficult, it is stipulated that there are at least three possibilities such that no conceivable set of individual orders thereof is ruled out a priori.

The 'conditions of correspondence' laid down by Arrow can be formulated as follows.[2]

This paper first appeared in the *Journal of Political Economy*, 60 (Oct. 1952). University of Chicago Press, 1952. Permission to reproduce is gratefully acknowledged.

The paper is a comment on a work by Professor Arrow. The author is indebted to P. A. Samuelson, G. Warnock, and H. Brotman for various helpful comments on an earlier draft.

[1] K. J. Arrow, *Social Choice and Individual Values*, Yale University Press, New Haven, 1951, p. 59.

[2] Arrow actually has five conditions, but his first condition is not comparable with the others in that it merely sets the requirements for the problem indicated above, i.e., that the collective ordering be a true self-consistent ordering and that individual orders should not be unduly restricted a priori.

1. If one possibility rises or remains still in the order of every individual, then *ceteris paribus*, it must not fall in the collective order.

2. If the removal from or insertion into the set of possibilities of a certain possibility x results in no change in any individual order of the remaining possibilities, then it must cause no change in the collective order of those possibilities. This condition is named the 'independence of irrelevant alternatives'.

3. For all x and y, x must not rank above y in the collective order, regardless of the individual orders. This is called the condition of 'nonimposition'.

4. The collective order must not coincide with the order of any one chooser, regardless of the orders of the other choosers. This is called the condition of 'nondictatorship'.

Arrow has proved that no consistent collective order satisfying these conditions is conceivable. In his terminology, no satisfactory social welfare function is possible. By 'satisfactory' is meant 'satisfying the arbitrary conditions above'. By 'social welfare function' is meant 'a process or rule which for each set of individual orderings of alternative social states (one ordering for each individual) states a corresponding social ordering of alternative social states'.[3] In this definition the possibilities are interpreted as the different possible states of society. A 'social state' is defined thus: 'The most precise definition of a social state would be a complete description of the amount of each type of commodity in the hands of each individual, the amount of labor to be supplied by each individual, the amount of each productive resource invested in each kind of productive activity, and the amounts of various types of collective activity.'[4] The process of proof need not detain us here.[5]

2. RELATION OF THE ARROW THEOREM TO 'WELFARE' ECONOMICS

Let us suppose that each chooser orders different economic states strictly according to what he himself gets in each state. As is well known, this assumption enables one to isolate in principle an infinite number of 'Pareto-optimum' states, each of which is defined by the impossibility of selecting any alternative state which is higher on one man's order and lower on no one's.

Bergson suggested that this comparatively useless theoretical result could be improved on only if an 'economic welfare function' were postulated. What has this Bergson function to do with the Arrow function described above?

As I understand it, Bergson's welfare function was meant as a 'process or rule' which would indicate the best economic state as a function of a changing environment (i.e., changing sets of possibilities defined by different economic

[3] Arrow, op. cit., p. 23. [4] Ibid., p. 17. [5] See ibid., pp. 51–9.

transformation functions), *the individuals' tastes being given.* It may at once be noticed that Arrow's condition 1 above is inapplicable if tastes are given. Consequently, if I have interpreted Bergson's meaning correctly, then Arrow's result has no bearing on the possibility or impossibility of such a function.[6]

Arrow has a different interpretation. Thus, he writes:

> The ethical system is a rule which defines the Social state chosen from a given environment *as a function of the tastes of all individuals.* If, for a given set of tastes, the environment varies, we expect that the choices will be consistent in the sense that the choice function is derivable from a weak social ordering of all social states. Thus the Bergson Social Welfare Function has the form of a rule assigning a social ordering to each possible set of individual orderings representing tastes.[7]

I should agree that we must expect that, in principle, for a given set of tastes, as the environment varies, the choices will be consistent in the sense that they are derivable from a weak ordering. In other words, all logically possible social or economic states (not merely all scientifically possible ones) must be ordered. Then, as the scientific possibilities change, different states are selected as best. This is my idea of a Bergson function; or, if it is not what Bergson meant, it is what I think he should have meant. This conception has two important points of difference from Arrow's conception. First, tastes are given. If tastes change, we may expect a new ordering of all the conceivable states; but we do not require that the difference between the new and the old ordering should bear any particular relation to the changes of tastes which have occurred. We have, so to speak, a new world and a new order; and we do not demand correspondence between the change in the world and the change in the order.

The second important difference is that my interpretation of a Bergson function requires only that there should be an order. It does not require that it should be an order such that anyone would want to say of it that it represented the choices of society. To call an ordering a social ordering at all implies that one approves of the order, or of the mechanism (if any), through which it is determined by the individual choices or preferences. This is, of course, because 'social' is a persuasive word. In discussing the logic of welfare economics, there is no need thus to involve oneself in political philosophy. Thus, the so-called 'social welfare function', postulated by welfare economists, should on my view be regarded as a social ordering *only* in the sense that it orders states of society. Whether or not it is possible that such an ordering may be, in some further sense, a social ordering is a question we can, for the moment, leave on one side; we return to it later. The essential point here is that none of the advantages claimed for theoretical welfare economics, as a result of introducing such a function,

[6] I am indebted both to the Rockefeller Foundation and to Samuelson for a conversation with the latter in which he pointed out this divergence between his concept of the Bergson function (as elaborated in his *Foundations of Economic Analysis*, ch. viii) and that of Arrow.

[7] Arrow, op. cit., p. 72; italics mine.

depends in the least on the ordering of economic states being an ordering by society.[8] Instead of writing, with Bergson, $W = W(U_1, \ldots, U_n)$, we can write $W_i = W_i(U_1, \ldots, U_n)$ $(i = 1, \ldots n)$. There is no need, so far as pure theory is concerned, to introduce a further (social) welfare function of the form $W = W(W_1, \ldots, W_n)$. We can deduce the whole effective corpus of welfare economics from, say, $W_{10} = W_{10}(U_1, \ldots, U_n)$—remembering only to put 'in the opinion of individual no. 10' after 'welfare' whenever we use the term.

Arrow wants to go much farther than this in two directions. He wants a 'process or rule' which will produce a social ordering as a function of the tastes themselves. As I have tried to indicate, neither of these requirements really has anything to do with what is commonly thought of as welfare economics. Traditionally, tastes are given; indeed, one might almost say that the given individuals are traditionally defined as the possessors of the given tastes and that no sense is attached to the notion of given individuals with changing tastes. (Certainly, the individual's 'economic welfare' is not supposed to be comparable before and after a change of taste.)

Quite apart from condition 1, Arrow's other conditions are defined in terms of changing tastes. Nevertheless, it is condition 1 which is crucial, because the other conditions have analogues if tastes are given. Condition 2 need merely be modified to read 'The removal from or insertion into the set of possibilities of a certain possibility x must cause no change in the collective order of the remaining possibilities.' For, if the entry or exodus of a possibility *did* cause a change in the individual orders of the remainder, we should be faced with a new set of tastes which would require a new 'master'-order,[9] which, on my view, need not bear any relation to the old order. Condition 3, called 'nonimposition', can be modified to state simply that there must be some conceivable set of individual orders which precludes any given 'master'-order. In this form, 'nonimposition' is a traditional assumption of welfare economics equivalent to the postulate that, if someone prefers x to y and no one y to x, then x is better than y. Condition 4 ('nondictatorship') must also, if tastes are given, be modified to the effect that the 'master'-order must not coincide with that of any one individual if this order is exactly reversed for all others.[10]

While we must conclude that Arrow's work has no relevance to the traditional theory of welfare economics, which culminates in the Bergson–Samuelson formulation, it remains, of course, true that his wider conception may have advantages of its own. Let us therefore examine his conditions on their own merits.

[8] It is, incidentally, clear from Samuelson's work (op. cit.) that he would agree with me about this.

[9] I shall, where necessary, refer to a 'master'-order throughout the rest of this article, in order to try to avoid begging questions about the nature of the order.

[10] This form of the 'nondictatorship' condition is, in any case, a consequence of the above conditions; see Arrow, op. cit., pp. 53–4.

First, consider condition 1. Suppose that we have three individuals (defined independently of their tastes) and that the orders of three possible states are *xyz* for Mr A, *zxy* for Mr B, and *yzx* for Mr C. Let the 'master'-order be *zxy*. Then, let there be a change of taste such that *z* rises or remains still in each order, letting the orders become *xzy* for Mr A, *zxy* for Mr B, and *yzx* for Mr C. Condition 1 requires that *z* remain top of the poll. But, looking at the matter from an Olympian point of view, one can ask, 'Why on earth should it?' Could not, for instance, A's change of taste as between *y* and *z* justify a higher weighting of his first choice, so that *xyz* should become the 'master'-order? There is, indeed, nothing in Arrow's theory which prevents us from supposing that the rise of *z* in the first order is due not to a change of taste on the part of an ostensibly defined Mr A but rather to the substitution of a new individual for Mr A. There is then even less reason why one should accept the view that *z* must remain top of the poll. I may want to attach a high weight to the new man's tastes.

Take now condition 2, called the 'independence of irrelevant alternatives'. Arrow himself gives an example which throws some doubt on this condition. He writes:

> Suppose that there are just two commodities, bread and wine. A distribution, deemed equitable by all, is arranged, with the wine-lovers getting more wine and less bread than the abstainers. Suppose now that all the wine is destroyed. Are the wine-lovers entitled, because of that fact, to more than an equal share of bread? My answer is, of course, a value judgement. My own feeling is that tastes for unattainable alternatives should have nothing to do with the decision among the attainable ones; desires in conflict with reality are not entitled to consideration, so that condition (3) . . . is a valid value judgement, to me at least.[11]

It is, however, easy enough to argue the other way. Thus, I can argue that, if sacrifices must be made in an egalitarian society, then they should be equal sacrifices. But if the wine-lovers got only an equal share of bread, they would have lost more heavily than the bread-lovers. What one would think in an actual case would depend so much on so many circumstances. At all events, I know that I should hate to commit myself a priori to Arrow's value judgement.

Condition 3 ('nonimposition') needs no comment, since it has been discussed *ad nauseam* in the literature.

As put by Arrow, condition 4 ('nondictatorship') appears eminently acceptable. In his formulation, Tom is a dictator if, for all *x* and *y* and 'regardless' of the orderings of others, 'Tom prefers *x* to *y*' implies '*x* is higher in the master-order'. What Arrow evidently has in mind is that, if no change in the orders of others can upset the coincidence of Tom's and the master-order, then it would seem reasonable to call Tom a dictator. Here I should agree. But, when we discover that this condition, if combined with the others, produces the consequence that

[11] Ibid., p. 73.

no more need be known to dub a man 'dictator' than that his ordering of any pair of alternatives has prevailed against the reverse ordering on the part of everyone else, we may well begin to feel uncomfortable.

Take an example. Let there be three men and two alternatives, *x* and *y*. Let the orders be *xy* for Tom and *yx* for both Dick and Harry. The conditions then preclude *xy* as the master-order. The two (economic) states may be such that in *y* Tom has one piece of manna, while Dick and Harry both have ninety-nine pieces; in *x* Tom has three pieces and Dick and Harry both have ninety-eight pieces. Might not then the master-ranking *xy* be desirable? Use of the word 'dictatorship' suggests that Tom's preference for *x* over *y* somehow causes society to choose *x*. But, in fact, the coincidence of Tom's and the master-order may be a result of his poverty and not of his power. The plausibility of the 'nondictatorship' condition may come partly from the ambiguity of the word 'imply'. In ordinary language, it carries a suggestion of causation. But in logic '*p* implies *q*' means no more than 'not both *p* and not *q*'. Thus, poor Tom is deemed dictatorial merely because it happens to be the case that society agrees with him and not with the plutocrats. This may be an absurdly limited example (there being only three men and two alternatives), but, presumably, Arrow intended his conditions to be perfectly general. He does, it is true, find this sort of consequence paradoxical;[12] but he draws no conclusions from the paradox. The conclusion, to my mind, is that it is foolish to accept or reject a set of ethical axioms one at a time. One must know the consequences before one can say whether one finds the set acceptable—which fact sets a limit to the usefulness of deductive techniques in ethics or in welfare economics.

It is evident that Arrow has introduced a most interesting logical framework for possible critiques of the behaviour of economic systems under conditions of changing tastes and changing income distribution. He fills out the framework with a set of value judgements which yield him entirely negative conclusions. The fact that I have argued that I can see no reason to accept, and some reasons not to accept, his conditions does not, of course, imply that I think that any generally acceptable set of value judgements, which would turn the logical framework into something useful, is likely or even possible. In fact, I think the opposite, as should become clear from what follows.

3. THE GENERAL VERSION OF THE ARROW SOCIAL WELFARE FUNCTION IN ITS RELATION TO ETHICS AND POLITICAL PHILOSOPHY

In the preceding section it was supposed that each individual ordered states solely according to what he himself would get. Everything else which individuals

[12] E.g., Arrow, op. cit., p. 55.

thought significant could play its part only in determining the form of the function which would produce the 'master'-ordering from these original orderings. But of course, there is no need to suppose this. In general, Arrow assumes that the individuals take more into account than their own utility when compiling their original orders; more, indeed, than other people's utilities or welfare. In fact, quite generally, we may suppose that they arrange all states in order of what they regard as ultimately desirability, taking everything they know and feel to be significant into account. We shall call such an ordering a value ordering, although, of course, many of the discriminations made would not really be felt sufficiently strongly to be called value judgements. The problem, then, is to form a 'master'-ordering; in Rousseau's language, the problem is the well-known one of discovering the general will.

We must now make an important distinction which Arrow fails to draw. He calls his function both a social welfare function and a decision-making process. He believes that 'one of the great advantages of abstract postulational methods is the fact that the same system may be given different interpretations permitting a considerable saving of time.' Yes, but we must be careful not to give such a system a nonsensical interpretation, and it will be my contention that to interpret it as a social welfare function *is* to give a nonsensical interpretation.

Imagine the system as a machine which produces a card on which is written 'x is better than y', or vice versa, when all individual answers to the question 'Is x better than y?' have been fed into it. What significance are we to attach to the sentence on the card, i.e. to the resulting 'master'-order? First, it is clear that the sentence, although it is a sentence employing ethical terms, is not a value *judgement*. Every value judgement must be *someone's* judgement of values. If there are n people filling in cards to be fed into the machine, then we have n value judgements, not $n+1$. The sentence which the machine produces expresses a ruling, or decision, which is different in kind from what is expressed by the sentences fed into it. The latter express value judgements; the former expresses a ruling between these judgements. Thus, we can legitimately call the machine, or function, a decision-making process.

But what would it mean to call the machine a social welfare function? One would be asserting, in effect, that, if the machine decided in favour of x rather than in favour of y, then x would produce more social welfare than y or simply be more desirable than y. This is clearly a value judgement, but it is, of course, a value judgement made by the person who calls the machine a social welfare function. Thus, in general, to call the machine a social welfare function is to assert that x is better than y whenever the machine writes the sentence 'x is better than y'. Now we may suppose that the individual who calls the machine a social welfare function is one of those who has fed his own value order into it. It is clear that this person must be contradicting himself unless the 'master'-order coincides with his own value ordering. It follows that, if the machine is to be called a social welfare function, then anyone who is called upon to accept or reject the principles on which it is built (i.e. the conditions of correspondence) must refuse to accept any principle which ensures that the 'master'-order will necessarily not coincide with his own. This is because the conditions of correspondence determine the 'master'-order and because, by calling the machine a social welfare function, the person in question has accepted the 'master'-order. (It should be noted that accepting or rejecting a value sentence entails agreement or disagreement with the corresponding value judgement.) In other words, it is inconsistent both to call the machine a social welfare function and to accept the condition of nondictatorship.

This may appear very surprising. First, it may be objected that, as in the case considered in the previous section, a rich man may, like Bernard Shaw, easily *prefer* a state which yields him more manna but at the same time *disapprove* of it because he is an egalitarian and would therefore accept a rule which named as best a social state which yielded him less manna. This objection does not, however, apply in the case under consideration, because in this most general version it is presumed that the individual orders take the welfare of others into consideration. He would therefore *not* rank as higher the state which yielded him more manna.

It is true, of course, that, in the initial ordering, one thing which a person cannot take into consideration is other people's valuations, which he may very well regard as highly significant, if he is a tolerant sort of person. Even worse is the fact that valuations are expressed in value statements, whose whole purpose is to influence other people's value judgements and behaviour. It would consequently be surprising if an individual were entirely uninfluenced by the verdicts of others. Indeed, when a working agreement is reached, it is usually partly, if not wholly, the result of this kind of mutual influence. These are difficulties which Arrow does not seem to face. Nevertheless, they can, formally at least, be side-stepped. Thus, we can suppose that we can have as much revoting, or rearrangement of individual orders, as the individuals want when they learn the opinions and verdicts of each other. Accordingly, each order is, so to speak, a deadlock order. It is the individual order resulting when all persuasion has been used, and after an indefinite number of straw votes.[13]

Second, it will be objected that I may regard x as better than y but still be willing to submit to a ruling which proclaims y as society's choice. But it can easily be seen that this, though true, is no objection, for it interprets the machine as a decision-making process. I am not maintaining that there is anything inconsistent about accepting the nondictatorship condition when the machine is *thus* interpreted. The acceptability of the conditions of correspondence, given the decision-making-process interpretation, will be discussed in the next section.

[13] This consideration alone would seem to limit the applicability of the Arrow theorem to a very small society. Moreover, it is quite reasonable to suppose that no such deadlock, or equilibrium, set of orders would ever result, especially in a large society. The dynamics of value formation may imply that values are, as a result of mutual influence, in a state of permanent flux.

Third, some people might not find convincing my statement that the sentences which the machine produces cannot themselves be regarded as value judgements. They may think that judgements do not necessarily require someone to judge. Though I believe it to be a nonsensical supposition, let us suppose, for the remainder of this section, that the machine *does* produce value judgements.

Now, if I think *x* is better than *y*, and the machine announces that *y* is better than *x*, I have three choices. First I can say: 'I was wrong; *y* is better than *x*.' Thus, Rousseau claims: 'When therefore the opinion that is contrary to my own prevails, this proves neither more nor less than that I was mistaken.'[14] Rousseau's remark can be taken to mean merely that I was wrong in that my original vote was a guess at the general will which, *ex hypothesi*, is the majority decision. But Rousseau is nothing if not inconsistent, and the remark could be taken as an appeal to some mystical standard of right and wrong. But, since few philosophers now believe that value judgements can be verified or falsified (i.e. be said to be true or false in any objective sense), and since the fact that they cannot be thus verified is the whole basis of Arrow's work, this choice can be dismissed.

Second, I can say: 'I have changed my mind. I now wish to assert the same value judgement as the machine; *y is* better than *x*.' It is quite clear that we can dismiss this as a possibility for everyone; for, if everyone always changed his values to be in conformity with the machine, no problem could arise. There would always be unanimous agreement in the end, however perverse the machine was.

Third, I can say 'To hell with the machine; *x* is better than *y*, whatever it says.' If I always did this (and how could I do anything else, since, remember, we are supposing that all other people's values are already known; indeed, I have taken into account everything I think significant!), then I should naturally have refused to accept the condition of nondictatorship. It is in the nature of value judgements that the only order which I can fully accept is one that coincides with my own, regardless of the orders of other people. In other words, no one can consistently accept the condition of 'nondictatorship'. At all events, it is sheer nonsense to say, 'A is better than B, but everyone else claims B is better than A; therefore, since I don't want to be a dictator, B is better than A.' Yet this is what acceptance of condition 4 would imply in this general case. Once again, we are back at the conclusion that condition 4 makes nonsense of any interpretation of the Arrow system in ethical terms. In my opinion, this makes the title 'social welfare function' a dangerous misnomer.

Arrow presumably thinks differently, though it is difficult to be sure of this from his book. Thus, having shown that a 'social welfare function' satisfying his conditions is possible if individual orders happen to be of a certain form,[15] he proceeds to a brief discussion of some of the politico-ethical systems which various philosophers have vainly proposed, and rightly says that they are based on some idea of an initial consensus of values; he then writes: 'The results . . . show

[14] Rousseau, *Social Contract*, Everyman edn., 1913, p. 94.

[15] So-called 'single-peaked' preferences: see Arrow, op. cit., ch. VII, part II.

that the condition of unanimity is mathematically unnecessary to the existence of a social welfare function, and we may well hope that there are still other conditions [i.e., conditions as to the form of the individual variations] . . . under which the formation of a social welfare function will be possible.'[16]

The very use of the phrase 'social welfare function' suggests that, if such were possible, then somehow an objective moral code would have been erected. Political philosophers used to worry over the question 'Why ought I to obey the state (or society, or the general will)?' The pseudo-puzzle of how one can both be free and be subject to law is a variant of the pseudo-puzzle of how duty and self-interest can be reconciled. The philosophers tried to show that it was always really in one's own interest to abide by whatever the 'objective' code might be. Since, plainly, conflict must arise, at least in the absence of complete initial consensus, and since such consensus was obviously absent, they invented the doctrine of a metaphysical consensus. When people actually (i.e., really) disagreed about some matter affecting the common interest, they were really (i.e. metaphysically) agreeing. Rousseau, who was first responsible for this nonsense, found some difficulty in explaining how one found out what people were really metaphysically agreeing about when they disagreed, i.e., he found some difficulty in explaining the circumstances under which one could be sure that the general will had expressed itself.

We may illustrate all this with a few quotations:

'The problem is to find a form of association which will defend and protect with the whole common force the person and goods of each associate, and in which each, while uniting himself with all, may still obey himself alone, and remain as free as before.'[17]

'Each of us puts his person and all his power in common under the supreme direction of the general will.'[18]

'Whoever refuses to obey the general will shall be compelled to do so by the whole body. This means nothing less than that he will be forced to be free.'[19]

'The general will is always right and tends to the public advantage.'[20]

It is but a very short step from here (a step which Hegel took) to maintain that acceptance of the social order (or obedience to the state) is really only self-obedience. Arrow's problem clearly has so much in common with Rousseau's that it seems worth while to point out again the insidious danger of this approach. Modern totalitarian philosophy may be not altogether unjustly fathered on Rousseau.

Ever since the objectivity of utilitarianism was called in question, economists have been searching for that old philosophers' stone, a scientific ethic. Recently many philosophers, those of the linguistic school, have given up the search, because they have realized that any attempt to define ethical terms is necessarily

[16] So-called 'single-peaked' preferences: see Arrow, op. cit., ch. VII, part II p. 83.

[17] Rousseau, op. cit., p. 14. [18] Ibid., p. 15. [19] Ibid., p. 18.

[20] Ibid., p. 25.

also an attempt to lay down a moral code; i.e., any supposed definition of an ethical word in non-ethical terms is itself an ethical judgement. Thus, in view of the undoubted fact of disagreement about values, any assertion that such-and-such a given value statement is 'objectively true' is itself a value statement which persuasively twists words like 'objective' and 'true' in an attempt to get the given value statement accepted.

We can have an 'objective' ethic only when there is universal agreement. But when there is universal agreement ethics will have ceased to exist, since all moral judgements will have become futile and redundant. One does not tell people that they ought to do what they are doing or will do anyway. If everyone agreed, there would be no need to try to change other people's values and behaviour, which is the primary use of value statements. In Utopia, not only will the State have withered away, but also all morality; and naturally, since it is Utopia, not only all morality, but also welfare economics.

4. THE GENERAL VERSION OF THE ARROW SOCIAL WELFARE FUNCTION IN RELATION TO POLITICS AND DECISION-MAKING

We indicated in Section 3 that the so-called 'social welfare function' must be interpreted not (as the name might seem to imply) as a social welfare function but as a decision-making process. The question arises whether one can consistently accept Arrow's conditions, given this interpretation.

The importance of the distinction between a value order and a decision order, for our purposes, is as follows. In a given community, or committee, as many value orderings as there are individuals may coexist. On the other hand, as between two alternatives there can be only one effective decision. Thus, we may all have our conflicting opinions as to whether we ought to go to war or not. But the decision to do so or not to do so is unique and binding for everyone. Where values are concerned, everyone must be a 'dictator' (i.e., the logic of value judgements is such that one cannot consistently *accept* any value ordering which differs from one's own); where decisions are in question, everyone cannot be a dictator, in Arrow's sense, unless there is unanimity.

Thus, an individual will often be prepared to accept a decision which goes against him, because the same decision-making process (or 'procedure', for short) will be used for making many other decisions between other alternatives, some of which will go in his favour. This is, of course, true; but it is not an answer to the problem of why acceptance of Arrow's conditions does not imply inconsistency. I may be prepared, of course, to accept decisions which go against me because it is unwise to rebel against an established procedure with established sanctions. But this does not explain why, when I am free and still without my chains, I should accept certain a priori conditions to which any social contract must conform—a priori conditions which rule out all procedures which would ever decide in my favour against everyone else. To explain this, we require, I think, the hypothesis that, among the very limited number of procedures which would stand any chance of being established, none would make me dictatorial in Arrow's sense, together with the hypothesis that all such procedures would determine social states higher on my valuation than anarchy.

It may be suggested that the matter is much simpler than this and that I am making possible acceptance of the conditions depend too much on expediency and not enough on high moral purpose. Thus, it may be said that, although one values x above y, one might prefer to accept a procedure which would yield y, if the only way to get x were to impose one's will on society.[21] This is true; but it is not a sufficient reason for accepting Arrow's condition of 'nondictatorship', which, barring the name, contains nothing about power or force. This is not, of course, Arrow's fault, given his technique. It springs from the fact that causal and power relations are not logical relations. Thus, since 'dictatorship', in the ordinary sense, involves the idea of causation, it cannot be adequately described in terms of implication. Even so, one must add that it is probably true that most people would attach intrinsic demerit to a procedure which ever allowed a minority of one to win.

To sum this up, one may say that expediency might, in most situations, counsel one to accept condition 4 as applied to procedure. It may also be widely acceptable on moral grounds. Indeed, conditions 3 and 4 might be said to contain the bare essentials of democratic procedures—but, perhaps, only the barest essentials, since there is nothing in them to prevent, say, a minority of two in a million from carrying the day.

We may now briefly consider conditions 1 and 2, taken in conjunction with the others. It would seem unlikely that anyone would want to attach intrinsic merit or demerit to them. Consequently, one may suppose that individuals would decide whether or not to accept them on the basis of whether, in conjunction with the remaining conditions, they would be likely to admit or exclude procedures more or less likely to lead to higher or lower states more or less often than alternative procedures. Thus, the value of such conditions of correspondence would be derivative, though not derivative solely from one's own present, or even expected future, ordering, but also from a consideration of probable changes in

[21] It should be noted that to formulate this suggestion at all it is necessary to assume that the 'social states' contain only descriptions of the goods accruing to each individual. It presupposes that the procedures have intrinsic, and not merely derived, merit or demerit. In other words, since we are now dealing with decision-making processes or mechanisms, means may be valued apart from the ends attained by them. This distinction of 'ends' and 'means' could not, of course, arise when we were considering (or, rather, trying to consider) the function as a social welfare function. There cannot be procedures or mechanisms (means) for working out what is right or wrong. Means are, in the present context, means of arriving at a decision. It should be noted, however, that 'means' usually refers to social states which would necessarily precede some more distant social state aimed at. In this sense, the means are part of the ends in the present discussion: the individuals in willing the ends necessarily also will the means; they order the alternative future chains of social status.

other orderings as well. (E.g., if I disapproved of drunkenness very much and thought the taste for gin on the increase, I might not wish condition 1 to be satisfied for states involving alcohol.) The chief difficulty with any such 'conditions of correspondence' is that, for both logical and factual reasons, it is exceedingly difficult to see what they involve one in. Nevertheless, Arrow's conditions undoubtedly have some prima facie plausibility, probably mainly for the reasons of expediency discussed above.

5. CONCLUSIONS

It was concluded first that Arrow's system is quite different from, and has little relevance to, traditional welfare economics. Second, it was found that it cannot without inconsistency be interpreted as a critique of social welfare functions. Last, we found that it, and no doubt similar deductive techniques, are in principle applicable to decision-making processes. Whether, in this sphere, Arrow's conditions of correspondence are sufficiently acceptable as minimum conditions for a satisfactory democratic decision-making procedure for it to be said that he has proved that consistent decisions cannot be reached via such procedures must be left an open question. Some people will no doubt think that such a proposition requires no proof. Others will think that the essence of democracy is something which must escape definition in terms of any functional relation between decisions and individual preferences.

PART III

Development Economics

Life changed a good deal when in 1958 I accepted an invitation from Professor Rosenstein Rodan to join the India Project of the MIT Center for International Studies, of which he was the director. Thereafter I was primarily a development economist, and therefore a member of a sub-class then widely regarded as intellectually second-rate.

Indian Planning, Africa, and Aid (1958–1965)

The original MIT India Project team consisted of only three members: George Rosen, who was already working closely with the Reserve Bank in Bombay, and Trevor Swan and myself, who were established with an office in New Delhi. Our terms of reference agreed with the Government (that is, the Planning Commission) were very vague, but I think we were supposed to galvanize empirical economic research in liaison with four existing institutions: the National Council of Applied Economic Research under Dr Lokanathan, the Economic Growth Centre of the Delhi School of Economics under V. K. R. V. Rao (both in Delhi), the Indian Statistical Institute in Calcutta under P. C. Mahalanobis, and the Gokhale Institute in Poona under Dr Gadgil. These terms of reference were totally unrealistic for reasons of time, distance, personality, and lack of any research material. Outside government there were almost no up-to-date figures for anything, and we had neither the time (Swan and I were in India for only nine months) nor the resources to create data. Nor was this what we were supposed to do.

We were in despair of getting started on anything useful, when I met my previous boss, Sir Robert Hall (later Lord Roberthall), at a cocktail party and explained the predicament. He said 'You should get in touch with Pitamber Pant.' None of our Indian contacts, including our main official contact, the Secretary of the Planning Commission, had mentioned Pitamber Pant, who was the head of the perspective planning division of the Planning Commission. His official position was no measure of his influence. He was Mahalanobis's protégé and representative in Delhi, and he was Nehru's Secretary in his role as Chairman of the Planning Commission. On the run-up to the Third Plan, he was the arch planner.

We called on Pant. He showed us without hesitation a highly confidential paper which was to be the bones of the Third Five-Year Plan (see below). An intellectual love affair rapidly developed between him and Trevor Swan. We became in effect unofficial members of the perspective planning division, and did not thereafter lack either work or direction. This troubled others in the Planning Commission. The secretary complained to the head of the Ford Foundation, which was supporting the MIT India Project, that Swan and I were not doing research. Rosenstein Rodan managed to defuse the issue, and we carried on.[1]

Trevor Swan, whose contributions to economic theory are few but everlasting, was an eccentric and a heavy drinker. He never opened letters, or answered the telephone. Distant communication could be ensured only by telegram. We shared a house, our wives coming and going. Pitamber Pant often called in the morning, ebullient on his way to the office, for a tutorial with Trevor. When I warned him of Pitamber's approach, he would appear and palely try to swallow the cold cocoa which was the only sustenance he seemed to be able to take before noon. Then the tutorial began.

My work consisted of producing a plan to finance the 'real' plan that Pant had produced. This latter was the paper already referred to, entitled 'Certain Dimensional Hypotheses Concerning the Third Five-Year Plan' (never officially published). My paper was entitled 'Public finance and the Third Plan' (also unpublished).[2] The late Sukhamoy Chakravarty, who became the doyen of Indian planners, has referred to these papers as the Pant/Little model underlying the Third Plan.[3] A vigorous debate ensued as to whether a large public investment plan of the size adumbrated in Pant's paper could be realized without dire inflationary consequences. My paper argued that taxes could be raised sufficiently to finance such a plan without inflation. I thus supported the large plan, attracted Nehru's support, and helped win the day. I was right about the taxation potential, but I now believe that the Third Plan saddled India with a large inefficient heavy industrial complex, which crowded out investment in the light manufactured exports that would have contributed far more to India's growth and prosperity. In short, I was a bad influence.

I also wrote a paper just after my stay in India showing that on certain assumptions the shadow cost of labour was higher than the actual wage paid.[4] I now think the assumptions were indefensible.

Of the various papers that arose out of my first stay in India,[5] I include here only 'The Strategy of Indian Development', written in late 1959 or early 1960, as Paper 6. This purveys the Indian planners' thinking of the time, which I accepted almost unreservedly. The weakness of the reasoning (or rationalization) in support of the export pessimism that was an essential component of the Third Plan's logical structure is apparent now. However, I am afraid that my defence was plausible at the time. I include the paper as a warning against planning based on broad 'orders of magnitude' linked by tendentious guesses as to their relationship.

[1] The chequered history of the MIT India Project from 1958 to 1965 is recounted in detail in Rosen, *Western Economists and Eastern Societies*.

[2] The gist of the paper is however given and discussed in Little, 'Tax Policy and the Third Plan'.

[3] Chakravarty, 'The Mathematical Framework of the Third Five Year'.

[4] Little, 'The Real Cost of Labour, and the Choice between Consumption and Investment'.

[5] Besides those mentioned above, these include 'A Critical Examination of India's Third Five-Year Plan' (1962), and 'Atomic Bombay?' (1958). The latter argues that there was no economic case for nuclear power in India. I still like the title as being both witty and prophetic.

The second of the paper's conclusions is notable. It is a very clear statement that a foreign exchange 'gap' was prior to a savings 'gap'. The theory of the two gaps was later developed by Chenery and Bruno and became very influential.[6] Indeed, much of the economic research at the World Bank in the 1970s, under Hollis Chenery's vice-presidency, was inspired by the two-gap model. Gaps have since then multiplied. For many years now, I have declared myself to be an opponent of multi-gap theories.[7]

On my return to England in 1959, I tried to get myself recognized in Oxford as a development economist. But, with only two exceptions, no postgraduate student of the subject, or from a developing country, was assigned to me by the university before I became 'professor of the economics of underdeveloped countries' a decade later, and acquired some say in the matter. The two exceptions were from the Middle East. They were concerned with oil, and it was no doubt remembered that, many years earlier, I had written a book entitled *The Price of Fuel* (which dealt with coal, gas, and electricity—but not oil!). Development economics in Oxford was then the preserve of a sectarian leftist clique.

However, Nuffield College always appointed a college supervisor for its students in addition to the university supervisor, and in this way I did acquire a few students, the most famous of whom was Manmohan Singh, Finance Minister of India from 1991 to 1996. He wrote a thesis, subsequently published, on India's exports, which showed that their miserably slow growth was caused mainly by supply problems and not by sluggish world demand.[8] This was one of the influences that slowly lifted the veil of export pessimism from my eyes.

In 1963 the late William Clark, then head of the Overseas Development Institute (ODI) and later a vice president of the World Bank, suggested that I write a book on aid for them. It should be about aid from any source, but with some focus on British aid. He would provide a research assistant, and some travel expenses if need be. I agreed. My knowledge of developing countries, and of the problem of aid-giving, was limited to India. Ignorance of Latin America did not seem to matter, because it received virtually no British aid and not very much from anywhere. But ignorance of Africa had to be remedied. With a good deal of help from HMG, and also from Shell (the chief executive was a Visiting Fellow of Nuffield), I planned and carried out a highly concentrated tour of Africa, interviewing mainly donor and recipient country officials. I was at the time frightened of flying, a still persistent legacy from my war time experience. My wife and I went by boat to Cape Town, an irrational procrastination, since my trip could not subsequently be accomplished without many flights. From Cape Town we proceeded north to Addis Ababa and Khartoum, taking in Swaziland, Zimbabwe, Malawi, Tanzania, Kenya, and Uganda.

[6] Chenery and Bruno, 'Development Alternatives in an Open Economy: The Case of Israel'.

[7] Little, *Economic Development*; see also Joshi and Little, *India: Macroeconomics and Political Economy 1964–1991*, App. B.

[8] Singh, *India's Export Trends and the Prospects for Self-Sustained Growth.*

We crossed the African continent to Lagos by Ethiopian Airlines (I think this was then the only way of flying from East to West Africa) and visited also Benin, Togo, Ghana, Sierra Leone, Guinea and Senegal, ending with the Gambia, the only one that was still a colony. In all, we visited sixteen countries in sixteen weeks. The longest stay was a fortnight in Nigeria: the shortest was an excellent lunch in Benin, our first escape from 'anglophone' cuisine. In all there were twenty-six flights. I have never been afraid of flying since. This 'deep-end' cure was exhausting, but very worthwhile: after all, I could not be a 'development economist' and retain my fear of flying.

The trip contributed to the book on aid which I wrote with Juliet Clifford, the research assistant from the ODI. But before the main book could be finished I rapidly wrote a short book or pamphlet on aid to Africa, especially British aid.[9] Among the recommendations was that aid-giving should be concentrated in a single department. This was carried out by the incoming Labour government. I think I expected this, and naively hoped that I might become its chief economist. I had not reckoned with Thomas Balogh's close friendship with Harold Wilson and Barbara Castle, which ensured that most senior appointments to her new Ministry came, directly or indirectly, from the left-wing Oxford development establishment.[10] They included Dudley Seers, Paul Streeten, and Peter Ady.

Balogh reviewed my *Aid to Africa* in the *Guardian*. More accurately, he reviewed me, for it was obvious that he had not read the book. It was made very plain that I was not a suitable boy for any position of influence over aid-giving. The book was widely reviewed, unfavourably only by *The Economist* and Balogh. (I do not know who wrote the brief unsigned *Economist* review.) Balogh referred particularly to 'my obvious dislike' of the new African 'élite'. On re-reading the book, I find no trace of such obvious dislike. I did not in any case meet the élite—not Banda, Kenyatta, Nkrumah, Nyerere, Obote, Sekoutouré, or Senghor—among the leaders of the countries I visited. My interviews were at lower levels. My highest reach was Chief Festus Okotie Eboh, then the Finance Minister of Nigeria. He was on the telephone for the whole of the interview, buying and selling Mercedes Benzes. Whenever I tried to get in a word, he looked up and said 'no comment'. I did not report this interview in *Aid to Africa*! (He was murdered not long after.) I learned to dislike the 'new African élite' and their works only much later, as did most Africans. My obvious dislike of Lord Balogh came earlier.

It is ironical that one of the main recommendations of *Aid to Africa* was the creation of a large Development Institute in the UK. Like most of my recommendations, this was carried out, in the shape of the Institute of Development Studies (IDS) in Sussex. However, the IDS is smaller and quite different from the more multi-disciplinary institute I suggested, one of whose chief functions was to operate as a home base for technical assistance 'experts' in many fields.

[9] Little and Clifford, *International Aid*; Little, *Aid to Africa*.

[10] See Castle, *Fighting All the Way*.

When Barbara Castle left the new ministry, her most senior economic staff also left and took over the IDS.

My main book on aid came out a year later in 1965.[11] This two-year period spent on the role and problems of economic aid did not result in any article that could be included here. Aid, by which is meant the official transfer of resources by grant or on subsidized terms, needs a broad canvas. Its discussion involves moral and political philosophy as well as economic and political analysis. This explains my production of books, not articles.[12] It is impossible to summarize them adequately in a paragraph or two. But I can give a few highlights and indicate whether I have changed my mind since 1965.

The aim should be development that would sustain 'stable and independent governments based on mass support and rising standards of living'. The aim of development should not be compromised by using aid to promote the donor's commercial interests, e.g. by tying aid to exports, or to promote the recipient's pet projects if these were of little or no development value. Since donors should not expect to be paid back, grant aid should predominate. I supported aid for projects rather than plans, which were seldom operational or consistent. I dismissed the argument that, because of 'fungibility', a dollar tied to a project was no different from a dollar without strings.

I believed that the quantity of aid could usefully be increased. Most of the increase should go to India. Africa could not yet absorb large amounts of capital, but needed help with health and education, and government administration. More generally, the division between countries should depend on economic potential and the recipient's policies: if these were not conducive to development, aid would be wasted. However, international relations were also relevant: the Cold War was raging and one should not help one's enemies.

In what ways, if at all, have I changed my mind after the lapse of thirty-five years? Not in any way profoundly or dramatically. Indeed, most of what was then said is still disappointingly relevant. Only the Cold War has gone away. But the emphasis would be somewhat changed if I were writing on aid now. Although the books were not starry-eyed about development or planning, they still showed too much faith in government. I have become more conscious of the corruption of politicians and officials, largely because there is no doubt that it has increased, reaching highly counter-productive levels in Africa and South Asia. Worse still, the incidence of aggressive and cruel governments in the Third World has also increased. This makes aid for development and the relief of poverty more difficult, and increases the need for monitoring projects and policies. The upshot is that I still support aid, but cannot be as enthusiastic as I was.

It is notable that nothing was said about aid and macroeconomic crises, as these were very rare before developing countries began to be able to borrow on the

[11] Little and Clifford, *International Aid*.

[12] A later article, written in 1979 and included here as Paper 18, is, however, relevant to aid.

world's capital markets in the 1970s. But to go into this would be breaking new ground, which would be inappropriate in the present context.

In 1965 I had two invitations, both of which were of intellectual importance for me. The first was to visit India again on behalf of the MIT Centre for International Studies (MITCENIS). I arrived in the winter of 1965 with my wife, to find myself at the centre of a deep quarrel between MITCENIS and the Perspective Planning Division of the Planning Commission, of which Pitamber Pant was still the head. A planning model produced by MITCENIS economists seemed to show that concentration on heavy industry was not to India's maximum advantage. Although Pitamber Pant knew about work on this project, his mathematical intuition was insufficient to guess what the outcome would be. When it was produced, he saw MITCENIS and the authors as traitors.[13] As a result he would not speak to me, arriving at our house to apologize only on the eve of our departure.

It was clear that work, wearing an MIT hat, would be impossible. With the agreement of Rosenstein Rodan, I therefore attached myself to the Bell Mission from the World Bank which was then at work in India. Under its auspices I evaluated the heavy electrical plant at Bhopal. I concluded that this very large project was seriously flawed in conception, implementation, and current operations, and that it promised a very low rate of both financial and social return. The project evaluation work of other members of the Bell Mission suggested that Bhopal was no exception. If planning threw up many projects that seemed to have a very low rate of return, belief in planning—anyway, in planning as it was actually done—was undermined. A related lesson was that one of the reasons for the low calculated rate of return was that the advantages of international trade were being neglected. The consultants valued the project's tradable inputs and outputs at world prices, because they did not and could not know what domestic prices in India would be (largely determined, as they would be, by the government's taxes and controls). On reflection, it occurred to me that this was not merely a convenience, but could also be appropriate for assessing the real value to India of such a project.

This insight, blindingly obvious as it now appears, was then quite original, for the ethos of development economics at the time prohibited paying any attention to the advantages of trade. My consequential first thoughts on project selection and planning were given in a lecture at Delhi University in March 1965. A revised version of this lecture is included here (Paper 7). It incorporates, even if clumsily, all the essential ideas that later went into the OECD *Manual of Industrial Project Analysis* (1969), and *Project Appraisal and Planning for Developing Countries* (1974), henceforward referred to as LM(1) and LM(2), both written jointly with J. A. Mirrlees. These ideas were: (1) the use of border prices of tradable inputs and outputs; (2) the main method of valuing non-tradables; (3)

[13] This unfortunate episode is examined in Rosen, *Western Economists and Eastern Societies*.

the recognition that the shadow cost of labour might exceed the marginal product of labour because of the effect of employment on consumption; and (4) making the rate of discount equal to the marginal productivity of investment in the public sector. This last was achieved by assuming that the government decided the growth path of consumption so that the social discount rate became irrelevant, and also decided the division of industry between the public and private sectors, so that returns to investment in the private sector were also irrelevant. There were, however, certain features which I later came to think wrong, notably advocacy of a zero shadow wage rate (albeit under certain conditions). I revert in the following chapter to the history of my involvement in cost–benefit analysis for developing countries.

I am widely regarded as having shifted from uncritical belief in *dirigiste* planning to excessive trust in the price mechanism. Apart from the adjectives, this is broadly true. All economists are conversant with the faults of the price mechanism; some would suppress it altogether. Many liberals, including myself, wanted to tinker with it, and to rely on government to implement the tinkering. We were slow to realize that the most prevalent reason for market failure was government itself. Governments were driven by false economic ideology—heavy industry, protection, and import substitution—and also became increasingly self-serving and corrupt. My own change of emphasis is obvious, starting with Paper 6 and ending with the later papers on development that belittle economic planning and emphasize the benefits of an open economy. It was driven by experience and research. However, although the change was insidious from 1960 to 1990, my India visit of 1965 was a watershed. It led directly to my research programme at the OECD, and hence to increasing emphasis on free trade and the reduction of domestic controls.

The OECD: Trade, Industrialization, and Social Cost–Benefit Analysis, (1965–1975)

Shortly after returning to England in 1965, I received a telephone call from Paris asking me to come and submit myself as a candidate for the vice-presidency of the Development Centre of the OECD. I went and, after interviews with Robert Buron, the President, Thorkil Kristensen, the Secretary General, and Philip Tresize, the United States Ambassador, I got the job. I joined in September.

This was all orchestrated by the late Jo Saxe, who had been a student at Nuffield in 1954–6 (rarely putting in an appearance, since he was living in Paris with a heroine of the resistance) and was Kristensen's political adviser. My predecessor was Raymond Goldsmith of Yale University and the job was regarded as a US prerogative. Monty Yudelman, a US citizen of South African extraction, succeeded me. This goes to show that opportunities tend to come from personal contact, though I did not know Saxe very well at the time— only later. What one loses from the importance of personal acquaintance on one occasion, one may gain on another.

My main job at the Centre was to set up and participate in a research programme. My recent Indian experience obviously influenced my choice of trade and industrialization, since I had come to suspect that the neglect of trading opportunities might be resulting in very inefficient industrialization in other developing countries besides India. Robert Buron left the research side of the Centre entirely to me, and I was very fortunate in getting excellent researchers and authors for the five country volumes.[1] The final synoptic product, *Industry and Trade in Some Developing Countries* (hereafter referred to as LSS), was not at first universally acclaimed. Paul Streeten, reviewing it in the *Economic Journal*, wrote 'It will take its place, like some of the best books in economics, both among the literature of pamphleteering and that of scholarship.'[2] It became one of the most cited books on economic development ever published, and came to lead the way in a movement that finally resulted in an almost complete abandonment—twenty years later—of the previous doctrine of a paramount need for import sub-

[1] The five country studies are: Bergsman, *Brazil*; Bhagwati and Desai, *India*; King, *Mexico*; Lewis, *Pakistan*; Power, Sicat, and Mo-huan Hsing, *Philippines and Taiwan*.

[2] *Economic Journal*, 81: 148.

stitution policies. It was also the forerunner in a series of large multi-country comparative studies, promoted by Bela Balassa, Jagdish Bhagwati, Anne Krueger, and Deepak Lal. I include here as Paper 8 the unpublished script of a lecture I gave in 1968 at York University in Canada, which drew heavily on the work in Paris, and outlines much of what is important in LSS (now sadly out of print).

The other main product of my two years at the Development Centre was the OECD *Manual of Industrial Project Analysis*. This was jointly authored by myself and Jim Mirrlees (henceforth LM(1)). This was not the outcome of research that I had started. The Development Centre had already commissioned a French consultancy firm to produce such a manual, soon after it heard that the UN was doing so. A draft arrived, which I thought terrible. I criticized it fundamentally, and revisions were promised. I considered the revised draft which eventually arrived still unacceptable.[3] A small conference was called, most participants of which sided with me.[4] But I had to threaten resignation in order to stop the ball rolling. Buron was convinced that my opposition simply stemmed from an Anglo-Saxon attitude. He said my stance was improper for an international civil servant. The matter had to go to the Secretary General for resolution. I won. The French firm was to receive its full fee for producing Volume I, which consisted of straightforward discounted cash flow analysis, together with a set of industry profiles. I had to promise to write LM(1), the social cost–benefit analysis. I did not have the time to do this alone, and anyway felt need of intellectual support. Jim Mirrlees agreed to help. We met for only three days in Paris, and agreed the main outlines with an easy mutual acceptance of ideas. We then separated, and wrote the chapters we had agreed. I edited the whole, but we did not meet again before LM(1) was published. This seems to me to have come close to being an ideal collaboration.

LM(1) was strongly attacked by the development establishment, especially the Oxford branch. The use of border prices was anathema. It was felt that this meant that developing countries would be subjecting themselves to a neo-colonial tyranny of free trade, which in colonial times had ensured that they remained hewers of wood and drawers of water. The authors, of course, had no reverence for world prices: they were used because they were there, and constituted, as it were, invitations to trade; and trade should be optimally used in the best interests of the developing country. Twenty years later, this 'globalization' had become a cliché. The attackers were however quite shrewd, for the import substitution policies they had promoted were certainly threatened by the procedures of LM(1).[5]

[3] In technical terms, it was based on what is called 'the Effects Method'. The defects of this French method were later analysed in an article by Bela Balassa, 'The Effects Method of Project Evaluation'.

[4] It included Christopher Foster, Edmond Malinvaud, Goran Ohlin, V. K. Ramaswami, Tibor Scitovsky, and Maurice Scott.

[5] A 168-page symposium on LM(1) was published in the *Bulletin of the Oxford Institute of Economics and Statistics*, Vol. 34 (1972). The hostile articles were by Heather Joshi, and by Frances Stewart and Paul Streeten. Little and Mirrlees counter-attacked.

After returning from Paris, I got a grant from the Leverhulme Foundation to pursue with Maurice Scott the subject of cost–benefit analysis in developing countries. Several economists who have since become well known associated themselves, and produced published studies showing that the use of LM shadow prices was quite practical—these included Nicholas Stern, David Newbery, Deepak Lal, John Page, and Gordon Hughes. Maurice Scott himself produced a major study of land settlement in Kenya, which showed how shadow prices for non-tradables should be calculated.[6] I went to Malaysia in 1969 and wrote, with David Tipping, *A Social Cost–Benefit Analysis of the Kulai Palm Oil Estate, West Malaysia* (1972). Amazingly enough, this was the first ever published study of a social cost–benefit analysis of a project in a developing country.

As part of the project, my wife and I also went to India in 1970, visiting Indian businesses in Madras, Bangalore, Cochin, Goa, Bombay, Baroda, and Ahmedabad, mostly staying in company guest houses. This circuit was arranged by Sudhir Mulji. We ended in Delhi, where friendship with Pitamber Pant was renewed. I had cabled him before arranging the trip to ascertain whether I would be welcome in the Planning Commission for a few weeks, and got a positive response. My main purpose was to persuade him to try to set up what in LM(1) had been called the Central Office of Project Evaluation (COPE). To my surprise, I succeeded. (I had thought the chance of success was about one in ten.) There was some delay for political reasons, but in 1972 the Project Appraisal Division (PAD) of the Planning Commission was established. My favourite for the first director, the late Lovraj Kumar, was also chosen. In 1973/4 Deepak Lal spent a year in India calculating a set of shadow prices for the PAD to use.[7] I believe that over the next twenty years the PAD helped a little to improve public project selection, but it was not as influential as I hoped.[8]

In 1970 I became Professor of the Economics of Underdeveloped Countries in Oxford. Work on cost–benefit analysis continued on and off until the publication in 1974 of LM(2), and *Using Shadow Prices* (1976) with Maurice Scott.

Closely related to cost–benefit analysis, I did some work in this period on direct overseas investments. At the time, such investments were under heavy attack by the development establishment. This work included a paper on measuring the value of direct foreign investments in developing countries.[9] One of the main points was that such investments could reduce the national income of the recipient country, but only because of excessive protection of the domestic market. Rather than include this essay here (for it is much concerned with flogging horses which died long ago), I include as Paper 9 sections on the same subject from my 1982 book, which makes the important points more concisely.

[6] Scott, MacArthur and Newbery, *Project Appraisal in Practice*.

[7] Lal, *Prices for Planning: Towards the Reform of Indian Planning*.

[8] An assessment is made in Joshi and Little, *India: Macroeconomics and Political Economy*, pp. 321–2.

[9] Little, 'On Measuring the Value of Private Direct Overseas Investment'. This subject is explored in greater depth by Lal in *Appraising Foreign Investment in Developing Countries*.

Jumping ahead twenty years, Mirrlees and I published a latter-day survey of cost–benefit analysis for developing countries and our contribution to it. This is included here as Paper 10 (but the appendix on risk is omitted, since it was wholly Mirrlees's work and is characteristically much too mathematical for me to claim co-authorship).

I have devoted a good deal of time and effort to developing methods of social cost–benefit analysis. There was a promising acceptance and use of these methods in the 1970s by international banks and country donor agencies. But there was very little effective use in developing countries where the need was greatest. In the 1970s and early 1980s there was a plethora of public investment booms in these countries, mostly based on foreign borrowing (see e.g. Little *et al.*, *Boom Crisis and Adjustment*, and Paper 14). Many of these investments were ill-chosen, and their failure was a major cause of the debt crises of the later 1970s and early 1980s that were a tragedy for many developing countries. In *Boom, Crisis and Adjustment*, the authors concluded: 'The first and main lesson is that thorough cost–benefit analysis must be made that takes into account the need for export growth. . . . Countries should beware of huge dramatic government-inspired investments, whether in the public or private sectors. The lesson emerges from many countries, particularly from Côte d'Ivoire, Sri Lanka, Mexico, Morocco and even Korea.' I do not think this conclusion has struck home. I suspect that over-optimistic capital-intensive investment based on foreign borrowing has again played a part in the Asian crises of 1997.

The difficulty is that large public, or publicly subsidized, investments are a source of prestige, patronage, and huge kickbacks for those in power and their relatives and cronies. They do not want their projects submitted to hard-nosed appraisal by economists. A more successful way to reduce bad investment may simply be to reduce public investment, and government-inspired investment. Since some public investment is still highly desirable, especially in infrastructural sectors, this cannot however be an unqualified conclusion. And, like cost–benefit analysis itself, it is not a policy likely to appeal to many governments.

Korea, Taiwan, and the World Bank (1975–1978)

Returning again to the 1970s, I was invited in 1975 by the Asian Development Bank (ADB) to form a small team to evaluate the first ADB loan to the Medium Industry Bank (MIB) of the Republic of Korea. My team included Maurice Scott, Sudhir Mulji, and David Watkins of the Manchester Business School. We interviewed and evaluated twenty-eight medium-sized firms, clients of the MIB. My report is unpublished, but a few of the highlights are given in Paper 11, published twenty years later.

In 1975 I was also invited to write a survey chapter for a book on Taiwan edited by Walter Galenson,[1] and I spent about five weeks there in 1976 on the research, including many visits to manufacturing firms. I was assisted and encouraged by Wan-Yung (Shirley) Kuo. This experience confirmed much of what I had learned from South Korea. I distilled what I thought were the lessons in Paper 12, a paper given at an ILO conference on labour-intensive growth in Bangkok in 1980.

My experience of South Korea and Taiwan left a lasting impression of the huge benefits of their highly labour-intensive export-led development from about 1964–74. A major industrial revolution had occurred. The rate of growth of manufacturing employment, and the rise in real wages were unprecedented. The benefits of growth did not trickle down—they flooded down. The main 'secrets' were the maintenance of competitive real exchange rates for exports, and a free labour market with no protective labour legislation: the resultant exports of clothing and light manufactures were phenomenal.

Since 1979 I have had no direct experience of these countries. As real wages and savings rose, the economies of these countries naturally became more capital-intensive. They are now, and have been for many years, fully employed, labour-scarce economies. Growth continued to be very rapid, though not miraculously so, given the very high levels of savings and investment. Debate has raged over the role of government intervention and industrial policy. In Paper 11 I argue that selective government intervention was probably counter-productive. Korea finally ran into deep trouble in 1997 as a result apparently of mistaken macro-

[1] Little, 'An Economic Reconnaissance'.

economic policy, excessive borrowing, and unproductive investment. In contrast, Taiwan with its huge reserves has largely escaped the Asian crisis of 1997/8. However, it is too early, and anyway this is not the place, to analyse in depth the causes of this crisis.

I decided in 1975 to take the first two terms of the academic year 1975/6 as sabbatical leave. I was influenced in this by an invitation from the Secretary, Manmohan Singh, to spend some time as a special economic adviser in the Ministry of Finance, New Delhi. However, early in June, Singh telephoned to say that he was deeply sorry, but the political situation was such that it had become impossible to have a foreign adviser in the Ministry. A day of two later Mrs Gandhi's Emergency was declared. I had thought it rather remarkable that Manmohan had felt able to invite me anyway. Nevertheless, Mrs Gandhi had thrown my sabbatical plans into disarray.

My wife and I went to our house in La Garde Freinet to ruminate. There I received a letter from Ravi Gulati asking for suggestions to fill a vacant position of special adviser in the Development Economics Department at the World Bank of which he was the head. I suggested myself. We went to Washington, and after talks with Hollis Chenery an offer was confirmed and accepted. Although there was no security—it was only a two-year appointment, and intended to be temporary—I resigned the Oxford Chair to which I had been elected in 1970, and we moved to Washington.

The move was not quite as precipitate as I have made it sound. I had been thinking for some time that I really could not spend the rest of my life at Nuffield College. I had been a professor for only four years, but I did not think I was very good at it, and have never much liked lecturing. My wife had come to the end of a job she had been doing and, rather more strongly than I, wanted to get away from Oxford.

In 1976, soon after joining the Bank, I became a candidate for the presidency of the OECD Development Centre. For the second time since I left the Treasury in 1955, I was officially supported for an appointment. The first time was in 1969, when I became a board member of the British Airports Authority. Tony Crosland was then President of the Board of Trade. On this occasion Tony Crosland was our Minister for Foreign Affairs. I was given to believe that I was the front-runner, with the Secretary General in favour, and so I informally asked Hollis Chenery whether I could break my contract with the Bank if need be. He said there would be no difficulty. But then two events intervened.

First, Tony Crosland died in February 1977. Secondly, Dr Richard Jolly, then Director of the Institute of Development Studies, wrote to the Secretary General, and apparently convinced him that I was an unsuitable person for such a post. I was informed of this letter and its purpose by a member of the Foreign Office. I do not know the exact contents and date of the letter. In 1978 Jolly became a special consultant to the Secretary General on North–South issues. After this I was no longer in the running.

My main initiative at the Bank was to design and initiate a research project on small-scale manufacturing enterprises. I did so because there was a strong drive to lend to development finance institutions as a way of promoting small manufacturing units that were thought to be very labour-intensive. This was presented as part of McNamara's attack on poverty. I was suspicious, because the assumptions made seemed to have insufficient empirical support.

The project had barely got underway, under the management of Dennis Anderson, by the time that my wife and I left in April 1978 to take up residence in our house in La Garde Freinet. When I returned to the Bank six years later in 1984 it was still unfinished, with Dipak Mazumdar having succeeded Anderson. John Page, whom I had recruited to be a principal researcher on the project, was principally engaged on other matters. I managed to get the final book written. Although I played the major part in the rescue in 1985, I had done none of the basic work! There were further long delays caused by the publications department of the Bank which kept pushing it on to some back-burner. The book finally appeared in 1987, a decade after the research (which was supposed to take three years at most) began. I believe its findings are still of interest, and an article based on it is included here as Paper 13.

Mainly Self-Employment and Semi-Retirement (1978–1997)

Having built a house one kilometre from the village of La Garde Freinet in Provence, my wife and I intended to retire there in 1978. However, a little late in the day, I realized that I would be bored if I had no work to do. I toyed with the idea of changing subjects, but fairly quickly decided cautiously to stick with development economics. So I submitted to the Twentieth Century Fund a plan to write a survey of development theory and policy. This was accepted. The Fund wanted me to do it in two years. I insisted that this was impossible from my base in Provence. They agreed to three years, but would pay me for only two years. However, they were generous in allowing my wife to be paid as research assistant, so I agreed.

During these three years, I spent semesters as Visiting Professor at Boston University and at the Woodrow Wilson School, Princeton. I actually had to teach at Boston University, but the Woodrow Wilson School was so generous that my duties were limited to giving very few seminars. I still shudder with modest alarm when I recall that these were attended by Arthur Lewis and Albert Hirschman. I also spent a term at Oxford. These visits were necessary to give me library facilities. After three years to the day, in April 1981 I sent the text of *Economic Development: Theory, Policy and International Relations* to the Fund. They seemed a little surprised by the punctuality. The book sold quite well, about 7,000 copies. Some reviews were enthusiastic, and none, on this occasion, deeply critical.

We continued to live in La Garde Freinet for the next two and a half years. During this time I did some consultancy work for the OECD, drafting a report for the Secretary General on North–South interdependency. I seemed to have a good understanding with the Secretariat, and wrote nearly 50,000 words. Eventually an anodyne document appeared which bore no relation whatever to anything I had written. However, I was paid. I also spent an enjoyable semester at Colombia University at the invitation of Jagdish Bhagwati. I used my work on interdependency as material for the very few seminars I was called on to give. I wondered whether to publish this work on interdependency, but in the difficult circumstances of the time—my wife was suffering from cancer—did not have the heart to try to do so.

We left La Garde Freinet in September 1983, because of my wife's ill health. During the first summer of our quasi-retirement in 1978, Dobs had discovered a lump in her neck. We were due to go to Oxford in the autumn. Cancer was there diagnosed, and she had a major operation. We were told it was a secondary cancer, and the primary could not be found. Thereafter for five years, whether in France, England, or America, there was a monthly visit to a clinic. Several times a suspicious spot was found and Dobs had a minor surgical 'intervention', or radium treatment (in France). But the primary cancer was never found. In August 1983 in the Clinic in Nice a more serious 'anomaly' was found. By then, Dobs was not very happy with French medicine. We decided to return to Oxford and put our house in La Garde Freinet on the market. It was found in Oxford that her liver was affected, and her consultant recommended no treatment.

I had accepted a special Fellowship (for quondam Fellows) at All Souls College for two years when we decided to leave France. This meant at least that we had somewhere to live in Oxford, in one of the All Souls flats designed for Visiting Fellows. The hospice, Sobell House, under Dr Twycross, was most efficiently and kindly supportive. Dobs died on 20 January 1984. We had been married for thirty-eight years. She had accompanied me on all my major trips abroad, to India several times, to Africa and Latin America, to Korea, Taiwan, and Malaysia, usually acting as unpaid research assistant. Throughout the three years of working on and writing *Economic Development* she was formally research assistant, but also amanuensis and proof-reader.

In May I went to the World Bank for about two months to help complete the project on small-scale enterprises already mentioned. Sometime during that summer, it was suggested by Anne Krueger and Deepak Lal (respectively, Vice President in charge of research and Research Administrator) that I design and lead, with Max Corden, a major multi-country research project on macroeconomic management. Max and I suggested, and it was agreed, that Carlos Diaz Alejandro should join us—a proposal he accepted. I resigned the All Souls Fellowship, and went to Washington in October. Soon afterwards I visited the Australian National University (ANU) for several weeks to secure Max Corden's help with the design of the project and the writing of the detailed research proposal required for acceptance by the Bank. Very sadly, Carlos Diaz Alejandro died before he could make a significant contribution. His knowledge of, and contacts in, Latin America were irreplaceable. With the agreement of Max and myself, Richard Cooper was approached and agreed to take part. Max had joined the IMF, but he worked on the project with the Fund's agreement.

The project was accepted by the Bank, but it remained doubtful for some time whether it would go ahead. I felt I had been led to believe that I would be more effectively in charge, together with the other consultants, than turned out to be the case. Of course, a consultant could not be formally in charge; he could not give orders to staff members, hire consultants, sign cheques, etc. Thus, the project had to be located for administrative purposes in a division of the

Development Economics Department, and that of Sarath Rajapatirana was chosen by the Vice President, Anne Krueger. Sarath thus became the director of the project; he also became in every way a valued member of the team and one of the four authors of the final synthesis volume. His knowledge of the ways of the Bank, and of its members, was essential, especially in securing the cooperation of the departments responsible for each of the seventeen countries to be studied.

However, despite the above, I had thought that anything agreed by the three consultants that was compatible with Bank policy and procedures would go through easily. This was not the case. In particular, I felt I was being held largely responsible not only for the design but also for the quality of implementation of the whole project. This was incompatible with having no control over which and how many countries to include, and who to appoint as country-level consultants. It was all very different from my experience in promoting and managing the OECD Development Centre project on trade and industrialization (see the chapter above on the OECD).

Max Corden had his own doubts about the project, and more than once seemed to be on the point of slipping overboard. Dick Cooper seemed to have fewer doubts. Anne Krueger eventually managed to persuade us all to go ahead. I returned to Oxford after one year, but continued to participate from the base of Nuffield College. I left before some of the crucial decisions on countries and consultants were made. No doubt partly for this reason, I was not always consulted.

I had started work on the project in October 1984. The synthesis volume *Boom, Crisis and Adjustment* was published in December 1993. A summary of my main contribution to this volume is Paper 14. The last year for which economic data were used in the analysis was 1989. The long delays were partly the result of the huge size of the project; but they were also caused by the bureaucratic publication procedures of the Bank, and the low priority given to research results compared with the World Development Reports and special reports such as *The Asian Miracle*.

Eight of the country studies appeared between 1993 and 1996.[1] They were 'published' directly by the Bank in soft covers only. I believe that no bookshop will stock or take an order for such 'publications', for there is no agreement by which they receive any payment for this service. It takes a determined person to get hold of one of these volumes even if he has heard of it, wants it, and is keen to pay. Even this second-class treatment would not have been accorded without a generous grant from the Swedish International Development Agency. The Bank could not afford proper publication of the results of a project on which it had spent close to $3 million. I think the country-level authors got a raw deal.

[1] *Brazil* by D. V. Coes; *Colombia* by J. G. Garcia and S. Jayasuriya; *Cote d'Ivoire* by J. C. Berthelemy and F. Bourguignon; *India* by V. Joshi and I. M. D. Little; *Indonesia* by W. T. Woo, B. Glassburner, and A. Nasution; *Sri Lanka* by P. Athukorala and J. Jayasuriya; *Thailand* by P. G. Warr and B. Nidhiprabha; *Turkey* by Z. Onis and J. Riedel.

My awareness of the Bank's publication faults was heightened by the fact that I was myself a country-level author. Vijay Joshi and I wrote the Indian volume, *India: Macroeconomics and Political Economy 1964–1991*. This work of nearly 400 pages was much the largest and most comprehensive of the country studies. It was the first and only full macroeconomic history of India since the death of Nehru, and will, I hope, prove to be the definitive study of this period. It would have been anomalous for such a work to be lost in the jungle of World Bank paper. But in fact, Vijay Joshi and I were not thus submerged. It was agreed that there would also be a hardback Indian edition by OUP India, which duly appeared in July 1994.[2]

The World Bank project was my main occupation for nearly a decade. Was it worth it? For me, certainly 'Yes'. I was of retirement age when it started, and as a recently widowed person I needed psychologically the demands it made upon me. (Happily, before it ended I was again married, to Lydia Segrave in 1991.)

Was it a good use of Bank money? I am doubtful. Several valuable books were produced, which should contribute to good policy-making in developing countries. But the cost was excessive. I recall Max Corden remarking that we could have produced the synoptic volume without all those country studies. This may have been one of Max's rare incautious remarks. I think comparative empirical studies can be useful, but seventeen countries was far too many. There was also too much monitoring, with expensive conferences. In some ways, the Bank is a superb research base, providing easy contact with very experienced persons, and access to recent relevant research and to other information not easily obtainable elsewhere. But it also has the disadvantages of a large hierarchical bureaucracy, some of which I have described at or hinted at above.

The joint book with Vijay Joshi took the Indian story only up to the end of the 1980s. The Indian reforms, started in 1990/1, seemed to Vijay and myself to call for another effort on our part. This was especially appropriate for me since the chief architect and builder of the reforms, Dr Manmohan Singh, had been my pupil at Oxford (see the chapter above on India). This new project had nothing to do with the World Bank research described above. The UK Overseas Development Administration provided some funding, but was in no way associated with out work or findings. The resultant book, *India's Economic Reforms 1991–2001*, appeared in 1996. Paper 15, which originated as a lecture given at a conference on the reforms in Delhi in March 1994, draws heavily on the book.

During 1997 I edited, jointly with Isher Ahluwalia, a festschrift in honour of Manmohan Singh. The volume, entitled *India's Economic Reforms and Development* was presented to him in December by the Vice-President of India at a rather grand meeting in Delhi.

[2] The volume on Thailand is also exceptional in being distributed by OUP in Asia.

6

The Strategy of Indian Development (1960)

1. INTRODUCTION

India became independent in 1948. She is now in the final stages of preparing her Third Five-Year Plan for economic development. The First Plan ran from 1950/1 to 1955/6 (British financial years). It has no relevance to India's present problems. It was small; it was an amalgam of existing investment projects with little or no conscious economic philosophy behind it. The Second Plan runs from 1956/7 to 1960/1. The Third Plan starts in April 1961.

The scope of the Plans

The Plans contain quite detailed output targets for both agriculture and industry. These are important for assessing the economic coherence and strategy of planning, and also the performance achieved, but output and employment are not directly controlled. Consequently, the important operative decisions are the investment decisions.[1] Public investment expenditure (and Plan expenditure) is closely and effectively controlled.[2] Private investment expenditure, as such, is not controlled, but licences are required for increasing factory capacity, for foreign exchange, and for some materials—steel, for example. There is no direct way of ensuring that private investment reaches the planned figures, but this has not been a problem, and is not likely to become one. While effective means exist for damping down private investment, if necessary, it is impossible to give an accurate estimate of how closely it conforms to the planned figures. Indeed, there is considerable woolliness about both the concept and the magnitude of private investment. The Plan documents are imprecise about what is included. The only fairly firm figures relate to organized factory industry (that is, establishments

This paper first appeared in the *National Institute Economic Review*, 9 (May 1960). Permission to reproduce is gratefully acknowledged.

[1] Following Indian practice, investment and national income are, throughout, measured net of depreciation (for which allowances are very rough). Gross figures are not published.

[2] Plan expenditure and investment expenditure differ, for certain increases in current public expenditure are included in the Plan. But, throughout, only the estimated investment size and content of the Plans is referred to.

employing more than twenty men, or more than ten men with power), but this accounts for a very small part of private Indian output, though, doubtless, for a large part of investment. This is typical of the general difficulties of analysing Indian economic trends which result from the inadequacy of Indian statistics.[3]

Results so far

Planned investment in the Second Plan was £2,850 million for the public sector and £1,800 million for the private sector. This was about double the probable level of investment in the First Plan. The proportion of public investment (including stocks) allocated to industry, power, and the railways (the heaviest import users) rose from 47 per cent in the First Plan to 55 per cent in the Second. Some other details of investment in the Second Plan are given later in Table 2.

In 1957/8 there was a balance of payments crisis, and the Plan had to be cut, in spite of a hasty mobilization of greatly increased foreign aid. Imports had been seriously underestimated. There seem to have been two main reasons for this. First was the straight underestimate of the direct foreign exchange element in capital development, and of the material needs of full capacity working, due largely to inadequate information and inadequate work done on the problem. The second was that favourable monsoons during the First Plan had wrongly convinced people that an adequate upward trend in agricultural production had already been established. This resulted in the need for higher food imports than expected.

The real cuts were considerably greater than is evident from the figures in Table 2 below, since industrial projects, especially the steel plants, cost much more than was anticipated. This was partly because prices rose, but mainly because of faulty estimation. Industry, power, and the railways will have accounted for about 62 per cent of total public investment (including stocks). In spite of this, the real industrial investment achieved will have been considerably less than planned, although it was expenditure on the social services which was reduced most. Private investment may turn out to have been a little more than was planned in money terms, though not in real terms. Finally, foreign savings (the capital inflow, plus the fall in reserves, including some sales in silver to the

[3] It is impossible to let Indian figures speak for themselves. Sometimes they do not exist. Often they are years out of date. Always far more background is required for their interpretation than can be given in an article. National income figures exist, but are very unreliable. There is no series of investment figures, even for the public sector. Several different agricultural output estimates exist, and differ widely. Accurate output estimates exist for some particular industrial products. The balance of payments estimates are good, but trade figures are very unreliable for imports. In short, the reader must accept the author's judgement where figures are given or used, and must take them as orders of magnitude, except where the context implies otherwise, and he must not always expect sources or complete tables, which, if presented, would often shed more darkness than light. It is extraordinary what little fuss the Planning Commission makes about the poverty of Indian statistics.

United States) will probably turn out to have amounted to about £1,500 million, out of a total investment of a little over £4,500 million.

The growth of output under the First and Second Plans has been less than expected, but the growth of population greater. Since 1948, real national income may have grown by about 3 per cent per annum. Agricultural production, accounting for just on half of net national output, has probably risen about the same or slightly less fast. Since this latter rise owes nothing to population growth—there already being surplus population on the land in 1948—it is creditable by the standards of the past, though many other countries have done much better. The total rise of 35 per cent in the national income in ten years is probably as great as in the previous fifty years. But the population has risen by nearly 20 per cent, so that the growth per head is little more than perceptible.

Industrial production was very sluggish in the crisis years of 1957/8 and 1958/9. This was partly due to shortages of materials and components, resulting from the severe import controls instituted in the crisis, but also partly the result of a deficiency of demand for textiles. But production has now risen strongly again, and the figures for 1959, when they emerge, will probably show a 50 per cent rise over 1951—a growth rate of 5½ per cent a year. The heavier industrial investment of the Second Plan can have had little impact as yet, and there is reason to hope that industrial production will now begin to rise faster. However, factory establishments accounted for only 8½ per cent of national income in 1957/8 (the latest available figures) and total industrial production, including mining and workshop enterprises, for only 18 per cent. Less than 3½ million persons are employed in factories. For some time, therefore, industrial production cannot have any large effect on total income and employment. A rough division of the national income by sources is given in Table 1.

TABLE 1. Approximate division of the national income by sources in 1957/8

	%
Agriculture	47
Mining and factory establishments	10
Small enterprises	9
Transport and communications	5
Finance and commerce	13
Other services	17

The contents of the Third Plan

Little is yet known of the Third Plan, but provisional figures for the expected call on foreign aid, and for total public and private investment, and also a broad sectoral division of the planned investment, have been reported in the press, and given to the recent Bankers' Mission, headed by Sir Oliver Franks.[4] The figure given for public investment is £4,460 million, and for private investment £3,000 million. But prices have risen, and the definition and coverage of 'investment' has almost certainly changed. So a comparison of these figures with Second Plan figures is misleading; nor can price or coverage corrections easily be made. But the author's guess is that total planned investment in real terms is probably a little less than half as big again as in the Second Plan. The proportion of public sector investment (excluding stocks) devoted to industry, power, and the railways, is expected to be 59 per cent.

The Indians expect to need £1,575 million of foreign aid, inclusive of private capital, but excluding refinancing loans and any P.L.480[5] they may get. The latter two items may each add about £375 million. Thus, the total gross call on foreign capital may be £2,325 million, of which £1,950 million would represent new foreign savings. After making some allowance for private investment, net official aid might need to total about £1,700 million. If these figures were realized, it would imply that foreign savings would be financing about one-quarter of Indian investment, as compared with one-third last time.

The above figures on investment and foreign aid are summed up in Table 2, where some further detail is given.

2. THE PLANNING PERSPECTIVE

In spite of the growth achieved in the past decade, the state of India, on the eve of the Third Five-Year Plan, is still one of dramatic poverty. Dietary statistics suggest that the majority of Indians are slowly dying of malnutrition: the expectation of life is still under 40 years. Yet medical discoveries have recently reduced the death rate to about 20 per thousand. Since there is as yet no evidence of a fall in the birth rate, which is close to 40 per thousand, the population, now about 420 million, is increasing at 2 per cent, or 8½ million, a year. This rate of growth might increase still further.

Of the 420 million, about 90 million are town-dwellers, and their number is growing at about 4 per cent a year, as a result of migration from the country, while the rural population grows at 1½ per cent a year. Underemployment in

[4] See the letter to Mr Eugene Black from Sir Oliver Franks, Dr Abs, and Mr Sproule. The letter emphasizes India's basic needs, and generally accepts the strategy of her planning with only minor comments. It records the request for aid given below, but naturally could not commit itself to any view as to how much might actually be forthcoming, since this is a matter for the providing governments.

[5] This refers to the US Public Law No. 480, under which surplus agricultural products are disposed of against payment in local currency. These local currency payments are mostly held by the US Ambassador, before being ultimately lent or granted back to the purchasing government.

TABLE 2. Estimates of investment[a]
(*£ million at current prices*)

	Second Plan 1956/7 to 1960/1		Third Plan 1961/2 to 1965/6
	Plan	Probable out-turn	
Public investment	2,850	2,660	4,460
of which:			
Agriculture, community development, irrigation	595	485	890
Power	305	300	675
Railways	675	675	675
Other transport, communications	325	300	410
Industries and mining	595	675	1,100
Social services and other	355	225	410
Investment in stocks	(b)	(b)	300
Private investment	1,800	1,900	3,000
Total investment	4,650	4,560	7,460
of which:			
Investment financed directly or indirectly by foreign savings	840	1,500	1,950

[a] It must not be assumed that the operative definition of investment remains unchanged, particularly for private industry, for which the investment figures are very uncertain. Price changes also affect the figures for different sectors in different ways.
[b] Included under other heads.

both town and country is extensive, and almost certainly increasing; indeed, it is the most impressive feature of the Indian scene. It has been reckoned that 30 per cent of the labour force was underemployed in 1952–4 with as much as 12 per cent working quarter-time or less. This, however, overestimates the labour reserve because of the high incidence of sickness.[6] Registered unemployment is small (1.4 million in December 1959) but is rapidly increasing, having almost doubled in the last three years.

But, in spite of the poverty and malnutrition, the severe underemployment, and the gathering threat of open urban unemployment, it cannot be easily assumed that the overriding objective of the Third Five-Year Plan should be to increase consumption or employment. India's growth in the past few years has been heavily dependent on foreign aid (and reduced foreign exchange reserves). This will continue to be true for at least the next ten years, but it cannot go on

[6] *The National Sample Survey*, Report no. 14 (March 1959).

for ever. Consequently, India must also plan to develop and strengthen her economy in such a way that she can both rectify her severe foreign exchange deficit, and at the same time either make or buy the much larger quantities of capital goods which will undeniably be required to sustain a continued process of expansion. Moreover, the need for future consumption (including government consumption—for example, defence) may become even more acute than in the present. There is the threat both of China and of an increase in the rate of population growth. So the Third Plan must be seen in the context of the Fourth Plan at least. Theoretically, indeed, there is no time-horizon beyond which the planner does not need to try to peer; but the end of the Fourth Plan will do to be getting on with.

The broad objectives

The official aims of the Indian government, and their implied choice between the conflicting demands of the present and the future, are known. It is hoped to balance foreign payments without aid by the end of the Fourth Plan, that is by 1970, with a rate of net investment of around 16 per cent of net national income. At present the rate of investment is probably only 10 per cent with only 7½ per cent financed from domestic savings.[7] At the end of the Third Plan, in 1965, it is hoped that investment may have risen to 14 per cent, about 12 per cent being domestically financed. These figures are thought to be consistent with the investment of £7,460 million in the Third Plan, and of £11,250 million in the Fourth Plan. Thus, it is hoped that the proportion of national income invested and financed by domestic savings can about double in the next ten years.

The strain which this achievement would impose depends greatly on the rate of growth of output and income. Provided that income grows at 5 per cent or more, these targets can be attained or surpassed if consumption grows by one percentage point less than income. Put like that, the task appears manageable—for consumption per head would probably be growing a little faster than in the past. In effect, the idea is to devote to investment most of the 'proceeds' of the hoped-for increase in the growth rate. But the marginal rate of investment from domestic savings for the whole economy would need to be high—about 25 per cent. There is no possibility of this being achieved without increases in taxation which would be remarkable in the light of the recent past, although the resultant rates still need not be high by British standards. But if output fails to rise by 5 per cent a year, it would be difficult to increase investment to the extent indicated, and the hope of an adequate, self-sufficient, and soundly based growth by 1970 would probably have to be abandoned.

[7] Investment, and the use of foreign resources, have both fallen since the peak of 1957/8, and income has increased. Over the whole Plan, foreign resources may account for almost one-third of investment; see Table 2.

The above ideas have changed little since the beginning of the Second Plan. But, as noted earlier, success to date has been less than expected. Allowing for the change in prices (and a probable change in coverage), the Third Plan may be about 50 per cent larger than the actual achievement of the Second Plan, but it is about 20 per cent smaller than was originally envisaged in 1955/6.[8] It is certainly inadequate to the needs of the situation. Even if as successful as hoped, the standard of living will rise only slowly from its desperately low level, and it can make no great impact on the problem of underemployment. Moreover, if much more attention were successfully paid to consumption and employment within the framework of a plan of this size, then India would probably remain relatively as heavily dependent on foreign assistance as before. The question naturally arises as to whether the Third Plan should not be bigger.

3. THE NEED FOR AID

Figures for the Indian balance of payments for the last year of the First Plan, and the first 3½ years of the Second Plan are given in Table 3.

TABLE 3. India's balance of payments (£m)

	1955/6	1956/7	1957/8	1958/9[a]	April–Sept. 1959[a]
Imports (c.i.f.)	571	824	903	785	355
Exports (f.o.b.)	482	476	446	432	205
Trade deficit	89	348	457	353	150
Net invisibles (including private donations)	66	84	75	68	28
Current deficit	23	264	382	285	122
financed by					
Official donations	36	30	25	31	16
Official loans	1	23	69	162	63
Other capital transactions	18	−2	70	78	21
Drawings on IMF and fall in reserves	−15	212	221	32	20
Errors and omissions	−17	1	−3	−18	2

[a] Provisional.

[8] Roughly speaking, the levels of income and investment envisaged in 1955/6 for the period 1960–70, in terms of 1952/3 rupees, remain as targets. But they are now in terms of 1957/8 rupees. This means that the anticipated levels of income and investment for the next ten years, while bearing roughly the same relation to each other, are in real terms lower by 10–15 per cent than they were expected to be five years ago.

Savings and the pattern of trade

Owing to the present very small size of the capital goods industry and of the production of intermediate goods in India, programmes of industrial development result in a rapidly rising level of imports. More domestic savings can help to finance such programmes only to the extent that imports of consumption goods can be reduced, or exports expanded as a result of lower consumption at home. Some inessential consumption goods were imported before 1958. But the crisis of 1957 was not due to any large increase in imports of consumption goods, and by 1958 such imports had been reduced to a very low level.

Table 4 gives the author's estimate of the composition of imports in 1958/9.[9] Excluding the unclassified items, £195 million consisted of consumption goods. But of this, £140 million was food, of which about £85 million was received free as aid under P.L.480. Almost all the rest of the food must be imported as a condition of receiving P.L.480 aid. ('Normal marketing' must not be disturbed.) The small remainder of consumption goods (which includes at least £15 million of drugs) cannot be reduced much. By far the greater part consists of plant and equipment, and intermediates. Although some of the machinery and intermediates may be 'near-consumption' goods, needing little further processing, it becomes clear that more taxation, or more private savings, could have done little to reduce imports. No doubt, heavier taxation might have reduced imports of foodgrains, but this would merely have been saving free imports.

TABLE 4. Estimated composition of imports in 1958/9

	Value (£m)	% of total (excluding unclassified)
Machinery and defence	300	41
Materials and intermediates	340	33
Consumption goods	195	26
of which		
Foodgrains	115	16
Other food	25	3
Other consumption	55	7
Unclassified	50	
Total	885	100

[9] Official sources give a similar breakdown only for private imports, which are about half the total imports. The separate items are my estimates of the c.i.f. value of imports, whereas the total is an official payments figure. But it seems that the best estimate of total imports would be very close to the payments figure, which has therefore been used for the sake of convenience.

Table 3 shows a steady fall in export receipts in recent years. This is partly a price illusion. Also, of course, the usual divergences of balance of payments and trade figures enter in. The volume index, which is probably very rough, runs as follows:

1952/53	100
1953/54	100
1954/55	105
1955/56	115
1956/57	110
1957/58	107
1958/59	108

The fall in 1958/9 was not due to the pull of the home market, being almost entirely in textiles where there was a large excess capacity. Indeed, textiles and tea, in both of which, though for different reasons, internal demand has been an unimportant factor, dominate the Indian export position. In 1958/9, tea, cotton, and jute and their manufactures accounted for 54 per cent of exports, and other agricultural exports for a further 20 per cent; other manufactures accounted for only 14 per cent.

In the short run, there is in fact little that India can do to increase her export receipts significantly. The demand for tea (which accounted for 24 per cent of exports in 1958/9) grows only very slowly, and is price-inelastic. For jute manufactures, the next largest export, there is a static market. It is difficult to get a larger share of the declining world market in low-quality cotton textiles. Moreover, any increased share in these markets would be at the expense of other poor countries. Thus, while there may be a few products of which more could be exported if home consumption were reduced, for example vegetable oils, quantitatively the result would be very small.

One can conclude that domestic saving is no substitute for aid, so far as financing industrial expansion is concerned. India cannot herself produce the plant and equipment needed, and further austerity would not permit her to buy significantly more capital goods without foreign finance.

Aid for the Third Plan

What is true of the present will also be true for the Third Plan period. The need for aid will spring not so much from the limited saving potential of a poor country, but from the small size of the capital goods industry, and the very limited possibilities of expanding exports. The Third Plan will certainly require a very large increase in imports of machinery, and the invisible surplus will be much reduced by increased interest charges. In the category of intermediates, there should be a large saving in steel imports which may compensate for increases in fertilizers and probably in oil. Food imports may remain about the same, though it is expected that more will go into stock. As already remarked, it would in any case be absurd from the Indian as well as from the US point of view to attempt to do without P.L.480. Imports of other consumption goods will be kept down to approximately the present low level.

But it is impossible from this, or indeed from any other, distance to make a detailed assessment of the import requirements. They are extremely hard to predict, depending as they do not only on the import content of new projects, but also on the whole development of Indian output. (The more successful the output growth, the greater the import saving.) It has been seen that estimates of imports for the Second Plan were very low. But this time, they have been more carefully estimated. They certainly do not allow for any inflationary surge in the imports of consumption goods, and there is no reason to suppose that they are inflated beyond the needs of the situation.

On the export side, receipts are expected to increase by about 5 per cent a year, a considerable improvement compared with past trends. The biggest increases are to be expected in new products and intermediates or raw materials, especially iron ore and metals. It is very hard to suggest any road to a significantly better performance. Even allowing for the greater attention now being paid to exports, the growth expected may be optimistic.

Since no further use can be made of reserves, the expected need for foreign aid of £1,950 million implies an average deficit on current account from 1961/2 to 1965/6 of about £400 million. In view of the grave difficulties of estimation, this could be fairly wide of the mark; but I do not think there is any good reason to suppose that it is not as realistic an estimate as can be made.

Dispensing with aid

If India is to achieve her aims of increasing incomes by 5 per cent a year at least, together with a much higher level of investment, a very large increase is implied in the use of machinery, and of intermediate products such as steel, oil, cement, fertilizers, and other chemicals. Sufficient provision also has to be made for the non-traded goods and services, power, and transport. This implies either a very large increase in exports, or a large increase of import substitution, or some elements of both.

The present pattern of exports has been discussed. It is a most unpromising basis for expansion. Any major expansion of exports could come about only if India deliberately set about producing new manufactures for export on a large scale. This would seem to be unjustifiably risky. So far as heavy products go, her geographical position is unfavourable except for certain limited eastern markets. In light manufactured products, it is unlikely that the required quality for international markets, and the goodwill going with it, could be quickly achieved. High quality requires experience, or high capital intensity. The former is lacking, and the latter is just what the few advocates of much greater emphasis on building for export seek to avoid. There is also the established competition of Japan and Hong Kong to be reckoned with in this field, as well as the danger of import restrictions elsewhere, like the UK protection of Lancashire and Dundee. Moreover, it is very early for India to be able to guess where her comparative advantages will lie. There is also a more fundamental consideration that tells against a great expansion of exports: in a country the size of India, with a wide complement of natural resources, it would be surprising if it did not turn out to be economical for her to produce something of almost everything, and surprising if international trade should ever come to more than a small fraction of national income. (In 1957/8 imports were 10½ per cent, exports 5¼ per cent of national income.)

Thus, the relative attractions of import substitution are great. There is no doubt about the demand being there. One can, as it were, see what to produce. There are the obvious advantages of goodwill for domestic products, and transport costs act in favour, not against them. Lower-quality goods can be more easily absorbed. In short, the risks of failure are much less. This does not, of course, mean that export opportunities should not be explored. There is in fact a new awareness of the importance of exports. While India was certainly inadequately export conscious in the past, this is ceasing to be true. But there is no need to call in irrational autarky to explain the pattern of her planning today.

Imported consumer goods have been very largely replaced already. With the Second Plan, there began a phase of replacing the imports of intermediate products. The three steel plants formed by far the largest element of import substitution, and will have accounted for about 15 per cent of public investment. As a result, steel imports will be much lower from now on. (In the first three years of the Second Plan, steel accounted for 13 per cent of all imports.) Contrary to some impressions, investment in the production of capital goods—machinery, locomotives, and so on—was a tiny part of the Plan. In the Third Plan the major emphasis will shift to fertilizers and machinery. The forthcoming rapid rise in these imports will consequently level off, or might even fall, by the end of the Fourth Plan period, that is towards 1970.

4. THE PLANNED PATTERN OF OUTPUT

While the balance of payments deficit, and the rapidly rising need for machinery, steel, cement, oil, coal, and chemicals, play a large part in the determination of the pattern of industrial development, they by no means dominate it. In the Second Plan, public investment in the 'non-importables'—electricity, transport, and communications—will have been more than twice as great as public investment in industry, and more than equal to total investment in industry. This will probably also be true of the Third Plan. Even so, to date, the provision of these services has lagged behind the demand.

But, naturally, if anything can be said to dominate the output shape of the Plans, it is the provision of consumption goods and services, which are quantitatively of far more importance than anything else. They are not neglected.

Food

Probably about 60 per cent of consumption is food. Foodgrains are about two-thirds of food consumption, and the Third Plan output target for foodgrains will probably end up as 100–105 million tons against 73½ million tons in 1958/9—an increase of 36–43 per cent (around 5 per cent a year) compared with an expected increase in total consumption of about 30 per cent (4 per cent a year for seven years). Free grain imports under P.L.480 will continue, but even if they are 1–2 million tons less, it is difficult to see that people will eat so much; for, assuming other food production goes up at least *pari passu*, it would mean increasing the proportion of food eaten as income rises, contrary to all observation. This could come about only as a result of a large relative fall in food prices, or a large redistribution of consumption to the very poor, or both. Both may happen to some extent, but the price shift, to get so much food eaten, might need to be disturbingly large, unless there is a much greater increase in non-farm employment than seems to be planned.

Thus, the output targets for agriculture may well be excessive. This does not imply that the Plan expenditure will be excessive. Whether it will be or not is exceedingly hard to judge, because it is almost impossible to relate increased expenditure on agriculture to increased output. It is even impossible to say at all accurately what part of the Plan expenditure is devoted to more food. Thus, steel goes into dams for irrigation and into railways to deliver food, and so on. But a fair idea of the emphasis in different plans may be got by comparing the relative expenditures on agriculture directly, *plus* community development, *plus* irrigation and flood control, *plus* nitrogen production. Planned expenditure on these rose by about 40 per cent in the Second Plan, and may rise by 60 per cent in the Third. As a proportion of total Plan expenditure, it fell under the Second Plan but will rise under the Third.

Other non-food consumption can be dealt with briefly. Services form a large part, and aside from education and health (which there is no space to deal with here) can be left to look after themselves, as they require little equipment. Clothing, itself embodying a large agricultural output, is by far the most important of manufactured consumption goods, and there is at present considerable excess capacity. The rest is small, maybe 10–15 per cent of consumption. Much of it springs from cottage and small-scale industry, where production could probably be increased with little capital expenditure except for the provision of stocks.

In general, there is no particular reason to suppose that the provision for extra factory-made consumption goods is inadequate—and indirect taxation can be used to damp down excess demand for particular capital-intensive products such as electricity and passenger travel, or those with a large import content such as cars.

The general pattern

To sum up, the determination of the pattern of output in the Second and Third Plans (and probably the Fourth) can be described as follows. First, there is the aim to produce enough food, together with sufficient other agricultural output to provide those raw materials and exports which can be produced in India, for example, tea, cotton, jute, coffee. No one doubts the importance of this, and no one could possibly argue that the targets are generally inadequate. Secondly, there is the need to produce sufficient of the highly capital-intensive 'non-importables', electricity, transport, and communications. Thirdly, the remainder of the available investment (and this remainder is limited by the foreign aid to be received) is or will be primarily devoted to import substitution. Some outputs, and targets, are given in Table 5.

TABLE 5. Plan targets for some key items

	1955/6	1958/9	1960/1	1965/6 probable targets[a]
Output				
Foodgrains (m tons)	65.8	73.5	80.5	100–105
Tea (m lbs)	637	716[b]	700	
Jute (m bales)	4.2	5.2	5.5	
Electricity (capacity) (m kW)	3.4	4.3	6.4	12
Coal (m tons)	38.4	46.0	60.0	100
Finished steel (m tons)	1.3	1.3	4.3	9
Cement (m tons)	4.6	6.0	13.0	15.0
Cloth (m yards)	6,573	6,786	8,350	
Fixed nitrogen ('000 tons)	79	79	290	1,000
Cars ('000 tons)	25.3	27.2	57.0	
Bicycles ('000)	513	894	1,000	
No. of family planning clinics (established to date)	147	878	2,647	

[a] No official targets are yet published: these are the author's guesses.
[b] 1957/8.

The most common criticism of Indian planning is that it has been, and will be, too much orientated towards heavy industry. It is true that agricultural production failed to rise fast enough in the Second Plan period. But it is being wise after the event to say that more attention should have been paid to it. Moreover, it does not follow from the relative failure of output that there should have been more direct investment in it. Probably the surest way to have increased output more would have been to have had more heavy industry in the shape of more fertilizer plants.

Apart from food and agricultural materials, it is clear that, if India is to develop successfully, the most rapidly increasing demands will be for the products of mining and heavy industry—steel, electricity, coal, heavy chemicals, cement, oil, and so on. Who can seriously suggest that she ought to import these things—especially when in some of them at least (coal, steel) she has a marked comparative advantage? Yet she cannot plan to produce all she needs of everything. This brings one to the problem of an adequate use of India's own resources, which, above all, means an adequate use of her abundant manpower.

5. INDIA'S OWN RESOURCES

The need for making the greatest possible efforts to increase output is undoubted. Furthermore, the Second Plan did not provide enough jobs to keep pace with the increase in the labour force. It is doubtful whether the larger Third Plan will do more than keep pace, even assuming it is realized without any setback. No real attack will have been made on the problem of underemployment. More employment would be of value in itself. But there is also a strong *prima facie* argument to the effect that output would also be greater if the available capital were combined with more labour.

Labour in industry

There is an apparent dilemma here. It has been seen that demand considerations tend to suggest that, outside agriculture, investment should be concentrated on typically capital-intensive products. The surplus of labour suggests the opposite. The best pattern of output is inevitably a compromise between these conflicting tendencies. Yet, even within a policy of import substitution, there is some choice. India cannot, and does not want to, replace more imports than necessary. To take an example, it seems more sensible to go in for heavy machinery than oil refineries (unless, of course, as may be the case, some foreign resources are tied to oil refineries). Apart from this, one conclusion at least appears to emerge. Whatever is produced should be produced, if possible, by relatively labour-intensive methods. Against this, however, it can be argued that technology gives one little latitude. Nevertheless, there is often some room for manoeuvre. Even if Western-produced or designed machinery gives little possibility of usefully employing more labour on the central productive process, there are ancillary processes—for example materials handling and packaging—which need not be mechanized, but sometimes are. Outside factories there is probably more choice. Building can usually be of masonry, not steel and concrete. Atomic energy and the most capital-intensive hydroelectric schemes can be looked at suspiciously, and so on.

It is important to note, at this point, that the price mechanism in India is a poor guide to what to produce. That the most profitable things should be best presupposes that prices properly reflect the relative scarcities of different goods and services. But capital, labour, and imports are all very wrongly priced in this sense. Imports are much too cheap, the rupee being greatly overvalued. Capital is also too cheap, and labour too expensive. The price mechanism thus inevitably gives a strong bias to too great a capital intensity, too free a use of imported goods, and too little use of labour. It is tempting to suggest that efforts should be made to make prices more realistic. But there are considerable difficulties in the way. While devaluation would increase the rupee price paid for imports, which is as it should be, it seems quite probable that foreign exchange earnings would be reduced by a devaluation, unless export taxes, or similar discriminatory methods, were adopted. Also, whatever might be possible so far as import prices and interest rates go, wages certainly cannot be made to reflect the abundance of labour. The distortion of prices puts considerable difficulties in the way of rational planning, since planners inevitably work from the basis of estimates of actual cost and actual returns. In private industry, which follows the guide of profit without the correcting bias which planners can to some extent impose, all decisions tend to be slanted towards using too little labour, too much capital, and too many imports.

However, it is important not to exaggerate the possible benefits which might flow from an increased use of labour in industry and construction. Not only is industry limited in its flexibility, but it is also small: less than 3½ million are employed in factories. Also, most construction, although there is some unnecessary use of steel and concrete, is still highly labour-intensive. Thus, it is mainly in agricultural investment that any possibility exists of a greatly increased use of labour, though, to a lesser extent, possibilities also exist in the social services.

Labour in agriculture and the social services

Once agricultural and rural development is admitted into the argument, there is no doubt that many more men, many millions more, could be employed with the equipment that could be made available, even in the next five years. Men can work on improving the land with negligible equipment—shovels and baskets—

which would not divert capital from industry. Agricultural reports testify to the almost unlimited work of this kind that could be done.[10] All of it might not be very productive, but some would. The list includes contour bunding, terracing and levelling, drainage, irrigation ditches and minor canals, digging wells, fencing, and making local roads and other constructions from indigenous material which can, again, be got with shovels and baskets. Some social services also fall within the class of needing negligible equipment, for example primary education and birth control. (Education is certainly the main cost in birth control.) In this connection it should be noted that there is serious unemployment among those with university degrees.

But there is the well-known problem of preventing such greater employment from increasing consumption too much. This might result in inflation in the short run, and in the longer run it would be necessary to make a greater provision of capital for the production of factory-made consumption goods. This would in turn imply a slower build-up of the capital goods industries, and hence a further postponement of the date when India can grow by her own resources. On the other hand, the presence of unemployed resources makes it possible that their fuller employment could yield, after some lag, both more investment goods and more consumption.

It has been suggested that there is no potential inflationary barrier in the way of putting idle hands to work, because agricultural production (and well over half India's personal consumption comes from agriculture) would quickly increase.[11] This is a mistake, for the men employed on land improvement schemes must be paid; and any extra output, however quickly it materializes (and in fact there must be a lag), will add to peasants' incomes as well as to output, so that the extra output is an offset only to the extent that the peasants save more of their higher incomes. Thus, the ability or willingness to tax is a limit not merely to the size of the Plan, but to the amount of employment it can offer. A larger plan with less employment may put less strain on the fiscal system and on a politician's courage than a smaller and more labour-intensive plan.

To put it another way, the limitation on employment is not employment opportunities, but the immediate supply of consumption goods, primarily food. Thus, more employment depends on the Government's willingness or ability to redistribute consumption sufficiently in favour of the newly or more intensively employed men. It is the barrier round which many believe that China has found a way. This suggests the possibility of a larger Third Plan.

[10] For instance, *Report on India's Food Crisis and Steps to Meet It*, Ford Foundation Agricultural Production Team, 1959.

[11] Ibid.

6. A LARGER THIRD PLAN?

Before turning to the fiscal difficulty, there are two other possible problems to consider: organization, and the balance between agriculture and other production.

Organization could be a limitation which would bite before any fiscal limit. But it is my impression that it is the latter which is now operative. There seems to have been some disagreement between the Ministry of Agriculture and the Planning Commission over the agricultural allocation for the Third Plan. This suggests that the former believes that it could usefully spend more. India has many monuments to the power of unassisted labour in the shape not only of vast forts and palaces, but also canals and railways. Of course, more is needed than merely recruiting large numbers of men, and setting them to work, if the result is to be as productive as it might be. But, by now (though this was not true some years ago), agricultural and other departments probably have the skill to organize more work than is planned.

The balance of agriculture and industry

It has been argued that the agricultural targets are, if anything, too high already. Would not much further employment on land improvement certainly result in too much food? This objection can be answered. First, there is no certainty in agriculture. Secondly, there is the matter of timing. For several years such further employment, which would increase each year as the programme was built up, would add more to food demand than supply; and the problem would be to prevent excess demand for food. If it subsequently became apparent that the eventual increase in supply would be excessive, certain of the more capital-intensive ways of producing more food (major irrigation and fertilizer plants) could be cut back. Fourthly, some combination of falling food prices and increased indirect taxation of factory-produced consumption goods could always steer the extra consumption towards food. This would be necessary to prevent too large a part of future plans from being devoted to the provision of manufactured consumer goods, with a consequent delay in the establishment of a sufficient industrial basis to provide for enough capital investment without foreign aid.

The fiscal problem

This is the heart of the matter. If a much larger programme of land improvement were added to the Third Plan, the need for taxation would surely be increased in the initial years at least. As it is, the Third Plan will demand considerably higher taxation. But the increases in taxation will certainly not be excessive provided the Plan is a success. This needs no argument, for total consumption is planned to rise by 4 per cent a year, and the increased taxation will be needed only to prevent it rising faster. At a very rough guess, assuming that India obtains the aid she hopes for, £75 million worth of additional taxes, or increased rates, might be needed every year. This is more every year than any finance minister has yet added in any one year. The idea horrifies the middle classes, which are the backbone of the Congress Party. Yet very few need actually be made poorer, and those not for long.

Some people have the impression that tax rates are high in India. This is wrong. Only corporation tax and direct personal tax on the very rich are high, and the latter is not effective. Other rates of tax are mostly low. In fact the middle classes, say those with over £180 a year, are very lightly taxed: even on paper, the direct tax paid does not match British standards below about £4,000 a year, and indirect taxation is far lower. Administratively, it is harder to tax in India. But there is no doubt that the fiscal requirements of the Third Plan are very well within the administrative limits. Yet one fears that fiscal pusillanimity is a danger, especially in view of the relative inability of the central government to get the States to increase the taxes reserved to them. These include all taxation of land, and of incomes derived from the land.

If the Third Plan were enlarged in the manner indicated, a still greater taxation effort would be required in the first few years. This would need to be directed towards damping down the demand for food. All taxation will do this to some extent. But increases in land taxation—which, in real terms, has been declining for decades—would probably be most appropriate, not only because the peasants would be the chief beneficiaries of the absorption of underemployed members of their families, and of the subsequent increases in output and the value of their land, but also because they eat a higher proportion of their incomes than others. Unfortunately, increased land taxation not only depends on the co-operation of the States, but is also of particular repugnance to the Congress Party, much of whose support derives from the richer farmers. But if agricultural output responded well, then the shift of emphasis should pass to indirect taxation of manufactured consumer goods.

It should finally be noted that the higher paid wage-earners in India are scarcely touched by taxation. The only way to restrain the rise in their consumption is to stop real wages rising. This sounds harsh until it is realized that the average wage in organized industry is about four times as high as the lowest wage in India. It is insufficiently realized that high real wages help to limit the numbers who can be employed, as well as providing employers with an incentive to use more capital. This is of secondary importance only because the number of well paid employees is still small.

In spite of the political difficulties involves in raising taxes, and restraining generally the consumption of those with sufficient work, it is hard for an economist not to believe that the best use of Indian resources requires a still larger and more labour-intensive Plan. This assumes that sufficient aid will be forthcoming for the industrial development and other import-using projects. If this is not so, then the programme of industrialization will have to be cut, but it should still be possible to put more effort into the labour-intensive sector.

7. CONCLUSIONS

1. The broad strategy of Indian planned development is eminently sound. The Third Plan is part of a series designed to raise the proportion of investment in a rising national income, and reduce and eventually eliminate that part financed by foreign savings. One cannot quarrel with this aim, and few who have really studied the problem doubt that it involves a rapid increase in industrialization, involving the building up of heavy industry roughly on the scale planned.

2. A large element of foreign aid is, for a decade at least, indispensable. This is not so much because it is impossible to increase savings in India, but because savings cannot be translated into the kind of capital development which will later permit India to grow without continued reliance on foreign aid. In other words, saving is at present no substitute for aid.

3. It is very difficult to judge the amount of aid which will be necessary for the Third Plan to be viable. But there is no good reason to suppose that the figures put to the recent Bankers' Mission are exaggerated. The Mission itself did not hint that they might be.

4. There is a good case for saying that India has failed, and is failing, to solve the problem of putting idle hands to work. Increased savings can be turned into greater employment on land improvements without increasing the need for aid. Fear of inflation has been a barrier to such increased employment. Consequently, a greater willingness to tax (and to stop or moderate wage increases for those already employed) would pave the way for significantly greater output and employment. It follows that there is a good case for a larger Third Plan.

5. If India does not obtain the aid she needs (and there is, of course, considerable doubt about this), the industrial part of the Third Plan would have to be cut. She might partly compensate for the loss of income by an increased effort towards agricultural improvement, and in the social services. But the day when India can ensure her own growth, from a level of abysmal poverty, would surely recede even further into the future.

7
Public Sector Project Selection in Relation to Indian Development (1969)

1. INTRODUCTION

As a result of the influence of input–output analysis, there is a tendency to think that, once the final outputs of an economy—the consumption, investment, and exports—are chosen (from the range of possibilities), then the output of all goods is determined by the set of technical coefficients.

This is wrong for two reasons. First, the input coefficients are not independent of the pattern of demand, unless by fiat. This is not a criticism of technocratic planning, with which we shall be concerned in this essay. Secondly, the model makes no provision for the determination of what shall be imported and what produced domestically—unless it be by assuming that important coefficients (those proportions of particular inputs into an industry, or directly into final demand, which are imported) remain unchanged. It is obvious enough that this assumption is absurd in India's situation, and is indeed absurd for any industrializing economy. The import pattern, as well as the export pattern, must be chosen by some criterion or other, which is the same as saying that one must choose what to produce domestically; in other words, production is not determined by ultimate goals expressed in terms of living standards at some future date—not by a long chalk.

The above is obvious to the point of being trite. Nevertheless, it can be, and has been for years, forcibly argued that the circumstances of India are such as to virtually determine the desirable pattern of India's production without recourse to any economic criterion which involves optimization, i.e. making the best of one's resources. If there is only one possibility, there is no room for economics to help decide the pattern of production. It might still play some part in determining how a particular product should be produced—e.g. electrify a railway or not—but that would be all.

A first draft of this article was written when the author was a member of the Indian project of the MIT Centre for International Studies in March 1965. He is indebted not only to MIT, but also to members of seminars at Delhi University and Nuffield College, who made valuable suggestions; and to Dr Grossman of the Ford Foundation, New Delhi, for various helpful criticisms.

The present version originally appeared in A. V. Bhuleshaker (ed), *Indian Economic Thought and Development* (1969). Permission to reproduce is gratefully acknowledged.

What is the argument? It runs as follows.

1. Export growth, mainly determined by world conditions, will be slow—slow enough to substantiate argument 4 below. This will be the case even if all economically justifiable efforts are made to promote exports.
2. Net foreign aid must be eliminated after a decade.
3. Therefore a very limited amount of foreign exchange will be available.
4. India must grow fast, and will therefore require rapidly increasing exports of things which cannot physically be produced or found in India in sufficient quantities—oil, non-ferrous metals, and some chemicals. These, plus interest on aid already received, will swallow up all the foreign exchange.
5. Therefore India must produce everything that can physically be produced in India.
6. Therefore, if the demand is established, that alone is a sufficient reason for embarking on production (unless the good is an item of luxury consumption, the demand for which can reasonably be suppressed).[1]

This is a powerful argument. It is, we believe, accepted by many, including many members of the Planning Commission and some foreign visiting economists. It was argued, in effect, in the Second Plan and in the Third Plan.

What is wrong with the argument? First, unless there is a catastrophic change in the climate of world opinion, India will not need to do without aid in a decade. The choice always to plan to do without aid in a short time is the Indian Government's choice, and absolutely unjustified in the light of India's great poverty and the high probability that economic aid will, in a decade, still be flowing from developed to developing countries, possibly even on a much larger scale than now. Admittedly, some donors, notably the United States, like to see a country planning to do without economic aid: but surely not India in a decade. Pakistan, for example, also plans to eliminate aid, but only in 20–25 years, a long enough period for such a stipulation to have no influence on the present pattern of investment. So the hurry to achieve a high degree of independence from foreign suppliers is not as desperate as the Indian Government claims.

Secondly, even if some unforeseen political catastrophe were to result in a cessation of the flow of public capital from rich to poor countries, the argument does not hold water, because the scarcity of available resources during the next decade will almost certainly be too great, and time too short, to enable India to establish the industrial base required to achieve *both* the rapid growth postulated from 1975 onwards, *and* a viable balance of payments.

The relevant basic scarcities are: (*a*) foreign exchange, and (*b*) domestic skills and experience sufficient to create and run an enormously expanded industrial nexus in a very short time. There is not going to be enough foreign exchange in

[1] Where an element of choice has been admitted to be necessary, there has been a tendency to choose the heaviest kind of industry. The general argument—a demonstrably false argument—that the stage of production most remote from final demand saves most foreign exchange, has been put forward as a justification of this tendency. But it is doubtful whether anyone believes this any more.

the next decade to do the job of setting up factories to make everything that can physically be produced in India in the required quantities for a 6–7 per cent rate of growth. But, even if there were enough foreign exchange, which could result only from a great 'leap forward' in aid, a decade or even fifteen years is not long enough for India, with her present knowledge, political organization, and administration, to be able to plan and establish the required industrial capacity; nor is it long enough for her to acquire the industrial skills and discipline, and the managerial expertise, to get the desired output from the large increases in capacity contemplated.

The argument has been rebutted. If India cannot do everything in a decade, then there is a problem of choosing what it is best to do. *Not* choosing results in a waste of capital. Wrong things get started. Almost worse, too many things get started, and not enough finished. This ties up capital unproductively, and results in bad labour relations, and thus slows up the rate of growth; which in turn means that less capital is available—not merely domestic capital, but also foreign capital, both public and private; for there is nothing that foreign investors, including foreign governments (especially the USA), like to see so much as a rapid growth of output.

Overlong gestation periods and lagging output have been one of the important lessons of the last few years—i.e. since large plans got under way. There is no doubt that more careful project selection and project planning—above all, more attention to project and sectoral costs—would help to reduce the magnitude of this problem. It is not sufficient to establish that the demand is there. Costs too are important.

Demand can claim to be a sufficient criterion for production only in the case of goods and services which cannot be imported, such as power, internal transport, construction, and various services. Thus, an important distinction to be drawn in this article is between 'tradables' and 'non-tradables'. It corresponds to the distinction drawn by Professor Tinbergen between 'national' and 'international' industries.[2] We shall not be specifically concerned with non-tradables, where the economic choice lies between different ways of achieving the same output (in which case different projects are 'incompatible').[3] The division between

[2] This paper is based on a seminar given at the Delhi School of Economics in March 1965. At the seminar, Professor J. Bhagwati pointed out how closely my project selection criterion was related to methods being advocated by Professor Tinbergen to planners in Turkey. I was unaware of this at the time. Professor Tinbergen's views are outlined in 'Projections of Economic Data in Development Planning', *Planning for Economic Development in the Caribbean*, Caribbean Organisation Hato Rey, Puerto Rico, 1963. While my treatment of non-tradable and tradable inputs corresponds exactly to Professor Tinbergen's 'semi input–output method', Professor Tinbergen did not, in the article cited (which is without special reference to the conditions of a particular country), propose any such precise methods of valuing inputs and outputs in a cost–benefit analysis as are suggested here. Nor did he go into the problems of discounting.

[3] But the analysis of costs, which is made in this article, is just as relevant to the choice between incompatible projects of this kind as it is to the choice between those compatible projects with which we are more immediately concerned.

tradables and non-tradables is not absolute. In a few countries, for instance, some electricity can be more economically imported than produced. 'Non-tradables' can be taken to mean those goods or services for which it is absolutely obvious that it is more economical to produce them at home rather than import them, and where profitable export sales are vastly unlikely. (Sometimes almost the whole supply of a good is obviously non-tradable, but a small proportion can be imported or exported—e.g. electricity to a frontier village. Such exceptions present no great difficulty.)

It should also be noted that we are concerned only with project selection in the public sector. This is for two reasons. First, the validity of the criterion developed depends upon the choice between public and private sector having been made on non-economic grounds. (The public sector is not, by assumption, competing with the private sector for savings.) Secondly, the criterion could not be applied to private sector projects.

Finally, our intention in this article is to find a *practical* criterion for project selection. We aim to build a bridge between rather high-brow theories of optimization, and the welter of conflicting arguments (some based on false theory) which, through some process of compromise, influence the actual decisions taken. (The decisions themselves influence, but do not determine, what actually gets done.)

2. SOME BASIC ASSUMPTIONS

One's criterion must depend on the broad politico-economic framework. Two assumptions are made about this. The first, as we have seen, is that the division between the public and private sectors is determined on political grounds. The choice between the relative amounts of investment in the public and private sectors is thus deemed to have been taken. This assumption is made because it is, broadly speaking, true; and also because it enormously simplifies the problem of choice, as we shall see.

Secondly, the Government is assumed to set a target for the growth of consumption (probably in the region of 4–5 per cent), which will not be allowed to rise above the target path, unless something other than domestic savings prevents investment from being increased. It is assumed that the fiscal system is powerful enough, and that political courage is great enough, for this to be possible. Considering how valiantly finance ministers have raised taxes in the face of the disappointing outputs of the Third Plan, and the very disappointing rise in consumption (partly due, of course, to unexpected defence expenditures), this is a fair assumption provided that one is not too pessimistic about future production possibilities. The point of this assumption is that, in choosing between two projects (of equal size), we need not worry abut whether one is more conducive to saving than the other. If we choose the less conducive to saving, the Finance

Minister will look after the difference. The effect of relaxing this assumption will be discussed at a later stage.

Thirdly, foreign exchange is assumed to be a bottleneck which operates prior to domestic savings. This might not be true if the shape of investment were changed. But I think it has been true, and would remain so for some time even if our criterion were adopted. If our criterion pulls away the ladder by which it is created, no matter. We shall change the criterion when that happens!

Let us approach the problem of project selection by considering two of the most common criteria used (or, perhaps, one should call them merely 'considerations'), these being profitability and the capital/output ratio. Nothing new is said about them, but their failings serve as a useful introduction to better methods of project evaluation.

3. PROFITABILITY

In a perfectly competitive economy, where prices correctly measure scarcities and benefits, the profit and interest resulting from some investment in a particular year is equal to the increase in real national income caused by that investment in that year.

We take each year's profit or loss (including interest), after allowing for replacements, and discount it back to the present, and add up. We also take the original capital expenditures, discount them back to the present, and add up. The ratio of the sum of discounted profits to the sum of discounted capital expenditures is the proper measure of profitability. This is a form of cost–benefit analysis. Sales = gross benefits. Costs = costs. Profits = net benefit. Let us defer consideration of the rate of discount. For the moment we are concerned with evaluating the costs and benefits of the project this year, next year, and so on.

But profits are not always a very satisfactory measure of net benefits. This is the case when the prices of goods and services do not properly reflect the relative opportunity costs. In India, this is the case. In particular, profits and interest do *not* measure the increase in real income resulting from an investment, if there is a surplus of labour. If the surplus of labour is absolute, the capital/output ratio has a certain plausibility as a criterion. To this we now turn.

4. CAPITAL/OUTPUT RATIOS

If the proper shadow price for labour is zero, and if labour is the only current input, then output in the sense of value added is the proper measure of net benefit, for it represents the increase in real national income which results from the capital expenditure. Labour is not counted as a cost, because its employment need not reduce labour used elsewhere, and hence need not reduce output elsewhere. In such a case value added is simply the sum of wages, interest, and profits; and is also identical with the gross value of output, or sales. Even with these simplifications, this result is subject to the proviso that sales must be made at prices which reflect the gross benefit to the economy.

But labour is seldom, if ever, the only current input. Purchases of inputs from other enterprises must be subtracted to arrive at value added. If value added is to be a proper measure of benefit, these purchases must be correctly valued. If *ex hypothesi*, labour's proper value is zero, then the actual prices of indigenous purchases cannot represent their true value, for the actual wages paid in India will be a component of the price. There are also other reasons, such as an exchange rate which does not reflect the scarcity of foreign exchange, for rejecting actual prices.

So the capital/output ratio is not an acceptable criterion, even if it is correct to value labour at zero. We shall have to investigate further the price not only of labour, but also of all other inputs and outputs. Before doing this, however, it is worth mentioning that capital/output ratios, as often quoted, are usually extremely misleading for another reason than that the prices used may not reflect scarcities. They normally relate the maximum output or value added, which, in a large public sector enterprise, is usually attainable only several years after completion (sometimes, in Indian conditions, this lag can be as long as ten years), to the capital expenditure (which may, or may not, have been properly compounded at a meaningful rate of interest). Such a statistic has no value whatever. It is essential to discount (or compound) all capital expenditures and receipts, and all annual estimates of value added, to the same point in time. In fact, the author has never seen a capital/output ratio quoted in this, the only meaningful, form.

The proper rate of interest to use will be discussed later. Until then, we shall be concerned only with measuring costs and benefits in particular years—that is costs and benefits which are contemporaneous.

Let us turn now to a discussion of the 'shadow' prices of current inputs and outputs, i.e. those prices which should be used in evaluating and selecting projects.

5. THE PRICING OF CURRENT INPUTS AND OUTPUTS IN COST–BENEFIT ANALYSIS

The shadow price of labour

It is surely much nearer the truth to say that more labour can be employed in a public sector enterprise in India without thereby reducing output elsewhere, than it is to say that paying another man Rs 100 a month will cause output elsewhere to fall by Rs 100 a month. But can we assume that the marginal product is always zero—i.e. that increased employment in a public sector enterprise will never tend to cause any withdrawal of labour from other uses with a resultant fall in output? Obviously not, but the question asks too much. In searching for a general and applicable criterion, we need a good working rule which distorts the truth less than any other such rule. It is suggested that open and growing urban unemployment and heavy underemployment in rural areas, together with the fact that there is little chance (at least unless labour-intensive development is greatly increased) that job creation can match the growth in the labour force for many years, makes the assumption that the marginal product of labour is zero a reasonable working rule.

Let us, however, consider briefly some of the objections often made to this assumption. The most usual objection is that the labour which is suitable for industrial enterprise is not the raw landless labour which is surplus in rural areas, nor the completely uneducated urban proletariat. This is, of course, true. Skilled labour is scarce. Nevertheless, I do not think this a valid objection. Skilled labour for new industrial enterprises is formed by taking matriculates, or at least those with some education, and giving them training in the special skills required in the industry in question. Now Indian educational programmes are surely going to produce an excess of this 'raw material for skilled and semi-skilled workers' anyway. This education is not itself a cost of the enterprise, because political considerations are going to ensure that it is provided in any case. Thus, general education becomes a free good so far as industry is concerned. There remain only the special skills. These of course are a cost to the enterprise, and should be reckoned as such. The cost of such training will often, perhaps normally, be included in the project report as part of both the initial capital and continuing expenses of the enterprise. It is just part of the project, and presents no special problem.

Of course, the wages and salaries bill will include the salaries of a number of people, whose skills are not acquired as part of the project, and who have a very real opportunity cost which, for top management, is probably far in excess of their salaries. In theory, therefore, it is totally illegitimate not to count their salaries as a cost. But, in practice, doing so is unlikely to bias the results. Salaries are only a very small part of costs. So, for the sake of simplicity, it is probably not too serious a distortion to treat this as a '*de minimis*' consideration. On the other hand, if sufficient resources are available for project evaluation, it is obviously more accurate to separate out those categories of the staff which are clearly scarce, and cost them accordingly.

Let us turn now to another class of objections, those concerning the transfer of labour from the countryside to the towns. First, despite the evident surplus supply of labour in agriculture most of the time, it is said that, in some areas at least, there is no excess at certain peak periods.[4] Whether, nevertheless, the same

[4] The seasonal nature of agricultural projection makes it inevitable that either men (where agriculture is very labour-intensive) or machines (where agriculture is capital-intensive) will be underemployed for parts of the year, even if people work exceptionally hard at peak times.

crop would somehow be planted and harvested with fewer hands, most of the time in most places, by virtue of long hours, mutual assistance, and so on is hard to say. Even if not, the objection is sustained only if the drift to the towns would not take place independently of the demand for workers in the towns. If this drift is going to occur anyway, and is not *caused* by industrial employment opportunities, then greater demand for labour in public sector urban enterprises does not itself restrict agricultural output, and there is no social cost to such employment.[5]

Secondly, it is often argued that there are costs involved in urban living, and that these represent an inescapable social cost. This is a different kind of objection, which is separate from the argument about the marginal product of labour. In this connection, two kinds of costs should be distinguished. The first is the capital cost involved in housing, transport, sanitation, etc. The second is the higher current costs of living in cities, which makes it inevitable that urban workers should consume more. So far as the first is concerned, many new public sector enterprises have a township attached, whose costs form part of the project, and are not municipalized. Now if, in project selection, township costs are allowed for, it is clear that the extra capital costs associated with urban living cannot also be adduced as a reason for using a higher-than-zero shadow wage. However, we shall argue later that charging township costs to a project is more likely to distort the choice between projects than otherwise. Even so, it does not follow that the capital expenditure involved in urban living is a good reason for attributing some real cost to the employment of urban labour. For instance, as we have seen, it does not follow that urban drift would occur in any case. Furthermore, we must remember at this point that it has been assumed that the prime scarcity in India is foreign exchange, and capital expenditure on towns is not very import-intensive.

Turning to the second kind of cost which was distinguished above, it must be agreed that higher consumption by those actually employed is an unavoidable concomitant of urban employment. But this brings us to a quite different objection to attributing zero marginal social cost to the employment of labour. It is not enough that the marginal product of labour be zero, and that no indirect capital costs be associated with employing labour. It must also be true that the total amount of consumption is independent of which projects are selected. Yet, prima facie, it is certain that a labour-intensive project will add directly to consumption more than a capital-intensive project of the same capital outlay: in which case more effort (and foreign exchange) has to be devoted to investment in consumption goods. This is precisely why we have assumed that aggregate consumption is planned to rise at a certain rate, and no more—which means that,

[5] It may, further, be argued that, even if the marginal product is zero now, it will not be in a decade, especially now that more active and promising efforts to control births are being made. In this connection it should be noted that, with projects that last 20 years, the first 10 years have much more weight than the second 10 in any cost–benefit analysis. Furthermore, however effective birth control becomes in, say, 5 years' time, it will have no effect on the huge growth of the labour force for 20 years.

the more labour-intensive the projects selected, the more taxes the Finance Minister must impose in order to combat the direct effect on consumption of those projects. It follows also, more generally, that the inevitably higher consumption levels associated with urban employment are no reason for assigning to labour a shadow wage greater than zero.[6]

Some may think this assumption much too strong. We think the truth depends very much on how widely one's criterion is applied—a question to which we have not, so far, given a precise answer. Suppose it is applied only to industrial projects. Valuing labour at zero would tend to shift choice both towards the production of goods which can be produced by relatively labour-intensive methods, and towards the selection of more labour-intensive means of production. But we would not expect any increase in the job-creating capacity of plans to be at all dramatic. First, within the industrial sector, probably few things can be made very labour-intensive. Secondly, the criterion would not operate easily at the project design stage. (At that stage, one can only tell the consultants that you do not want mechanization where more labour-using methods can be used, and will not prejudice too much either the speed of operation of the process or the desired quality of the product.) Thirdly, many Indian enterprises are overstaffed anyway. More labour-using methods will often tend to save capital per unit of output by increasing the utilization of the labour force employed, rather than actually increasing employment. So we would expect the adoption of a zero shadow wage in project appraisal to be more insidiously beneficial than dramatically effective. This being so, we feel it fair to assume that the Finance Minister can still prevent consumption rising too fast, despite the not-altogether-to-be-regretted tendency to somewhat greater employment.

If the criterion is also applied to agricultural projects of all kinds, so that industrial projects are compared with agricultural, the results could be more dramatic. (We know too little about evaluating the benefits of health and education to be able to apply it at all in these sectors.) If it appeared that such a major shift to labour-intensive agricultural projects (especially those of relatively long gestation) was indicated, that employment and consumption threatened to diminish total investment (or cause over-rapid inflation), then it would appear that the shadow wage had been set too low.

We must now sum up our discussion of the price of labour. It has been rather long, but it is, or should be, the crucial issue in Indian planning. First, it is certain that the shadow price of labour is much below the actual wages paid in the public sector (themselves well ahead of the private sector). The real problem is

[6] We have shown elsewhere that, if the marginal product of labour in agriculture (and other consumption good industries) is zero, then, if the Finance Minister *cannot* prevent consumption rising above some target rate, as a result of more employment in capital creation, the correct shadow wage is the actual wage multiplied by the marginal propensity to consume. In this article, however, we are making (with qualifications) the opposite assumption; see I. M. D. Little, 'The Real Cost of Labour, and the Choice between Consumption and Investment', *Quarterly Journal of Economics* (Feb. 1961).

whether one can use a zero shadow wage, or must opt for some compromise between zero and the actual wage. The author's feeling is that none of the arguments against a zero shadow wage are very compelling. If it is believed that something close to zero is the right answer, then there are good reasons for settling for zero: this is because it simplifies project appraisal considerably. Moreover, with a zero shadow wage, the calculation of net benefit will approximate (after certain other adjustments, to which we come later) to net value added—a well-known, familiar, and hence more or less acceptable measure of benefit.

Probably the crucial question is whether the criterion, which we are approaching, is extended to comparisons of industrial with agricultural projects. If this is done, it might be prudent to settle for, say, half the actual wage as the shadow wage. If it is confined to industrial projects, the author would advocate a zero shadow wage.

Before considering the price to be assumed for other inputs (purchases from other enterprises at home and abroad),[7] let us consider the price of the output.

The shadow price of the output

It can be seen that, although we have earlier dismissed 'net value added' as a good measure of benefit, nevertheless we are approaching an 'adjusted net value added' concept of benefit, if it is accepted that labour should be valued at zero. 'Net value added', as estimated by national income statisticians, is the difference between the actual value of sales and purchases from other enterprises. But we have already given reasons why actual values may not measure benefit properly. How then should the value of output be measured, if not by actual prices obtained?

Consider first the process of import substitution, which accounts for a large part of Indian industrialization. The import is displaced normally by a higher-priced domestic output. Clearly, the actual net value added is not a measure of the real increase in net national income, if we use Indian domestic prices. If we do that, we have built in a price rise as part of the real output increase, which is false. So we must not use prices higher than the landed prices of the input. But we also measure net national income at factor cost, so tariffs must come off too. Therefore the price to be used is the c.i.f. price.[8] Indeed, in the case of lower priced goods, which are either displaced or would have had to be imported if the project in question had not been chosen, the benefit of the

[7] Land is ignored as a cost throughout the text. Where relevant, i.e. where it has some significantly valuable alternative use, it should be added to the capital cost of the project. The same is true of other natural resources, where either possible alternative uses or conservation policy require that some inherent value be put upon them.

[8] In theory, the marginal c.i.f. cost. But this is seldom likely to differ significantly, in the case of industrial goods, from the c.i.f. price.

output to India is quite clearly the rupee equivalent of the foreign exchange cost. This follows from the fact that we have assumed that foreign exchange is the operative bottleneck.[9]

Let us anticipate some objections. One might argue, for example, that fertilizers are worth more to India than their c.i.f. prices, by virtue of the extra output they cause. So how can we take the c.i.f. price as a measure of real value? Or, it may be argued that most things are worth far more in India than their c.i.f. prices, because of an overvalued exchange rate. The answer to this is that, since we are concerned with choosing what to make in India, we are interested only in the relative benefits of different projects. If it is foreign exchange that is scarce, valuing things in terms of foreign exchange gives the correct relative valuation. But it might be further argued that, while most other things are worth, say, double their c.i.f. value, fertilizers are worth treble because of the foreign exchange saving of increased food production. If this is true, it follows of course that not enough fertilizers are being used. But it by no means proves that India should be making fertilizers. That can be decided only by reference to what it costs to import them. We are, in fact, trying to arrive at a criterion which will select projects according to India's comparative advantage. (Very probably fertilizers should be made, but that is not the point.)

But now suppose the Indian substitute can be produced at lower cost than the price of the import. The extreme case of this is a strictly non-tradable good whose import price can be deemed to be infinite. Does it matter if the shadow price used is the import price? Not if one is deciding merely whether the good should be produced in India at all. Take the case of a virtually non-tradable good, like electricity, which could presumably be imported at some gigantic price. All that happens, if we put the shadow price of electricity at, say, Rs 1,000 a unit, is that the criterion tells us that electricity must be produced in India. But it does not tell us how much to produce. It was said earlier that the production of non-tradables can be determined by demand. But, of course, the amount demanded varies with the price. More strictly, then, the output of non-tradables should be planned to satisfy the demand, *given the right pricing policy*. The right pricing policy depends on costs, which themselves must ideally take account of the shadow prices of labour and other scarce factors of production. (All non-tradables can ultimately have their long-run marginal cost structure analysed into labour and tradable inputs.)[10]

The above paragraph also applies to a tradable good provided that the unknown unit (shadow) costs of the marginal productive unit are less than the price of imports, and provided also that such costs are greater than the export

[9] Of course, India is a large country, and sometimes the imported good at the port may be nearer or further from its market than the home-produced good at the factory gate. Thus, an allowance may need to be made for internal transport on both. Internal transport is a non-tradable, and its treatment is considered later.

[10] Again, land is ignored (and also other resources in their natural state).

price.[11] We can thus have a complication where there is a considerable divergence between c.i.f. and f.o.b. prices. The proper price lies somewhere in between—but, without a full evaluation of the costs (at shadow prices for all factors of production), one cannot say exactly where this price lies.

This complication, however, by no means destroys the utility of the criterion towards which we are working. It is a problem which primarily concerns the optimum output of non-tradables, and only to a lesser extent tradable goods for which there is a significantly large divergence of import and export prices, and then only those for which Indian costs (at optimum shadow prices for all scarce resources) would be lower than import prices. In other words, it is a problem of the optimum output of those goods which India has a sufficient comparative advantage to make, but not a sufficient comparative advantage to export. With all goods, it is correct to value output at the import price so long as some of the good is actually being imported. Equally, it is correct to value at the export price if some is exported, and none imported. The problem arises only over the optimum output of goods which are neither exported nor imported. (It is a problem which would take us too far afield to explore here: but, given that the long-run marginal costs of such goods can be resolved, as near as makes no matter, into labour and import costs, a solution using a shadow price for labour, and actual import prices, can be found.)

There may finally be some cases where, owing to transport costs and market imperfections, the good is both exported and imported. One then has to guess *ad hoc* whether the projected new production, taking account of the proposed site, would save imports or increase exports, and value the output accordingly. (It must do one or the other, as compared with what would have happened if there had been no new production—assuming a free market, i.e. no excess internal demand.)

To sum up, our thesis on the price to be assumed for tradable outputs is really quite simple. If the good is being imported and not exported, take the import price. If vice versa, take the f.o.b. price (or marginal revenue in appropriate cases). If both, take whichever price seems more appropriate. If the good is produced but neither imported nor exported, it must be assumed that it would pass our criterion for import substitution, but is not worth exporting. Whether more should be produced for the home market is a matter of pricing policy, into the full details of which we do not enter here, but which must rest on an analysis of the long-run marginal costs into labour and foreign exchange costs (together with a rate of interest—of which more anon).

We turn now to tradable inputs. It should be no surprise that much the same treatment is appropriate for them as for tradable outputs. Nevertheless, there is some difference, and a brief discussion is appropriate.

[11] In theory, again, it is the marginal revenue which is relevant. Usually, however, in the case of a new export project, a market survey will suggest that there is a market for a certain quantity as a certain price; provided other Indian exports are not competing, this is the price to take.

The shadow price of tradable inputs

For imported inputs, we obviously use c.i.f. prices.

For indigenous inputs, we also propose to use c.i.f. or f.o.b. prices, whichever seems in the particular circumstances more appropriate. As with tradable outputs, there will occasionally be cases where the good is produced, but neither exported nor imported, non-tradables being extreme members of the class of goods for which this is likely to happen. As before, this raises a problem. One could, of course, treat all goods which in fact are neither imported nor exported as non-tradable (see below). But this might multiply the number too much. It must, in this connection, be remembered that we are searching for a practical criterion. Non-tradables can include, for practical purposes, only a few very generally used inputs which are neither significantly imported nor exported. We believe, however, that outside these it will be rare to find indigenous inputs where a wide divergence of the potential c.i.f. and f.o.b. prices gives an arbitrary element to the price. In such rare cases, we would suggest taking the actual price, provided it is less than the potential c.i.f. price (assuming in effect that the results of an overvalued rupee and an overvalued wage cancel each other): if not, take the potential c.i.f. price.

Normally it will be found that Indian prices are much higher than import prices. It is a wrong valuation of such inputs that we chiefly have to guard against. Their actual prices must *not* be used. The real cost to the Indian economy of using a high priced indigenous component can seldom if ever be more than the import price.[12] If the import price is not used, one biases the choice of projects against those which use indigenous components.[13]

[12] If use of an indigenous component causes, in the short run when output potential is fixed, a shortage rather than an increase in imports, then this shortage could do more damage than is measured by the cost of imports. But, of course, we have to assume that the inputs used by the projects under consideration are in free supply, or can be freely imported. It makes no sense to choose a project which can only achieve its output by starving other productive units of essential imports. Rational calculation is impossible in such circumstances. This is quite consistent with foreign exchange being the bottleneck on growth, and with an overvalued exchange rate.

There is, however, another reason why the true cost to the Indian economy of an input could be above the c.i.f. price, which is valid only if the shadow price of labour is above zero. In that event, there are basically two shortages operating—foreign exchange and domestic savings—in which case a labour-intensive indigenous input could theoretically cost the Indian economy more than the foreign imported substitute would have done. But since this case can arise only if it is decided to use a positive shadow wage, and since even in that event we would very much doubt its importance, we ignore the possibility in formulating our criterion.

Finally, it is conceivable that a non-zero shadow price for land or minerals could make the real cost of an indigenous input greater than the c.i.f. price. This seems a remote possibility which we also ignore.

[13] Using the rupee equivalent of the c.i.f. price in such cases has the same directional effect as using a shadow rate of exchange higher than the actual rate. Both methods guard against biasing project choice in favour of those using the actually cheaper imported component. The shadow rate of exchange method is to increase the valuation of the imported component (100 per cent import content) relative to the indigenous component with a lower import content. Our method is to reduce the valuation of indigenous supplies.

Where Indian prices are actually lower than the import price (and where also there are no imports), then as we have seen we would use the actual price (net of tax) provided it is higher than a price at which the good can be advantageously exported.

External economies

This concept has played a large part in economic literature. Should we now somehow allow for external economies in arriving at the shadow prices of inputs and outputs? In particular, it may be argued that we have left out of the account external economies connected with the supply of indigenous materials and components. Some projects will enlarge the market for such supplies, and so should lead to economies of scale elsewhere: they may make economical the production in India of some things which could not otherwise have been made since the domestic market was previously too small, or non-existent. Perhaps, in using c.i.f. prices for components, we underestimate the benefits of the project, if it eventually leads to India having a comparative advantage in such components.

Now it must be remembered that we are trying to arrive at an applicable criterion which will help choice between public sector projects (and not determine the size of the public sector). So the question is whether one project will give rise to significantly more such external economies in the shape of economies of scale elsewhere than another project. No doubt, this would occasionally be the case: but it is a consideration which it is virtually impossible to quantify. In the interests of getting an applicable criterion, it is a consideration which probably has to be neglected. The concept of external economics is a real danger to good applied economics. It has been said that when external economies enter in at the door, economics flies out of the window. Admitting them into the argument is dangerous, because if any non-quantifiable consideration is to be allowed, then it is difficult indeed to draw the line. Every kind of special pleading becomes admissible.

The case when a project will permit the manufacture of a component in India, which would not otherwise have occurred, may, sometimes, be different. Where there is a clear case of this, then it may make sense to regard the manufacture of this component as an integral part of the project, and consider the two together. (The treatment of the component is then analogous to the treatment of non-tradable inputs, which we consider below.) But they should also be considered separately, for it may well be the case that the component should *not* be made in India.[14] Such lumping together of projects is plausible only when the investment

[14] It is sometimes taken as an argument in favour of a project, that components which are actually imported will later be made in India, and it is claimed that the import-saving potential of the project will thus improve. This, of course, is quite illegitimate double-counting. When this happens, the import saving can be attributed only to the new investment undertaken to make the components in question. It is only when such investment could never have been undertaken without the initial project's demand that there may be a case for considering the two together.

required to make the component can be clearly identified, and when the initial project constitutes the major part of the market for the component in question. It is again suggested that this kind of treatment will only rarely be justified, and should normally be ruled out of court in the interests of getting a workable and reasonably simple criterion of selection.

6. THE TREATMENT OF NON-TRADABLE CURRENT INPUTS

We now come to indigenous non-tradable inputs—power, inland transport (including port facilities), construction, and perhaps also one or two semi-nontradables like cement. These have to be treated on a different principle altogether. The current flows cannot be imported, and so their use necessarily starves other production, unless there is surplus capacity, which one must generally assume not to exist (since one must work on the assumption of good planning). It follows that further investment in power, transport, etc., must be undertaken, as a direct consequence of the project. Quite often, in fact, a project could not operate without such investment, as there is no power or transport available in the right place.

So we must consolidate power and transport with the project. This is very easy for power. Instead of subtracting from sales the actual cost of power to the project, we estimate the number of kilowatts required and the marginal c.i.f. cost of a kilowatt in India, and add the product of the two to the capital cost of the project. From current sales we subtract, at c.i.f. cost, only the fuel costs of the power used (assuming labour's shadow price is zero)—using marginal fuel cost to the Indian economy, which is probably imported oil. We do likewise with transport, although the calculation will often be more difficult in this case. We add the capital cost of the extra transport required to the capital costs of the project itself, and subtract as current costs only the non-labour current costs of transport.[15]

It should be noted that an important advantage of this procedure is that we have removed the main source of the kind of external economies and diseconomies which would arise from incorrect pricing by other enterprises. It should also be noted that what we have done, in effect, is to produce a 'consolidated' project whose inputs and outputs other than labour are all tradable, and hence can all be valued at world prices.

Provided this treatment, as 'non-tradables', is limited to only a few industries, the method is not too difficult to apply. Wherever possible, standard costs for different regions of the country, e.g. for power, should be laid down from time to time. Then these costs can be very quickly applied to project evaluation.

[15] In so far as electricity is a current input into transport, in principle this cost must in turn be split into a capital cost and a current non-labour cost of the project. In practice, this second stage of the 'limited input–output' method can probably be safely neglected.

As already noted, this method is identical with that of limited input–output proposed by Professor Tinbergen. There should be sufficient knowledge to use it for the very small number of industries proposed. There is the happy coincidence to note that, not only would there be insufficient knowledge to apply it more widely, but also, wider application would be unjustified since input–output methods are inadequate to deal with optimum project selection when imports are an alternative to production.

7. CAPITAL COSTS

Following common practice, we here deal with capital costs separately, although, in evaluating a project, as we shall see below, there is no basic distinction to be drawn between capital and recurrent expenditures and receipts.

It will be remembered that we have already assumed that foreign exchange is even more scarce than domestic savings. This means that the stream of net benefits, as calculated from the adjusted values of current inputs and outputs, must be related to the foreign exchange components of the stream of capital expenditures.

Apart from site labour, investment consists mainly of expenditures on steel, concrete, plant and machinery, stocks, and payments to operative staff before sales can cover such payments. To estimate the foreign exchange component, one first ignores site labour and other wages. All other expenditures are on tradable goods. (If it were decided to treat, e.g., cement as a non-tradable, then it would disappear as an item in the 'composite project' investment under examination.)

Now the foreign exchange cost of such tradables, even if actually procured in India, will generally be equal to the c.i.f. value. This is obvious if Indian production is not expanded, for then Indian procurement by the project merely means that other importers import more. If Indian production *is* expanded, but some of the good is still imported, then it is still true that extra demand for the capital good results in greater imports of it into India than otherwise. Only if import substitution has been complete, and remains complete, may the foreign exchange cost of a tradable (procured in India) fall below the c.i.f. value. It can, of course, never fall below the f.o.b. marginal revenue.[16]

From the above paragraph, it can be seen that the rules for valuing capital inputs in order to produce a good estimate of the direct and indirect foreign exchange cost of a project are identical with the rules already given for valuing current inputs and outputs so as to produce a good measure of net benefit.

[16] If it lies between these limits, one could in principle make a cost analysis in order to estimate its foreign exchange component. In practice this would be a great complication. In these circumstances (zero imports), one is not likely to go very far wrong by taking c.i.f. or actual price, whichever is the lower—which is what we suggested as the rule for current indigenous tradable inputs.

Indeed, so long as it assumed that labour's shadow price is zero (which implies that foreign exchange is the only bottleneck on growth), the two measures are identical. In evaluating net benefit, we were really estimating the total direct and indirect foreign exchange savings of the project.

If, however, labour's shadow price is not deemed to be zero (on the ground that, if projects were selected on the basis of not reckoning labour as a cost, consumption could not be prevented from growing faster than the government desired), then there are two shortages operating, foreign exchange and domestic savings. In this case, cost and benefit are not reckoned exclusively in terms of foreign exchange. Nevertheless, the rules given for valuing the output, and indigenous inputs, of tradable goods remain valid (as near as makes no matter) (see fn. 12).

There remains one item, consisting mainly of capital costs, which deserves separate mention: that is township costs. It seems best to exclude township costs altogether from project evaluation, on the following grounds. Some projects will be sited where a township is necessary, others not. The inclusion of township costs might badly bias the issue against the project with a township. This is because there will often be no reason why, if A has a township and B not, they should not have been switched in location, and B therefore look worse than A instead of vice versa. To this it may be objected that some projects are necessarily sited, by virtue of sheer size or their raw material supply, away from existing towns. Even then it is not clear that one should reckon the township as a cost, because more industrial housing is essential in India, and the fact that one project necessarily has a township merely contributes to a quantum that must be supplied anyway, and thereby permits some other project to draw on existing housing which otherwise could not have so done.

The running costs of a township are normally subsidized by the project. This 'fringe benefit' should count as an addition to wages; i.e., loss on the township should not be subtracted from sales value in calculating the net benefit. (There is admittedly a danger in thus excluding all township costs from project evaluation, which is that the tendency to excessively high standards is reinforced. But we must assume that this is guarded against by administrative fiat rather than economic constraint.)

8. RECAPITULATION

Thus far we have explored a practical method of valuing the inputs and outputs of a project in order to arrive at a time stream of costs and benefits. The final evaluation of these streams requires a discussion of discounting, which is reserved for the final section.

The optimum values can in purest theory be arrived at only by solving a dynamic planning problem, which would also throw up a shadow value for all scarce factors of production. These shadow values could in turn be used to determine the shadow values of all goods and services, and so be used to evaluate projects. But this would, of course, be redundant—for the problem had to be solved first, i.e. all projects be selected, in order to determine the shadow values!

Our procedure is essentially to guess shadow values, which do not require much computation, and which will be sufficiently close to the optimum values to determine a choice of projects which will approximate the optimum choice. We believe we have given good reasons why the methods of valuation we have suggested will reflect true scarcities (but we left the shadow price of labour open, while suggesting ourselves a zero shadow value if the method is used only to choose between industrial projects).

We have leant heavily on world values. We believe this is correct. It is also practical, for import and export prices are often better known than internal prices. They are certainly better known to foreign consultants, who still must needs be relied on extensively for the estimates on which the project appraisal is based. The estimates required could quite easily have been made in the case of the one major project which the author has himself looked into. It is however important to remember that the physical inputs and outputs are themselves estimates which can go quite seriously wrong. Thus, theoretical and practical zest in estimating exactly what prices to use can be carried too far. What is important is to get agreement on a criterion, which is certainly on the right lines, and to use it. Almost certainly, quite a number of things have been undertaken in India which no sensible criterion that gave due weight to the real scarcities and benefits would have let through. It is also probable that some relatively unfashionable types of production might, by the systematic use of a criterion, be seen to be very advantageous.

Finally, we do not want to leave the reader with any impression that we claim to have exhausted the subject of public sector planning. We have envisaged a choice between projects which have already been designed in broad outline (the feasibility stage) or in detail (the project report stage). But a very important part of planning is that projects in particular sectors should be properly designed to take account of the scarcities and possible benefits. The use of a choice criterion operating between projects has only an indirect influence on this. Also, of course, this article is mainly concerned with tradables; and we have not considered the difficult problems involved in the optimum planning of the non-tradable sectors. Finally, we have not considered the problems of phasing, or of when, even if a project is acceptable, it should be deferred because it becomes even better. Nor, again, have we considered the relation between the rate of growth and the optimum size of project. (This is another aspect of sectoral planning—of the optimum design or projects in a particular industrial sector.)

We turn now to discounting—that is, to the evaluation of costs and benefits accruing at different periods—but, again, we warn the reader that time is considered only in relation to already designed possibilities, with an estimated flow of such costs and benefits.

9. DISCOUNTING

Much highbrow theory has revolved round the problem of optimum rates of discounting the future. This discussion has descended to rather more practical problems in recent articles on cost–benefit analysis.[17] Even so, the economic administrator is likely to be perplexed. Moreover, practical exponents of cost–benefit analysis, such as the World Bank and consultant firms, still tend to use rates of interest which not only vary widely but also seem to have no theoretical derivation from the particular conditions of the country concerned.

Fortunately, we have already made two assumptions which help greatly to simplify the problem, and to rule out the more complicated solutions which would not only be very difficult to apply but also would carry little conviction with practical planners.

First, it was assumed that the politicians and planners themselves decide on a desirable future growth of consumption (bearing in mind, of course, their expectation of the rate of growth of the whole economy). This rate of growth of consumption is here assumed to apply for as long a period as one needs to take into account in cost–benefit analysis, say twenty years. The economic problem is then to maximize the value of productive resources in twenty years' time (in principle, this means that further decisions about the desirable pattern of growth after twenty years should be taken—but such decisions are not too crucial to the problem of what should be done now); that is, to maximize the growth rate of capital in this period, subject to the consumption restraint. In thus deciding the growth of consumption on political and social grounds, the politicians and planners have implicitly decided the value of what is known to economists as the 'marginal social rate of discount' (roughly speaking, the relative value of marginal additions to consumption at different times).

Secondly, it was assumed that the politicians have also decided on the public/private division of investment. This means that there is no problem, when deciding on public investment, as to whether the funds might not have benefited the economy more if invested in the private sector; or, to put it in a possibly less tendentious way, we assume that the politicians have already made the best decision. This means that we can forget what economists call 'the social opportunity cost' of public investment (roughly, what the percentage yield might have been in the private sector).

What then is our problem? We have to decide how a given quantum of public investment in the current period should be distributed between projects with differing time profiles of further (committed) investment and benefits, in such a way that this period's total investment makes the maximum (direct and

[17] A recent contribution which contains many references to the literature is M. S. Feldstein, 'The Social Time Preference Discount Rate in Cost-Benefit Analysis', *Economic Journal* (June 1964).

indirect) contribution to the value of the capital stock in, say, twenty years' time.[18]

In theory, to determine this we need to know the productivity of investment in each year (that is, the maximum contribution which more investment in that particular year can make to the terminal value of capital). This can be seen by taking a very simple case, and comparing, say, two expenditures of Rs 100 now, one of which produces a single return of Rs 200 in ten years and the other of Rs 400 in twenty years. We cannot say whether the first is better or worse than the second without knowing whether Rs 200 accruing after ten years can be reinvested to double itself in the second decade.

However, it is doubtful whether the limitations of our knowledge, together with the need to simplify, makes it sensible to assume anything except that the return on investment is constant for as long as makes no matter. This being the case, we can say that the proper rate of discount to apply is the marginal productivity of investment in the public sector. (We can also say that it is the marginal productivity of foreign exchange used in the public sector in saving or earning foreign exchange—assuming that the shadow wage is zero.) Thus, any switch of investments which produces Rs 100 extra next year at the expense of Rs 110 the year after is a good thing if the marginal productivity of investment exceeds 10 per cent, because (consumption being predetermined) the Rs 100 extra next year can be reinvested. It is thus a complete, but common, mistake to assume that taking the long view is inconsistent with choosing quick returns.

How then does one proceed in practice to try to reach an optimum decision on the allocation of investment? First, one has to guess the correct rate of discount. Then one discounts all receipts and all expenditure back to the present to produce a benefit–cost ratio for each project. One then ranks the projects by this ratio, and works down the list so as to exhaust the present period capital budget. The fact that projects can be started earlier or later in the present period gives some flexibility in achieving this objective. On the other hand, it means that one period's allocation (probably a year) cannot be settled without reference to future periods. For instance, one must not exhaust this period's budget with projects started late in the period, for that may commit so much expenditure in the next period that its budget is over-exhausted. This is the jigsaw-like problem of proper phasing.

Of course, sometimes a project will have been assessed on the basis that another project has already been carried out. One cannot then play around with the starting order, or even the relative starting times, without invalidating the cost–benefit calculation. This somewhat complicates the problem. Another difficulty is that the costs and benefits of a project are often not independent of the calendar time at which they are started (quite apart from inflation). Consideration

[18] So long as foreign exchange is the only bottleneck, this is the same as distributing a given amount of foreign exchange between projects in such a way as to maximize the foreign exchange savings in 20 years' time.

of such complications would take us too far afield, for this article is primarily about how to assess projects, and not about the dynamic problem of making up a programme for successive budget periods.[19]

If, however, the problem is correctly solved, the internal rate of return of the least good projects started in each period will be the same, or anyway very similar. If the correct rate of discount has been guessed in assessing the cost–benefit ratios, the internal rate of return of the least good projects will be equal to this rate of discount. If it is not equal, then in principle one must guess again and recalculate the cost–benefit ratios.

In practice, exactly the right rate will never be established. The sensitivity of the ranking of projects to changes in the rate can be established only by experience. But if the guessed rate is not very wrong, one can be fairly sure that it is right to chuck out, or get redesigned, the projects which come out of the comparison very badly.

10. FINALE

Of course, feasibility studies and project reports often differ very greatly from subsequent performance. With so many risks and unknowns, project selection will remain a hit-and-miss business. Nevertheless, we believe a lot of knowledge would be gained if all past reports were subjected to the analysis suggested, together with the outcomes, and if future reports were put through the same hoop. To do this, one must agree on and adopt a standard method. At present all sorts of criteria, some of them wrong-headed—profitability, import content, apparent direct import saving, employment, etc.—are given an airing. In a properly conceived criterion, all valid considerations are given their due weight, and applied to every project equally. Without such a criterion, bias and prejudice are inevitable.

It should finally be emphasized that nothing which has been said in this article has anything to do with how projects should be run, and how their performance should be evaluated after they are chosen. It is, of course, important that the quantities of the outputs achieved should be at least as high, and the inputs as low, as in the cost–benefit analysis. At the same time, in practice, the management has to work with actual prices, and try to maximize profits on this basis, subject possibly to a few administrative constraints (e.g. buy Indian). To achieve the best results, the tax system (plus any administrative constraints) must be care-

[19] For further discussion of some of these problems, see e.g. M. S. Feldstein and J. S. Flemming, 'The Problem of Time Stream Evaluation: present value versus internal rate of return rules', *Bulletin of the Oxford University Institute of Economics and Statistics* (1964); and S. A. Marglin, *Approaches to Dynamic Investment Planning* (North-Holland, 1963). The author is indebted to Mr Flemming for helpful comments on this section.

fully used to give the management the incentive to achieve or improve on the results planned at the project stage. It is also important to try to see that profits are possible, for the only practicable and economically sound general instruction to management is to maximize profits; and it is demoralizing for a management to be reproached for losses when profits are impossible. The problem is fortunately rendered simpler by the fact that the project design will often greatly reduce the range of choice for the management. For instance, it will not matter much that actual wages are higher than the shadow wage employed in the project design (assuming that the influence of the project selection criterion has filtered down to the project design stage), if the project design fixes the amount of employment within narrow limits. However, this problem of how best to run a project when actual prices do not reflect scarcities is a different problem from that which we have discussed in this essay, and we cannot pursue it further here.

8

Protection and the Industrialization of Developing Countries (1968)

I. INTRODUCTION

I have chosen this subject largely because I organized a research project on industrialization while I was at the OECD Development Centre in Paris. The project concerned seven countries: India, Pakistan, Taiwan, and the Philippines in the East; and Mexico, Brazil, and Argentina in the West. No African countries were included, mainly because, with the exception of Egypt, there is as yet very little experience of industrialization there, and therefore very little to work on.

The objective was to describe those policies which have affected industrialization; to relate policy to the out-turn; to assess the efficiency with which the process has developed; and, finally, to try to draw lessons from it. It was hoped not only that these countries might learn from each other if they knew more about each other, but also that other countries which have progressed less far could learn from the failures and successes of these seven.

A troop of economists has been, and is still, engaged on this work. I shall draw heavily on what they have done, and are doing.[1] Eventually, eight books and monographs should emerge—one on each country, and a final comparative volume.[2] What I shall be doing in this lecture is to give some personal impressions, based partly on my own experience and partly on the work described. But any conclusions are my own—and bind no one, not even myself later!

Let me now give a very brief quantitative description of these seven countries. Together they comprise a little over half of the developing world in terms both of population and GDP. They account for about 60 per cent of manufacturing

This is a slightly expanded and corrected version of the first Osler–Hammond Lecture given at York University, Toronto, on 20 March 1968.

[1] The main country-level consultants were Prof. J. Bhagwati and Mrs P. Desai for India, Prof. S. Lewis for Pakistan, Prof. Mo-huan Hsing for Taiwan, Prof. J. Power for the Philippines, Dr T. King for Mexico, Dr J. Bergsman for Brazil, and Dr J. Villanueva for Argentina. The project is co-ordinated by Prof. T. Scitovsky and M. Scott of the OECD Development Centre. Apart from these, I am indebted to Dr M. Corden for comments.

[2] In the outcome, six volumes appeared: Argentina dropped out, and the Philippines and Taiwan were merged.

in the developing world, but for only about 40 per cent of manufactured exports.[3] (This low percentage is due to the exclusion of Hong Kong!)

Between themselves, they vary greatly, from the giant of India with a population of 498 million to the very large countries, Pakistan (119 million) and Brazil (85 million), through the moderate-sized Mexico (44 million), Philippines (33 million), and Argentina (23 million), to the small but respectable-sized Taiwan (13 million). (I give 1966 population figures as estimated by the OECD Development Centre.)

In terms of income per head (1965), they range from the rich Argentina (about $1,170), fairly rich Mexico ($660), through Brazil ($360), Philippines ($180), and Taiwan ($180) to the exceedingly poor countries, India and Pakistan (less than $100). Of these, Argentina should not really count as a developing country; it has none of the outstanding characteristics, which include (1) low income per head, (2) a high proportion of the population in agriculture, and (3) a very wide divergence between labour productivity in agriculture and in industry.

So far as the absolute size of the manufacturing sector goes, which is what most concerns us here, India is the biggest; Argentina, Brazil, and Mexico are roughly comparable and about five-sevenths as large as India; while Pakistan, Philippines, and Taiwan are all still very small. Only in Pakistan and Taiwan is industrialization extremely recent: twenty years ago, neither had any industry to speak of. With the others, there was significant industrialization before the last war, going well back into the nineteenth century in the case of India.

The growth of industry has varied fairly widely in the post-war period. From the mean of the years 1950–2 to 1964–6, the growth of manufacturing output is shown in columns (1) and (2) of Table 1. (For sources, refer to forthcoming OECD Development Centre studies.) Column (3) gives the absolute size of the manufacturing sector in 1958. With the exception of Argentina, the more industry there was, the more slowly it grew over the whole period. In the last half of the period the same is true, except that the Philippines fell to fourth place. This inverse correlation is not too surprising. Any determination to industrialize will have a certain minimum force, which will be large relative to the amount of industry if the latter is of negligible proportions, as in Pakistan after partition. In the initial stages such an effort, even if very inefficient, is bound to produce a large percentage effect on the output figures, provided that the new industrialization is protected and its output is valued at local prices.

Column (4) gives the percentage weight of manufacturing in gross domestic product in 1958, and column (5), the contribution of manufacturing to the growth of total output from 1951 to 1965 (i.e. the rate at which output would have grown if manufacturing alone had grown at the rate of column (1), with other sectors stationary). Thus, column (5) takes account of the relative amount of industry in the economy and its growth rate. Despite its very small beginnings,

[3] European developing countries excluded.

TABLE 1. Selected statistics on manufacturing in seven countries, 1950–1966

	Manufacturing growth (%) (value added)		Manufacturing production (value added), mid-period 1958 (US$ bn)	% contribution of manufacturing to GDP, 1958	% contribution of manufacturing to growth of GDP, 1950–2 to 1964–6
	1950–2 to 1964–6	1957–9 to 1964–6			
	(1)	(2)	(3)	(4)	(5)
Taiwan[a]	13.7	14.9	0.18	16	2.9
Philippines	9.5	7.8	0.39	15	1.4
Pakistan	8.2	8.5	0.67	9	0.7
Mexico	7.9	8.2	2.26	22	1.9
Brazil	7.8	6.8	2.61	25	2.3
India	5.0	6.7	3.48	14	0.9
Argentina	4.4	4.1	2.51	32	1.4

[a] 1951–3 instead of 1950–2.

Taiwan's industrialization over the period was so fast that it made the largest contribution to growth of any of the countries. Mexico and Brazil come next, with their quite high weights for industry combined with a very good growth rate. The rest fall behind, either because there was relatively little industry (Philippines and Pakistan), or because the growth rate was not very high (Argentina), or both (India).

2. THE POLICY OF HIGH PROTECTION

So much for a brief description. Taking a look at the sort of policies that have been pursued in the post-war period, there is no doubt that the most important common feature is colossal protection of the home market. In many cases this has arisen from import quotas or bans, but tariffs are also of importance. Although in the project we looked at other aspects of policy towards industrialization, protection and export policy are of such dominant importance that I shall largely confine myself to these.

Before giving some idea of the orders of magnitude of protection, I must say something about 'effective', as opposed to 'nominal', protection. Consider first only tariffs. The nominal tariff may be expressed as a percentage of the c.i.f. price. Considered alone, it is, of course, an advantage to the domestic producer of a competing good. But the domestic producer may also have to pay more for materials, and for other inputs from either domestic or foreign producers, because these latter products are themselves protected. This may reduce, or even reverse, the effect on him of the tariff structure considered as a whole. Then, one has to ask, exactly what is one aiming to protect? The usual answer is 'value added', i.e. the factors of production used in the process. If value added is small, effective protection may become very large. But this gives rise to a problem. An industry will have non-traded inputs, like electricity. One *can* assume that their prices will not be significantly raised by the tariff structure, and treat these as zero-tariff inputs. This will not be quite correct, since electricity itself will have traded inputs whose price may be raised by tariffs on them. An alternative is to treat things like electricity as if they were part of what is protected. One then allows for the tariffs on electricity's traded inputs on the one hand, and includes its value added in what is protected on the other hand.[4] The difference between the methods is not too important for my purposes.

I shall rely generally on the second method. But I shall, anyway, be giving you only very broad orders of magnitude—for three reasons: (1) because the figures are, in any case, inevitably unreliable; (2) because 'effective protection' is a good measure of the degree of encouragement given to a particular industry only if fairly restrictive assumptions are made; and (3) because I do not want to quote any precise figures which would anticipate the results of the work of others.

As I have said, in most of our countries industries are protected not only by tariffs but also by quotas, or even by a total prohibition of imports. This, of course, can raise domestic prices well above what they would be if the tariff *only* were operative. If one can compare the c.i.f. prices of products with their internal prices, both for the inputs and the outputs of an industry or process, one can (analogously with effective tariff protection) find out the degree of protection inherent in the actual structure of prices, as they result from both tariffs and also other restrictions of all kinds. This I shall call 'total effective protection'. If it is greater than the tariff protection, that implies that it is the quotas that are really operative. But it does not imply that all the *potential* 'total effective protection' is being used. If, on the other hand, the total effective protection is less than the tariff protection, this implies that, although the effective tariff protection is available, it is *not* being used. Lastly, let me remind you what effective protection is supposed to measure: that is the percentage amount by which value added per unit at domestic prices *can* be raised as a result of the tariff system—and, where other restrictions bite, the percentage by which value added at domestic prices *is* raised by the actual structure of prices compared with what it would be under free trade.

[4] Effective protection was fully understood at least as early as the US tariff of 1867, when manufacturers were 'compensated' for duties on their inputs, and received 'net protection' on top of this. See Joint Report of Wool Manufacturers and Wool Growers, 'Revenue Report for 1866', p. 430, quoted by F. W. Taussig in the *Tariff History of the United States*, 6th edn. (Putnam's, New York, p. 204, fn. 1). Taussig himself uses the term 'net effective protection'.

Now I can turn to a few orders of magnitude. Take India first. Total effective protection is very high indeed. For manufactures it is rare to find cases where it is less than 100 per cent. There is a considerable spread in the range of 100–500 per cent. Figures of over 500 per cent can be found. If you take effective tariffs alone, cases of extremely high protection can also be found, but in many of these cases it is not fully used. The tariff structure seems to differ somewhat from total effective protection in that one can find more cases of relatively low protection, less than 100 per cent. One can even find cases of negative effective protection, i.e. where the producer is hurt more by the tariffs on his inputs than he gains by those on his outputs. But in almost all these cases of low or negative effective tariff protection, the import restrictions take charge. Thus, the variability as between industries and products of total effective protection, though enormous, seems to be rather less than the variability that might arise if protection were afforded only by tariffs, and if all this tariff protection were used (internal competition playing no part). To put it in another way, although the structure of relative internal prices is wildly out of line with relative duty-free c.i.f. prices, it seems to be not quite so wildly out of line as a study of 'effective tariffs' above would suggest.[5]

I shall say rather less about the other countries. In Pakistan effective protection exceeds 200 per cent for quite a number of products. For almost all classes of manufactures, it is import restrictions that bite rather than tariffs. Protection tends to be highest for consumption goods, and rather lower for intermediate and capital goods.[6] This is a common feature for most of the countries, though it is less marked in India than elsewhere. It arises largely because the countries have gone in for fairly complete import substitution of consumption goods, before intermediates and capital goods. Heavy protection of the latter may then be opposed by consumption good producers, for it is against their interests. It does not follow that capital goods and intermediates need less protection; nor does it follow, because consumption goods came first, that these countries may not have a comparative advantage in, at least, some capital and intermediate goods. Consumption goods may have come first because import restrictions, imposed for balance of payments reasons, are most justifiably and heavily imposed on consumption goods.

In the Philippines, effective tariffs seem to be around 200 per cent for any consumption goods, but are considerably lower for other classes of goods.[7] For Taiwan, I can give no figures for effective protection, but nominal tariffs are fairly high. There is, however, an interesting exception to this. Taiwan has established an industrial free trade zone, operating entirely for the export market. It appears that industrial expansion has proceeded very rapidly there, despite there being zero protection.

[5] This paragraph is based on work by W. R. Panchamukhi, J. Bhagwati, and P. Desai.

[6] This is based on work by S. Lewis.

[7] This is based on work by J. Power and G. Sicat.

Turning to Latin America, Brazil still protects very heavily, although tariffs were reduced in 1967. The tariff is now the main weapon, unlike most of our other countries (although there is also a complicated 'law of similars', which has some additional protective effect). For many classes of goods, effective protection averages over 100 per cent, even including cotton textiles. When one comes to individual products or processes, the range extends from negative on some goods to over 500 per cent on others.[8]

I can say very little about Mexico or Argentina. I am told by Professor Balassa that, despite the import restrictions on which Mexico mainly relies, total effective protection may not be very high.[9] The possibility of very heavy smuggling from the USA prevents producers exploiting all the protection that is potentially available. In contrast, in Argentina, which has from time to time used the whole gamut of protective devices, from tariffs to special exchange rates and import restrictions, protection is almost certainly very high.

I have now said enough to support the proposition that protection is extremely high, and that it varies enormously from product to product. It is much higher than in the USA, Europe, or Japan, where it would be rare to find effective protection of over 100 per cent, and where most rates tend to fall in the 20–50 per cent range.

3. WHY SHOULD PROTECTION BE SO HIGH? THE ECONOMIC ARGUMENTS

The first thing that might be argued is that it need be so high only because exchange rates are overvalued. Of course, this is true. Nevertheless, the argument ignores the nature and effects of protection. Protection of the domestic market for manufactures does not merely see to it that domestic producers can compete with imports: it has two other major effects, which a lower exchange rate would not have.

First, it favours manufacturing over agriculture. These two major sectors compete for scarce resources—if not for labour, then for investment as well as for scarce organizing ability and attention on the part of the government. Furthermore, protection of manufacturing changes the internal terms of trade against agriculture. It raises the prices of manufactured inputs into agriculture, thus resulting in negative effective protection for agriculture. It also raises the prices of manufactures which farmers consume. On both counts, it reduces the incentives for investment in agriculture and for increasing agricultural output.

[8] Based on work by J. Bergsman. All the above work will be incorporated in studies for the OECD Development Centre.

[9] Professor Balassa is engaged on work on effective protection for the IBRD, and the work on Brazil and Mexico has been carried out under his project.

Secondly, protection favours production for the home market as against exports. It does not merely *not* encourage industry in its export markets (as compared with *laissez-faire*, and an equilibrium exchange rate), but it actively *discourages* it by raising the domestic export prices of manufactures above the level that they would assume if there were no protection of the home market.

Thus, even though overvaluation of currencies is a reason for protection, whether by quota or tariff, the latter is not a good substitute for a lower value for the currency. It has quite different effects.

Now let us look at the main reasons why economists, and others, have suggested that industry in LDCs should be protected. These can be divided into two categories, the first concerned more with static efficiency, and the second with more dynamic efficiency. Both kinds of argument must be essentially concerned with divergences between decentralized costs and benefits as reflected in the free operation of a price mechanism, and real social costs and benefits.

Arguments of a mainly static kind

(a) The wage in industry does not reflect the social opportunity cost of labour

I am not going to discuss the empirical truth of this argument. I shall merely say that the evidence in all our countries (except possibly Argentina) points to its truth. But, prima facie, it is not an argument for protecting, by tariffs or quotas, the home market against competing imports. In principle, it is an argument for subsidizing labour. Of course, it could also be an argument for actually reducing wages in industry relative to agriculture. This may well be justifiable in some countries.[10] In others, however, the industrial wage level may be justified in terms of promoting labour efficiency through a tolerable standard of living, or for other reasons. The whole of the difference between industrial and rural wages or earnings cannot be taken as a 'distortion'.

(b) General external economies

Labour training is the most common case cited. Industry not only has to train its labour force, but also to pay for it in terms of higher wages. Other more dynamic external economies are also suggested—e.g. that industry breaks down traditional attitudes, makes for inventiveness, promotes punctuality, inculcates economic attitudes to resource allocation, etc. Economies of agglomeration are also cited: it is cheaper to operate some industries in close contiguity with an industrial environment (apart from the labour force argument already mentioned).

[10] E.g. W. A. Lewis, 'Reflections on Nigeria's Economic Growth', OECD Development Centre, 1967, ch. VII.

This is all more debatable. For instance, the Gandhian movement in India considers that modern industry has severe external diseconomies which result from the destruction of traditional patterns of behaviour and modes of thought. It should also be noted that most of our countries already have extensive industrial areas. Nevertheless, let us accept that there is something in these arguments. The existence of such external economies is also, in general, a reason for subsidies, on the basis of either employment or production.

(c) A deficient infrastructure, in the widest sense, i.e. one that has inadequate or very expensive power, transport, telephones; a lack of adequate general educational and training facilities; or a lack of a well-functioning capital market

Certainly, we can accept the fact that infrastructure is deficient in most of our countries, perhaps most clearly in Brazil, but also in India, and probably elsewhere.

But, if there is not enough infrastructure, that is more of an argument for promoting or providing it (but not for subsidizing it) than it is for protecting manufactures. Things like electricity and transport may be inevitably expensive, because of a lack of economies of scale. We also know that the installation of plant is always more expensive in developing countries. But this does not mean that there is a divergence between apparent cost and true social cost. Furthermore, the inadequate infrastructure may handicap agriculture as much as industry. In principle, the exchange rate should take care of such 'absolute' disadvantages from which less developed countries suffer.

(d) A failure to respond to normal economic incentives; overestimation of risks; lack of foresight; inertia; in general, lack of entrepreneurial attitudes and abilities

This is rather a rag-bag: but I am sure you know the sort of thing I mean. In our countries, which have progressed some way along the path of industrialization, this set of arguments seems much less compelling that it may be in, say, parts of Africa.

But these are arguments which suggest not that industry would be unprofitable, but rather that people will not respond to reasonable expectations of profits. Making profits unreasonably high, by very high protection, is not obviously the best method of dealing with pessimism, inertia, and shortsightedness. Furthermore, it should be noticed that most of these arguments apply as strongly, and some even more strongly, to agriculture as to industry.

Are these arguments, then, really arguments for favouring industry against agriculture? It is very questionable. But, even if they are, then they seem to be arguments not so much for protection as for direct efforts to create entrepreneurial attitudes, for starting management schools, providing industrial extension services, and so on. Thus, in many countries an entrepreneurial class seems to have sprung up quite easily, and its development seems to be limited more by lack of resources, knowledge, and training than by any innate inertia, pessimism, or inability. Even so, in the early stages, a lack of private entrepreneurs may sometimes be a good reason to start industries in the public sector (possibly selling them later, as has been done in Japan and Pakistan).

(e) Inelasticity of foreign demand or supply

This is certainly not a good argument for general protection of industry, since the foreign supply of manufactures is generally very elastic. It is primarily an argument for export taxes, especially on a few agricultural products.

Before turning to the more dynamic arguments, it should be noted that we have suggested that the static arguments examined are in each case (except (*e*), which itself is no good argument for industrial protection) not so much arguments for protecting industry as they are arguments either for subsidizing it or for providing services to it, including technical assistance and training.[11] But subsidies, and some kinds of services—notably education, training, and roads—cost the government money. In contrast, tariffs raise money. Thus, the economic argument for protection, as so far developed, seems to stem fundamentally from either an inadequate fiscal system or excessive government expenditure on non-developmental items. This is despite the fact that quotas, which do not raise money, have since 1945 been extensively used as the means of protection.

Arguments of a mainly dynamic kind

(a) 'Infant industry' argument

The first argument comprises what seems to be the essence of the 'infant industry' argument, as discussed, e.g., by List, Mill, and Taussig. A new industry is difficult to establish in the face of competition from an established industry abroad: the managers and workers lack experience, and even if techniques can be acquired the know-how that goes with them always takes time to learn. Thus, costs will inevitably be high for some years. But, in some cases at least, these disadvantages will prove to be temporary. The industry will become competitive. This argument has been applied in highly developed high-wage countries as much as to the LDCs. But the case is stronger for the less developed countries,

[11] Many other authors in the field of international trade have made the same point. For a recent discussion and further references, see e.g. J. Bhagwati, *The Theory and Practice of Commercial Policy: Departures from unified exchange rates*, Special Papers in International Economics no. 8 (Princeton University Press, 1967). Static arguments, which are 'first-best' arguments for tariffs, can be found, but they do not seem to be arguments that are very relevant to development policy.

because it is surely harder to acquire industrial know-how and suitably trained labour in a non-industrial environment.[12]

But the fact—if it is a fact—that the industry in question will eventually become a good industry for the country in question is not necessarily a good reason for starting it. No doubt many industries which are relatively footloose as far as resources are concerned could eventually have a comparative advantage in almost any country. (It may be chance—e.g. a fortuitous invention—which determines where they first become established.) But, given that others have got a start, the cost of catching up may be too high, from the point of view of dynamic advantage.

If the 'infant industry' argument is really to be an argument for giving some special encouragement, whether by protection or by any other method, then a divergence of social and private advantage must be shown. (If proper methods of project evaluation are used, such industries would always be approved for the public sector.) This divergence must stem from one of three reasons: (1) the private entrepreneur fails to anticipate increasing profits through lower costs; (2) he overdiscounts the future (or the risk) from the social point of view; or (3) he fails to gain enough from lower future costs because the process of learning cannot be kept to himself, i.e. 'internalized', so that domestic competition will spring up.

It appears from the above that the best way for a country to deal with the 'infant industry' argument may be to start the industry in the public sector, since all the above inhibitions can easily be allowed for in choosing industries for the public sector. But if public industry has, or is thought to have, disadvantages of its own, then other means may be necessary. The causes of the initial period of high costs can be directly attacked by providing technical assistance, and by subsidizing training. If this is not enough, some period of subsidization may be theoretically appropriate. Many developing countries go some way towards this by extending tax holidays to new industries and ventures (usually on top of heavy protection). This can help provided that losses can be carried forward, but it may not be enough.

Finally, it is worth emphasizing that the 'infant industry' argument is really very general. It can apply to the adoption of any new technique, even in a closed economy. It can apply to agriculture also. A farmer may anticipate high costs, and early losses, with a new technique which he and his men or relatives have not mastered. He may realize that it will be better in the end, but he has a high rate of discount, and an understandable aversion to risk.

(b) Industry as a source of savings, and taxation

It is often argued that industry saves a lot, and also provides a source of taxation, and so should be specially encouraged on these grounds. This implies not only

[12] It should be noted that it is hard to keep the 'infant industry' argument distinct from that of external economies arising from labour and management training—but we treat it as distinct.

that industry should be encouraged to expand at normal profitability, but even that high profitability should be encouraged.

Who really pays for these taxes, and makes these savings? Obviously—the other sectors, i.e. agriculture and services. So heavy protection of industry, leading to high prices and profits, can be seen as a way of squeezing, or taxing, the rest of the economy.

Thus, once again, we see how closely protection is bound up with public finance. It would surely be better in principle to tax these other sectors in a more direct manner, and to channel the public savings towards industry via development banks, which would also assist in the creation of a capital market. I say this for two main reasons. First, while high gross profits admittedly increase savings and the government's tax receipts, they also raise the consumption of the rich, as well as adding to their wealth. Secondly, and I think this is very important, the protection, when it is unnecessarily high, may well lead as much to inefficiency as to high profits. The Brazilian textile industry appears to be a particularly good example of this.

Summing up on the justifiability of the level of protection

First, if there were no fiscal problems, and if equilibrium exchange rates could be maintained, there would seem to be little reason for protection at all! Everything it is supposed to do, which we have examined above, can be done better in other ways. Protection would then be more clearly seen to be what it often is, merely the protection of inefficient vested interests, of industries that have lost or never had a comparative advantage.

But, secondly, let us admit a fiscal problem, and suppose at least that subsidies cannot be given to industrial employment; or, to take account of external economies, suppose in fact that the government feels it necessary to use protection as a (poor) substitute for bounties.[13]

Now, in the kind of relatively capital-intensive industries that we have looked at in the course of the OECD project (and we have done quite a number of detailed plant and project studies), direct manual labour cost is a small proportion of value added at domestic prices, usually less than 10 per cent. Figures given in *The Growth of World Industry 1938–61*,[14] suggest that wages *plus salaries* are fairly typically around 30 per cent of value added in the average of manufacturing industry in developing countries. Unskilled wages alone would be considerably less than this. W. A. Lewis also gives a figure of 30 per cent for Nigeria for salaries and wages,[15] but Nigerian wages and salaries constituted only 21½

[13] There has has as yet been little formal analysis of optimum trade policy in the face of a fiscal constraint; but see V. K. Ramaswami and T. N Srinivasan, 'Optimal Subsidies and Taxes when some Factors are Traded' (mimeographed).

[14] United Nations (1955).

[15] W. A. Lewis, *Reflections on Nigeria's Economic Growth*, OECD Development Centre, Paris, 1970.

per cent, so that unskilled wages would be well under 20 per cent of value added. These figures are far lower than in the highly industrialized countries, where wages and salaries are typically in the range of 50–60 per cent of value added. The reason is that profits and capital charges are very high relative to wages in most developing countries.

Now suppose that, on grounds of the efficient allocation of resources, a subsidy of 50 per cent should be given to industrial labour—quite a high figure—and that we want to protect industries where the wage bill accounts for 20 per cent of value added. This would need an effective tariff of only 10 per cent to have the same effect. If one tried to quantify the value of labour and management training, as the chief external economy of manufacturing in general, this could, I think, add only another few per cent at most; of course, if profits were lower, and in the case of more labour-intensive industries, the figure could go higher. Guessing wildly, I would say that one cannot really imagine that these more or less rational economic arguments could justify protection of more than, say, 30 per cent even for the most deserving, i.e. labour-intensive, industries. Incidentally, it is interesting that it is the labour-intensive industries that probably most deserve protection according to these *a priori* economic arguments; but it is often the capital-intensive industries that, for devious reasons, actually get the most protection.

But what about the dynamic arguments? Take the 'infant industry' argument. First, except in the least developed countries, where all industries are new, it cannot be an argument for generalized protection. Secondly, its validity can be and is being reduced by technical assistance, and should be further reduced by governmental provision of training and opportunities to acquire technical knowledge. Thirdly, it is much less true than in the days of List that inexperience of new methods applies only in the industrial sector. If—and it is a big if—governments can spot industries to which the argument really applies, then there is a case for special measures, which must be temporary. As an argument for general protection of industry, it can make sense only for a decade or two at the very beginning of a country's industrialization process—and even this is questionable.

Turn now to the argument that manufactured goods should be made expensive in order to 'tax' the service and agricultural sectors. Surely, the answer here is that excise taxes, falling equally on domestic production and imports, are what is required. If one has designed the proper degree of protection for manufactures, there should be no need to raise it further for fiscal reasons. The only counter-argument is that it is easier to tax imports than domestic production, because the former flow through a few ports and the latter may come from many factories. For many industries there is no weight to this argument, because domestic sources of production are in fact few. Indeed, sometimes the argument can go the other way: in some countries, smuggling can make it easier to tax domestic production than to tax imports; and under-invoicing can permit customs duties as well as excise duties to be evaded. In fact, the argument is valid only for small-scale industry.

Admittedly, it is politically easier to tax imports than domestic production. Although the consumer suffers either way, foreign producers cannot lobby against tariffs in the way that domestic producers may do against excise taxes. On the other hand, it is encouraging that internal indirect taxes have been greatly raised in some developing countries; indeed, as import substitution has cut down imports of manufactures for consumption, this change has been almost forced on some governments. There is nothing illogical about having an indirect tax on a good, whether imported or domestically produced, while at the same time spending money to encourage the domestic producer, whether by subsidies or in some other way. Only if the appropriate encouragement were a subsidy to production (for the rather unlikely static reason that some external economy flows from the actual production of that good, rather than the employment of some factor) is there an apparent conflict. There is then a dynamic reason to tax the good (it must play its part as a revenue source, since revenue is needed for dynamic reasons—to raise savings), and a static reason to subsidize it. Both arguments can be valid, and the upshot is merely that the good should be taxed less than a good whose production yielded no external economies.

In suggesting that not much protection is required in order to promote the right amount of industrialization, I am aware that all the highly industrialized countries except the UK have industrialized behind protection. But my impression is that such protection has not always been very heavy, certainly not as heavy as now is the case in the less developed countries. In the USA, for instance, protection was quite moderate in the early stages of industrialization; it became very heavy only after the Civil War. Even before then, the argument that it was necessary to protect against efficient established industry in the UK had largely given way to the argument that it was necessary to protect against the low wages in Europe.

There are also some examples in developing countries of industrialization without any protection. For instance, Indian industry grew before 1921, when there was no protection, though admittedly not so fast as in the LDCs now—maybe at a rate of 4 per cent per annum. But how much faster might it have gone with a government that was favourable to industrialization, and was prepared to start industries itself, prepared to foster management and industrial training, prepared to provide government finance through development banks, etc.? The British government may not have actively discouraged industry in India: that is debatable. But it certainly did not actively encourage it. Another example is the growth of industry in free trade zones. Again, it is possible to find some industries in our countries which exist both without protection and also with heavy overvaluation of the currency.

3. WHY AND HOW HAS THE PRESENT SYSTEM GROWN UP?

There seem to be four answers to this question, all of some relevance in most of our countries.

Wars

Wars cut off imports. There is then a natural protection, behind which industries emerge. The least essential and most bulky imports are often most heavily cut, so that there is some tendency for luxury and semi-luxury consumer goods to be most protected by war—though this is probably not so true of wars as it is of quotas imposed for balance of payments reasons. After the war, protection follows to defend the industries which have grown up. These will have been established for short-run reasons, which may have little relation to the country's long-run comparative advantage.

The Great Depression

There was a 'natural', but short-lived, change in the terms of trade in favour of industry during the 1930s. In addition, increased unemployment made many governments protect in order to try to create employment in industry. As with wars, it seemed necessary later to protect these industries when the terms of trade for primary products improved.

Inflation and balance of payments problems

These have, since 1945, played a major role. Since balance of payments trouble arises very largely when a government tries to do too much, including too much investment in industry relative to available savings, industrialization has certainly been one of the causes of increased protection. The pattern is familiar, and applies to most of our countries, though to some more than others. For one reason or another, a balance of payments crisis has arisen, and import controls have been imposed. Such reasons include excessive government investment, partly in industry—or excessive encouragement of private industry by deliberate policy, including fiscal reliefs and tariff protection—but also a deterioration in the terms of trade and crop failures. The result is very like a war, but more so. All kinds of production suddenly become very profitable, especially that of luxuries, because a scarcity price emerges which may make even extremely inefficient small-scale production profitable.

Similarly, inflation itself, together with a reluctance to devalue enough or often enough, has made it increasingly necessary to offset an overvalued currency by import controls—thus magnifying the degree of protection of the home market for manufactures, and magnifying the 'anti-protection' accorded to exports and agriculture. This applies most to India and Pakistan in recent years.

Deliberate policy

More research is certainly needed as to the effective influence of deliberate policy. Import controls and tariffs have been deliberately used to foster selective industrialization in Mexico, Taiwan, and Argentina—and perhaps to some extent elsewhere. Tariffs have also been used—for instance in India between 1921 and 1956, when quotas began to predominate.

What I can say confidently is that nowhere has a protective tariff been designed such that the government could then sit back and let industry develop behind it. Industries have been selected or encouraged on other grounds, and tariff or quota protection has followed—almost automatically. Until at least very recently, very little attention appears to have been paid to costs. Alternatively, very general import restrictions have produced a flood of applications to industrialize, some of which a harassed bureaucracy would have had to turn down without usually having the time, expertise, or information to apply any economic criteria.

Perhaps the main deliberate influence of governments has been to give preference to heavy industry. On the other hand, their unintentional influence has often favoured consumer goods. Perhaps Brazil has gone furthest in successfully seeing that import substitution has been deep, i.e. covering intermediates and capital goods. But she has been assisted in this by having the largest domestic market and the best material advantages, except perhaps for India. She has also had more time than India.

4. WHAT HARM DOES EXCESSIVE PROTECTION DO?

There are several kinds of harm: (1) inhibition of exports, and consequent lack of scale economies; (2) choice of wrong industries even for the domestic market; (3) promotion of inefficiency through excessive coddling; and (4) promotion of delays, waste of time in getting round the bureaucracy, corruption, etc. This last sort of harm applies mostly where quotas, imposed for balance of payments reasons, are the mode of protection, as in India, Pakistan, and Ceylon. Only in these cases does one get the phenomenon of not enough imports of materials and components to keep existing capacity operative. Lastly, (5) agriculture may be over-discouraged—there is clear evidence of this in India.

I shall enlarge only upon (1) and (2), which anyway hang together. It is obvious that protection inhibits exports—I have already spoken of that. The average bias in favour of production for the domestic market[16] has sometimes been enormous—it reached almost 400 per cent in Brazil in 1958, though it has been greatly and progressively reduced since then.[17] It must have been very high also in India and Pakistan before the recent schemes to subsidize exports. The bias shows up all right. Mexico, Argentina, and the Philippines export only 2 per cent, 0.7 per cent, and 1 per cent of their manufacturing production measured in terms of value added.

Without the heavy bias in favour of the home market, one would have expected a greater growth in industries in which the economy had some natural advantage, together with a greater realization of economies of scale, and economies of specialization. There would have been less variation in the degrees of protection afforded to different industries, which at present range from zero to several hundred per cent.

The Latin American countries are increasingly realizing the disadvantages and losses involved in heavy protection. Industry in these countries (indeed, in all our countries) has grown, of course, much faster than the domestic demand for industrial products. This can happen only by reducing the proportion of imports, or increasing that of exports. Except for Taiwan, our countries have overwhelmingly chosen the former path. They are now worrying because they are 'running out of import substitution'. There is rather little room left. Mexico and Argentina now probably import less than 10 per cent of their total consumption of manufactures. In pushing 'import substitution' to such lengths, it is inevitable that these countries have gone in for less and less suitable industries. Now, rather late, the Latin American countries are seeing the light, and realizing that they have saddled themselves with some very high-cost industries and production units, which is a poor basis from which to keep up the momentum of industrial advance by entering export markets. Surely, industrialization would have been more efficient with less concentration on the home market—and the transition would have been eased.

5. TWO OBJECTIONS TO MY THEME

Could much more have been exported?

I must now answer two arguments. The first is that they could never have exported much anyway: the industrialized countries would not have let them. I

[16] The percentage by which the average effective import rate of exchange (e.g. cruzeiros per dollar, including the tariff) exceeds the average export rate.

[17] See Joel Bergsman, *Brazil, Industrialization and Trade Policies*, OUP (forthcoming).

think this is too pessimistic. Admittedly, there is the notorious textile agreement, which has done much psychological as well as actual harm. There are other quantitative restrictions, especially by France. Also, quite a number of countries apparently discriminate against Hong Kong. More work is being done on this, but my impression is that the position is not too serious apart from textiles. Nevertheless, the LDCs certainly think that there are, or would be, extensive restrictions.

One could add that those few late industrializing countries or territories that have trusted to manufactured exports—principally Japan and Hong Kong, but most recently Taiwan—have succeeded. A further 'straw in the wind' is the finding of Professor Hal Lary to the effect that exports of less developed countries of 'labour-intensive' manufactures to developed countries have grown by 13 per cent per annum from 1953 to 1965.[18] Furthermore, those of our countries which have introduced special incentives for export—India, Pakistan, and Taiwan—have as a result increased their manufactured exports quite rapidly, and Taiwan spectacularly so: her exports of industrial products quadrupled between 1958 and 1961, and then doubled again between 1961 and 1964; they now account for about half her total exports.

Of course, it has to be admitted that, the more LDCs that try and succeed, the stronger and more foolish may be the 'defences' of the rich countries. But, as against this, there is the fact that many of the less traditional manufactures—less traditional than textiles—are not generally so regionally concentrated, and have a more expanding market than textiles, and therefore are not so politically sensitive as textiles (or as food products). Other non-food non-textile manufactured exports are now rising much faster than textiles. But the position is still rather dominated by Hong Kong, which in 1965 accounted for over a quarter of all the manufactured exports of the LDCs, while the whole of the Western Hemisphere LDCs accounted for less than 20 per cent, about the same as India.

The second point to be made is that developing countries might export much more to each other. The increasing interest in free trade areas and common markets is a natural reflection of the tremendous protection which the LDCs have erected against each other. Reduced protection could go a long way towards reducing the need for such schemes which, apart from LAFTA, still embrace only very small markets. Thus, the Central American Common Market—the most successful so far—consists of only about 11 million people. If protection must remain rather high, the LDCs could nevertheless remove the barriers to their mutual trade by subsidizing exports, or by some form of dual exchange rate. If it is worth giving special encouragement to industry, then it is worth giving it for export markets equally with the home market. In this way, the LDCs would protect against developed countries, but not effectively against each other—because the tariff of one would be offset by the export subsidy of the other. If a

[18] Hal B. Lary, *Imports of Manufactures from Less Developed Countries* (National Bureau of Economic Research, 1968).

specially favourable exchange rate for manufactures were adopted by all LDCs, it becomes even more obvious that their home markets would be protected *vis à vis* developed countries, but not *vis à vis* each other.

In this connection, one must remark that the world trade rules laid down by the IMF and the GATT are inappropriate so far as LDCs are concerned—given that a case for *some* protection is admitted. They fail to recognize openly that special exchange rates, tariffs, quotas, and export subsidies all fulfil the same function of creating a divergence between relative import and export prices, and relative home market prices. Yet tariffs and quotas are permitted, and also export taxes, but multiple exchange rates and export subsidies are frowned on. Through the medium of tariffs or quotas, a LDC can have as many effective exchange rates for imports as it likes. It can also have multiple exchange rates for primary exports, and many of them do. But the rules insist that it *cannot* have the same effective exchange rate for manufactured exports as for manufactured imports (unless it adopts free trade). The rules are thus shaped to lock these countries into their own small markets. The best that one can say for them is that they do not seem to be applied, at least in the case of export subsidies (although the economic inefficiency of the Indian Export Subsidy Scheme was apparently increased by the need to pretend that it was not really a subsidy scheme).

Does not the rapid industrialization achieved prove that international trade does not matter much?

The second objection to my theme—that excessive protection is very harmful—is that the rates of industrial growth in our countries have been very fast. So what am I fussing about?

I have already remarked that it is not too difficult to grow fast when one grows from nothing. This applies to Taiwan and Pakistan and, to a slightly lesser extent, to the Philippines.

The second point is that performance must be related to the resources invested in industry. Unfortunately we have no reliable measures of investment in industry for our countries; but, relative to the pre-existing size of industry, it has clearly been large in Taiwan and Pakistan, which have received large amounts of aid (for 1960–5, 6.4 per cent and 5.9 per cent of GNP respectively—but aid to Taiwan was much higher in the 1950s). Aid plus foreign private investment for the other countries has been low relative to GNP (ranging from about 1 per cent in the case of Argentina to about 3 per cent for India). Admittedly, Taiwan has continued to grow extremely fast in the 1960s, when American aid has tapered off. But then, since 1959 Taiwan, alone of our countries, has adopted a strongly export-oriented policy.

Of our remaining countries, Argentina's performance is clearly rather poor. But in the most recent period for which I have given figures (1958–65) Mexico,

Brazil, and India had apparently good rates of industrial growth (8.2, 6.8, and 6.7 per cent). Of these, Mexico and Brazil have both certainly had an impressive sustained growth since 1945, although Brazil has fallen off since 1963. India's rapid industrial growth began only in 1958, and has fallen off again since 1965. Over the entire period, Mexico's performance is the most impressive, and Mexico seems to be considerably less protected than the others, and has used quotas as a mode of protection only selectively. Admittedly, there are also many other differences. For instance, Mexico has a fully convertible currency, with no restriction on capital movements. It has also had less inflation than the other countries.

Finally, it is reasonable to look at the figures with a certain suspicion. It is sometimes argued that the growth is underestimated, because out-of-date and therefore low weights (in terms of value added) are given to the rapidly growing industries. This could be the case in some countries, although theoretically it need not be true if prices in expanding industries fall rapidly enough. Nevertheless, it seems much more probable that the figures overstate the real rise for the following reason. The weights used are, of course, value added at domestic prices, and we have also seen that a large part of manufacturing growth has come from import substitution. Now it is an oft-heard traveller's tale that value added at world prices has been negative in some import substitution industries (and even for some exports, when a badly designed export subsidy scheme is in operation). Our research has substantiated these tales. We found quite a number of examples where the local activity subtracts value at import prices. What does 'value subtracted' mean? It means that the foreign exchange saved by the production of the good is less than the foreign exchange cost of the inputs. Since the foreign exchange costs are opportunity costs, so far as the country is concerned, this means that the diversion of domestic resources to such activities actually reduces the real income of the country. In Pakistan, for instance, motor car assembly appears to subtract value; in other words, the country could import the assembled car for less than it imports the components which it then assembles. This gives no addition to the national income. Yet it shows up as an increase in industrial production. In India, in particular, we found quite a number of examples of value subtracted.

Value subtracted is an extreme case of overweighting of protected products. In general, if new products which are heavily protected are inserted into the manufacturing production index at domestic value added weights, and if their output then grows fast, the index will exaggerate the effect of manufacturing on the national income.

Apart from suspect index numbers, another indication of the success of industrialization might be the contribution it has made to employment. Of course, we all suspect, for several *a priori* reasons, that industry has been too capital-intensive in these countries. In Argentina, always the exception, industrial employment actually fell between 1953 and 1963. In the other countries the annual rate of growth of industrial employment between the early 1950s and early 1960s has ranged from 1.8 per cent in the case of Brazil to 6.1 per cent in the case of Mexico. Only in Mexico, India, and Pakistan has industrial employment grown faster than the population as a whole—thus making some contribution to an absolute reduction in underemployment in other sectors. But in view of the low weight of manufacturing employment in total employment, the contribution has been small—about 0.5 per cent per year to total employment in India and Pakistan, and about 0.8 per cent in Mexico.

6. CONCLUSION

I do not think that the actual industrialization performance of these countries makes worry about the efficiency of their industrialization at all redundant. I think that, if they could have devised a system of incentives, and influences or controls, which paid more attention to costs and efficiency, industry could have grown significantly faster. Alternatively, industry could have grown as fast with less discouragement of agriculture—for we should remember that a failure of agriculture to grow faster has certainly inhibited overall growth in India and Argentina, as well as in Pakistan in the 1950s. The same probably applies, though to a much lesser degree, in the other countries. Finally, the problem of 'import substitution running out' would not now be threatening growth, as it is in our Latin American countries.

Of course, divergences between prices and social costs and benefits exist everywhere. But it is very difficult not to believe that they are far and away more serious in the countries we have been looking at than in the more fully industrialized countries. Much of this distortion comes from excessive protection. Yet protection is intended to reduce distortion, by removing obstacles in the way of industrialization, and not to exacerbate it. I have argued in effect that more than moderate levels of protection—a maximum rate of say 30 per cent—are extremely hard to justify on any rational grounds; and that, even then, steps should be taken to see that such protection does not inhibit exports. (At least, drawbacks on exports should be given, even if subsidies or dual exchange rates are not used.) The exchange rate should do the rest. Probably many would agree with this for the seven countries discussed, but might argue that almost prohibitive protection is needed to get industry started in the least industrialized countries. The proof of the pudding is in the eating. It makes sense to see whether sufficient demand for industrial investment, having regard to the resources available and the needs of other sectors, cannot be created with rather less protection. Certainly, many developing countries have created conditions in which the demand for industrial investment is excessive, so that steps then had to be taken to restrain it.

One final word, however. Nothing that I have said is incompatible with the belief that some of these countries have done better by promoting industry, even by the extraordinarily inefficient methods adopted, than they would have done under *laissez-faire*. I myself have little doubt that industry should be given some special encouragement in LDCs. But I think that colossal protection falls far short of being the best way to encourage it—even in the case of the least developed countries.

9

The Transnational Corporations: The Economics of International Direct Investment (1982)

If written a dozen years ago, this section would, without change of subject, have been entitled 'Private Foreign Investment' (PFI) or 'Private Overseas Investment' (POI). Terms were changed in the late 1960s, as authors wanted to emphasize the size and widespread activities of the some 2,000 large corporations that accounted for the bulk of overseas investment, as well as the fact that they might in some measure escape the surveillance of any one nation, and especially the host country. Since, for various reasons, including low real interest rates and risk reduction, foreign corporations often borrowed locally as much as possible and therefore brought in little capital, the change of title was also associated with increased emphasis on the part they played in the transfer of technology and managerial expertise, and in marketing.

Soon afterward, the United Nations adopted the term 'transnational' in order apparently to emphasize further the presumed threat to national sovereignty. Although the basis of the powerful emotional reaction against the transnationals stems largely from their size (as well as the nationality of the parent company), it should be noted that any company with any overseas subsidiary or affiliated company over which it has some control, however small, is included in the definition. There are about 10,000 transnational corporations.[1] It is also worth noting at the outset that the dropping of the word 'private' is appropriate. There is a significant number of very large *public* companies with overseas investments.

We are concerned only with LDCs, which account for barely one-quarter of the stock of overseas assets.[2] For about the first fifteen years after World War II, governments and economists in MDCs, with a few exceptions, assumed that PFI was beneficial to 'host' countries, and LDC well-wishers welcomed any moves by more developed Countries (MDCs) to encourage the outflow to LDCs. PFI was seen as a complement to aid. The LDCs were capital-hungry. Aid could

This is taken from *Economic Development: Theory, policy and international relations* (Basic Books, New York, 1982). Permission to reproduce is gratefully acknowledged.

[1] UN Commission on Transnational Corporations, *Transnational Corporations in World Development* (New York: United Nations, 1978), p. 35.

[2] Ibid., p. 8.

do more to help as far as social and economic overheads were concerned, but private investment was more appropriate in mining and manufacturing, areas in which governments had little or no expertise. LDC attitudes were more ambivalent. India, for instance, adopted quite restrictive policies—and, partly as a result, has received very little foreign investment. Latin America vacillated between a perceived need, both for the finance and the technology, and political suspicion, which, however exaggerated, was deeply rooted in the past.[3]

Research on multinationality exploded in the 1960s beginning with S. Hymer's 1960 study, published in 1976,[4] and was followed by notable contributions from R. Caves, C. Kindleberger, and R. Vernon.[5] This work was in the industrial organization tradition. Its chief aim and result were to show that foreign corporate investment could be understood only in the framework of monopolistic and oligopolistic theory. The essential idea was that some special advantage, of the kind familiar in the barriers-to-entry literature, was required to offset the disadvantages inherent in operating in a strange country, disadvantages that might be expected to give local firms a competitive edge. The special advantage of the foreign firm usually lay with its technological lead. This literature concentrated on the reasons for American investment in Canada and Europe. Much of it is rather irrelevant to LDCs.[6] The chief reasons for foreign investment in the latter have been different, and there is much less need to explain why the foreign firm could do well in the face of local competition. In the natural resources field, the objective has been to reduce risks in material supply and to capture part of the rents inherent in a good find. In manufacturing, the main reason has been to preserve sales in markets that were cut off, or threatened to be cut off, by the import-substituting policies of the host country, or sometimes to invade such a protected market, taking the place of previous foreign suppliers. More recently, in some countries, the reason has been to take advantage of cheap labour in making goods designed largely or wholly for export to MDCs. The 'host' country very often prohibited foreign investment where there was any established local industry, and encouraged it when there was little or no comparable local production and none in sight.

There was a remarkable absence of any hard analysis of the costs and benefits that might accrue to a LDC host. G. D. A. MacDougall made a careful neoclas-

[3] For a good balanced account of Latin American attitudes, see V. L. Urquidi in *Obstacles to Change in Latin America*, ed. C. Veliz (London: Oxford University Press, 1965). For a later account, see C. Diaz Alejandro in *The International Corporation*, ed. C. P. Kindelberger (Cambridge, Mass.: MIT Press, 1979).

[4] S. Hymer, *International Operations of National Firms: A Study of Direct Foreign Investments* (Cambridge, Mass.: MIT Press, 1976).

[5] This work is reviewed by C. F. Bergsten, T. Horst, and T. H. Moran, *American Multinationals and American Interests* (Washington, DC: Brookings Institution, 1978), ch. 7.

[6] This is also pointed out by D. Lal, *Appraising Foreign Investment in Developing Countries* (London: Heinemann, 1975), chs. 1 and 2. He argues that the industrial organization literature, especially the 'product cycle' model, was mainly concerned with sophisticated products or techniques; whereas a substantial part of private foreign investment in the least industrialized LDCs was in simple technology products.

sical analysis for Australia in 1960.[7] It was a macroeconomic analysis in the sense that it estimated the effects of an increment to the foreign capital flow, without specifying into what it flowed. For this reason, it could not easily be applied to LDCs, where, in view of the distorted prices, net benefits must depend greatly on the particular projects associated with the increase in the foreign capital inflow.[8] MacDougall concluded that the main benefit was likely to be the direct tax the foreign company paid. We shall see below how far this needs to be modified in the case of cost–benefit studies of particular investments in LDCs. But in any case, this article was not followed up in a LDC context.

The development establishment was more concerned with the 'external' economic and political effects of foreign investment than with the visible measurable effects of the net value of the labour and other inputs, and the outputs—the sort of quantities that appear in company accounts. Externalities centred on two questions: whether the entry of foreign enterprise stimulated or discouraged actual or potential local entrepreneurs, and the extent and depth of the technical knowledge that was transmitted to nationals. The second can only be a benefit, though it may be negligible. The first could go either way. In a famous article, A. O. Hirschman put forward the hypothesis that private direct investment helps to create local initiatives in early stages of development but later discourages them. On the basis of this hypothesis, he proposed 'an Inter-American Divestment Corporation', a sort of giant Crazy Horse Saloon.[9] Latin American countries have in fact done a lot of divestment in the post-war period, often accompanied by an exacerbation of US–Latin American relations. The political attraction of an orderly, friendly, and fair process of nationalization is clear, clearest perhaps for the United States. But that Latin America would have gained economically is highly questionable.

By the late 1960s, hostility to private foreign investment had been built up by a mass of scarifying literature that claimed that national sovereignty was threatened. But the more narrowly economic literature began to concentrate on unearthing and emphasizing possible deleterious effects. Much attention was concentrated on the fear that transnational corporations might worsen countries' balances of payments, and it was pointed out that transnational corporations often raised loans in the local market and transferred relatively little from abroad while repatriating profits. LDC fears in this regard resulted in UNCTAD commissioning a study of the balance-of-payments effects of foreign investment. There

[7] G. D. A. MacDougall, 'The Benefits and Costs of Private Investment from Abroad: A theoretical approach', *Economic Record* (March 1960); reprinted in *Bulletin of the Oxford Institute of Economics and Statistics*, 22/3 (1960), and in American Economic Association, *Readings in International Economics* (London: Allen & Unwin, 1968).

[8] MacDougall was writing before the effective protection literature had begun to demonstrate that the benefit to the host country of producing a particular commodity might vary greatly—in other words, that the domestic price could not be taken as a measure of benefit.

[9] A. O. Hirschman, 'How to Divest in Latin America, and Why', *Essays in International Finance*, no. 76 (Princeton University Press, 1969).

are some serious errors involved in this fearful approach. First, it is absurd to try to measure balance-of-payments effects by looking at the associated financial flows, since imports and exports are also affected. Second, there can be no objective balance-of-payments effect attributable to the investment alone, since what happens depends on how much real expenditure changes, in response to the real income changes induced by the investment, and this is a matter of fiscal and other policies. Last, a government should be designing its policies to accommodate beneficial foreign investments, whatever their inestimable balance-of-payments effects. In other words, what matters are costs and benefits.

That the only valid way of dealing with the economics of foreign investments was by cost–benefit analysis of individual investments seems, surprisingly enough, to have been first suggested by the present author,[10] who had already been responsible for the first published *ex post* cost–benefit analysis of any investment in an LDC, an investment that also happened to be a foreign investment.[11] Since then, there has been a small spate of such studies, using the so-called Little/Mirrlees methodology.[12] Even the UNCTAD study referred to above ended up, after some considerable methodological strife, using this methodology in a very rough form, although the authors were strong believers in the importance of immeasurable factors.[13]

It is easy to state the net benefit (or cost) of a wholly foreign investment. It consists of:

1. the taxes (less subsidies) the host country receives, *plus*
2. any excess of the amount the foreigner pays for indigenous inputs over their social cost (or shadow price), *less*
3. any excess of the price the local user pays for the output over its social cost (or shadow price).

Ex hypothesi, these shadow prices take full account of any excess demand for foreign exchange. They can also include all *measurable* externalities. Of the above, (1) needs no comment; (2) is normally positive, since wages paid usually exceed the real social cost of employment, but a negative item arises if the enterprise raises local finance at any interest rate less than the 'accounting' or socially optimum rate;[14] (3) is usually positive in a protected market (the consumer is subsi-

[10] I. M. D. Little in *The Gap between Rich and Poor Nations*, ed. G. Ranis (London: Macmillan, 1972).

[11] I. M. D. Little and D. G. Tipping, *A Social Cost Benefit Analysis of the Kulai Oil Palm Estate* (Paris: OECD Development Centre, 1972).

[12] The methodology is well explained, and justified, by Lal, *Appraising Foreign Investment in Developing Countries*, Part 2.

[13] S. Lall and P. Streeten, *Foreign Investment, Transnationals and Developing Countries* (London: Macmillan, 1977). See also a review of this book by D. Lal in *Overseas Development Institute Review*, no. 2 (1978).

[14] In the case of mining ventures, a scarcity rent may be included in the shadow prices in the case of an exhaustible resource. The lack of such a rent is the basis of most of the complaints of historical exploitation, or 'theft', of the raw materials of LDCs in the past.

dizing the enterprise). It is thus not surprising that empirical studies almost invariably show that export investments are socially beneficial. (This could be reversed only if exports were heavily subsidized.) Import substitution ventures, however, quite often show negative social returns—in a highly protected market, the consumer is subsidizing the foreigner.

No mention has been made above of the foreign financing, that is, the capital inflow from and the profits accruing to the foreigners. It is indeed wholly irrelevant to an assessment of the host's benefits, if no domestic alternative is available.[15] But if a local entrepreneur could have carried out the projects with local savings, then the country should prefer this if the rate of return is higher than that to be expected on other average new investments in the economy. In principle, such alternatives should always be investigated. Even when no such domestic alternative is possible, it is useful from the point of view of bargaining to know both the country's own benefits and the return to the foreigner. If the latter is high, it may be possible to bargain harder, and so increase the former.

The above analysis can be directly applied to divestment or nationalization as well as to investment. A fair price for an asset from the foreigners' point of view would be the present value of future expected returns, discounting at the expected rate of return on risk capital in his own country. The host would gain at this price only if his accounting or social rate of interest was lower (assuming the expected returns under his management were the same). Only if a LDC has rather limited investment opportunities relative to its level of savings is such nationalization likely to constitute an economic benefit. But when we add in the political advantages, and the fact that the host country may well be able to nationalize at a lower price than the investor thinks fair, without causing undue political repercussions or preventing other new desired foreign investments, then one should not be surprised to see quite a lot of nationalization in the manufacturing field, as soon as LDCs can operate the enterprises successfully. Nationalization of mining ventures, which has been on a large scale, may be a pointer to the future.

Joint ventures have always been popular with developing countries and have been increasing as US companies have weakened their resistance to them, and as European and Japanese firms, always less resistant, have increased their share of the transnational corporation market. LDCs have, at the same time, toughened their attitudes, and in many countries, in some or all sectors, local equity participation or even control is mandatory. The reasons for this must be largely political, for the economic arguments rather tend to suggest that providing local finance for such joint ventures may not be a particularly good use of a country's savings (unless local bureaucrats or entrepreneurs are very clever at spotting

[15] This can be most vividly seen by imagining an enclave, which sells nothing to the local economy and buys only labour from it. (We can imagine it operating on wasteland, or even on a ship moored offshore.) If labour is surplus, there is a gain to the host country, which has and need have no notion of how the enclave is financed, or what profit it makes.

which are likely to be the most profitable ventures to opt into). The foreign company is less likely to transfer secret processes and know-how to an affiliate over which it has less than full control, and access to foreign markets may be more restricted. Local equity holdings may also give an incentive to transfer pricing. It is notable, perhaps, that joint ventures are much less common in MDCs, where political fears are less pronounced.[16]

We turn, very briefly, to two of the most frequently asserted complaints against transnational corporations. The first is 'transfer' pricing as between different units of the transnational corporation in different countries. Although there is often no way of establishing an arm's-length price, and so no way of saying what is a 'proper' division of the transnational corporation's profits between different centres, there is no doubt that many transnational corporations have some latitude of choice as to where they will declare profits, although revenue and exchange control authorities try to reduce this latitude. In most LDCs, corporate taxes are lower than in MDCs, and so there is an advantage in using transfer pricing in favour of LDCs.[17] The US tax authorities seem to believe it works in this direction: but development economists have almost invariably assumed the opposite. There may, however, be reasons for transferring profits, despite a tax disadvantage, if the host limits dividends or exercises price control based on costs or import prices, practices that are quite frequent. Apart from balance-of-payments emergencies, limitation of dividends constitutes an attempt to increase the inflow of foreign investment (by reinvestment of profits). On balance, it seems likely both to have the opposite effect and to decrease the host's benefits from such investment, by reducing the tax take. A number of reports and commentators have made this point. But no doubt the practice will continue, since host governments tend to believe that profits that legally belong to foreigners nevertheless in some sense belong to the host country when they arise from operations in that country.

Firm empirical evidence on transfer pricing is extremely scanty and mostly involves pharmaceuticals. It does not support a presumption that it works on balance against the interests of LDCs.[18] It is also, perhaps, worth noting that local firms have almost as much opportunity, and often a greater incentive, for transfer pricing as have foreign firms, by over- and underinvoicing of

[16] There is evidence on the points in this and the two succeeding paragraphs in, e.g., 1978, *Transnational Corporations in World Development*; G. Reuber, *Private Foreign Investment in Development* (Oxford: Clarendon Press, 1973); R. Vernon, *Storm over the Multinationals* (London: Macmillan, 1977); and I. Frank, *Foreign Enterprise in Developing Countries* (Baltimore: Johns Hopkins University Press, 1980). Balasubramanyam, 'Multinational Corporations' Choice of Techniques and Employment in Less Developed Countries', also sums up much of the evidence, in the spirit of what is written here.

[17] High tariffs also favour underinvoicing of imports, and hence profit transfers to LDCs. For a review of the fiscal incentives for transfer pricing, see G. F. Kopitz, 'Taxation and Multinational Firms' Behavior', *International Monetary Fund Staff Papers* (November 1976).

[18] For a review of evidence, see UN Conference on Trade and Development, TD/B/C2/167 (1978).

imports and exports; and there is plenty of anecdotal evidence that this is not uncommon.

Transnational corporations may use tax havens to avoid tax in either home or host country. By establishing a trading subsidiary in such a haven, the TNC can realize profits there by manipulating intrafirm prices. These profits, which by definition are untaxed or very lightly taxed, may then be used for investment elsewhere. Tax on undistributed profits is thus avoided. Home governments, especially that of the United States, have taken steps to prevent or limit the use of tax havens, but with what success one does not know. There seems to be no evidence concerning the amount of profit accruing in tax havens from offshore operations.

The second common ground for attack on TNCs is that they introduce inappropriate technology and products. In so far as all foreign technology is inappropriate, of course TNCs introduce it. But there is no evidence that, on balance, sector by sector, they introduce more capital-intensive methods, or adapt less, than do local firms, public and private, which acquire foreign technology by licensing, consultancy contracts, etc. The anecdotal evidence cuts both ways.[19] Turning to inappropriate products, whatever one may think of Coca Cola and Nestlé's baby food, it is a little one-sided to forget the very large range of chemicals and other products that no one would claim to be inappropriate, or the fact that local firms also produce many Western proprietary products that advocates of the simple, hard, indigenous, childbearing life would condemn.

If one can sum up the economic arguments in a single sentence, it would be: 'they greatly exaggerate the difference between indigenous and foreign enterprise'. Problems of monopoly, technology, and products arise in either case. Both foreign and domestic enterprises may do harm in overprotected markets. The only significant difference is that excessive profits belong to nationals in one case, and foreigners in another. But one can make too much even of that. There is zero national social value to be attached to adding unnecessarily to a foreigner's wealth, but the social value of adding unnecessarily to a local tycoon's wealth may be very close to zero.

[19] Balasubramanyam, *Multinational Enterprises and the Third World*, Thames Essay 26, London, Trade Policy Research Centre 1980, and L. J. White 'The Evidence on Appropriate Factor Proportions for Manufacturing in Less Developed Countries', *Economic Development and Cultural Change*, October 1978 briefly review the Evidence.

10

Project Appraisal and Planning Twenty Years On (1991)

In the late 1960s there was considerable development of methods for applying social cost–benefit analysis to investment in developing countries. In the 1970s, these methods began to be applied. From 1974 to 1982 there were massive public sector investment booms in many of the developing countries. It appears that much of this investment yielded little or nothing. Were the methods flawed in principle? Were they ignored? And if so, why? Was the possible effect of project appraisal swamped by unforeseen events that rendered potentially valuable investments useless? We do not provide definitive answers to these questions, but we hope to contribute to their answers by discussing the current state of the theory of project appraisal and the current practice and influence of social cost–benefit analysis, particularly within the World Bank.

1. REFLECTIONS ON THE PRINCIPLES OF PROJECT APPRAISAL

In our book (Little and Mirrlees, 1974) we provided a method for social investment decisions. In brief, we proposed the following techniques:

- Measuring the values of outputs (benefits) and inputs (costs) with shadow prices
- Using border prices as shadow prices for traded inputs and outputs, or—in cases where demand or supply is not independent of price—using the marginal revenue or cost to the country in foreign exchange as a first approximation
- Where possible, using costs, themselves measured at shadow prices, as shadow prices for non-traded inputs

†This paper, written jointly with J. A. Mirrlees, originally appeared in the *Proceedings of the World Bank Annual Conference on Development Economics* (International Bank for Reconstruction and Development, Washington, DC, 1991). Permission to reproduce is gratefully acknowledged. The title of the paper alludes to that of the authors' book on project appraisal; the paper does not deal with planning directly. The authors wish to acknowledge discussions with economists in the World Bank and with J. D. MacArthur, J. M. Healey, and J. Wilmshurst.

- Using conversion factors, estimated separately for a number of different broad categories of inputs and outputs, to calculate shadow prices from market prices for most minor inputs and outputs
- Using as shadow wage rates (SWRs) market wage rates discounted by a conversion factor estimated from an overall study of the economy, and depending in particular on a judgement that public income is more valuable at the margin than private income
- In cases where no other rule is applicable, using a standard conversion factor (SCF) to deduce the shadow price from the market price, to be estimated by comparing (domestic) market prices with border prices for traded goods, and others for which a sound estimate of the shadow price is available
- Estimating the private and public parts of the net (social) costs and income of the project, so that private income and costs could be discounted relative to public income and costs, and giving a low weight to private profit income
- Basing the shadow prices used on forecasts of border prices and market prices, not usually on their current values
- Discounting net social profits so calculated by means of an accounting rate of interest (ARI) that is high (or low) enough to be expected to ration investment projects in the whole economy to the funds available—a rate that could well vary over time—but in no case using a discount rate less than the rate available for investment in international capital markets
- Allowing for uncertainty only to the extent that the profitability of the project was expected to be correlated with the general state of the economy
- In the case of large projects, allowing for changes in prices brought about by their introduction, and estimating the incremental value of outputs and inputs by 'surplus' calculations
- Converting all external effects of the project to numerical terms by making some estimate of the cost or value in terms of public income and including them directly in the calculation of the present social value of the project.

These features of the method proposed had grown out of wide debate and discussion among economists. Other studies of cost–benefit analysis which reflected that debate in their own way differed in some respects, but there was much in common.[1] We attempted to provide a systematic procedure that would correct all the important distortions. The method we proposed is not a theoretical ideal. It was intended to be practical, and therefore it simplifies and approximates. Even so, some aspects have been found hard to implement. In later sections we discuss implementation. The present section deals with some aspects of these methods, particularly the more controversial features.

[1] See e.g. the famous UNIDO Guidelines (UNIDO, 1972), written by Dasgupta, Marglin, and Sen; work by international trade theorists, much of it presented in Corden (1974); a notable series of studies by Arnold Harberger, collected in Harberger (1972); other work collected or referred to in the useful collection by Layard (1972); and an earlier formulation of our own (Little and Mirrlees, 1969).

An extensive literature in the last twenty years has subjected the methods, or at least some of the principles embodied in them, to critical analysis.[2] Arising from that, there are some respects in which expansion, development, or revision of these procedures seems to us to be warranted. But to a large extent we stand by them.

Traded goods

Much of the literature on methods of social cost–benefit analysis has concentrated on the issue of optimal shadow prices under perfect certainty. Squire (1989) in the *Handbook of Development Economics*, concludes that the literature has shown that the border price principle for traded goods is quite robust.

In the case of a small country, for which border prices are essentially independent of the amounts imported and exported, quite weak assumptions are sufficient to justify the border price principle. When price varies with the amount of trade, it is not exactly right to use marginal revenues and costs. This was pointed out in Little and Mirrlees (1974, p. 229), but it has tended to be neglected. A more extensive treatment has been given in Bhagwati and Srinivasan (1978). The point is that the change in exports, say, affects not only the price received by the country in world markets but also the prices received by domestic producers and paid by domestic consumers, for these prices are generally linked—by taxes, or by the workings of price control systems—to the world price. These changes in market prices involve changes in the welfare of consumers and the actions of producers that ought not to be neglected. The calculations required in principle are similar to those required for the correct pricing of non-traded factors of production. The attractive idea that one could look only to the external environment when estimating shadow prices is not justified—or, at least, it is not exactly justified.

This is only one example of the widespread effects that should in principle be estimated to calculate shadow prices. Although it is reasonable—in the absence of a good applicable model of the economy—to guess that these hard-to-trade effects would not much modify a first approximation based on marginal foreign revenue alone, that is a guess, warranting at least testing in plausible models.

Non-traded goods

A major simplifying idea behind the shadow pricing methods suggested is that, given an estimate of the shadow wage rate and an estimate of the accounting rate of interest, it would be possible to calculate shadow prices for many non-traded

[2] Two recent surveys (Drèze and Stern, 1987; Squire, 1989) give accounts of the literature, particularly on shadow pricing.

goods on the basis of input–output data, describing costs of production. This is based on a general principle that the shadow price for a commodity produced under competitive conditions and constant returns to scale is equal to its average cost, calculated using the shadow prices of the inputs into its production (including labour and capital).[3]

Granted the often reasonable approximations of constant returns and competitive conditions, this social cost principle seems common sense, but there is a hidden difficulty, one that has struck economists who consider economies in which the number of traded goods appears to exceed the number of non-traded goods and factors—too many equations chasing too few unknowns.

The difficulty can best be brought out by contemplating a strikingly unsatisfactory, but not unrealistic, state of affairs. Suppose that two private producers are producing the same commodity, using only labour as an input, and one of them is more efficient than the other. Suppose also that subsidies are provided to the less efficient, so that in fact both firms operate. Costs of production in the two firms are different, when measured using shadow prices. Therefore, the social cost principle does not give an unambiguous rule for calculating the relationship between output and input shadow prices.

The analysis of Diamond and Mirrlees (1976) assumed that equilibrium was unique. This is a common assumption, but it is not always warranted. In the situation described, we can only say that the appropriate output shadow price depends on what will actually happen when demand for the product changes. Marginal social cost should be calculated, but what that is depends on the shares of the two firms in the change in aggregate output. There is no good reason to expect marginal cost to be equal to average cost in this case.

The main areas in which these considerations are relevant is when import substitution is subsidized or when quantitative controls are used to achieve the same effect. Then the border price principle is correct when trade can be expected to adjust to changed demand. Otherwise, economic theory cannot predict how much domestic production will be allowed to supply. The project appraiser has to guess what will be allowed to happen. The appraiser should also make recommendations about sources of supply and point out the possible impact on the value of the project. The right answer to the project question may not be yes or no, but rather 'only if these inputs are imported instead of being produced domestically'.

The social cost rule is incomplete in the sense that it does not enable appraisers to calculate theoretically satisfactory shadow prices for all goods. Sieper (1981) and others have found relatively simple rules that may sometimes be used for calculating the shadow prices for non-traded goods in some of the more difficult cases. (For the main results of Sieper's unpublished paper, see Squire, 1989.) The last resort is to derive the shadow price from the market price by applying a standard conversion factor based on comparisons of shadow and

[3] A general theorem with this consequence was proved formally in Diamond and Mirrlees (1976).

market prices for commodities (such as traded goods) where the shadow price has been satisfactorily estimated. Despite the weakness, we believe that our proposals take good care of the major distortions. In the simplest terms, our rules would not permit projects making cars at a greater foreign exchange cost than by direct purchase abroad.

Another aspect of the social cost procedure has drawn comment (see e.g. Srinivasan, 1982). It is essential for applying the principle that there be some means of making prior estimates of shadow wage rates and discount rates. We proposed basing these on simple macroeconomic models, and calculations of that kind have been done for one or two countries. (In other cases, estimates of conversion factors for other countries have been used, and the ubiquitous 10 per cent accounting rate of interest does not derive from any serious model.) There is no economic theorem that says that the strategic shadow prices calculated in this way are, in some sense, best unbiased estimators; nor is it easy to conceive how such a theorem could be formulated. As with other features of practical welfare economics, the recommendation to use simple macroestimation is essentially intuitive.

Income differences

The presumption that public income is more valuable than private income has been challenged. That presumption forms the basis for arguments that the shadow wage rate should be a substantial proportion of actual wage rates (after adjusting from market prices to shadow prices for consumption goods).

The reasons for it were, first, that government could use additional revenues for further socially profitable investment to a greater extent than private income earners; second, that there are administrative costs to raising tax revenue; and, third, that raising tax revenue creates distortions. The first consideration is weak for countries in which public income seems to be spent on, or diverted to, many objects of little value. The second is not very large. The third argument, which is emphasized by Squire (1989), seems to need further analysis.

Claims about the cost of public funds in developed countries that are based merely on the existence of distorting taxes are invalid. In any economy, there are distorting taxes on labour and commodities. Revenue is rightly raised that way, because discriminating lump-sum taxes are not possible. In many economies there are also elements of the tax system, such as income tax allowances, that approximate a uniform lump-sum subsidy. If that uniform subsidy is at an optimal level, then a public expenditure that brings about equal income increases for a representative sample of people is just as valuable as a project that increases public income by the same amount. That is because one can be transformed into the other, at the margin, without distortion. Projects that augment private incomes, however, generally do so differentially, though not necessarily benefiting the rich more than the poor. Taking the usual view of the relationship between income and welfare, private income changes accruing to those above mean income levels are worth less than public income changes; but in the opposite case, they are worth more.

The above argument may not be very relevant for developing economies, where scarcely any policy tools approximating a uniform subsidy exist. Typically, a reduction in government income or a rise in expenditure would be offset by an increase in the 'inflation tax', or, after some delay, by taxes on consumer goods, reductions in other public services, or indeed a cutback in investment. Again, a judgement on the relative value of public and private income turns, in part, on a welfare judgement of the relative value of income to people with different incomes.

When changes accrue to those of average incomes, a useful guide is the Ramsey model of an economy with identical individuals and all government revenue raised by taxes proportional to sales and purchases of commodities (that is, no tax allowances or general subsidies). For such an economy, plausible specifications of consumer preferences yield a 20–40 per cent premium for public over private income. (One attempt to estimate this for the US economy is Ballard, Shoven, and Whalley, 1985). When private income accrues to those with income much above the income of the average taxpayer (often quite a low income level in developing countries), its value relative to public income is correspondingly lower.

Uncertainty

It has been argued that careful project appraisal is worth little when uncertainty about the project and about the environment within which it will operate is great. Project appraisal is costly, and the benefits of better decisions could fail to justify that cost. But it is by no means clear that the benefits of improved decisions are slight in a *very* uncertain environment. We have considered this question and find that there can be a reduction in the value of appraisal because of general uncertainty. But in principle it remains considerable.

One can think of cost–benefit analysis as the elimination of error—not all error, but some of the error implicit in decisions by hunch or apparent financial profitability. A theory of these matters is sketched in the appendix [not reproduced here]. It is shown, using a plausible simple model, that in the context of project appraisal we should expect some reduction in the value of appraisal when general uncertainty is greater. A simple rule of thumb for judging the benefit is developed. It says that the value of a system of project appraisal is (at least) 10 per cent of the standard deviation of the errors removed by appraisal, multiplied by the ratio of that standard deviation to the standard deviation of errors not removed. In Section 3 below we discuss some evidence suggesting that the ratio of these standard deviations is around unity. The variation in observed rates of return is very great. It is not implausible to suppose that the standard deviation of errors removed by appraisal is at least a quarter of the mean net value of projects. With good appraisal it ought to be much more. On that basis, one can claim that appraisal is worth at least 2 per cent of the mean net value of projects appraised.

In our book on project appraisal, we recommended allowing for uncertainty by subtracting from the expected value of net social profitability of the project in any year an amount equal to $A\,\mathrm{cov}(P, Y)/E(Y)$, where $\mathrm{cov}(P, Y)$ is the covariance between social profit P and national income Y, $E(Y)$ is the mean expected value of national income, and A is a measure of risk aversion known as the coefficient of relative risk aversion, for which we suggested the value 2. Another way to express this is to suggest that the net value of a project in a year be taken as

$$E(P)(1 - A\,r\,\mathrm{CVP}\,\mathrm{CVY}), \tag{1}$$

where r is the correlation coefficient between the project's social profits and national income, CVP is the coefficient of variation (ratio of standard deviation to mean) for social profit, and CVY is the coefficient of variation for national income. The justification for these rules is provided in the appendix [not included here].

Estimating these correlation coefficients and variances and means is a matter of skill, requiring training, not least in the concepts and judgement of appropriate values in well-specified examples. Frequently there would be very little data to go on. One could use data for similar industries in similar countries where there is more relevant experience. The task is essentially equivalent to the use of 'beta coefficients' by financial managers, and it is as hard or easy as that.

Some allowance for uncertainty should be made, though it seldom is. The appropriate allowance can be substantial, especially in the later years of a project. But for most countries, the coefficient of variation for national income is not very large, looking forward for a decade or so, if one may be guided by time series; and therefore in most cases the allowance for uncertainty is not a large adjustment in the value of the project. It should be noted that the allowance could take the form of an increase in the value of the project, if it were negatively correlated with national income.

In our book we also pointed out that allowance should sometimes be made for inflexibility, for the cost of irreversible commitment in projects, though we claimed that such an adjustment should seldom be required. We probably understated the importance of this consideration (see Henry, 1974, for an analysis). In a sense, the issue of flexibility is the desirability of continuing appraisal during the life of the project. At the time of initial investment appraisal, the project can develop in many ways; and some projects have more possibilities of development and adjustment than others. The more flexible projects are worth more for that reason. How much more they are worth depends on how much, and when, flexibility is expected to be exercised.

Because of discounting, flexibility that can occur only after decades (as in the choice between projects that are long-lived and ones that are not quite so long-lived) is not likely to be worth a great deal. Flexible response to variations in prices may well be exercised before many years have passed. Granted the great uncertainty in many prices, such flexibility may be of considerable value. The specific rules we listed in our book neither draw attention to this nor provide rules of thumb for evaluating it. In principle, flexibility is already valued in the estimation of expected profit, because the probability distributions of social profit for various more or less flexible projects or programmes should have been compared, allowing for the response of the project to varying circumstances. But project reports seldom if ever allow for responsive alteration in production, such as closing (temporary or permanent) or expansion. They should.

At least, they should when it could be important. But this seems to be a difficult and costly task. For a substantial price, consultants will construct a model and do a computer simulation of many alternative futures. It may contain many fairly arbitrary assumptions, and it may ignore shadow pricing, which is likely to be quantitatively even more important. In large projects, where flexibility could be substantial in the first two decades, it may be worth attempting such an analysis, but the appraiser needs to keep close track of just what possibilities are being simulated. This is an area in which it is too easy to make spurious claims which add to the apparent value of the project.

Appraisal incentives

This last line of thought brings us to the question of the environment within which project appraisal itself may operate. Appraisers—like workers, managers, and politicians—have their incentives, and they may be expected to respond to them. Space allows little systematic discussion here. The obvious difficulty is that appraisers will be judged on the number of 'good' projects they find relative to the numbers that others find. More and more often, as a system of appraisal operates, the standards on numbers of projects found will be based on past performance, and it will not be surprising if arguments and analysis are shaded to continually increase that number. As we discuss below, such a phenomenon appears to have occurred in the World Bank. We have no doubt it has also occurred elsewhere.

The difficulty is that the obvious basis for incentives—comparison of appraisals with results—is almost impossible to use, because of the great length of time that elapses between initial recommendation and final results. And if comparison is used, the reappraisal process could be corrupted. There are other possibilities: independent reappraisal of randomly selected projects shortly after the original appraisal, or explicit grading of project appraisals by quality, as judged by independent inspectors, paying attention not only to analytical method and conformity to standard procedures but also to checking the empirical basis of the appraisal. If good project appraisal warrants expenditure of resources, as we argue in Section 4, so does good appraisal of appraisal. We do not argue for any further levels of appraisal, though that raises an interesting question.

2. THE RISE AND FALL OF COST–BENEFIT ANALYSIS IN THE WORLD BANK AND THE STATE OF THE ART ELSEWHERE

During the 1970s there was a remarkable development of both the methodology and the use of shadow pricing in estimating the true national value of projects in economies in which, primarily because of government taxes and controls, the allocation of resources was distorted. This happened first because of an increasing realization of the degree of these distortions, and second because of a desire to apply systematic decision procedures where previously there had been haphazard action and arbitrary plans. We would claim that our development of a method by which a set of consistent shadow prices could be estimated had some part in it (Little and Mirrlees, 1969; Dasgupta, Marglin, and Sen were also devising guidelines for project appraisal; see UNIDO, 1972). Within two or three years, most donor agencies and a few developing countries were using some simple version of the methodology. But among donor or lending agencies the methods were most fully used and further developed by the World Bank. (The first major demonstration of how to estimate a full set of shadow prices was by Scott; see Scott, MacArthur, and Newbery, 1976.) The World Bank's own version of the methodology was published in Squire and van der Tak (1975). This methodology incorporated 'social' prices whereby consumption was weighted according to the income of the consumer. If such distributional weights were not used, then the shadow prices were (tendentiously) called 'efficiency' prices. Efficiency pricing was based on the remarkable and extreme presumption that a dollar's worth of consumption had the same social value to whomsoever it accrued. Efficiency prices were also based on the presumption that all kinds of income and all uses of income were equally valuable. Our book (Little and Mirrlees, 1974), which also incorporated distributional weights, was published at about the same time. But it is important to note that Little and Mirrlees (1969), which did not use distributional weights, had not assumed that all *uses* of income were equally valuable. As in UNIDO (1972), investment was presumed to be worth more than consumption. In Little and Mirrlees (1974) the numeraire was changed to uncommitted government income, which was also presumed to be worth more than average consumption.

A battle raged in the World Bank during the 1970s about whether social prices should be used. Formally, the 'social price brigade' won, in that guidelines on the use of distributional weights were actually incorporated in the *Operational*

Manual in 1980. In practice, we believe, they were hardly ever used except in an experimental manner in a few cases. But aside from this battle, there was a good deal of debate, interest, and research. Guidelines flowed from the Central Projects Department under Warren Baum, which also ran a long series of workshops. With or without distributional weights, a fairly full set of sectoral conversion factors and shadow wage rates was estimated by staff members or consultants for nearly twenty countries. The use of the foreign exchange numeraire became standard practice in the World Bank and remains so.

Multiple conversion factors are an important, indeed essential, feature of the Little–Mirrlees and Squire–van der Tak methodologies. We suppose that they were used for the countries for which they were estimated. Shadow pricing in the World Bank reached its apogee around 1981. Yet, inspection of a sample of completion reports of projects approved in the 1970s suggests that the Squire–van der Tak system was far from being fully adopted, either intensively or extensively. Many country economists were still unconvinced, either because they were overworked or lazy or because they were genuinely unsure of the usefulness or validity of the system. At the same time, there have always been senior World Bank staff members who have remained suspicious of economic analysis, especially when it conflicts with their hunches about what is good for development—whether it be integrated rural development, afforestation, or steel plants.

In the 1980s there was a decline in the use of shadow pricing at the Bank. In terms of interest, attention, guidance, supervision, and research, the decline is steep. The change in actual working practice may be less dramatic. We say this partly because the Bank, even at the apogee, had been less than thoroughly permeated by the Squire–van der Tak methodology, and partly because it is difficult to describe the present state. The difficulty stems from the fact that there is no longer a Central Projects Department, offering common advice and exercising common quality control over project appraisals. We do not know whether regions now diverge significantly, but we guess probably not (or not yet, anyway).

There have always been sectoral differences, particularly in the case of power (but also telecommunications and water supply), and these remain. The benefit of power is generally taken to be measured by what it is sold for. This must often yield an underestimate of benefit, where tariffs are controlled at low levels. We were told during interviews we conducted at the World Bank in the process of writing this paper that the World Bank's loans are made conditional on tariffs being raised (though such conditions are not always fulfilled) if this is required to show a 10 per cent return. In fact, we found one appraisal report of a hydroelectric project in which the benefit was reckoned to be the cost of power from a thermal project (based on imported oil); the benefit was thus grossly overestimated, because the World Bank grossly overestimated the future price of oil. We have mentioned this methodological divergence because we return below to the proper appraisal of power and other non-traded goods projects.

However difficult they are to make, some general propositions as to present practice are essential, although we have not made sufficient inquiries to be sure they are altogether correct. We believe the following:

- Social pricing, using distributional weights, has been abandoned.
- No distinction is made between public and private income, or between the uses of income—whether saved or invested.
- Sectoral conversion factors are rarely if ever calculated and used.
- Shadow wage rates are not systematically used or estimated.
- The values of non-traded goods are mostly converted to border values by a single standard conversion factor. To put this in another way, there is seldom if ever any attempt to estimate the actual foreign exchange consequences of using or producing particular non-traded goods. It is also equivalent to saying that the relative prices of non-traded goods are assumed to be undistorted (except perhaps that taxes may be subtracted).

If the above propositions are correct, they amount to saying that, apart from the cutoff economic rate of return, only one shadow price—a standard conversion factor or shadow exchange rate—is used (and it is unclear how this is estimated, or whether it is estimated in the same way for different countries). This is probably not very different from the practice in the 1960s, when shadow exchange rates were used (and even shadow wage rates) when required to make the rate of return good enough. The only important improvement may be some greater use of border prices for tradable goods. It is doubtful whether the World Bank can now be said to have a standard methodology. It is certainly not that of Squire and van der Tak (or of Little and Mirrlees, or even of UNIDO).[4]

Before speculating about the reasons for this withering, we briefly survey the situation in the regional banks and other donor agencies, and in developing countries. Here, nothing much seems to have changed in the past ten to fifteen years. There was no buildup of interest and development of the methodology similar to that in the World Bank, nor consequently any subsequent withdrawal. Those adopting in the mid-1970s a limited version of Little–Mirrlees, whether directly or following the World Bank, include the Asian Development Bank (ADB), the Inter-American Development Bank (IDB), the Overseas Development Administration (ODA) in the United Kingdom, and the Kreditanstalt für Wiederaufbau in Germany. Japan also claims to follow the World Bank. France and the European Commission still use the 'effects method', despite its errors, as pointed out by Balassa (1976). Other countries seem to follow no particular methodology, or hardly use cost–benefit analysis at all. The Canadians and the British agree, however, that most consultants are familiar with the World

[4] In a recent Development Assistance Committee review of *Project Appraisal Criteria and Procedures* (Development Assistance Committee, OECD, 1987 [87]11), the methodology used by the World Bank is described as being that of Squire and van der Tak. Presumably the World Bank supplied this information, but it seems to be more of a travesty than the truth.

Bank methodology and use it. (And the British add that they are required to do so.)[5]

The IDB is still active in calculating national parameters using input–output methods. Current work apparently includes estimates for Colombia, Panama, and Venezuela. But we do not know what use in practice is made of them. Apart possibly from the IDB, the British ODA seems to be the most persistent upholder of the principles adopted in the mid-1970s. It also appears to be more convinced of the practical value of the methodology than other agencies. A third edition of the ODA's *Appraisal of Projects in Developing Countries* (ODA, 1988) retains guidelines for the calculation of sectoral and other conversion factors, for shadow wages, for the incorporation of different values for saving and investment, and for the use of distributive weights. Although the latter two adjustments are rarely used, examples are given of the careful calculation and use of multiple conversion factors.

Information on the state of the art in developing countries is spotty. Chile, partly inspired by Harberger (1972), has a well-developed system of appraisal operating at all government levels. In India, the project appraisal division of the Planning Commission continues to operate, but it appraises only about one-third of public sector projects. Lal (1980) worked out a full set of national parameters, but practice has degenerated to the use of a single shadow exchange rate which never changes. The Development and Project Planning Centre, University of Bradford, has recently on request calculated national parameters for Ethiopia and Jamaica. Work has begun on China and Sri Lanka.[6] Squire (1989) reports, on the basis of information from World Bank staff members, that (of twenty-seven countries surveyed) Côte d'Ivoire, Ethiopia, Republic of Korea, Pakistan, Philippines, Sierra Leone, Thailand, and Yugoslavia undertake project appraisals using shadow prices (how rigorously is not clear). Personal information suggests that Malaysia should be added to the positive list.

We here mention some reasons for the rather poor penetration, because they differ from reasons applicable to the World Bank and other lending agencies. Public projects derive from ministries or other agencies with departmental, sectoral, or regional interests (not to speak of personal, monetary, or political interests, which also sometimes intrude). Only the central government and the ministries of planning and finance can at best be expected to look to the national interest. Some conflict is inevitable and essential, because project proponents do not welcome central control, which constrains the extent to which they can make projects serve their own purposes.

Even financial control has proved difficult in many countries, and soft budgeting has resulted in the subsidization of many decentralized agencies. So a central system of project appraisal must always be unpopular, and therefore it

[5] These observations are based mainly on Development Assistance Committee, OECD (1987), interviews with the United Kingdom ODA staff, and hearsay (for the ADB and IDB).

[6] We are indebted to J. D. MacArthur for this information.

needs strong political backing at the highest level. This may be lacking for many reasons, among them the fact that, at least until very recently, many planners and politicians in developing countries sensed that the methods proposed would conflict with the import-substituting industrialization policies that were at the heart of their development philosophy.

3. SOME REASONS FOR THE DECLINE OF INTEREST IN SHADOW PRICES AND COST–BENEFIT ANALYSIS IN THE WORLD BANK

The decline proclaimed in the title of this section assumes that the general propositions of the previous section are not very far from the truth. If so, it is a shattering indictment, because a shadow price is the marginal effect on social welfare of any quantity change. Shadow prices are fundamental to the evaluation of policy changes, not merely investment projects. This is well recognized in the normative theory of taxes and subsidies, but it also applies to the evaluation of quantitative controls—quotas and rationing.

Shadow prices and cost–benefit analysis are inseparable. Sometimes actual prices coincide with their shadow values, as if on the equator in the midday sun. Only then is financial analysis also cost–benefit analysis. For public sector projects and enterprises, a decision has to be made about pricing. A good guideline is to make prices coincide as nearly as possible with their shadows, which requires knowledge of the shadows. Sometimes, however, it is impossible or obviously undesirable to charge at all—for example, in the case of most roads. But the shadows are still required to plan the roads.

It is sometimes argued that the thrust of policy should be to get the prices right, and it is suggested that this is an argument for forgetting about, or at least de-emphasizing, shadow prices. To the extent that activities are private, and there is no price or profit control, this is feasible and may be desirable. But in the public sector, or whenever there is public regulation, getting the prices right implies knowing the shadow prices.

Less room for project analysis? The growth of non-project, health, and education loans

Despite the importance of our introductory remarks, cost–benefit analysis and shadow pricing are closely associated with investment projects, in the normal narrow sense of the word 'project'. The decline of interest may thus be related partly to the relative decline of project lending. Structural adjustment loans and other non-project loans—such as those to development finance corporations—account for an increasing proportion of World Bank lending. There may also be no identifiable project in the case of sectoral adjustment loans. In the case of loans for health and education, no economic rate of return (or present value) is estimated; shadow pricing is still relevant for cost effectiveness, but we do not know whether it is used. In a few countries—such as Brazil—World Bank lending now includes almost no projects to which cost–benefit analysis can be applied. Nevertheless, overall, there are still a great many projects; and, furthermore, sectoral adjustment loans also lend themselves to analysis that makes use of shadow prices. The growth of forms of lending other than straight project loans has probably caused a diversion of attention out of proportion to their relative importance.

Institutional reasons

The World Bank is a relatively unsuitable and unstable institution for time-consuming and dedicated quality control (via technical and economic appraisal at all stages) of the investments it finances.

Ironically, in the 1970s, when the World Bank's Central Projects Department was trying to engineer an improvement in economic analysis, its president, Robert McNamara, was presiding over a huge increase in the volume of lending, which put pressure on country and project staff to get enough projects approved. There is no doubt that this created tension. When the pressure is on to get the money out, it is not surprising that demands for more complex analysis are unwelcome. Worse than this, project analysts would never get promoted if they were honestly compelled to report unfavourably on several projects. Promotion would come from writing good reports that would help steer the project through the processes of approval, and not from improving projects or improving project selection. Economic rates of return (ERRs) on projects became more and more optimistic, without justification. No one we have spoken to denies that the incentives facing the staff worked toward a deterioration in the quality of project work or asserts that this was a trivial matter; it is well known as the 'McNamara effect'. It parallels what was happening in the commercial banks.

The present situation is not very different. The World Bank is again under pressure to lend, because of the debt crisis. The debt crisis has in turn arisen largely because the massive lending from 1974 to 1982 was matched by investments that turned out to have very low or negative returns. Almost all developing countries raised the share of investment in gross national product (GNP) in this period, some by a great deal, and the increase was predominantly in the public sector. The World Bank was not immune from promoting or supporting some very bad investments, for which its own price projections were partly responsible.

The reorganizations of the World Bank in the 1980s have clearly contributed to the decline of cost–benefit analysis. There is now no Central Projects Department to promote common methods and to exercise quality control.

Regionalization need not, of itself, have had this result. But it has. There is now no fully independent watchdog over the quality of project work. We have the impression of widespread deterioration. This is not only in economic analysis. Fewer resources are apparently devoted to project work. There is, we are told, less continuity and expertise in project teams than earlier on. Technical, financial, and institutional analysis may have suffered. Obviously economic analysis would not be immune.

New concerns

New concerns may have complicated the project analyst's task. There was a new emphasis in the 1970s on projects that would benefit the poor directly. Cost–benefit methods were adapted to make the poverty impact quantifiable and to integrate it into the cost–benefit analysis. That this has been rejected reduces the work load, for it is difficult to trace the beneficiaries of a project and assess their wealth. Yet we gather that for some kinds of projects the analyst is still expected to do this. (Only, having done so, the analyst must not apply weights to these differential benefits—it could be argued that this is incurring the costs of the analysis without the benefits.) Now the development of women has been added as a project concern. Surely this is an irrelevant consideration in most projects. Then there is the environment. All effects of a project—including on the development of women and the environment—that might seriously affect its value should always be considered and quantified if possible. But there is a cost to insisting that in all cases the appraiser should be seen to have spent considerable resources on trying to identify kinds of consequences that are unlikely to be of any importance. This is not to say that apparently remote environmental damage may not be large and important. In some areas, the specialist's assessment of these magnitudes is much to be desired.

Sustainability has come to be used in recent years in connection with projects. This is more of a buzzword—probably derived from the environmental lobby—than a genuine concept. It has no merit. Whether a project is sustainable (for ever?—or just for a long time?) has nothing to do with whether it is desirable. If unsustainability were really regarded as a reason for rejecting a project, there would be no mining, and no industry. The world would be a very primitive place. In defence of sustainability, it will be said that the concept has drawn attention to some often disregarded reasons for project failure. But it seems much better to detail what these reasons are.[7]

We were told in our discussions with World Bank Staff that on occasion the same analyst would give a project a high ERR but would say it was unsustain-

[7] Sustainability is also described as a 'central notion' in the extraordinarily vapid document, *Principles for Project Appraisal* (Development Assistance Committee, OECD, 1988).

able. Of course a reason for this could be that sustainability was irrelevant, as with the possibly rapid extraction of an ore body. But this is not what was meant. What was meant was that the same analyst could give a project a high ERR but could also say that it would probably fail (that is, end up with a low *ex post* return). This could arise because the project analyst, wearing the hat of ERR analyst (rightly), thinks that it is up to him to take account only of limited kinds of risk—for example, that future prices will be worse for the project than predicted, or that agricultural response has been overestimated. The analyst does not, in writing a project report, assess such risks as that the dictator will be shot and the subsequent economic management will be so muddled that a major slump will be unavoidable, or even that the economic administration will deteriorate to the extent that the project will be starved of funds for recurrent costs. He is also probably in no position to assess whether the country is overborrowing or planning more investment than it can possibly handle efficiently.

It appears that the 'division' of labour is as it should be. The project appraiser should make it clear which risks have been taken into account and which have not. The appraiser, or some other person familiar with the political and macroeconomic situation of the country (or maybe the administration of a sector), may comment that no project in that country (or sector) is at present likely to succeed, whatever the calculated ERR.

Methodological defects

We have been considering some institutional reasons for the decline of cost–benefit analysis. But cost–benefit analysis, or the World Bank's version of it, may have been its own worst enemy. The methodology may have been unsound. We discussed this in Section 1 above. There has been some sniping from theoretical perfectionists over the years. This may have reduced its acceptability, but probably only among those already disposed to attach a high value to comprehensive countrywide planning. Little–Mirrlees methods have stood up to intensive theoretical discussion remarkably well, and on balance the large outpouring of theory consequent on the original publication of Little and Mirrlees (1969) has confirmed the correctness of the authors' original intuitions.

The other way in which the methods could have been self-defeating is that they were too complex, so that the simplifications we have described may have been both inevitable and all to the good. This argument is best examined after reviewing the evidence provided by the World Bank's Operations Evaluation Department (OED). Here, we will remark only that simplification and theoretical soundness are not good bedfellows.

4. EVIDENCE FROM WORLD BANK DATA ON THE VALUE OF COST–BENEFIT ANALYSIS

The World Bank's annual review of evaluation results for 1988 gives some information on nearly 2,000 projects approved in the period 1968–80 and subsequently evaluated. The World Bank's OED provides original appraisal ERRs and re-estimated economic rates of return (RERRs) on more than 1,000 projects approved in the period 1968–80, together with figures for original and completed costs and expected and actual gestation periods. Gerhard Pohl and Dabrarko Mihaljek (1989) have analysed these OED data, and this section draws on their work.[8]

RERRs are taken from project completion reports usually made by those responsible for the project, which could lead to bias. They will normally allow for known changes in capital cost and any known changes in the mix of inputs and outputs. But actual experience of operation either will be limited to a short period or will be non-existent. Changes in price predictions also will be fed in. The difference between the ERRs and the RERRs is mainly a difference of expectation. The methodology of the estimation of the ERR will not normally be changed. Obviously, the RERR is very far from being a post-mortem ERR.

To the extent that resources permit, the OED conducts an 'audit' on top of the project completion report and ranks projects as 'satisfactory' or 'unsatisfactory'. In the case of projects with calculated RERRs, there is in most cases a coincidence of an unsatisfactory rating and a RERR of less than 10 per cent. But there are exceptions, in which a project with a high RERR is deemed unsatisfactory. In such cases it is clear that the OED does not believe the RERR. But it does not have the resources to make an independent estimate, so the incredible RERR is recorded.

Over the years 1968–80, there was a remarkable and continuous rise in appraisal ERRs. They averaged 17 per cent in 1968 and 29 per cent in 1980. There was no similar trend in average RERRs for projects approved in that period, which, apart from the years 1970 and 1980, were in the range 13–17 per cent.[9] As a result, a large gap between ERRs and RERRs has arisen and has excited some attention. It casts some doubt on the objectivity and stability of appraisal, there being no reason to think that investment possibilities were rapidly improving. The rise in appraisal ERRs was common to all regions and sectors

[8] Note that in many cases the so-called economic rates of return are really modified financial rates of return. That is true for power, telecommunications, water supply, and possibly some other subsectors. It is important to remember this limitation in the following discussion.

[9] We have no explanation for the high average RERR of 21 per cent in 1970. We distrust the high figure for 1980 (24 per cent), because relatively few projects approved in that year have been evaluated, and because there is a tendency for good projects to have short evaluation lags. We do not know how negative rates of return that could approach infinity are reckoned. From Pohl and Mihaljek (1989) it appears they may all be counted as -5 per cent. In view of this arbitrariness, it would be useful to know the median rates.

but was most marked in Asia and Africa, and sectorally in agriculture and rural development and in transport and tourism. We do not know to what extent the apparent euphoria was genuinely felt, or to what extent it was due to the McNamara effect.

The RERRs of 1968–80 were calculated over the period 1974–88, with an average lag between approval and reappraisal of nine years. One would expect the RERRs to be importantly affected by the year of reappraisal, particularly by the euphoria that may have continued until mid-1982. After that, the reappraisers' expectations of project performance would surely have been scaled down, in view of the difficulties in which most developing countries found themselves, and all sectors would have been affected. Almost no projects approved before 1971 were evaluated in 1983 or later (see Table 1).

TABLE 1

Year of approval	Percentage of projects evaluated after 1982
1971	16
1972	23
1973	35
1974	66
1975	86
1976	90
1977	92
1978	96
1979	98
1980	98

All other things being equal, one would expect, with scaled-down expectations and with the rising proportion of reappraisals done after 1982, falling RERRs, especially for the projects approved from 1973 to 1976. The data do show low RERRs (13 per cent) for projects approved between 1973 and 1976, but they then rise (to about 16 per cent) for the projects with 1977, 1978, and 1979 vintages. We leave the reader with this puzzle. We do not have figures for appraisal ERRs in the 1980s.

The proportion of unsatisfactory projects is of interest, as are average RERRs. As we have seen, an unsatisfactory rating usually coincides with a RERR of less than 10 per cent, but not invariably so. The average percentage of unsatisfactory operations among those approved in the period 1968–73 was 15 per cent; in the period 1974–79 it was 23 per cent. This deterioration occurred in all regions except Europe, the Middle East, and North Africa. It would be of interest to know whether this can be accounted for by a shift to more difficult sectors (agriculture and rural development) and regions (Africa), or whether there was some general deterioration in project identification and appraisal, again possibly resulting from the McNamara effect.

We turn to Pohl and Mihaljek's (1989) analysis. They regress RERRs on a number of independent variables, including ERRs. Except for regional and sectoral dummies, few of these variables are significant. The simplest equation of all, regressing RERR on ERR alone, gives a coefficient of 0.44 for ERR, which is highly significant, explaining 19 per cent of the variance. Sectoral dummies for transport and urban projects are significant and raise the yield by 7–9 percentage points compared with agriculture. Regional dummies are also significant. Asian projects are better than Europe, the Middle East, North Africa, and Latin America, whereas sub-Saharan Africa trails badly. But of course, project appraisers know which region and what sector they are in. The coefficient for the appraisal ERR is hardly affected.

The essential findings of the analysis, relevant to assessing the benefits of cost–benefit analysis, are that there was an unjustified rise in revealed optimism about project returns in the 1970s; and that the ERR is a highly significant explanatory variable for RERRs, with a coefficient of 0.44, but it explains only about 20 per cent of the variance ($R^2 = 0.19$).

The main conclusion drawn by Pohl and Mihaljek (1989, p. 32) is that:

> cost–benefit and rate of return calculations seem to be most useful in the case of large and capital-intensive investment projects. A sufficiently high minimum rate of return criterion, say 10 percent, will help to screen out large and capital-intensive projects with potentially low rates of return. But further refinements in the methodology, such as allowing for distorted prices resulting from overvalued exchange rates, while intellectually appealing, do not seem to make much difference in practice.

This conclusion is far from clear. Taken literally, it seems to suggest that all shadow pricing is futile and that even financial rates of return should be calculated only for large, capital-intensive projects. Worse, there is nothing in the analysis reported above that has any bearing on the conclusions. There was no analysis relevant to the question of whether refinement of method would improve ERRs (that is, make them better predictors of RERRs), or of whether such improvement would justify its cost.

Pohl and Mihaljek (1989, p. 32) do say that:

> this was brought out by an analysis of industrial projects for which both financial and economic rates of return were available. Appraisal of financial rates of return were just as good a predictor of ex post economic rates of return as ex ante economic rates of return. The adjustments for price distortions seemed to make little difference, at least for projects that had been accepted for World Bank financing.

For this, a statement is hardly enough: supporting evidence needs to be closely considered. It is hard to believe that one can do as well aiming at the wrong target. If so, it seems to be unnecessary to take thought at all. Pohl and Mihaljek's final twelve words should be noted. For industrial projects, the main point of shadow pricing is to spot projects in which financial returns are misleading, say, because of protection. If some of these are successfully rejected, there will be a bias towards some coincidence of financial returns and ERRs.

Taking the figures for pre- and post-project evaluations at face value, it is important to appreciate what the apparently low incidence of association between them is saying. A linear regression of the RERR on the ERR is not appropriate, or at least, it is not to be interpreted in the way one might usually interpret a regression coefficient. To interpret the statistical results reported by Pohl and Mihaljek (1989), we need a properly specified underlying model.

A simple plausible model is that the *ex ante* and *ex post* estimates of rates of return are attempts to assess the true value of the project, both subject to additive errors. (Multiplicative would be better, but Pohl and Mihaljek have used additive, and we are interpreting their results.) We can interpret the regression as revealing the value that is common to the two observations. Write C for the common element of the two evaluations. It is subject to errors u and v, independent of one another, and of C. We then have ERR $= C + u$; RERR $= C + v$.

The regression coefficient of the RERR on the ERR is cov(RERR ERR)/var(ERR), where cov is covariance and var is variance. With this additive model, that is equal to $\text{var}(C)/[\text{var}(C) + \text{var}(u)]$. The regression coefficient therefore shows the proportion of total variability that is due to the common element.

At least, that would be correct if the error, u, were independent of the common element, C. It is not. The common element is made up of the true value of the project and any source of error common to the two appraisals. Because the worst observations in the first round, having rates of return below 10 per cent, are (largely) rejected, there is a negative covariance between the common value and the error u (assuming that the mean return in all projects assessed is above the cutoff value). The regression coefficient is then $\text{var}(C)/[\text{var}(C) + \text{var}(u) + \text{cov}(C, u)]$. This means that the regression coefficient actually underestimates the ratio of the common variance to the error variance.

We are interested in the variance of the true value of the project and the extent to which it seems to be picked up by these observations. We cannot directly tell how much of the common element is the true value and how much is the common sources of error. Because many sources of error (such as utilization estimates and prices) changed greatly between the two evaluations, we believe that the true value is a rather substantial part of the common value. All in all, a regression coefficient of 0.44 for ERR, when regressing RERR on ERR alone in Pohl and Mihaljek's simplest equation, suggests that the variance of the true value of the project may be nearly as large as the variance of error in an evaluation.

The 'proportion of the variance explained' in the regression equation is the product of that regression coefficient and the corresponding one for RERRs. Even allowing for the selection bias, it appears that errors in the reevaluation may not be much less than errors in the initial evaluation. It should be appreciated that the low proportion of variance explained is in fact a compound of the error magnitude at the two evaluations. It is not surprising that it is as low as 20 per cent. That is not in itself evidence of a particularly low common element.

These errors in the project appraisals are substantial, but they are not immense. Taken literally, they are quite good news for the users of project appraisals. We show in the appendix on uncertainty [not here reproduced] that the value of project appraisal can be measured roughly by taking 10 per cent of the standard deviation of true project values times the ratio of that standard deviation to the standard deviation of measurement errors. If the two standard deviations are of about the same magnitude, as seems to be implied by the data, the value of project appraisal is truly substantial.

Several considerations suggest that the data may considerably understate the precision with which projects can be appraised. First, we should not pay excessive attention to the average divergence. Given the World Bank's selection methods, it makes no difference if a project yielding 20 per cent was appraised at 40 per cent. Excessive optimism is likely to be important only if it pushes a bad project over the 10 per cent barrier. One would hope that around that level, appraisals would have been done with greater care. We believe that the association between ERRs and RERRs is greater around these low appraisal levels. More generally, the simple model we have used to interpret the data gives too much weight to outliers.

The data suggest some further observations, comparing the World Bank's experience of evaluations with that of countries for which they are done. Improving the World Bank's portfolio may not improve that of the country. There is the problem of fungibility between project funds and the general budget. The value of project aid has often been called into question over the past forty years. Despite this long history, we do not know of any empirical work devoted to ascertaining first what difference is made to a country's investment by the involvement of donors and lending agencies in project preparation and selection. We do not know how many projects are effectively invented by the World Bank (and whether these were particularly successful or unsuccessful); we do not know what happened to projects the World Bank rejected; and we do not know whether, if carried out, the projects had high or low returns.

It has been repeated ad nauseam that economic appraisal at a late stage very rarely stops a project. It must be applied early on to stop work on the project or to effect improvements in the design of a project that will finally go ahead. If one asks whether such improvements are made—and we have asked this question of a few people in the World Bank, in ODA, and in India's Project Appraisal Division of the Planning Commission—one is always told that they are. But there is no way of assessing the magnitude of this benefit of the appraisal process, which is already incorporated in reported ERRs and helps the borrower even if fungibility were complete.

Thus, we do not know to what extent the high average RERRs on World Bank projects are achieved because the World Bank improves projects or invents good projects, and to what extent they come simply from skimming the cream from the country's own proposals. (Nor do we know whether the World Bank helps the country to achieve a higher-yielding portfolio by convincing it not to go ahead with unpromising ventures the World Bank rejects.)

There is a lot we do not know. There is no doubt, however, that the World Bank's average RERR is high for the projects of the 1970s—about 16 per cent. Of course, as we have pointed out, RERRs are not true *ex post* rates, which may be significantly lower. Even if the true return is several percentage points lower, it would still be above the real foreign borrowing rate. (An ERR calculated using border prices and conversion factors for non-traded goods will be a good approximation to the foreign exchange yield.) This is more than one can say for total investment in many, if not most, developing countries. Because almost all did use their borrowing to support or raise the ratio of investment to GNP, there would be no debt crisis if total investment had yielded even half that of the World Bank-financed investments.

India is a country with no debt crisis because it did not borrow commercially until recent years. India engineered no foreign-debt-supported public investment boom, as did many other countries in which the rise in investment was so rapid that it can only have been hastily planned and executed. But, in work in progress, Joshi and Little (1990) have calculated nevertheless that the return on public sector investment in India over the period 1974–5 to 1984–5 was no more than 6 per cent.[10] The average RERR (both weighted by size of project and unweighted) over roughly the same period for projects in India was very high, about 23 per cent. (Negative returns arbitrarily put at −5 per cent.)[11]

This makes India one of the great stars for World Bank-financed investments, although it is not only Joshi and Little who find the returns to investment in India to be low. It is also notable that the apparent high performance of World Bank investments is not attributable to the World Bank having avoided agriculture, which has low returns in other countries. More than half the projects are agricultural, and even in value terms they amount to about a third of World Bank-financed investment in India, with average returns about as high as in other sectors.

RERRs may be grossly overestimated, the World Bank may be very good at creaming off projects, or the World Bank is very good at creating or improving projects. It is clearly of great importance for World Bank policy to know how much weight to give to these different possibilities. We cannot tell. But if the

[10] Joshi and Little's work is a draft chapter, entitled 'Macroeconomic Management, Investment and Growth in India, 1960–61 to 1984–85', of a contribution to the World Bank research project on macroeconomic policy and growth. The calculation is made at market, not shadow, prices. Recalculation at shadow prices would raise the yield in so far as the benefits from public sector investments are not reflected in public sector value added. This may be considerable. An offset, however, is that a good deal of public sector industrial value added would be even less than it is if calculated at shadow prices. It should also be noted that similar calculations for total manufacturing investment (public and private) show returns of about 10 per cent.

[11] The averages are taken over a total of 68 Indian projects evaluated by the OED for the period 1974–87 for which an RERR was calculated. Lipton and Toye (1990) also found an average RERR of about 23 per cent on 33 projects for which the OED provided them with evaluation documents.

World Bank is good at discovering and improving projects (and rejecting poor projects in countries with limited alternative sources of finance), then there is a strong case for the World Bank to do all it can to teach countries to improve their selection of investments, or to make its influence felt over a greater value of investments than it actually helps to finance. (This should be possible in the case of sectoral loans.) But whatever the value of the World Bank's involvement in projects, including economic appraisal, it remains true that cost–benefit analysis would be much more effective if done in the country. It can then be applied to all large projects, and there is no problem of fungibility.

We have very briefly reviewed above what little we know of the use of cost–benefit analysis for public sector investments in developing countries. In most it is non-existent, and in only a very few is it better than rudimentary. There is, of course, more to planning public sector investment than project appraisal. (In Little and Mirrlees, 1974, we did try to show how the two can, and should, be integrated.) From this wider perspective also, it seems that in only a minority of developing countries is there any coherent and rational control over ministries and other public agencies, with the result that far more projects get started than can be financed without interruption.

The World Bank does not seem to have played a leading role in the promotion of rational public investment planning. Yet there would appear to be room for the World Bank to have a considerable beneficial influence. It is surely an essential part of continuous (sustainable) structural adjustment that public sector investments be well chosen. This applies both at the most central level, where intersectoral choices are required, and at sectoral levels, whether or not sectoral adjustment loans are being made.

For the World Bank to have such an influence, it must have—and be understood to have—the necessary skills. These include a thorough understanding of cost–benefit analysis and shadow pricing. They also include experience of the control of public expenditure.

The declarations of ignorance in this section suggest the need for research on how far the World Bank's activities improve the productivity of investment in the borrowing countries. Because examination of rejected project proposals and what happened to them is essential, and very many projects need to be examined, a deeper analysis than the OED has the resources for is warranted. A pilot study of one cooperative country (if such can be found) could throw much light on the possible value of a wide-ranging study.

5. THE COSTS OF COST–BENEFIT ANALYSIS

We have discussed the benefits of cost–benefit analysis in general, and of shadow pricing in particular, at some length. What are the costs?

No one suggests that industrial or other 'commercial' projects should be approved without even a financial analysis. Nor does anyone suggest that any old road should be approved without a traditional estimate of its benefits in terms of expected vehicle cost savings, time savings, and traffic generation; that an irrigation or settlement project be approved without some estimate of the value of the extra crops expected to be produced.

What more is required for an economic rate of return? For traded goods it is now generally accepted that border prices are to be used. But this is little or no extra work, because the future international prices of such goods will be needed in any case for a financial analysis. Otherwise present practice merely involves multiplying some of the rows by the standard conversion factor (SCF), adding up, and recalculating the ERR and present value—a few minutes' work at most for the project analyst on a personal computer. The country economist supplies the SCF. This could take some time if conscientiously done, but, knowing how often it has been 'calculated' as 0.8, the economist may get away with this and just write a memo saying 'SCF = 0.8'.

The benefits, as we have argued above, are immensely greater than the costs of applying these procedures. They would justify much more extensive work, both on national parameters and on the specifics of the individual project. This cost–benefit analysis at least seems to give a very clear answer. It is less easy to generalize about the value of refining the appraisal (as opposed to the use of simplifications and often justifiable shortcuts) and about the loss from cutting short an analysis when important aspects have not been adequately allowed for.

6. THE TRADE-OFF BETWEEN COMPLEXITY AND RELIABILITY

Here, we comment briefly on the value of refining calculations at both the national and the sectoral or project level.

National parameters

How sophisticated should be the analysis that goes into the calculation of national parameters, such as discount rates and shadow wage rates? There is no very short answer. Most of the national parameters calculated by the World Bank are out of date. The IDB and the Development and Project Planning Centre, Bradford University, have calculated recent sets for a number of countries, whether for their own use or at the country's request. (The introduction of Little and Mirrlees's methods to China with a set of national parameters is still a victim of Tiananmen Square.) Where do the priorities lie? Given the World Bank's policy of using a single accounting rate of interest, unvarying by country and time, there may seem to be little point in estimating this parameter. (The rate is almost always 10 per cent, but 12 per cent is used for a few cases.) Yet, in theory, variations should be one of the main responses to changing external or exogenous conditions. There is a case for more serious attention to these issues.

The shadow wage rate, or the conversion factor from which it is derived, is a parameter that can vary substantially by region, and for which local information specific to the project should influence the figure used. Here, we consider its estimation at the national level.

Employment is one way in which the benefits of a public sector project 'leak' into the private sector. This arises when the increased demand for labour raises wages or when the wage paid is above the supply price of labour. Part of the resultant increased private income is a cost to the economy if, as we have insisted, it is worth less than public income. Given this, the calculation of a shadow wage (the real cost of employing someone) becomes very complicated. It is hard to estimate not only the loss of output elsewhere but also the increase in private income.

Regarding modern sector urban wages, there is a consensus that the shadow wage is probably not very different from the wage paid, despite the presence of a wage gap between the 'organized' and 'informal' sectors. Given that modern sector projects are also capital-intensive, it is reasonable to assume that the actual wage is as good an approximation of the shadow wage as can be found.

Research in recent years has tended to suggest that rural labour markets, and informal sector markets generally, are active and that the wage paid is probably close to the marginal product. With some large-scale agricultural projects, however, wages in the area may well be raised, with some loss of producers' surplus and some gain in private incomes. Some agricultural projects have foundered as a result of lack of knowledge of, or enquiry about, labour supply conditions. Such effects as those suggested above certainly need to be investigated, whether or not they are formally used to quantify a shadow wage rate (SWR).

Sectoral costs and benefits

Specific conversion factors for the use of important non-traded goods were regarded as an essential part of the Little–Mirrlees or Squire–van der Tak methodologies. But we also need to consider the numeraire value of the outputs of projects in these sectors. We take power as an example, mention transport and construction more briefly, and must bypass the important subject of irrigation for lack of space. Public utilities (defined as public enterprises for whose output little or no charge is made) present special problems.

Power

Perhaps the most important non-traded good is power. The World Bank has power projects in most countries, and power is an input into all other projects—occasionally a very large input.

We have seen that the output of power projects was never normally valued in the Squire–van der Tak manner. This was reasonable. It would be absurd to calculate an ERR for every power station financed. The ideal procedure is to obtain agreement with the country on an appropriate tariff system. Normally this will be based on long-run marginal cost (LRMC) at accounting prices. When the tariff is in place, demand at those prices must be estimated and should be satisfied (obviously by the least-social-cost mode). Sectoral loans can then be made, and there is no need to calculate a power conversion factor for other projects. There is an equilibrium, and the price is already 'right'. Unfortunately, things get more complex when there is serious excess supply or demand at a price equal to LRMC (which still needs to be calculated). There may then be a good case for charging less or more than LRMC, as the accounting price diverges from LRMC for several—even many—years. When there is excess demand, as in India, the value of power is its marginal product, not its marginal cost. However, the stipulation of serious excess supply or demand at a price equal to LRMC at least makes it clear whether any investment in power is justified.

Construction and transport

A construction conversion factor may be desirable on the ground that construction enters importantly into many projects, and that it may be very labour-intensive. If the latter is the case, a lot in turn depends on whether SWRs should be used. This could make a construction conversion factor significantly different from (lower than) the SCF.

Construction is of course virtually the only input into road programmes, which are a large component of World Bank lending in several countries. Sectoral lending seems to make good sense for roads, where a component of an ongoing programme that can be separately and validly assessed may be impossible to identify. As with power, the World Bank may then want to assure itself that road programmes are designed and assessed according to its own guidelines (noting that roads are public utilities to the extent that there is little or no cost recovery; see below). It would then, and only then, be willing to lend on a sectoral, and not a project, basis.

Transport costs also enter into almost all projects. Although transport is non-traded, its use may have quite large foreign exchange implications, making a special conversion factor desirable.

The extent to which multiple conversion factors should be calculated by the World Bank depends on the country (how distorted are the relative prices of non-traded goods?), on the sectoral composition and size of the World Bank's lending programmes, and on the extent to which the country itself is willing to adopt good cost–benefit analysis on a sectoral (even if not a countrywide) basis. If a set of consistent conversion factors calculated by input–output procedures is not available, the project analyst can often make a good guess at one that is particularly relevant, by back-of-the-envelope methods.

Public utilities

Public utilities are special. Their costs are (generally) borne by the public sector, whereas a large part of the benefit accrues to the private sector.[12] A transfer to the private sector occurs when, as often happens with electricity, gas, and water supply, there is no full cost recovery.

We have argued that public income in most developing countries is worth more than private income because of the administrative costs of taxation and the absence of anything even approximating a general lump-sum subsidy, so that taxation is necessarily distorting at the margin in the relevant sense. These considerations are sometimes strengthened when most saving comes through the public budget. The argument for assigning a greater weight to public than private income holds even if no distributional weights are acknowledged. In brief, increasing the public sector deficit is costly, and projects that do increase it should be penalized.

As we have already mentioned, differential weighting of public and private income is ignored in cost–benefit analysis done by the World Bank and other agencies. We would urge that the fiscal effect of all projects should be estimated and included in appraisal reports. As far as possible, this should include indirect effects, such as changes in tax payments by recipients of additional income. If that is done, it will be clear how the present value of a project can depend on the way it is financed. Public utility pricing policy and project appraisal results are inseparable. If, as we suspect, public income can have a much greater value than private income, the impact of pricing on the value of the project could be very substantial. Estimation of the administrative and distortional costs of taxation in developing countries is a matter on which more research would be valuable.

7. CONCLUSIONS

Social cost–benefit analysis is not as widely, as well, or as effectively practised as its expected net value might lead one to hope and expect. We have covered, or at least touched on, many aspects of its theory, practice, and effects. We have claimed that much in the rules we collected and prescribed in 1969 and 1974 has survived analytical scrutiny, that these procedures are capable of being used effectively, and that many important aspects of them have been neglected by project evaluators. We have found that the extent to which they are used and have real influence is not great, even in the World Bank. We have examined some of the data appearing to show considerable randomness in the evaluations performed within the World Bank. We went on to consider the bearing of the very consid-

[12] This section owes much to Squire (1989).

erable uncertainty that has been shown to attend project appraisal upon the value of the appraisal activity itself. We argue that the value is indeed probably diminished by that uncertainty but is nevertheless very large.

In aggregate, much of the investment in developing countries has had very low returns. This is evident in the low growth of many of these countries during the 1980s. Project appraisal is an essential part of the business of avoiding these mistakes in the future. Good project appraisal is done by people with their own incentives, within organizations that, wittingly or not, set these incentives. Both environments of project appraisal, the intellectual and the political–organizational, are keys to the quality of selection overall. This needs to be most seriously considered by those who manage and create these environments.

References

Balassa, B. (1976), 'The "Effects Method" of Project Evaluation', *Oxford Bulletin of Economics and Statistics*, 38: 219–31.

Ballard, C. L., Shoven, J.B., and Whalley, J. (1985), 'General Equilibrium Computations of the Marginal Welfare Costs of Taxes in the United States', *American Economic Review*, 75: 128–38.

Bhagwati, J. N., and Srinivasan, T. N. (1978), 'Shadow Prices for Project Selection in the Presence of Distortions: Effective rates of protection and domestic resource costs', *Journal of Political Economy*, 86: 97–116.

Corden, W. M. (1974), *Trade Policy and Economic Welfare*. Oxford: Clarendon Press.

Development Assistance Committee, OECD (1987), *Review of Project Appraisal Criteria and Procedures*, (87)11) Paris: OECD.

——(1988), *Principles for Project Appraisal*. Paris: OECD.

Diamond, P.A., and Mirrlees, J. A. (1976), 'Private Constant Returns and Public Shadow Prices', *Review of Economic Studies*, 43: 41–7.

Drèze, J., and Stern, N. H. (1987), 'The Theory of Cost–Benefit Analysis'. In A. Auerbach and M. Feldstein (eds.), *Handbook of Public Economics*. Amsterdam: North-Holland.

Harberger, A. C. (1972), *Project Evaluation: Collected Papers*. London: Macmillan.

Henry, C. (1974), 'Option Values in the Economics of Irreplaceable Assets', *Review of Economic Studies*, 41(S): 89–104.

Joshi, V., and Little, I. M. D. (1990), 'Macroeconomic Management, Investment, and Growth in India, 1960–61 to 1984–85'. Oxford University, processed.

Lal, D. (1980), *Prices for Planning: Towards the reform of Indian planning*. London: Heinemann.

Layard, R. (ed.) (1972), *Cost–Benefit Analysis: Selected readings* Harmondsworth: Penguin.

Lipton, M., and Toye, J. (1990), *Does Aid Work in India? A country study of the impact of official development assistance*. London: Routledge.

Little, I. M. D., and Mirrlees, J. A. (1969), *Manual of Industrial Project Analysis*, ii. Paris: OECD Development Centre.

——(1974), *Project Appraisal and Planning*. London: Heinemann.

ODA (Overseas Development Administration) (1988), *Appraisal of Projects in Developing Countries*, 3rd edn. London: HMSO.

Pohl, G., and Mihaljek, D. (1989), 'Project Evaluation in Practice: Uncertainty at the World Bank'. Economic Advisory Staff, World Bank, Washington, DC, processed.

Scott, M. F. G., MacArthur, J. M., and Newbery, D. M. G. (1976), *Project Appraisal in Practice*. London: Heinemann.

Sieper, E. (1981), 'The Structure of General Equilibrium Shadow Pricing Rules for a Tax-Distorted Economy'. Unpublished paper, Department of Economics, Australian National University, Canberra, processed.

Squire, L. (1989), 'Project Evaluation in Theory and Practice'. In H. Chenery and T. N. Srinivasan (eds.), *Handbook of Development Economics*, ii. Amsterdam: North-Holland.

——and van der Tak, H. G. (1975), *Economic Analysis of Projects*. Baltimore: Johns Hopkins University Press.

Srinivasan, T. N. (1982), 'General Equilibrium Theory, Project Evaluation, and Economic Development'. In M. Gersovitz and others (eds.), *The Theory and Experience of Economic Development*. London: George Allen & Unwin.

UNIDO (UN Industrial Development Organization) (1972), *Guidelines for Project Evaluation*. Project Formulation and Evaluation Series, no. 2. New York: United Nations.

11

Trade and Industrialization Revisited (1994)

1. LSS AND SUBSEQUENT EVENTS

In 1970, the book *Industry and Trade in Some Developing Countries* by myself, Tibor Scitovsky, and Maurice Scott was published (referred to henceforth as LSS). It exposed the bad effects of the import substitution policies which had been the prevailing mode of industrialization in developing countries for a long time. It advocated the elimination of quotas and a uniform tariff of 10–15 per cent. The exchange rate should be adjusted to ensure that exports were competitive. If any industry was, exceptionally, to receive more promotion than that implied by the low tariff, this should be by some form of subsidization which should not exceed another 10–15 per cent of domestic value added. LSS is, I believe, still the most quoted work on the subject.[1] It was quite closely related in theory to the methods of cost–benefit analysis proposed by Little and Mirrlees (1974) (referred to henceforth as LM).

While the influence of LSS on the development literature was extensive, neither it nor LM would seem to have had any influence whatever on the policies of most developing countries for a decade. This is, perhaps, the normal fate of policy-oriented books. Korea and Taiwan continued with the export policies they had already initiated. Admittedly, these policies eliminated the bias against exports inherent in protective policies, a bias that LSS had castigated. But Korea, and to a lesser extent Taiwan, also reverted in the 1970s to the selective promotion of some mainly capital-intensive industries (referred to as Heavy and Chemical Industries (HCI) in Korea) producing tradables. In Korea, towards the end of the 1970s, it is possible that LSS played some part in the modification of the HCI drive. But only in Chile was the policy of a low uniform tariff, as advocated by LSS, wholly adopted. Chile has stuck to this policy.

Elsewhere in the developing world, the new availability of international finance at very low interest rates during the 1970s resulted in public sector investment booms. Fifteen out of eighteen countries studied in Little *et al.* (1993) experienced

This article, based on the Iqbal Memorial Lecture, first appeared in the *Pakistan Development Review*, 33 (Winter 1994). Permission to reproduce is gratefully acknowledged.

[1] It was followed by Bhagwati (1978) and Krueger (1987), works which further explored the relationship of trade regimes and development, and used the same comparative country research as LSS.

these booms. Some of them resulted in almost incredible rises over periods of two to four years in the ratio of public investment to GDP. In Morocco and Nigeria, the ratio more than trebled; it doubled (approximately in Côte d'Ivoire, Mexico, Pakistan, Thailand, and Sri Lanka.

Poor choice of investments, with little or no attention paid to their ability to earn or save the foreign exchange needed to service the loans, was a major contributory cause of the debt crisis that ensued at the beginning of the 1980s. More generally, inward looking policies combined with heavy foreign borrowing was a recipe for disaster. Eight of the eighteen countries studied both experienced severe recessions in the early 1980s *and* rescheduled their debt.

I shall later be paying particular attention to East Asia. None of the three East Asian countries studied in Little *et al.* (1993)—Korea, Thailand, and Indonesia—rescheduled. They remained credit-worthy. Korea and Indonesia had brief recessions in 1980 and 1982 respectively, but after a few years recovered famously. All three showed flexibility of macroeconomic policies. The heavy industry investment booms were cut back, Korea in particular reverting to much less selective investment policies. All devalued, ensuring competitive real exchange rates, and liberalized imports. Their recoveries were based on very rapidly expanding exports of manufactures—over 20 per cent per annum from 1982 to 1989 in dollar terms. These countries certainly moved in the 1980s towards LSS policies.

The same is widely true elsewhere, the main exceptions being the countries of the French franc zone, which eschew flexible exchange rates.[2] Most developing countries have adopted flexible exchange rates, and have reduced import quotas and tariffs. Most also go some way towards offsetting the anti-export bias implicit in their remaining protection. Even India, the arch-protectionist, has been making major reforms since 1991. Thus, during the 1980s there has been a strong movement towards LSS policies. Only Chile is exactly there, and has been for a decade or more. But Korea, Taiwan, and Singapore are virtually there, after a decade of slowly reducing the remaining protection of their domestic markets. Hong Kong, of course, has always been a free-trader.

This is not to say that the policy-makers who may have absorbed the logic of LSS when they were 20–25 years old are now in power and putting into effect what they then learned. More probably, the recasting of economic policies in favour of exports, and higher trading, have occurred mainly as a result of the debt crisis. Countries were more or less forced to improve the current account of their balance of payments. This could not be done by reducing imports, without creating recession. Only by increasing exports could they avoid a recession, or climb out of one. Every cloud has a silver lining.

After this highly condensed account of the course of economic development since 1970, I turn to another question. Has anything occurred, either in the realm of ideas or in the experience of development, in the past twenty-five years to

[2] But the CFA franc was devalued by 50 per cent in December 1993.

make one want to modify the guidelines of LSS (or LM), and hence to question the wisdom of the movement towards liberal policies in the 1980s? This is no empty question, for there are some strident critics of what they term the neoclassical model (which I am supposed to embrace with blind fervour), who call for 'a new paradigm'.

2. NEW IDEAS

Perhaps the most important advance since 1970 in the realm of ideas is the so-called New Growth Theory, associated in the USA mainly with the names of Romer and Lucas. The distinguishing feature of the new growth theory is that technological progress is endogenized, and not left as a residual (or error) in growth equations. As yet this theory has hardly been applied to developing countries, though there is a recent article, in which Lucas (1993) is mainly concerned to modify growth theory so as to permit episodes of *miraculous* growth such as he believes to have occurred in Korea. Since this article is not closely relevant to my main theme I shall pass it by (though his conclusions are sympathetic to uninhibited trading). But I shall be using an earlier version of the New Growth Theory, attributable to Scott (1989), below.

The notion of asymmetrical information, attributed to J. Stiglitz, has been of importance. It has become clear that the concept of perfect competition cannot be applied to most credit markets. Lenders will often ration credit rather than let the interest rate rise to clear the market, because of the possibility that high interest rates result in adverse selection. Under certain circumstances the peculiarities of credit markets may make it advisable to cap interest rates.[3] This argument has been used by some writers to justify credit allocation by government, and indeed to attribute miraculous growth in Korea and Taiwan partly to such allocation. But it does not follow that it is better for government to direct the rationing of credit by commercial banks rather than to allow them and other lenders to be guided by expected profitability in arranging their portfolios. This, however, seems to be presumed by those authors who see an alliance of government, the banks, and very large companies (the *chaebol* in Korea) as analogous to intra-firm planning in large companies, basing themselves on recent industrial organization literature. There is no doubt that in Korea credit allocation was influenced by such tripartite consultation, but those who stress this feature of the economy, calling it 'government-led internal organization' (GLIO), offer no evidence that the results were good, let alone better than what the banks would have done in pursuit of profits.[4] GLIO theory cannot be applied to Taiwan, for there are no

[3] See McKinnon (1990).

[4] See Yoon and Hellman (1993). I have elsewhere questioned whether the inevitable departure from perfect competition that is to be found in most credit markets should be called market

very large private companies in Taiwan and the government had no policy of close consultation with private firms, or credit allocation. (Nor, of course, can it be applied to Hong Kong.)

Next, we have to consider the 'New Trade Theory'. It points out that even a small country, which cannot generally affect the world price of commodities, may nevertheless by imposing a tariff be able to secure a reduction in the c.i.f. price when the foreign supplier is a monopolist. (It is perhaps contestable as to whether there is anything new in this argument.) Paul Krugman, one of the main progenitors of the New Trade Theory, after admitting the difficulties of realizing any advantage from this theoretical possibility, has written: 'Imagine a small country with a highly competent and honest administration. Would it be unreasonable for such a country to centralise its purchases of a few commodities when we know that large buyers are able to negotiate substantial price discounts?[5] India, which in terms of economic theory is a small country, did just that, though for more than a few commodities. I know that a former chairman of the Indian State Trading Corporation, a friend of mine, would regard any claim that India thereby got its imports more cheaply as laughable.

The second main line of argument of the New Trade Theorists is known as 'strategic trade policy'. It is held that government by some subsidization may play a role in securing oligopolistic or monopolistic rents for their country that might otherwise accrue to other countries. It can apply only where a very few firms compete for the world market. The obvious example is large passenger aircraft. Nuclear reactors may be another. The UK has practised strategic trade policy in these two fields since 1945, some forty years before the idea entered the trade-theoretical literature. In civil aircraft the UK tried many times to jump ahead of the USA and earn the supposed rents of being first or early in the field. This policy started with the Princess Flying Boat, the idea being that one could only reach across some long distances by landing on water (on Lake Victoria or Nyasa, in the case of flights from Europe to South Africa). Then came the first jet-liner, the ill-fated Comet. Then came the VC10, a fine aircraft hopelessly eclipsed by the far more economical Boeing 707. Then the Concorde, another beautiful folly whose development was hugely subsidized by the poor British taxpayer. It was the same with nuclear energy. The UK was early in the field, spending huge sums on the wrong technology expecting to monopolize the world market:[6] I do not know that we have exported a single nuclear power plant. Beware strategic trade policy!

failure. It should perhaps be noted that the idea of comparing economic management in Korea to that of a large corporation is not new. To quote 'The management of the Korean economy resembles the operation of a business corporation with the leaders of the Government and of private business sitting in the management board and jointly deciding the strategic choices, and the execution of these choices' (Datta-Chaudhuri, 1981). For a critique of credit allocation policy in Korea, see Dailami and Kim (1991).

[5] Krugman (1989).

[6] British losses incurred in developing Concorde and the Advanced Gas-Cooled Reactor have been estimated by Henderson (1977).

3. INFANT INDUSTRY REVIVED

The strategic trade idea is related to the infant industry argument. Economies of scale or learning by doing are closely involved: otherwise the premiss of only a few suppliers for the world market would not be realized. It is essentially the infant industry argument that is invoked by recent 'revisionists', the most influential of whom seem to be Amsden (1989) and Wade (1990). They claim that government intervention, especially in the form of selective protection or other promotion of industries, was an essential element in the success of Korea and Taiwan, a fact that was wilfully ignored by such neoclassical writers as myself. The infant industry argument is not necessarily linked to exporting. But these and other authors who favour government intervention in industrial development feel the need to dissociate themselves from the inward-looking protection policies pursued by almost all developing country governments until recently. They therefore stress the need to achieve *international competitiveness* (presumably without subsidies). Since they also stress 'heavy', increasing-return, and high-technology industries, where learning by doing is important, it seems that their arguments are closely akin to those of strategic trade policy. Indeed, one of the industries in which Korea's achievement is most praised is shipbuilding, and Korea and Japan are now much the largest suppliers of big ships to the international market. So are Korea's ships great rent-earners, or are they more like British aircraft? I shall be suggesting the latter.

Although the subject of transfer of technology does not involve any new theoretical ideas, and has always been part of the development literature, I should note that it has attracted a lot of empirical work since 1970. This too is closely related to the infant industry argument. Westphal, for instance, has argued that developing countries starting up an industry that is new for them may lag far behind in total factor productivity, even though the 'best practice' technology can be imported. It may require heavy protection or subsidization for as much as a decade before 'international competitiveness' is achieved. The cost of this may be so great that a country should not think in terms of thus protecting or promoting more than a very few lines of activity (Westphal, 1982, p. 267).

The presumed growth in productivity is a necessary condition for public promotion as an infant industry, but it is not sufficient. It also has to be shown that eventually the returns will be high enough to offset the decade of losses, and that the private entrepreneur for one reason or another cannot or will not take advantage of this. Westphal accepts this and recognizes that the proper test is the social rate of return. Elsewhere he (with Howard Pack) has written of Korea: 'Our knowledge of the evidence leads us to conclude that the average social rate of return on investments in selectively promoted infant industries has been relatively high if the most serious mistakes made in pursuit of objectives unrelated to market performance are omitted from the valuation.'[7] Presumably the main

[7] Pack and Westphal (1986).

unrelated objective was increased self-reliance in the manufacture of armaments. One does not know what investments he would omit on the grounds of being related to non-market objectives. Nor do the authors tell us what *ex post* social cost–benefit analyses of promoted and other investments constitute the evidence referred to. I shall later give some evidence on social returns, and some guesses.

The revisionists give no evidence of high social returns. They seem to think that it is enough to show (*a*) that there was a good deal of specific intervention by government in Korea and Taiwan in favour of particular industries, and (*b*) that some of these promoted industries survive, and export. They also, like the technology buffs, point to the rapid acquisition of technological expertise in these countries attributing at least some of this to government institutions. This seems to support the idea of infants growing up. Apart from this, and appeals to market imperfections, the revisionists, especially Wade, try to buttress their case by entirely unjustified and easily refutable attacks on some 'neoclassical' writers for falsifying the development story of Korea and Taiwan by ignoring protection and other forms of government intervention.[8]

4. KOREA AND TAIWAN: THE ISSUES

The reader cannot but have noticed the close focus on Korea, and to a lesser extent Taiwan, on the part of those who want to prove the value of industrial policy, that is, of having government choose industries to develop, while implementing this policy either by creating the industries in the public sector or by using incentives or guarantees to secure their development in the private sector. The reasons for this obsession with Korea are clear. The Korean government directed the process of industrialization to a greater extent than any of the other fast-growing Far Eastern economies, though her rate of growth of GNP per head has been a little lower in the period 1960–85 than those of Hong Kong,

[8] I give in refutation three quotations from Little (1979). The first two concern Taiwan, and the third Korea.

'The effect of the new policies [late 1950s and early 1960s] was not to create *laissez faire* conditions for the whole of industry, let alone the whole economy. They created a kind of dual economy in which exports, but only exports, could be manufactured under virtually free trade conditions—a policy soon copied by Korea.'

'Although import controls were being reduced [1963–73] there was no reform of the tariff structure, which remained, potentially, highly and erratically protective.'

'The degree of planning in Korea is probably greater than in Taiwan. There the Economic Planning Board controls the budget, unlike the Economic Planning Council in Taiwan. Taiwan has no equivalent to the Korean Development Institute, a parastatal body concerned with economic research and planning. There is the same promotion of capital-intensive intermediate industry. Import controls have probably been more extensive, still persist, and are used selectively to promote favoured domestic industries such as recently the machine tool industry . . . '

Other quotations from such authors as M. F.G. Scott and G. Ranis could be adduced.

Singapore, and Taiwan.[9] However, many other countries directed the process of industrialization through protection and in other ways, to a greater extent than Korea; indeed, until recently this is arguably true of almost all developing countries, perhaps most especially India, and it is, of course, true of all the ex-Communist countries. It is now hardly controversial that these policies retarded growth with no countervailing advantage in terms of equity, independence, or any other objective. So logic seems to suggest that the proper question to ask is why Korea succeeded with policies that failed elsewhere.

Some commentators do indeed claim to give reasons why industrial policy in the form of protection and subsidization was beneficial in Korea (and Taiwan) but not elsewhere. They all perceive in Korea some facet of their own speciality—be it credit, trade, industrial organization, or technology—that suggests market failure and a role for government leadership. They do not question the proposition that industrial policy was successful. To quote Wade (1990, pp. 305–6), 'the balance of presumption must be that government industrial policies, including sectoral ones, helped more than hindered. To argue otherwise is to suppose that economic performance would have been still more exceptional with less intervention *which is simply less plausible than the converse*.' Since the less interventionist Hong Kong, Singapore, and Taiwan grew faster than Korea, it is unclear why Wade thinks it simply less plausible that less intervention would have been better, given also the widespread failure of government industrial policies elsewhere. I find it simply more plausible that Korea grew fast despite its industrial policies, than because of them. I shall be giving some positive reasons for this view later.

Thus, it is claimed that those who have ascribed Korea's or Taiwan's rapid growth largely to the reforms around 1960, which undeniably led to the rapid development of labour-intensive low-technology industry and exports, a development right in line with the Heckscher–Ohlin explanation of comparative advantage (a scarcity of capital and abundance of labour), wore blinkers, and neglected the role of government in creating comparative advantage.

Very few economists now contest the view that the reforms which resulted in the removal of the bias against exports were of great importance, and that the rapid growth in exports was in large measure the cause of the rapid growth in output. What is at issue is partly the extent to which some export industries were more favoured than others, whether by protection of the home market, or by subsidies, or by superior export incentives, but mainly about whether such discrimination between sectors was beneficial for growth or welfare.

On the first point, the revisionists suggest that the government's purposeful distortion of the market has been large and perhaps not even much less than in many other developing countries. The evidence seems to be against this view at least for the early 1970s. For 1973, Lal and Rajapatirana (1987), calculated

[9] See World Bank (1993, fig. 2).

accounting ratios (essentially ratios of import or export prices to local prices) for 56 traded commodities in Korea. The mean ratio was 0.883 with a standard deviation of 0.178. For India, a similar calculation gave a figure of 0.675 with a standard deviation of 0.294. This indicates both higher protection in India, and greater variability of protection. Balassa's figures for effective protection show relatively low rates for both Korea and Taiwan (Balassa, 1982). Howard Pack, reviewing the evidence in the case of both Korea and Taiwan, refers to 'the relatively low variance in protection across sectors' (Pack, 1992*b*, p. 296). In the case of Taiwan, he writes 'Thus old and new sectors grew because of relatively neutral incentive policies, new ones also benefiting from some promotional measures' (Pack, 1992*a*, p. 83); and again, 'Anecdotal evidence collected by Wade (1990) and often cited in journalistic accounts suggest that in some selected sectors effective rates of protection have continued to be very high up to the present time. The absence of systematic evidence precludes analysing the possible anomaly of rapid and efficient growth in sectors that have continued to be protected' (Park, 1992*a*, p. 84). Presumably 'up to the present time' must mean, say, 1987 or 1988, since Wade's book was published in 1990. One might add that in very recent years, that is in the 1990s, it seems that there is very little protection left in either country.

The precise degree to which some industrial sectors were protected or subsidized relative to others does not perhaps matter very much. No one doubts that such discrimination existed in these two countries. That being the case, one can search for evidence as to whether, first, the relatively highly promoted sectors expanded faster than others, and secondly, if so, whether such expansion was beneficial for the growth of GNP per head. *The East Asian Miracle* (World Bank, 1993) (henceforth the *Miracle* for short) seeks to answer the above two questions, and hence to establish whether industrial policy made an important contribution, or indeed any contribution, to the supposedly miraculous growth of the high performing Asian economies (HPAEs), as the *Miracle* terms them.

5. IS THERE A MIRACLE?

Before we examine the *Miracle*'s argument concerning the possible contribution of industrial policy to miraculous growth, we logically need to establish whether there was anything miraculous about East Asian Growth.

The HPAEs have grown exceptionally rapidly, from about 1958–73 in the case of Japan, and from about 1965–89 or later in the case of the other seven. If, however, this high growth can be attributed to very high ratios of investment to GDP and a very rapid growth in the quality and quantity of the labour input, that is to conventional inputs, then there is nothing very mysterious. There would be no need to posit superior industrial policy. What would need to be explained is how very high levels of investment, education, and training could be achieved. However, if this is *not* the case, then the enquiry is opened up to more difficult and elusive factors, such as what governs the efficiency of investment, and the allocation and use of resources more generally. The *Miracle* does have a good deal to say about levels of savings and investment, and education and training, but it also seeks to establish that these conventional inputs do not explain everything. This it does in two ways.

First, it does a 113-country cross-economy regression analysis of real per capita income growth (1960–85) on the following five variables: (1) relative GDP to that of the USA in 1960—this is a '*catch-up*' variable, introduced on the assumption that the poorest countries have the greatest opportunities to grow, by copying the methods and techniques used, or once used, by the richer countries; (2) primary school enrolment in 1960; (3) secondary school enrolment in 1960; (4) growth of population; (5) the average investment ratio to GDP.[10] The resulting coefficients are then applied to the same variables for the HPAEs. It is found that, except for Hong Kong (44 per cent), between 60 and 87 per cent of growth is explained. This compares with a R^2 of 0.43 for the whole sample. On this basis, it could be said (but is not) that there is *relatively* little that is not explained by the growth of capital, by labour inputs, and by a rise in the quality of the labour force. (The educational variables are, presumably, meant to be proxies for the latter.)

However, it is argued that little of the *difference* of growth between the HPAEs and the countries of Latin America (17 per cent) or Africa south of the Sahara (36 per cent) is explained by differences in the variables. This suggests (though it is not said—after all, the authors want to explain the Far Eastern 'miracle') that what most needs explanation is the relatively poor performance of Latin America, and the extremely poor performance of Africa south of the Sahara (where a good many countries had *negative* growth, despite positive investment and often quite high expenditure on education).

However, I do not believe one can put much trust in this regression. For many of the 113 countries, the figures for *all* of the variables must be extremely unreliable. Nor do they all measure what is wanted. Thus, 'growth of population', even if it means 'growth of the economically active population', is a poor measure of actual labour input, since average hours worked per annum can change markedly. More important, perhaps, primary and secondary school enrolments in 1960 can hardly be considered to indicate relative improvements in the quality of the labour force from 1960 to 1985 which is what is wanted. Although primary school enrolment turned out to be highly significant, it is not clear what this is telling us, especially as recorded primary school enrolments may bear little relation to the numbers that complete primary schooling or even a year of it. For instance, the 90 per cent primary school enrolment recorded for India in World

[10] See table 1.8 of the *Miracle*. The variables are not well defined. The table reads 'growth of population' and the text, 'growth of economically active population'. Presumably the latter is intended as a crude measure of labour input. It is not stated whether the investment variable is gross or net.

Bank data is a gross exaggeration of the quantity and quality of primary schooling. It is not surprising that the fit of the equation is poor ($R^2 = 0.35$). Given these weaknesses, I am not sure that any significance should be attached to the different extents to which individual country performances differ from those predicted by this regression.

Secondly, there is an analysis of total factor productivity (TFP), or, in other words, of the residual left after 'explaining' growth by the stock of capital, the stock of 'educational attainment', and the growth of the labour force,[11] the coefficients of these explanatory variables having calculated from a Cobb–Douglas cross-country (87 countries) production function. The coefficient for capital was very low for the whole sample. Since this result was strongly affected by the thirteen developing countries with negative growth, the production function was re-estimated on the basis of the high-income countries only.

The coefficients thus calculated were then applied to the eight HPAEs. The results are shown in Table 1.

TABLE 1. Total Factor Productivity Growth from *The Asian Miracle*[a]

Countries	Calculated from the full sample (87 economies)	Calculated from the high-income sample
Hong Kong	3.6	2.4
Japan	3.5	1.4
Taiwan	3.8	1.3
Thailand	2.5	0.5
Korea	3.1	0.2
Singapore	1.2	−3.0
Malaysia	1.1	−1.3
Indonesia	1.3	−0.8

[a] World Bank (1993).

M. FG. Scott has cogently criticized the use of the conventional capital stock concept in such calculations of TFP, and the same remarks as made earlier about the regression apply to the measurement of labour inputs and to the general reliability and comparability of the figures for 87 countries. I cannot comment on the measure of 'educational attainment' (which presumably stands for the human capital stock), not having seen the source given. The large difference between the two columns also suggests that these estimates of TFP are worth little. With the full sample, the coefficients of the three explanatory variables were: capital, 0.18;

[11] The reference for the capital stock is Nehru and Dhareshwan (1993), and for 'educational attainment', Barro and Lee (1993).

educational attainment, 0.15; and labour input, 0.67. With the high-income sample they were 0.40, 0.27, and 0.33. Since the inclusion in the full sample of countries with positive investment and negative growth makes no sense, it has to be presumed that the second set of estimates, however bad, is more indicative of 'normal' elasticities of output, and therefore that the second column of figures for TFP growth is to be preferred to the first column. It should be noted that the figure for Korea is 0.2 per cent. The unweighted average is 0.1 per cent. It therefore seems misleading to state 'The final outstanding characteristics of the HPAEs is their rapid productivity growth' (*Miracle*, 1993, p. 46). This could be justified only by taking the 2.5 per cent mean of the first column. I am not sure that TFP means anything more positive than simply 'error of estimate', but I am quite sure that no significance should be attached to TFP figures derived from a cross-country Cobb–Douglas production function with observations of ill-measured variables taken from countries ranging from the USA to the least developed countries with the most unreliable statistics.

The upshot is that I am not sure whether there has been a miracle (in the sense explained). We know of course that there are huge differences in growth among developing countries that cannot be explained by differences in investment—the extreme examples are those with negative growth and positive investment. But it is not clear that returns to investment (or education) have been exceptionally high in the HPAEs *relative to the richer countries*, which did not, of course, suffer the debt crisis and deep recessions that plagued many developing countries (but none of the HPAEs) in the 1980s.

I shall return to the estimation of investment returns after describing the *Miracle*'s attempt to assess the value of industrial policy.

6. THE INDUSTRIAL POLICY FINDINGS OF THE *MIRACLE*

Despite the above criticism, we now accept for the sake of argument the claims that growth was miraculous. It therefore becomes a possible hypothesis that the miracle was in part due to the industrial policies pursued. First, it is asked whether the policies were effective.

Did promoted industries grow faster than might have been expected? Consider the pattern of development in Japan, Hong Kong, Korea, and Singapore as compared with 'normal' patterns based on GDP per head and size (in terms of population).[12] Two sectors (out of nine)—textiles and clothing, and metal products and machinery—stand out as super-normal in their *shares* of GDP, in all four. The super-normality of the share of textiles and clothing increased from around 1970 (1963 in the case of Japan) to around 1990 in all four countries, while that

[12] The norms are taken from Syrquin and Chenery (1989).

of metals and machinery rose only in the case of Korea. The typically 'heavy' sectors—chemicals, non-metallic minerals, and base metals—were at or below normal at both dates in all four countries, the only exception being basic metals in Korea in 1988.[13]

In the period considered, textiles and clothing were not especially promoted. Korea at least was trying to reduce its dependence on exports of textiles and clothing. However, some elements in the metal products and machinery sector were promoted. There is some ambiguity in terms of capital intensity. Some parts of textiles (man-made fibres) are capital-intensive, and some parts of metal products and machinery are very labour-intensive (e.g. the assembly of calculators). For this reason, the *Miracle* probed a little deeper.[14]

Tests were carried out in the case of Japan and the four 'tigers' to discover whether sectoral growth (at the two-digit ISIC level) seemed to accord with simple Heckscher–Ohlin expectations. Did the share of the labour-intensive sectors rise as exports exploded? If industrial structure is determined primarily by market forces, then low wages and low capital intensity at the beginning of the period of active industrial policy will, despite intervention, predict the pattern of growth. If industrial policy to promote capital- and knowledge-intensive sectors were successful, then high wages (a measure of human capital intensity) and high capital intensity at the end of the promotion period should 'predict' changes in industrial structure. The results were inconclusive for various reasons in the case of Japan, Hong Kong, and Singapore. In Korea, the most interventionist country, the sectors that grew most (in the period 1968–88) were the more labour-intensive low-wage sectors. Government intervention in favour of the capital and skill-intensive sectors was evidently not strong enough to prevent this. In the words of the *Miracle* (p. 333), 'the quantitative importance of government intervention to alter the structure of production is not confirmed at the sectoral level'.

Nevertheless, it does not follow that industrial policy had no effects. First, the comparison with Syrquin–Chenery norms does not show this, because the 'norms' are not patterns produced by *laissez faire*. Almost every developing country has an industrial policy of import substitution. Secondly, common sense tells one that the timing, scale, and pattern of investment in heavy industry—especially cars, shipbuilding, and petrochemicals—was markedly different from what would have occurred under *laissez faire* (or under some non-selective industrial promotion).

We can therefore usefully ask, as the *Miracle* does, whether the promoted sectors had greater productivity growth than others, as measured by total factor productivity (TFP). Sectoral growth rates of TFP are available only for Japan and Korea. In the case of Korea, 'there is no simple correlation between TFP and promoted sectors' (*Miracle*, p. 335), and 'The major reason for Korea's manu-

[13] They were also mostly below normal in Indonesia, Malaysia, and Thailand, the exceptions being chemicals in Singapore and non-metallic minerals in Thailand.

[14] Possibly also because the Syrquin–Chenery norms are themselves affected by industrial policies.

facturing success lay in high individual values [of TFP growth] for most sectors in most periods' (p. 336). In the case of both Korea and Japan, the metal products and machinery sector (ISIC 38) grew abnormally fast, and exhibited relatively high productivity growth. Since some branches of this sector were promoted, it was calculated how much less overall manufacturing TFP growth would have been if ISIC 38 growth had been normal. In both countries there would have been a small reduction in TFP growth; since, however, only some branches of this sector were promoted, one cannot be sure that this small contribution to TFP growth (and very small contribution to value added growth) was the result of promotion. Promotion aside, Dollar and Sokoloff (1990) show that TFP growth in the most capital-intensive sectors was less than half that in the most labour-intensive sectors. Electrical goods; rubber, leather and plastic products; furniture; and clothing and footwear all show above average TFP growth.

The degree of correspondence of domestic and international prices[15] is highly significant for the growth of TFP in cross-country regressions (51 observations) (see *Miracle*, table A6.3). This was taken as a measure of openness. It could also be taken as a measure of the efficiency of the use of resources. Neoclassical authors and common sense would, of course, claim it was both. The proportion of manufactured exports in total exports was also significant.[16]

On the above bases, what does the *Miracle* conclude concerning selective intervention? 'The most successful selective intervention in the HPAEs—the commitment to manufactured exports—was also the most general' (*Miracle*, p. 325). Eliminating the double-talk, this should read 'The least selective intervention in the HPAEs—the commitment to manufactured exports—was the most successful.'

The above analysis of productivity, which showed that the capital-intensive sectors that have been proclaimed as infant industries exhibit below-average productivity growth, are of course based on TFP estimates. We have earlier cast considerable doubt on TFP analysis. There is, however, a big difference between the country and the sectoral results. The estimates that purported to show that growth was miraculous in the HPAEs were based on inter-country production functions with all the problems of unreliable and incomparable statistics. The sectoral estimates of TFP for Korea are likely to be based on more reliable statistics. Furthermore conceptual and measurement errors in the explanatory variables are more likely to cause absolute errors in the TFP estimates than to affect the sectoral relativity of such estimates, and it is the latter which enter the argument.

[15] As measured by Dollar (1990).

[16] I would have thought that the proportion of manufacturing output exported could have been a more relevant determinant of TFP growth. In 1973 Taiwan, Korea, and Singapore exported 40–50 per cent of manufacturing output (sales/value added). In Argentina, Brazil, and Colombia this share was 3–8 per cent.

7. ESTIMATES OF INVESTMENT RETURNS

We saw earlier that what matters for growth and welfare are the social returns to investment. This is recognized by the *Miracle* and other authors cited, e.g. Pack and Westphal (1986). It is therefore strange that the *Miracle* tries to assess whether East Asian growth was miraculous, and the value of industrial policy, by the roundabout method of estimating total factor productivity growth. No attempt was made to estimate returns, and such estimates as exist were ignored.

I have calculated the returns to gross investment for the non-residential 'business' sector of Korea (i.e., excluding housing and government) for the period 1963–82 and some sub-periods from figures estimated by M. FG. Scott.[17]

The formula, also due to Scott, is

$$r = \frac{G_Y - [G_{LA}\,(WL/Y)]}{I/Y},$$

where r is the exponential rate of return, G_Y is the fitted exponential growth rate of output, G_{LA} is the fitted exponential growth rate of the quality-adjusted labour input, WL/Y is the share of wages, and I/Y is the gross investment ratio. It should be noted that *all* growth that is not ascribed to an increase in quality-adjusted labour is ascribed to investment. The estimates for various periods are given in Table 2.

TABLE 2. Calculation of Returns to Investment in Korea

Years	G_Y	G_{LA}	WL/Y	I/Y	r (Exponential)	r (% pa)
1963–82	0.0877	0.0651	0.523	0.235	0.228	25.6
1963–73	0.0934	0.0660	0.545	0.213	0.270	31.1
1972–82	0.0604	0.0551	0.496	0.263	0.126	13.4
1974–79	0.0838	0.0758	0.503	0.271	0.168	18.3

In Table 3 the figure of 31.1 for Korea for the period 1963–73 is compared with estimates for Japan, UK, and USA, calculated from Scott (1979, table 7.1, col. (2)), using exactly the same methodology, for the same 'non-residential business' sector, for similar periods ending in 1973.

The order of Japan and the UK relative to the USA is as expected given a 'catch-up' factor. For the same reason, one might expect Korea to head the list provided that economic policies or some special features of underdevelopment did not dampen the process of catching up. However, the Korean figure of 31.1

[17] Mr Scott's figures are in turn based on Kim and Park (1985). The raw figures are available on request.

TABLE 3. Comparative Estimates for Returns to Investment (% per annum)

Korea	1963–73	31.1
Japan	1961–73	23.6
UK	1964–74	20.4
USA	1948–73	16.9

is certainly notable.[18] But this notable performance applies *only* to the period 1963–73. The figure for the 1974–82 period of 13.4 constitutes a grave lapse into mediocrity. The investment ratio rose and the growth of output slackened. This is the period of the HCI drive. Towards the end of the period, in 1980, there was a recession (output fell 1.3 per cent) largely caused by a fall in agricultural output, though probably to some extent the result of fiscal action to cool the overheating of the economy in 1979 that resulted from the HCI drive. The recovery of output in 1982 and 1983 was sluggish by Korean standards. Thus, the low investment returns in this period were partly caused by macroeconomic disturbance, and are not therefore a fair measure of what the return would otherwise have been. For this reason, we have estimated the returns in the period of 1974–9 when the economy was booming. The returns, at 18.3 per cent per year are far below those of the decade 1963–73. It is possible that some fall in the rate of return was inevitable. Unfortunately, I do not have figures for later years which would show whether or not high returns reappeared after the emphasis on heavy and chemical industries, and more generally on industrial policy, was reduced. Nevertheless, the figures given above are bad news for heavy industry fundamentalists, and those who stress the importance and value of the government's industrial policies.

The high returns to investment in the period 1963–73 did not come as a surprise to me. In 1975 I led a small team which investigated on behalf of the Asian Development Bank the performance of 28 randomly selected medium-size firms which had received loans from the Medium Industry Bank (MIB). Since the MIB was government-owned, it might be thought that our sample firms were selectively promoted. This was not so. The government's guidelines to the MIB gave priorities which covered every kind of industry except non-traded luxury consumer goods. (The MIB agreed that confectionery was probably the only

[18] Mr Scott has estimated a cross-country regression using the investment ratio, growth of the quality-adjusted labour input, and as a catch-up variable (*cu*) the ratio of quality-adjusted labour productivity to that of the USA (see Scott, 1989, p. 294, eqn (10.3)). The USA (1948–73) and Japan (1961–73) lie almost exactly on the regression line, and the UK (1964–73) slightly above it (see Scott, 1989, table 10.2). It is interesting to see where Korea lies. On the assumption that *cu* was the same for Korea in 1963–73 as for Japan in 1952–61, the figures already given for Korea show that Korea's actual growth was nearly 1 per cent below that indicated by the regression line. So Korea's growth, while noteworthy, does not show any exceptional efficiency in the use of capital and labour.

exclusion.) This, incidentally, suggests that the extent to which the government directed finance (because it owned the banking system) is sometimes exaggerated by the revisionists. The average employment size of the sample was about 200 in 1969, rising to about 500 in 1974 (a 20 per cent per year rate of increase!). About one-third were textiles or textile-related, another third miscellaneous metal products (zippers, cutlery, crown caps, bicycle parts, etc.), and the rest very miscellaneous (special chemicals, paint, printing, electronic parts, toys). The unweighted average export ratio of sales was 44 per cent. The unweighted average of the constant price rates of return of these firms over the period 1969–74 was calculated (earlier investments back to 1963 were recorded—very few had an earlier investment than that) to be 22 per cent. The average shadow or social rate of return (using simplified LM procedures) was a little higher, 27 per cent. The figure of 22 per cent compares with that of 31 per cent given above for investment in the business sector, over roughly the same period.

It was largely from the experience of conducting this survey, involving visits to the firms ranging from 1.5 to 3.5 hours, that my own impression of such matters as the acquisition of technology and skills on the part of the labour force, of the intensity of work, and of marketing were formed. I also visited a number of high exporting medium-size labour-intensive firms in Taiwan in 1976. I have recorded my conclusion on such matters in Little (1979). Two points are mainly relevant in the present context. First, the technology was simple, non-proprietary, and easily acquired.[19] The suppliers of the standard machines, which were quite often second-hand, would teach the purchasers how best to lay them out and use them. Secondly, both Korean and Taiwan workers were very quick to learn. Employees would usually reach the expected high level of productivity within a few weeks. This would probably not have been the case if the standards of primary education had not been high.

Such little evidence as there is does not suggest high financial or social returns for those industries which believers in Korea's industrial policies mostly cite when they write about creating comparative advantage. These include shipbuilding and cars, petrochemicals and steel.

The main steel company (POSCO, the only important state enterprise in the industries mentioned) has had low financial returns throughout its twenty-year life despite heavy subsidization of its non-traded inputs, including the real interest rate which has been negative throughout most of its life. It has also received protection. (The import tariff on steel was 25 per cent until recently.) Despite this, pre-tax income as a percentage of assets averaged only 4.6 per cent from 1973 to 1987. Even that figure would be exaggerated if assets were not revalued

[19] For some confirmation of this, see Westphal *et al.* (1981). Howard Pack also writes: 'formal methods of knowledge acquisition were undoubtedly dwarfed by the ability to absorb non-proprietary knowledge in the relatively uncomplicated sectors that formed the basis of the early industrialisation drive' (Pack, 1992, p. 82).

with inflation. These figures suggest that POSCO may even have had negative social returns.[20]

I visited in 1986 Hyundai's shipyard at Ulsan where operations began in 1973. I marvelled at their technological progress. A Scottish firm on the Clyde had taught them. The professor of marine engineering at Ulsan had studied at Glasgow University. He told me: 'You British could teach us to make ships, although you could not make them yourselves.' However, there had been seriously mistaken investment decisions, and a top executive disclaimed economic success. They were still enjoying subsidized interest rates; only this, together with much lower wage rates, permitted them to compete with Japan.

It also seems very unlikely that Hyundai's cars have contributed much to the dynamism of Korean industry. I met the late George Turnbull, ex-Chief Executive of British Leyland, in Seoul in 1975. He was setting up production of the Pony car. He was amazed at the speed with which production in Korea could be initiated from a 'green field' site. But ten years later exports were still subsidized and the domestic market was totally protected (imports of cars being banned). To quote, 'Hyundai initially exported at a loss to Asia in order to boost scale benefits and required large subsidies until the mid-1980s' (Auty, 1993). Hyundai entered the Canadian market in 1984 with the help of a preferential tariff, but it earned a profit of only $50 per vehicle (Auty, 1993). It later, in 1985, entered the US marked helped by Japanese Voluntary Export Restraints (VERs). It was recently reported that 'in the US market its cars are a byword of poor quality' (*Financial Times*, 3 June 1993). The petrochemical industry is heavily protected. Naphtha-based plants can be internationally competitive only when the price of oil is very low. This applies in Korea despite her efficiency in plant construction (see Auty, 1991).[21]

The doubts I have expressed concerning steel and petrochemicals in Korea apply also, perhaps *a fortiori*, to Taiwan, despite some glowing accounts of the progress of these industries.[22] I visited the integrated steel plant of the China Steel Corporation in 1976. It was still under construction, so I was surprised to read in Wade (1990, p. 99) that it 'came on line' in 1974. From a long interview with a very frank vice-president, I was able to make a back-of-the-envelope

[20] This paragraph is based on Auty (1991).

[21] Cost–benefit analysis of six promoted projects in Korea are reported in Stern (1990). These use the shadow prices given in Sabin and Kato (1989). These studies are not based on actual operating data. First, there is a social cost–benefit analysis based on the project proposal. The project data are then corrected only for price changes, and a second estimate of social returns produced. As admitted, the latter is not an *ex post* appraisal. It assumes that the *quantities* of all inputs and outputs are as originally projected. It therefore shows only the extent to which an appraisal may go wrong as a result of incorrect assumptions about future prices. For what they are worth, it is not claimed that the results contribute a good case for selective intervention. It may also be noted that the same paper categorizes POSCO and Hyundai's car production as successful. This categorization is not, however, based on cost–benefit analysis or on financial returns. Indeed, the ascription of 'success' does not even follow from the discussion of the ventures.

[22] For instance in Gold (1986).

cost–benefit analysis. Sales to exporters, especially shipbuilders, would have to be made at world prices. But sales to the construction sector, which was remote from exports, could be made at protected prices, and it was expected that this, together with low interest rates supported by government guarantee, would enable the plant to be viable. I guessed that it might have a very low positive return at shadow prices. I also visited a petrochemical plant, which almost certainly produced negative value added at world prices.

8. THE MOVE TO CAPITAL AND SKILL INTENSITY

It has been my contention that the outstanding success of Korea and Taiwan from the early 1960s to the mid-1970s was based on a phenomenal growth of labour-intensive manufactures. This branch of manufacturing took off because exports were highly profitable once the previous bias against manufacturing for export was removed. The high profitability also depended on a relatively well-educated hard-working docile labour force which was, apart from the natural rate of increase, fed by a large movement out of agriculture (a process not very different from the famous Arthur Lewis model of growth with unlimited supplies of labour). High profits and increased earnings for recruits to the industrial labour force led to a very rapid rise in savings. There was thus a virtuous circle.

The *Miracle* agrees that the rise in savings is best explained by growth itself. It points to various government inducements given to savings and investment: but these are also widely prevalent in much less successful developing countries. The profitability of exports was a strong enough inducement to invest (and to save, on the part of industrialists). Thus, the principal role of government was to 'get the prices right' for exporters, and to give them confidence, by its own commitment to export-led growth, that exporting would remain profitable. It also helped to maintain the docility of the labour force by making strikes illegal and in other ways. It did little to assist in the acquisition of technology: there was no need.

But the need for a transition to more capital and skill-intensive technologies, which might present problems of acquisition and learning, was obvious as real wages and savings rates rose in the 1970s. The issue is whether government intervention was needed to effect or speed this transition. We have seen that the Korean government thought so, and this was one of the reasons for the HCI drive. I met the same belief in Taiwan in 1976. I expressed my doubts about the wisdom of this, observing that every firm I visited had plans to make their operations more capital-intensive (Little, 1979, p. 504). Of course one cannot prove that either Korea or Taiwan would have done better with less selective intervention; but the finding that returns have been very low in some of the main areas of promotion, together with the finding that productivity rose faster in the 'old' industries than in the infant industries, must certainly count as evidence against selective intervention. The exception to these findings is light electrical and electronic machinery, largely consisting of consumer goods. Confusingly enough, these labour-intensive activities count as heavy industry in Korea. They were promoted and were probably highly profitable, both from a private financial and a social point of view. But governmental promotion in this instance was giving a passing winner a pat on the back (Yoo, 1990). It is interesting that the manufacture of semi-conductors at the high-technology end of the electronics industry was developed without subsidy and apparently profitably by a private firm (Yoon, 1991).

There may be a case for the public promotion of institutions to facilitate the absorption of sophisticated foreign technology when the increasing scarcity of labour makes the most labour-intensive modes of production obsolete. Korea and Taiwan have created such institutions, and are still struggling with the problems that arise when labour becomes scarce and demanding. Many other developing countries have promoted institutes of technology, and supported research and development. There is certainly a *prima facie* case for this, as research and development must often give rise to external benefits; and ultimately a country may and should want to go beyond absorbing foreign technology by developing an indigenous scientific or technological capability. What determines success in this area is beyond my knowledge. All I need to say here is that this kind of promotion of research and development is not a high priority in the early stages of industrialization.

9. CONCLUSIONS

The rapid growth of a number of East Asian countries is fully explicable in conventional economic terms, that is very high rates of both material and human investment, together with the absence of the macroeconomic disasters that overtook many developing countries in the early 1980s.

However, in Korea, and very probably Taiwan, the returns to investment were exceptional in the period 1963–73. This was because industrial capital was combined with a lot of labour. This in turn occurred because reforms to the system of incentives permitted these countries to realize their comparative advantage in labour-intensive manufactures—a comparative advantage that was reinforced by a hard-working, docile, moderately educated labour force.

Selective intervention by the government was minimal in this first period. It later reduced the rates of return in Korea by premature promotion of heavy industry. The acquisition of technological capability was no problem in the early period. It became a problem later as more sophisticated techniques became appropriate. The extent to which government help may then be useful is an open question.

Many developing countries still have an abundancy of labour that scratches a living in extremely unproductive activities. But their industrial development absorbs little labour. It is to the Korean and Taiwan policies of the early period that they should be looking. Apart from 'getting the prices right', what is most needed is an improvement in the quality of the labour force, and labour legislation that encourages employment.

Lastly, let me revert to the trade policy recommendations of LSS with which I began. I have recently been trying to convince the Indian government that it should abolish quotas, institute a low uniform tariff, ensure that the exchange rate is such that the manufacture and export of tradables is adequately profitable, and rarely, if ever, subsidize particular industries; that is, in short, it should adopt the recommendations of LSS. This means that I have found nothing in either theory or experience in the past twenty-five years that makes me want to modify what was then recommended.

References

Amsden, A. H. (1989), *Asia's Next Giant: South Korea and Late Industrialisation.* New York: Oxford University Press.

Auty, R. M. (1991), 'Creating Comparative Advantage: South Korean Steel and Petrochemicals', *Tigdschrift voor Econ. en Soc. Geografie*, 82: 1.

——(1993), 'Sectoral Targeting: Auto Manufacture in Korea and Taiwan'. Lancaster University Working Paper no. 92: 10.

Balassa, B. (1982), *Development Strategies in Semi-industrial Economics.* Baltimore: Johns Hopkins University Press.

Barro, R. J., and Lee, J.-W. (1993), 'International Comparisons of International Attainment'. World Bank.

Bhagwati, J. (1978), *Autonomy and Consequences of Exchange Control Regimes.* Cambridge, Mass.: National Bureau of Economic Research.

Dailami, M., and Kim, E. H. (1991), 'The Effects of Debt Subsidies on Corporate Investment Behaviour'. World Bank Working Paper no. WP 727.

Datta-Chaudhuri, M. K. (1981), 'Industrialisation and Foreign Trade: The Development Experiences of South Korea and The Philippines'. In E. Lee (ed.), *Export-Led Industrialisation and Development.* Geneva: ILO.

Dollar, D. (1990), 'Outward Orientation and Growth: An Empirical Study using a Price-Based Measure of Openness'. Washington: World Bank, processed.

——and Sokoloff, K. (1990), 'Patterns of Productivity Growth in South Korean Manufacturing Industries, 1963–1979', *Journal of Development Economics*, 33: 309–27.

Gold, T. B. (1986), *State and Society in the Taiwan Miracle.* New York: East Gate Books.

Henderson, P. D. (1977), 'Two British Errors: Their Probable Size and Some Possible Lessons', *Oxford Economics Papers*, 29: 2.

Kim, K. S., and Park, J. K. (1985), 'Sources of Economic Growth in Korea 1963–1982'. Seoul: KDL.

Krueger, A. O. (1987), *Foreign Trade Regimes and Economic Development.* Cambridge, Mass.: National Bureau of Economic Research.

Krugman, P. (1989), 'New Trade Theory and the Less Developed Countries'. In G. Calvo *et al.* (eds.), *Debt, Stabilisation and Development: Essays in Memory of Carlos Diaz-Alejandro*. Oxford: Basil Blackwell for WIDER.

Lal, D., and Rajapatirana, S. (1987), 'Foreign Trade Regimes and Growth in Developing Countries', *World Bank Research Observer*, 2: 2.

Little, I. M. D. (1979), 'An Economic Reconnaissance'. In Walter Galenson (ed.), *Economic Growth and Structural Change in Taiwan*. Ithaca, NY: Cornell University Press.

——(1981), 'The Experience and Causes of Rapid Labour-Intensive Development in Korea, Taiwan Province, Hong Kong, and Singapore and the Possibilities of Emulation'. In E. Lee (ed.), *Export-Led Industrialisation and Development*. Geneva: ILO.

——Scitovsky, T., and Scott, M. (1970), *Industry and Trade in Some Developing Countries*. London: Oxford University Press.

——and Mirrlees, J. A. (1974), *Project Appraisal and Planning*. London: Heinemann.

——Mazumdar, D., and Page, J. (1987), *Small Manufacturing Enterprises: A Comparative Analysis of India and Other Economies*. New York: Oxford University Press.

——Cooper, R. N., Corden, W. M., and Rajapatirana, S. (1993), *Boom, Crisis, and Adjustment: The Macroeconomic Experience of Developing Countries*. New York: Oxford University Press.

Lucas, R. E. (1993), 'Making a Miracle', *Econometrica*, 61: 2.

McKinnon, R. I. (1990), 'Monetary Stabilisation in LDCs'. In L. B. Krause and K. Kilwan (eds.), *Liberalisation in the Process of Economic Development*. University of California Press.

Nehru, V., and Dhareshwan, A. (1993), 'A New Database on Physical Capital Stock'. International Economics Department, World Bank.

Pack, H. (1992*a*), 'New Perspectives on Industrial Growth in Taiwan'. In G. Ranis (ed.), *Taiwan from Developing to Mature Economy*. Boulder, Colo.: Westview Press.

——(1992*b*), 'Technology Gaps between Industrial and Developing Countries: Are There Dividends for Latecomers?' In *Proceedings of the World Bank Annual Conference on Development Economics 1992*. Washington, DC: World Bank.

——and Westphal, L. E. (1986), 'Industrial Strategy and Technological Change', *Journal of Development Economics*, 22: 1.

Sabin, L. L., and Kato, H. (1989), 'Shadow Price Calculation and Application: A Case Study of Korea'. Harvard Institute for International Development, Development Discussion Paper no. 313.

Scott, M. FG. (1989), *A New View of Economic Growth*. Oxford: Clarendon Press.

Stern, J. J. (1990), 'Industrial Targeting in Korea'. Harvard Institute for International Development, Development Discussion Paper no. 343.

Syrquin, M., and Chenery, H. B. (1989), 'Patterns of Development 1950–83'. World Bank Discussion Papers, no. 41.

Wade, R. (1990), *Governing the Market: Economic Theory and the Role of the Government in East Asian Industrialisation*. Princeton, NJ: Princeton University Press

Westphal, L. E. (1982), 'Fostering Technological Mastery by Means of Selective Infant-Industry Protection'. In M. Syrquin and S. Teital (eds.), *Trade, Stability, Technology and Equity in Latin America*. New York: Academic Press.

——Rhee, Y. W., and Pursell, G. (1981), 'Korean Industrial Competence: Where It Came From'. World Bank Staff Working Papers, no. 469.

World Bank (1993), *The East Asian Miracle*. Washington, DC: World Bank.

Yoo, J. (1990), *The Industrial Policy of the 1970s and the Evolution of the Manufacturing Sector in Korea*. Seoul: Korea Development Institute.

Yoon, C. (1992), 'International Competition and Market Penetration: A Model of the Growth Strategy of the Korean Semiconductor Industry'. In G. K. Helleiner (ed.), *Trade Policy, Industrialisation, and Development: New Perspectives*. Oxford: Clarendon Press.

Yoon, J. C., and Hellman, T. (1993), 'The Governments' Role in Japanese and Korean Credit Markets'. World Bank Working Papers no. WPS 1190.

12

The Experience and Causes of Rapid Labour-Intensive Development in Korea, Taiwan Province, Hong Kong, and Singapore, and the Possibilities of Emulation (1981)

PERFORMANCE OF THE FOUR ASIAN COUNTRIES

There is good reason to ask what can be learned from South Korea (hereafter, 'Korea'), Taiwan Province (hereafter, 'Taiwan'), Hong Kong, and Singapore—the 'four', as I shall call them for convenience. Korea, Taiwan, and Singapore had all achieved in 1973 a growth rate of gross domestic product (GDP) of over 10 per cent per annum for the previous decade. Hong Kong only just missed this magic figure; but the latter's growth over the longer twenty-year period, 1953–73, was better than that of the other three. Hong Kong, Taiwan, and Korea were also by 1975 the largest exporters of domestically produced manufactures in the developing world: each exported over US$4 billion worth, the next in order being Yugoslavia, Brazil, India, and Mexico, all of which were in the US$2 billion league.

Exports are only a means to an end and growth of GDP is not everything. But the quality of growth has been exceptional. There is probably less inequality in Taiwan than in any other developing country, and it did not increase during the period of most rapid growth.[1] Korea is also among the group with relatively little inequality, and experienced no increase in inequality in the period of most rapid growth.[2] There is much more inequality in Hong Kong; one estimate of

This paper first appeared as a chapter in E. Lee (ed.), *Export-Led Industrialization and Development* (ILO, Geneva, 1981). We are grateful for permission to reproduce.

This paper draws quite heavily on W. Galenson (ed.), *Economic Growth and Structural Change in Taiwan*, Cornell University Press, Ithaca, 1979, especially my own chapter in that book.

[1] W. Y. Kuo, 'Income Distribution by Size in Taiwan Area: Changes and causes', in *Income Distribution, Employment and Economic Development in South East and South Asia*, Council for Asian Manpower Studies, Manila, 1975.

[2] I. Adelman and S. Robinson, *Income Distribution Policy in Developing Countries: A Case Study of Korea*, Oxford University Press, Oxford, 1978; B. Renaud, *Economic Growth and Income Equality in Korea*, World Bank Staff Working Paper no. 240, 1976; D. C. Rao, 'Economic Growth and Equity in the Republic of Korea', *World Development*, March 1978.

the Gini coefficient for 1971 is 0.49, which would make Hong Kong fairly typical of a middle-income developing country.[3]

Real wages have risen impressively. In the period 1965–75 in Korea, real wages in manufacturing and agriculture rose respectively at annual average rates of 7.75 and 4.8 per cent.[4] In Taiwan, the corresponding figures are 4.3 and 7.5 per cent.[5] In 1975 in Taiwan, the daily agricultural wage exceeded that of the factory worker! In Hong Kong real wages, which rose at 5.4 per cent per annum during 1964–73,[6] fell during the recession, regaining their previous level only in 1976. This did not happen in Taiwan, nor in Korea in manufacturing. (There was, however, a fall in real agricultural wages in Korea in 1974.)

In both Taiwan and Korea, the unions are virtually powerless, and there is no government influence to raise wages. (There is no minimum wage in Korea, and in Taiwan it is far below any wage paid.) These wage rises therefore indicate a relatively inelastic supply of labour. The concepts of full employment and surplus labour are notoriously slippery. But the now falling agricultural labour force in Taiwan, the low unemployment figures (2.6 per cent in 1976) emanating from surveys, the rising female participation rates, long working hours, rising real wages, falling skill differentials, and complaints of labour shortage all indicate that Taiwan at least is much more fully employed than most industrialized countries. Many, though not all, of these features are also true of Korea; but, even if some observers might claim that there is still some surplus labour in Korea, it is nevertheless coming close to being a full-employment economy in that further increases in the demand for labour relative to the population of working age are not likely to increase the total participation rate very much. Most observers would probably say that Hong Kong achieved something like full employment in the early sixties, and Singapore probably in the late sixties.

The usual social indicators also show high levels of achievement. The expectation of life for males and females in Taiwan (1975) is 67 and 73 years respectively; in Korea 63 and 67 (1970), in Hong Kong 67 and 73 (1968), in Singapore 65 and 70 (1970).[7] Calorie consumption per caput was 2,700 in Taiwan (1975) and 2,500 in Korea (1970).[8] Primary education in both these countries is almost universal, and literacy high.

This sort of performance is almost unique among developing countries in the post-war period: and the pre-war period never saw anything remotely approach-

[3] See T. Y. Cheng, *The Economy of Hong Kong*, Far East Publications, Hong Kong, 1977, tables 6.1–6.4. It is, of course, hard to compare the income distribution of a city state with that of a normal country. Distribution in urban areas is normally more unequal than in rural areas.

[4] L. E. Westphal, 'The Republic of Korea's Experience with Export-Led Development', *World Development*, March 1978.

[5] E. Thorbecke, 'The Agricultural Development of Taiwan', in Galenson, op. cit., table 20. An alternative source gives the rise in industrial hourly wages at 5.7 per cent per annum, which may not be inconsistent; see Cheng, op. cit., E. Lundberg, 'Fiscal and Monetary Policies in Taiwan', in Galenson, op. cit., table 10.

[6] Cheng, op. cit., table 14.1.

[7] *United Nations Demographic Yearbook.*

[8] FAO, *State of Food and Agriculture, 1975.*

ing it. Only Israel is comparable in that she achieved a growth rate of 10 per cent per annum in the 1950s, and has done almost as well since. But Israel, which is also a relatively egalitarian country, started from a far higher level of income per head and human expertise. Brazil has also achieved very high growth rates, but income is extremely unequally distributed, and the distribution worsened with high growth. No one would claim she had achieved full employment.

Korea and Taiwan tend to look to Japan, among the new developed countries, as a model. But the latter's 'miraculous' growth started from a much higher level than that of the 'four'. She is also far larger, and the absolute size of her GDP was many times that of Korea or Taiwan, let alone the two city states. Furthermore, it seems to me that the quality of her growth was lower. Inequality was much greater, at least until very recently, and even now it might be claimed that she has a more dualistic economy.

I shall concentrate on the period from the early fifties to 1973, though with occasional references to the situation in 1975 or 1976. These countries have continued to do very well since the oil crisis and the world recession, despite their high dependence on imported energy and export markets. All except Korea suffered quite seriously from recession in 1974 and 1975—though less seriously than most of the industrialized countries. All rebounded with phenomenal growth in 1976. But the period since 1973 raises rather different issues to those discussed here. Chief interest centres on their different reactions to the world inflation, the oil crisis, and recession: and, now that they all have rapidly rising real wages, on the policies they adopt to further greater capital intensity. But our subject is labour-intensive development. Both for this reason, and because the latest years are least researched, I shall not attempt to examine the post-1973 period in any depth. I shall also concentrate on Taiwan and Korea (and especially the former) with only occasional glances at the city states. This is because I know more about the former countries (and the figures and the research are better), and because they are more normal countries.

Except for Hong Kong, very rapid growth began only in the sixties, in each case after a marked change of policy from import substitution to export promotion. It makes sense to divide the post-war period into three—from reconstruction to the change in policy, and then to the oil crisis and world recession, and beyond. But as already indicated, I shall say little about the last period.

It will be the thesis of this paper that the success is due almost entirely to good policies and the ability of the people—scarcely at all to favourable circumstances or a good start. Therefore, before looking more closely at the above mentioned periods, we must examine the circumstances of these countries and the initial conditions in the early fifties.

PRECONDITIONS

Circumstances

The 'four', like Japan, are poor in minerals. From 1963 to 1970 mining accounted for 1.6 per cent of Taiwan's GNP, and it was less than this in Korea, negligible in Hong Kong, and non-existent in Singapore. Mineral exports are insignificant. This contrasts with the average developing country. Even excluding oil exporting countries, the average contribution of minerals to exports was almost 20 per cent in 1973. The 'four' are thus heavily dependent on imported energy. Taiwan, for example, was importing over two-thirds of the energy used in 1975.

Apart from a few city states (including Hong Kong and Singapore), Taiwan and Korea have also, together with Japan, the highest population densities in relation to cultivable land of any country in the world; higher even than Egypt and Bangladesh, and about four times as high as India. The *average* farm size in Taiwan is just under one hectare, about the same as Korea. In both countries, the maximum legal ownership size is three hectares. Obviously the people in such countries can become well off only through industrialization. Not only this, as they get richer they are likely to become more and more dependent on imported materials, and even food. They can become rich, therefore, only through increasing trade in manufactures.

Lack of land might be interpreted as an advantage. It is very rare for agriculture to grow faster than 5 per cent per annum in any country where agriculture is an important part of the economy. Therefore, the less important agriculture is, the easier it is to achieve high growth rates of GDP. Perhaps this is what people have in mind when they dismiss Hong Kong and Singapore as irrelevant. But it does not apply initially to Taiwan or Korea (nor to Japan). In the mid-fifties, one-third of Taiwan's output was from agriculture, and about one-half of Korea's, these figures being typical of low and very low-income countries. The proportions were reduced to 23 and 28 per cent respectively by 1973. Japan, in 1953, was already more industrialized: 21 per cent of her output was from agriculture, although 42 per cent of employment was still there.[9]

It is an advantage if there are only a few people to share some natural asset. This is the explanation of the growth and wealth of countries like Kuwait. We have seen that none of the four has significant mineral wealth. But Hong Kong and Singapore, with populations 4.2 and 2.2 million respectively, have fine well-placed ports, which have undoubtedly contributed to their relatively high income per head. Korea and Taiwan have no similar locational advantages. Taiwan, indeed, is notably lacking in good harbour sites. Nor are these two countries very

[9] Figures from K. Ohkawa and H. Rosovsky, *Japanese Economic Growth*, Stanford University Press, Stanford, 1973.

small. Korea is among the largest developing countries, with a population of 33 million. Taiwan, with its 15.4 million people, is from a human point of view considerably larger than Australia, and ranks in population with such developing countries as Afghanistan, Morocco, and Peru.[10]

All these countries are islands or peninsulas, which confers certain advantages. Nowhere is it far from the sea, and there are economies of internal transport. They are naturally open economies, and they can benefit more easily from foreign trade than very large or land-locked countries. But having a long coastline per square kilometre is of little help if the countries' policies offset the natural openness which their shape determines: one has only to cite the poverty of Sri Lanka as an example. One circumstantial advantage, which they share with Japan, is that of internal cohesiveness. Taiwan and Korea are not plagued by ethnic, tribal, or religious differences. All have strong and stable governments which have been intent on development, and do not need to look to what is immediately popular.[11]

Initial position

The initial position, i.e., that of the early fifties, requires some discussion. It should not be thought that there is any precise set of preconditions of rapid growth, or any level of income per head which is a *sine qua non*. Nevertheless, there is some evidence that countries starting from a very low level of development—as crudely measured by income per head—find it harder to grow fast. In the last decade, for example, the 'middle-income' developing countries (with income per head of between US$200 and US$1,000 in 1973 prices) have managed to grow significantly faster than the poorest. Although the city states certainly started in the early 1950s with greater wealth than the great majority of developing countries, this was not so true of Taiwan or Korea. Working growth rates backward from 1973 estimated levels, one arrives at a net per capita income, in terms of 1973 dollars of US$222 and US$145 respectively for Taiwan and Korea in 1953. This would have put Korea at par with Thailand, South Vietnam, and the Philippines. (But one must remember that Korea was still dislocated by the war.) Taiwan was better off than these, though well below Malaysia, which on the same reckoning had an income per head of US$360. In terms of other parts of the world, the initial per capita income of the ex-Japanese colonies of Korea and Taiwan was higher than that of South Asia and Africa south of the Sahara, but below the level of the countries which border the Mediterranean, and well below any South American country.[12]

[10] The above population figures are as of 1973.

[11] Hong Kong, with its extreme *laissez-faire* philosophy, may be regarded as an exception: but the authorities there argue that *laissez-faire* is the best way of being intent on development.

[12] Figures in this paragraph have been calculated from IBRD, *World Tables 1976*.

Of course, the initial position cannot be adequately described in terms of income per head alone. Indeed, it is only a proxy for wealth, i.e. the physical and human assets which are the potential sources of income. We have already briefly discussed the non-reproducible physical assets, the land and minerals, the geographical situation, the relation of land to the size of the population. We now turn to the man-made infrastructure, and the human resources.

Korea and Taiwan were Japanese colonies from around the turn of the century to 1945. Taiwan was developed by the Japanese principally to supply rice, sweet potatoes, and sugar. They introduced irrigation, fertilizers, new seeds, and cooperative institutions. Indeed, there was a 'green revolution', and agricultural technology was far ahead of most of Asia when the war broke out. Communications were also widespread—much better than in most colonies because of the nature of the exports which the Japanese wanted. (That they concentrated on foodstuffs was also, of course, an advantage from the point of view of the immediate post-war period.) It is notable that road and rail mileage did not have to be extended in the post-war period up to 1975, although great improvements were made (e.g., the percentage of paved road rose from 7 to 55 per cent from 1952 to 1975). The Japanese creamed off probably as much as 10 per cent of GDP in the latter half of the colonial period, in the form of food exports. This agricultural surplus, when agriculture had recovered from its war-time decline, could be, and was, devoted to the maintenance of the army and to the industrialization of Taiwan itself. There was also some industrialization in the colonial period, but mainly in food processing and cement manufacturing until the 1930s, when for strategic reasons the Japanese introduced some heavy industry. There was extensive primary education; by the end of the Japanese era, three-quarters of the appropriate age-group (6–12) were enrolled in primary schools. There was, however, very little secondary or higher education, e.g. less than 2,000 college students. Quite apart from war damage and greatly reduced agricultural output, there was a skill vacuum when the Japanese left. This resulted in chaotic conditions, including massive inflation, until the vacuum was filled by the arrival of the mainlanders (about 1½ million including half a million military—a 25 per cent increase in population) in the period 1947–9. Taiwan thus suddenly acquired an effective administration, and also a very large army relative to her size.

Extensive land reform was initiated in 1949, and took eight years to complete. Real output probably reached pre-war levels in 1950 or 1951, but inflation remained high. Large-scale American aid began in 1951 which helped bring inflation under control in 1952. Real output per head reached pre-war levels in 1953.

Hong Kong has some similarities to Taiwan. The city was derelict in 1945 when the Japanese surrendered. The population was 600,000 compared with 1.6 million in 1939. The entrepot trade, which was her mainstay in the 1930s, was totally disrupted (just as were the markets for Taiwan's sugar and rice). Former residents then returned, and there was a massive influx of refugees from the mainland, bringing with them, as in Taiwan, industrial skills and capital (and trebling the population in two and a half years). This, and her free trade policies, together with the further shock to her re-established entrepot trade in 1951 (when trade with China was embargoed as a result of the Korean war), set Hong Kong on a course of rapid industrialization, through manufactured exports, a decade before it happened anywhere else.[13] Hong Kong became the model for the first free trade zone established fifteen years later in Taiwan.

The Korean story is very different. Korea had a shorter period of development as a Japanese colony from 1910 to 1945. The Korean climate makes agriculture less naturally productive, and the Japanese appear to have paid less attention to it. There was rather more industrial development than in Taiwan, but more than half of this, and a very high proportion of heavy industry and electricity generation, was in the North. Although Korea did not suffer physically during the 1939–45 war, the departure of the Japanese, and partition, caused a catastrophic economic set back for the South. The Japanese owned and managed all the medium and large industrial establishments. As in Taiwan, the Japanese had concentrated on primary education. Unlike Taiwan, few came to fill the resulting skill gaps. The 1945 partition was also highly damaging, especially as a result of the crippling lack of electricity, and the South's immediate inability to earn foreign currency to buy the material inputs which previously came from the North. It is reckoned that industrial production in 1948 was only about a fifth of what is was in 1940.[14] There was also a flood of mainly unskilled refugees from the North, so that total population rose from about 16 to 20 million between 1945 and 1948.[15] The North invaded in 1950, over-running the whole country except for the Pusan perimeter. About 1.3 million South Koreans were killed, and physical damage was of the order of one-and-a-half to two years' GDP.[16] Although the fighting stabilized after 1950 and reconstruction could begin before the Armistice of 1953, it is clear that the year 1953, when official National Income figures start, is far from being a year from which one can date any process of long-term growth. Indeed, industrial production was probably not much more than a third of the level of 1940,[17] and millions of refugees roamed the country, homeless. Heavy American aid began after the Armistice, but it seems likely that reconstruction and recovery were not complete before 1958.[18]

[13] My brief references in this paper to Hong Kong and Singapore owe much to T. and F. M. Geiger, *Development Progress of Hong Kong and Singapore*, Macmillan, London, 1975, and also to Cheng, op. cit., in the case of Hong Kong.

[14] Bank of Korea, *Economic Statistics Yearbook, 1949*: quoted in C. R. Frank, K. S. Kim, and L. E. Westphal, *Foreign Trade and Economic Development*, Columbia University Press, New York, 1975.

[15] D. C. Cole and P. N. Lyman, *Korean Development: the Interplay of Politics and Economics*, Harvard University Press, Cambridge, Mass., 1971.

[16] Cole and Lyman, op. cit., and Frank, Kim and Westphal, op. cit., refer to estimates of $2 and $3 billion respectively.

[17] Frank, Kim and Westphal, op. cit., p. 9.

[18] The year given by Cole and Lyman, op. cit., as the end of post-war recovery.

Thus, in the early 1950s, Korea was in a miserable state compared with Taiwan. But, for what it was worth, there had been a great levelling down process as a result of the departure of the Japanese and the destruction of property. Also, a very similar land reform to that of Taiwan had been initiated as early as 1947 under American auspices. But no one could conceivably have guessed that such a desperately poor and overcrowded country, with a severe lack of industrial or any high-level skills and natural resources, would within a decade embark on a fifteen-year period of miraculous growth.

FROM THE EARLY FIFTIES TO NEW POLICIES IN THE SIXTIES

Discounting recovery periods, growth in both Taiwan and Korea was good, but not spectacular. In both it was supported by heavy US aid. In both, industrial development was import substitution, mainly in consumer non-durables, both countries having been still heavily dependent on imports of clothing and textiles at the end of the colonial period. In both, there was a spectacular interest in secondary and higher education, largely private. In both countries agricultural output grew rapidly.

The change of policies affected agriculture much less directly than industry. We shall, where convenient, therefore extend the discussion of agriculture in this section beyond the early 1960s. From 1952–4 to 1966–8, the agricultural output of Taiwan and Korea both grew at about 4.5 per cent per annum, a rate exceeded by very few other countries. In Taiwan, however, the higher levels of yields resulted in a net agricultural export surplus, which increased until the mid-1960s and then declined and turned into a deficit by 1973. In Korea, there was a steadily increasing agricultural deficit. Similarly, agricultural savings have contributed more to overall savings in Taiwan than in Korea.[19]

Many analysts of Taiwan's development set great store by the contribution of agriculture. Certainly the Taiwan authorities succeeded in combining a squeeze on agriculture (through land taxes, but mainly the rice fertilizer barter arrangement) with an excellent rate of growth of output. In the first part of the period (up to 1957) the land reform was proceeding. It turned Taiwan in less than a decade from the common pattern of inequality, with tenancy predominating, into a country of tiny owner-cultivators. It is clear that neither the squeeze nor the land reform could have been combined with a 4.5 per cent rise in output (much faster in the recovery period up to 1953) without a high level of integrated support. This was provided by that unique institution, the Joint Committee for Rural Reconstruction (JCRR). Agricultural planning was thus 'integrally intertwined with the US foreign aid process', and 'a final essential characteristic of the land

[19] On this see C. H. Fei and G. Ranis, 'A Model of Growth and Employment in the Open Dualistic Economy: the Cases of Korea and Taiwan', *Journal of Development Studies*, January 1975.

reform process was the immediate implementation of a whole set of complementary policy measures which included, inter alia, the provision of credit, extension services, and strong organisational support in strengthening farmers' associations, and continued public investment in traditional agriculture'.[20] The JCRR not merely planned, but implemented. It is notable, however, that the Japanese had also provided a high level of services to agriculture; they had created the Farmers' Associations, which provided in the early 1930s one extension worker for 32 farm households!

Agricultural development was also labour-intensive. Presumably the tiny holdings contributed to this—there being wide evidence that labour-intensity goes together with small holdings. But in addition, it can be said that the increased inputs were complementary to increased use of labour, taking the form of improved seeds, fertilizers, irrigation and drainage, leading to an increase in multiple-cropping. Although fertilizer use rose, the increase must have been limited by the rice fertilizer barter tax. On the other hand, this 'hidden tax' helped to diversify agriculture away from rice, which fell steadily as a proportion of agricultural output, in favour of the most rapidly growing elements, namely vegetables, fruit, and livestock. Presumably, these latter not only provided higher incomes for smallholders, but were also more labour-intensive than rice. After the foreign trade reforms, the development of the famous mushrooms and asparagus also increased labour intensity. Apart from power tillers, there was no mechanization until the 1970s, when labour had clearly become a limiting factor. Power tillers are not thought to be labour-displacing, and certainly seem mainly to have taken the place of draft cattle whose numbers have fallen rapidly since 1958. The upshot was that man-days per cultivated hectare rose from about 275 in the early fifties to about 325 in the early sixties, peaking at 343 in 1966, and subsequently falling. Although there was a slow increase in the number of workers until 1967–8 (0.4 per cent per annum from 1953 to 1968), man-days per worker rose from about 165 in the early fifties to a plateau of about 200 in 1966.[21] Perhaps 200 days a year is close to the maximum that non-mechanized farming can ever use.

I can say little about Korean agriculture in either this or the later period. It appears to have been much less studied (and I had no original sources on hand while writing this paper). The use of fertilizer and crop yields are high by Asian standards, though lower than in Taiwan or Japan. As we have seen, growth has been very good. There are said to be well developed research and extension programmes. Both the labour force and man-days per worker have continued to increase slowly. Mechanization has, until recently, mainly taken the form of

[20] Thorbecke, op. cit.

[21] Ibid., table 9. There is a large discrepancy between these figures and those of Ishikawa, *Labour Absorption in Asian Agriculture*, ILO-ARTEP, Bangkok, June 1978, who gives a figure of 469 working days per hectare for Taiwan in 1964. But even 325 is high compared with the figures he gives for India and mainland China, though low compared with Japan (Ishikawa, table 2).

tillers. All in all, the descriptions I have seen of Korean agriculture make it seem very like Taiwan, but with everything a little less so—which may be fully accounted for by poorer soils and a harsher climate.

As already noted, industrialization in both countries was mainly import-substituting until the early 1960s. In both countries, it was the so-called easy, or primary, phase of import substitution, mainly manufacturing of consumer goods, such as textiles, clothing, and wood and leather products; in Taiwan there was, however, also some development of the producer goods industries established in the 1930s by the Japanese and inherited from them. Nevertheless, Ranis characterizes this phase as very mild import substitution; i.e., there was very little investment in capital-intensive intermediates. This is confirmed by the fact that effective production never became very high.

After the recovery period, the growth of industrial production in Taiwan was erratic from year to year. Over the period 1953–63 the rate of growth of manufacturing was 10.3 per cent, but in the late 1950s the policies followed came to be increasingly questioned, and there was good reason to do so. Growth was apparently slowing. The economy was still highly dependent on US aid for imports, which were severely controlled. Taiwan could not expect, with her rapidly growing population and poor resource base, much (if any) improvement in the primary product balance. Import substitution in such things as beverages, tobacco, textiles, clothing, paper, and cement had been virtually completed. Taiwan in the late 1950s was indeed in a situation which is by now very familiar. She had a heavily overvalued currency, supported by complete import control. Often the import control resulted in excess profits for importers, rather than cheap inputs for producers. There was little or no incentive for private industry to export. There was excess capacity in manufacturing. Controls and irregularity of supply resulted in industrial inefficiency. Investment was virtually stagnant during 1953–7, and the government was promoting the domestic production of things, such as non-ferrous metals, which were surely not in Taiwan's comparative advantage to make. The reforms did not come all at once. They were concentrated around 1960, when exchange rates were unified at NT$40 to the US dollar, a rate which was maintained until the small revaluation in 1973. Imports were then increasingly liberalized, and exporters came to be able to buy their inputs at world market prices (whether actually imported or not).[22] There are some additional tax reliefs for exports. The response was little short of fantastic, as we shall see below.

In Korea in the second half of the fifties, expansion was slow, GNP growing by only 3.8 per cent per annum. Manufacturing, of course, grew faster (in terms of value added at 10.3 per cent per annum), but the base was very small. In 1955 manufacturing was only 7.9 per cent of GNP. Manufactured exports began to

[22] The Taiwan reforms are more fully described in M. H. Hsing and Scott, 'Taiwan', in M. H. Hsing, J. H. Power, and G. Sicat, *Taiwan and the Philippines*, Oxford University Press, and M. F. G. Scott, chapter V in Galenson, op. cit.

grow fast in 1961, but from the negligible level of US$9.4 million. There was an abortive attempt at exchange rate unification and liberalization in 1960, which failed, partly because there was no resultant increase in export incentives. The economy was almost stagnant from 1958 to 1962. The successful reforms were initiated in 1964, when the exchange rate was unified and heavily devalued. This time there was a considerable increase in the incentive to export (and vice versa for imports). Export incentives, which had started in 1959 with tariff exemptions on imported intermediates, became more extensive. By about 1966, there was in Korea, as in Taiwan, a virtual free trade regime for exporters, plus some further incentives which apparently gave some slight preference to exports over production for the home market. It is also important to note that deposit and lending rates were doubled, giving real interest rates of over 10 per cent.[23]

The effects of these reforms in terms of effective incentives have been fully and authoritatively analysed by Westphal[24] for the year 1968. At the time, and during the sixties, it was quite widely believed that Korea had gone overboard on export promotion and that social value added by exports was very low. This can be attributed to an *a priori* distrust of trade rather than any actual analysis. Total effective protection for manufacturing was zero. It was primary production which was, on balance, protected. Within manufacturing there was quite heavy protection for the domestic sales of a number of primarily import-competing sectors, and for some sectors which were both import-competing and exporting (both imports and exports exceeding 10 per cent for these sectors). This was counterbalanced by negative protection on domestic sales of the exporting sectors, and those with virtually only home market sales.[25] It is thus important to realize that the virtually free trade regime applies only to exports, and that these were not over-subsidized. Westphal is able to conclude that, after allowing for a small overvaluation of the won (9 per cent), 'the average net effective subsidy rate on manufactured exports was virtually zero. Thus value-added on the given volume of exports was about the same as under a free trade regime.'

A further important point to note is that, unlike Taiwan, Korea continued with a high rate of inflation. Since the won was not floating, it became periodically overvalued. Export incentives were then increased, but reduced again when the won was devalued. The Korean authorities by these devices managed to keep the profitability of exporting relatively constant. Their commitment to the export drive, and that their actions corroborated this commitment, must have played a

[23] The Korean reforms are more fully described in Cole and Lyman, op. cit., and Brown, *Korean Pricing Policies and Economic Development in the 1960s*, Johns Hopkins University Press, Baltimore, 1973.

[24] Westphal, op. cit.

[25] There was quite high legal protection in all sectors. But this is of little significance since many tariffs were rebated, and many were redundant. The same is true of Taiwan, where however, effective protection of the home market is higher than in Korea. For 1969 it was estimated at about 17 per cent; see T. H. Lee *et al.*, 'The Structure of Effective Protection and Subsidy in Taiwan', in B. Belassa (ed.), *Development Strategies in Semi-industrialised Countries*, World Bank, Washington, forthcoming.

large part in inducing business to invest heavily in exporting. It is also notable that the incentives given to exporting were relatively invariant between industries, unlike protection for the home market.[26]

RESPONSES TO THE NEW POLICIES, 1963–73

From Hong Kong's performance with a perfect free trade regime (no tariffs, no taxation of intermediates other than gasoline, no controls, no subsidies), it should perhaps have been expected that the reaction would be startling. But it was certainly far greater than either the Taiwan or Korean planners expected—exports, and growth in general, were always heavily underestimated. Their indicative planning gave wrong indications.

Only a brief description of the industrial revolutions that ensued is necessary. For Taiwan, Table 1 tells the overall story, and broadly distinguishes the pre-reform and post-reform periods. It shows clearly the acceleration in growth after 1963, and that this was almost wholly accounted for by manufacturing growth. One can, in turn, ascribe manufacturing growth to the growth in exports and in the home demand for manufactures. (Import substitution was negative for manufacturing as a whole, probably in both periods.)[27] Such statistical ascription is, however, of very limited value. Exports themselves cause an increase in the domestic demand for manufactures, both because they generate income and through backward linkages, which robs statistical accounting of any causative significance. The point is that manufactured exports were clearly the leading sector especially in the second period. In fact, their accelerated growth started earlier than 1963, very soon after the reforms of 1959–60. Thus, the annual growth rates (from initially an almost negligible level of US$10.7 million) in five four-year sub-periods from 1953 on (in terms of US dollars) were 15, 44, 27, 39 and 49 per cent—bringing us to 1973.

[26] The proper place for the free trade zones (and bonded factories) in the two countries is a footnote. They began in 1965 in Taiwan, and 1970 in Korea, copying Hong Kong, which is itself a free trade zone. They were attractive, mainly because they cut down the cumbersome procedures, quite costly in time and money, involved in importing duty free, and claiming other export incentives, in the rest of the country. But there is still a lot of paperwork compared with the system in Hong Kong, as one Hong Kong businessman in the Kaohsiung Zone told me; also, shipping facilities are not as good as in Hong Kong. The more streamlined the virtual free trade regime for exporters outside the zones, the less point the latter have. They may have attracted some foreign investment which would not otherwise have come. In 1972 they accounted for 8 per cent of Taiwan's exports, much less in Korea. While useful in Taiwan and Korea, similar institutions could be much more beneficial in less open economies. For further details see Scott, op. cit. for Taiwan, and B. J. Choe, 'An Economic Study of the Musan Tree Trade Zone', in W. Hong and A. O. Krueger, *Trade and Development in Korea*, Korea Development Institute, Seoul, 1971.

[27] See W. Y. Kuo, 'Labour Absorption in Taiwan 1954–71', *Economic Essays*, vi, National Taiwan University, Taipei, 1977.

TABLE 1. Indices and Annual Growth Rates of Total Production and Exports in Taiwan*

	Production				Exports			
	Agriculture and mining	Manufacturing	Others	Total	Industrial products	Processed agricultural products	Agricultural products	Total
Indices								
1953	40 (40)	11 (11)	49 (49)	100	1 (1)	8 (8)	2 (2)	11 (11)
1963	53 (28)	36 (19)	97 (53)	187	13 (7)	14 (7)	4 (2)	31 (16)
1973	78 (16)	157 (32)	235 (52)	484	249 (49)	22 (5)	21 (4)	282 (58)
Annual growth rates (%)								
1953–63	3.0	12.5	7.1	6.5	29.6	4.8	10.3	10.6
1963–73	3.9	15.7	9.9	10.0	34.2	4.8	17.7	24.9

* The estimates are at 1971 prices with total production in 1953 taken as 100. Figures in parentheses are percentages of the total product in 1953.

SOURCES: Total production refers to real net national product and is from *National Income*, 1976. The distribution of production and the calculation of total real exports are from the same source. The composition of exports (using current dollar values) comes from *Taiwan Statistical Data Book*, 1977, table 10.8. Clearly, these figures are not perfectly comparable, but they suffice to show the orders of magnitude. It should also be noted that exports of industrial products include some minerals, but this is very small. This table is an amended version of table 7.2 in Little, chapter VII, in Galenson, op. cit.

Table 2. Korea: Growth Rates
(% per annum at constant 1970 won)

	1955–65	1965–75
GNP	5.0	10.4
Manufacturing (value added)	11.0	19.9
Total exports	20.1	30.6

The Korean response was very similar. A few illustrative figures will suffice. (The decades compared in Table 2 are shifted forward two years for convenience—but it is also appropriate because reconstruction in Korea was far from complete in 1953, and because the trade and other reforms occurred about two years later in Korea than in Taiwan.) The second period includes the world recession of 1974/5.

In terms of dollar value, in the decade 1963–73, Korean-manufactured exports grew from US$44 million to about US$2,700 million, a growth rate of over 50 per cent per annum. Taiwan's went from US$129 million to US$3,680 million, a growth rate of about 40 per cent per annum. The latter had just caught up with Hong Kong, whose exports were almost identical in value (if re-exports are excluded).

Singapore had a short period of protection before adopting, like the others, a free trade regime for exports. Protection began around 1960 but was restricted to a few products until 1965. Although it went on increasing until 1969, when effective protection for the home market was estimated at the relatively low figure of 18 per cent,[28] there was a shift to export promotion beginning with political independence and the collapse of the union with Malaysia in 1965. It was then that a virtual free trade regime for exports was instituted. Between 1965 and 1972 the average annual rate of growth of manufacturing output was 26 per cent per annum.[29] Between 1965 and 1973 the dollar value of exports rose at the rate of 27 per cent per annum, bringing them to about US$1,600, just ahead of India in the latter year (though there are some re-exports in this total).

HOW COULD THERE BE SUCH AN EXPLOSIVE INDUSTRIAL REVOLUTION?

First, there must be opportunities for investment which are socially very profitable. The word 'socially' is very important. It is always possible to make some

[28] See C. S. Yue, *Size of Market and Export Oriented Industrialisation in Singapore*, Institute of Development Economics, Tokyo, 1974.

[29] Ibid.

sectors profitable by subsidy or protection. But then the rest of the economy pays, growth in other sectors is handicapped, and higher savings in the protected sectors are offset by reduced savings elsewhere.

Secondly, there must be the savings to create the required investments; and where there are foreign inputs, there must be enough foreign exchange to pay for them.

Thirdly, there must be people willing to seize the opportunities, and capable of organizing production efficiently.

Fourthly, there must be an elastic supply of both capital and current inputs, including labour.

Fifthly, the relative prices must be such that the available factors of production, capital goods, and labour are efficiently used.

Let us look at these (interrelated) conditions in turn. I shall term these last three conditions the 'production conditions'.

Socially profitable opportunities

If the conditions of production are good, it is not surprising that labour-intensive activities should provide highly profitable opportunities. If labour can be efficiently used, and is paid (in efficiency units) a small fraction of what it earns in the industrialized countries, then highly socially profitable production is possible. Naturally, the advantage of low wages must not be offset by discriminating protection of labour-intensive industries in the high-wage-cost countries. Although there was some such discrimination, the record shows that it was very far from offsetting.

It is equally true that the macroeconomic management of trade in the developing country must be such that labour-intensive exports are not discriminated against, and that such discrimination is not expected. We have already made it clear that this condition was fulfilled in our four countries (and only in them).[30]

Lastly, there is the problem of marketing. The foreign markets may be there. But they have to be reached. The strange thing is that this supposedly serious problem seems to have been no problem at all. Unfortunately, I found no research into marketing, and had to rely on my own interviews, not primarily directed to the subject of marketing, with businessmen in Taiwan and Korea. In many cases, foreign buyers came and either simply bought standard products (e.g. towels), or arranged for production according to their own designs (e.g. higher-quality clothing, sporting equipment, some consumer electronic

[30] Although by now many other countries have used export subsidies, it remains true that no other developing country (or anyway none whose foreign trade regime has been studied) has adopted virtual free trade regimes for exports. See B. Balassa, *Export Incentives and Export Performance in Developing Countries: A Comparative Analysis*, World Bank Staff Working Paper no. 248, January 1977.

products). In other cases Japanese trading houses, or other foreign agents, were used. Some quite small businessmen themselves went abroad to make contacts (and contracts). At least one very large furniture maker had set up his own re-assembly and sales organization in the USA. No doubt, foreign investors provided the marketing where they came in. But foreign investment was quite limited, and dominant only in the electronics industry (in both countries). Thus, in total, sales of subsidiaries to parent organizations played only a very minor role. Only in very recent years has there been some development of indigenous marketing houses and cooperatives with government encouragement.

The big markets for Taiwan and Korea have been the United States and Japan. But between 1962 and 1972 the Japanese share of Korea's exports fell from 43 to 25 per cent, and of Taiwan's exports from 24 to 13 per cent. Over the longer period, 1953–75, exports to Japan rose only about half as fast as total exports. Japan has never been an important market for Hong Kong or Singapore. For all four, exports to the slow-growing American market have been rising many times faster than to the fast-growing Japan. The reason is clear. For manufactures, the USA was a far more open market, and also her wage costs were higher than in Japan. In recent years, the share of Japan and the USA taken together has begun to fall in the case of Korea, as she has expanded exports to Europe and elsewhere very fast. Inter-trade among the four is also very small; paradoxically, the largest flow is capital-intensive synthetic textiles from the relatively low-wage-cost Taiwan to Hong Kong. Thus, neither regionalism nor Japan's growth have been very important factors.

Savings and foreign exchange

Taiwan relied heavily on US aid from 1951 to 1962. Her total current deficit over this period was about US$1.3 billion. This was covered to about US$1.1 billion by US aid and about US$0.2 billion by private capital inflows. Other loans and transfers were very small. The position from 1963 through 1973 was very different. There was about US$370 million of US aid in the pipeline. Total Overseas Development Assistance and multilateral loans at concessional rates remained at a level of about US$5 per capita until 1968;[31] thereafter such loans became negligible or negative, as repayments were made. However, private foreign investment, which had been very small, built up quite rapidly after 1966, rising from US$29 million to a peak of US$250 million in 1973 after which it declined considerably in 1974–76. The net capital transfers went to build up Taiwan's reserves, for the current account was in substantial surplus over the whole period 1963–73, to the tune of about US$900 million.

[31] OECD, *Development Cooperation*, various series. Of course, as GNP was rapidly rising, US aid as a proportion of GNP was rapidly falling; it fell from 6–7 per cent of GNP in the years 1958–61 to almost nothing in 1968.

Korea has been still more heavily aided than Taiwan. From 1953 to 1960, it received US$1.9 billion from the UN Korean Reconstruction Agency and USAID, a level of about US$10 per head.[32] But in recent years, most of the capital inflow has been in the form of commercial and near-commercial loans. Private direct investment has been small, peaking at US$137 million in 1973.

Of the city states, aid to Hong Kong has ben negligible throughout, but Singapore has been heavily assisted, though mostly in the form of fairly hard loans. ODA and multilateral loans on concessional terms were running at a level of about US$12 per capita from 1969 to 1973. But the net result was largely to build up Singapore's foreign assets rather than to increase domestic investment.

The extent to which a country can and does use foreign resources is partly outside its control, but partly a matter of policy. Aid, which was the dominant form of foreign resources transfer until the mid-sixties, falls mainly in the former category. But the possibility of commercial borrowing, and also borrowing from the IBRD and the Asian Development Bank, depends largely on foreign confidence in political and hence economic stability, and on the growth of exports—and hence largely on success itself. These forms of borrowing have been the most important since soon after the export success became remarkable.

The overall degree to which a country relies on foreign savings for growth can be roughly measured by the ratio of the current payments deficit to domestic investment. In the case of Taiwan, this ratio ranged between one-third and one-half from 1951 to 1959. But during the period of Taiwan's most rapid growth (1963–73), the average value of the ratio was approximately zero. Korea has been much more dependent on foreign savings, which financed a very high proportion of gross domestic investment until after 1963. (The ratio averaged nearly three-quarters from 1959 through 1963.) Thereafter, there was a declining trend, but in contrast to Taiwan the ratio remained high on average—over one-third. Until after 1964, an even higher proportion of Hong Kong's investment was financed from abroad (though not by aid); then the proportion fell rapidly, so that Hong Kong apparently became a considerable net foreign investor after 1969. Singapore, since 1960, has also apparently been a net foreign investor (except for the brief period 1962–4), although she also borrowed considerably from the IBRD, ADB, and other sources. But there is an enormous 'errors and omissions' figure, resulting partly from the omission of trade with Indonesia from the official figures. All that is certain is that Singapore has rapidly built up its short-term foreign currency assets from 1966 to 1973.[33]

Investment was rising rapidly as a proportion of national income. This, together with the declining reliance on foreign savings, implied that gross domestic savings were rising very rapidly in relation to GNP. In Taiwan from 1952 to 1962, the ratio was low, in the range of 7.5–10.5 per cent, without a very marked

[32] Frank, Kim and Westphal, op. cit., p. 29.

[33] This paragraph is based on Little, op. cit., which in turn relied mainly on IBRD World Tables 1976.

trend. There was a jump to 17 per cent in 1963 with a rising trend until 1973, when the ratio reached 33 per cent. Gross investment as a proportion of GDP rose over the same period from 18 to 27 per cent.

In Korea, domestic savings in the 1950s were sometimes negative and always negligible. In 1962 they were still only 1.6 per cent of GNP. In 1963–5, the ratio rose to 7 per cent, and to 11 per cent in 1966, after which there was a fairly steady rise to 22 per cent in 1973. It should be remembered that part of the reform package was a doubling of interest rates on one-year deposits to 30 per cent in 1965, with real rates averaging about 15 per cent from then until 1970. The effect on bank deposits was stupendous. Time and savings deposits rose from 15 billion won in 1964 to 585 billion won in 1970, and M2 as a percentage of GNP rose from 9 to 35 per cent.[34] There is no proof, but I think there is a strong presumption, that high real interest rates cause higher savings, especially among the poor and those of moderate means for whom bank deposits are about the only available outlet for financial savings. But it was undoubtedly the growth of profits plus the rapid rise in personal incomes which did most to raise the savings ratio. Success brings the means for further success, with not much lag.

Conditions of production

Entrepreneurship and management are predominantly indigenous in both Korea and Taiwan. We have already seen how relatively little foreign investment there has been. Even in recent years in Taiwan (1967–75) it has been averaging only 6.5 per cent of fixed capital formation in manufacturing.[35] In Korea, it was 17 per cent during 1970–5,[36] but was far less in earlier years.

In Taiwan, it might be thought that the mainlanders provided most of the entrepreneurship. This may have been true in the early years, but the Taiwanese soon came into the picture. In 1976, of the top 300 corporations, 89 were owned by mainlanders (and 21 by foreigners). In Hong Kong, no doubt many of the successful entrepreneurs were immigrants, but we have no idea in what proportion. Singapore has relief on foreign firms to a far greater extent than the others. This is only partly because she has become an oil-refining centre, an activity based almost entirely on foreign capital. Her clothing and furniture industries were largely established by Hong Kong entrepreneurs, and the electronics industry by Japanese, Americans, and Europeans. Wholly foreign firms accounted for 65 per cent of exports in 1972, and joint ventures for another 22 per cent.[37]

There seems to have been little effort to create any specialized training in management. Technical assistance, and industrial extension, comes mainly from private sources, especially Japanese machinery suppliers. There are some official

[34] R. I. McKinnon, *Money and Capital in Economic Development*, Brookings Institution, Washington, 1973.

[35] Little, op. cit.

[36] Westphal, op. cit.

[37] Yue, op. cit., table 10.

sources of assistance, but I do not think they have played an important role in either Korea or Taiwan.

The upsurge in secondary and higher education must have played an important role, despite the fact that several of the greatest Korean and Taiwanese entrepreneurs had very little education. It also has to be noted that Hong Kong's educational levels are far below those of Korea or Taiwan. The drive, ambition, and capacity for hard work, of both Korean and Chinese businessmen, are notorious. Without this drive, education is probably of little avail.

In the development literature, the difficulty of finding sufficiently appropriate (i.e. labour-intensive) technology has been stressed. This, like marketing and entrepreneurship, seems to have been a non-problem for our countries. Indeed, one can say that they discouraged it, for the full access to imported duty-free machinery implied that there was some negative protection for the machinery industry.[38] There were some indigenous machines available, and in some cases (e.g. looms in Korea) it was more appropriate than imported machinery in use. Although now Taiwan, for instance, is selling turn-key plants abroad, it remains true that the vast bulk of the machinery used was imported, or imported designs were copied with little change. By using obsolete and quite often second-hand machinery, by not mechanizing operations that did not require to be mechanized for quality reasons (e.g. leaving out transfer machinery), by working long hours and in multi-shifts, operations could be and were made extremely labour-intensive. In addition, low construction costs helped to keep capital/labour and capital/output ratios low.

It is rapidly becoming fashionable to propose support for small and very small firms on the grounds that they employ more labour-intensive technologies. Personally, I regard it as an open question whether this is sensible. Here I shall note only that the development of the 'four' lends no support to this idea. There has been very little special support for small enterprises in any of these countries. As everywhere, the very imperfect capital markets, which still reign in Korea and Taiwan, discriminate against them. The idea that small modern firms (we are not speaking of traditional handicrafts, a negligible part of output in these countries) are labour-intensive may well be based on statistical aggregation of like with unlike. There is scattered evidence that with sufficient disaggregation medium and large firms have both higher labour and higher capital productivity. Casual observation supports this idea in Korea and Taiwan, where one can observe large firms in the clothing and footwear industries apparently employing the same techniques as smaller firms: it is then likely that there will be some savings of capital in buildings and inventories, and that the capability of meeting larger orders permits a more efficient production flow. This may be very industry-specific, and far more research needs to be done. Labour market conditions, and high interest rates, may also be critical in preserving labour intensity in those larger firms which do have good access to capital funds.

[38] But the indigenous machinery industry is now being protected in Korea. Negative protection of the machinery industry does not apply to Hong Kong.

Probably the most important factor making for labour intensity (in given sectors—we shall consider the sectoral composition later) was the elastic supply at low wages of reliable, obedient, unorganized, and hardworking people. Observers are impressed by the quality of Korean and Chinese labour—the skill, concentration, conscientiousness, and long hours worked. Above all, they give management no trouble (and are not allowed to do so). The cost of employing people is felt to be only the wage. This is in marked contrast to India, where, in a recent survey of small entrepreneurs, the interviewer reported that the desire not to employ labour, to mechanize at almost any cost, amounted to paranoia. I have also myself observed this unwillingness to employ.

The absence of union pressure (strikes are illegal in Korea and Taiwan), or government intervention in favour of high wages has also meant that there is no dualism in the labour market; i.e., organized or medium or large-scale industry does not have to pay more than is required to attract the kind of labour and the skills it wants. This makes for greater equality both directly (skill differentials have been falling), and because it does not reduce the demand for factory labour.

Real wages have risen throughout, very slowly in the fifties and early sixties, but slowly accelerating until in recent years they have risen fast. But they have risen only in response to increased demand. The demand curve for industrial labour has been shifting along a supply curve which was very elastic (but never perfectly elastic) in its early reaches, then becoming much less elastic as something like full employment was reached. Naturally, this implies that the capital intensity of output has to increase. Every entrepreneur I talked to had plans to increase labour productivity by increasing capital intensity, but only because labour was becoming expensive.[39] The relatively high demand for agricultural labour has also, of course, tended to shift the supply curve leftwards, and bring about wage increases earlier than otherwise.

It is an interesting question how far the universal primary education and very high degree of literacy has contributed to the quality of the labour force. I confess that, despite reading quite a lot on the subject, I still have no clear idea of the extent to which schooling, or literacy, or elementary numeracy, affects the productivity of unskilled and even semi-skilled labour, and how far this may vary between occupations. After watching electronic assembly operations in these countries, one is tempted to think that the main contribution of schooling may be to teach children to sit at tables and to concentrate.

LABOUR INTENSITY, OUTPUT MIX, AND EXPORTS

The sectoral composition of output has been greatly influenced by the growth of exports. It would be interesting to know how great has been the effect of this on

[39] Nowhere have I observed the famous Cambridge (England) theory of reswitching in action.

labour intensity. One can, through the input–output tables, attribute statistically so much direct and indirect labour to exports. But this is mere accounting. To say how much demand for labour was caused by exports, one would have to have an alternative counterfactual more import-substituting line of development. One could compare the relative direct and indirect labour intensity of the different patterns of output. But this would still not give the answer, because all comparisons with other countries go to show that the growth rate of output would have been much lower with the import-substituting development—because the social profitability and the savings generated would have been lower. It would also have been more likely that growth would have been interrupted or slowed by balance of payments crises, or by an excessive debt service ratio to export earnings. (Korea's and Singapore's massive borrowing would have been impossible without burgeoning exports.)

Nevertheless, it is worth giving a few partial indicators of the importance for employment of the main export sectors, and their relative labour and capital/output ratios.

Consider three industries in Taiwan: textiles (including clothing), footwear, and electrical machinery (including electronics and components) during the period 1966–71 when the export expansion was in full swing. Sixty-three per cent of the increased production of textiles and footwear was exported, and 33 per cent of the increased production of electrical machinery. Together, they accounted for 51 per cent of the increased employment in manufacturing, and 44 per cent of the increased value added. Their increased exports, assuming that exports have the same VA/L ratios as total production, would have accounted for only 11–12 per cent of the *total* employment increment. In fact, exports from the textile and clothing sector were much more labour-intensive than total production, since only 15 per cent of the very capital-intensive synthetic fibre production was exported in 1971, and over half the clothing output. At a guess, the rise in exports of these industries, which accounted for 63 per cent of incremental manufactured exports, were probably directly responsible for about 15 per cent of total incremental employment. Adding in the rest of manufacturing would bring the estimate to about 20 per cent.[40]

The most important question is whether, directly and indirectly, manufactured exports were more labour-intensive than total manufacturing. Some findings from Little are reported.[41]

Textile exports (including clothing) in 1966 were less capital-intensive than manufacturing as a whole, but more so in 1971. This was due to the increasing use of domestically produced synthetic fibre which is extremely capital-intensive. The same development raised the *K/L* ratio in clothing alone from about half to about three-quarters of the average for manufacturing industry (which was about

[40] This paragraph is based on Little, op. cit., which is in turn based on Kuo, op. cit.

[41] Based on K. Liang and D. H. Liang, 'Exports and Employment in Taiwan', in *Conference on Population and Economic Development in Taiwan*, Academica Sica, 1976.

US$4,000 per employee in 1971, more than double the 1966 figure). The *K/L* ratio for electrical and electronic equipment exports is about half the average. The same is approximately true of plastic products, plywood, other wood products, and the miscellaneous category, taken together.[42] The above industries account for about 70 per cent of manufactured exports.

Those manufactured tradables which are predominantly import-competing (less than 10 per cent exported) have an average *K/L* ratio about double the manufacturing average. The high *K/L* ratio is mainly accounted for by five products, which are (in order of capital intensity): artificial fibres, aluminium, petroleum products, industrial chemicals, and fertilizers. The rest were all relatively labour-intensive. (Note that Taiwan had no integrated steel plant in 1971.)

In sum, there is no doubt that manufactured exports were (directly and indirectly) considerably more labour-intensive than manufacturing in total and far more labour-intensive than the predominantly import-competing industries. But, as already stressed, this still does not go to the heart of the matter so far as the beneficial effects on employment are concerned.

In Korea, direct employment in production for exports has been reckoned at 18.9 per cent of manufacturing employment, and 5.1 per cent of total employment for 1970. Incremental figures, such as those given above for Taiwan, would surely be much higher. Average *K/L* ratios in manufacturing went, in terms of 1970 US dollars, from $1,620 in 1960, to $1,330 in 1966, to $1,480 in 1970, to $1,390 in 1973. At the same time, the *K/VA* ratio fell continuously from about 2 in 1960 to 0.9 in 1973. These figures are remarkable, even compared with Taiwan.[43]

Some critics have used the pejorative term 'shallow' to describe the development of Korea and Taiwan, by which is meant that there is relatively little backward linkage from exports. In that case, development in depth must be declared the enemy of employment and equality. All labour-intensive sectors have their *K/L* ratios raised by backward linkage, because all the intermediates—petrochemicals, artificial fibres, steel, non-ferrous metals, etc.—are highly capital-intensive. These intermediates are the curse of developing countries.

EQUALITY

Effects of labour intensity

The high degree of equality in Taiwan has been extensively studied.[44] It is obvious that the land reform has contributed, but it did not contribute to the fact

[42] All figures in this paragraph refer to the total (i.e. direct plus indirect) *K/L* ratios.

[43] They are quoted in Westphal, op. cit., but taken from W. Hong, *Factor Supply and Factor Intensity in Trade*, Korean Development Institute, Seoul, 1976.

[44] Kuo, op. cit., and Fei, Ranis and Kuo, op. cit.

that there was no increase in inequality during the period of the industrial revolution, since the early sixties.[45] Indeed, farm income fell from about 25 per cent of national income in 1960 to 10 per cent in 1972. Non-farm employment income rose faster than non-farm property income, from 46 to 55 per cent as against a rise in property income from 21 to 24 per cent. Within the category of employment income, equality increased markedly as between different occupations in a manner which is clearly attributable to a high demand for unskilled and semi-skilled labour.[46] Lastly, as we have seen, the high demand for labour equalized income as between households with mini-farms and those with more viable holdings.

The connection between a highly labour-demanding development and equality is surely obvious. Nothing else accounts for the maintained equality. The tax system and transfer payments were at best neutral. After the land reform there were no deliberately redistributive policies except for a reduction in the squeeze on farm incomes, which eventually in the 1970s turned into a support price system. The total effects of this on distribution are, however, very unclear.

For Korea, the Adelman–Robinson model confirms this:

> It is plain from our test results that the strategy of labour-intensive export-led growth has produced significantly higher incomes for the poorer half of the population and a far more equal relative distribution compared with a strategy of import substitution. As for slower growth strategy, supposing that had been Korea's choice, the government would have had to achieve it by exerting less pressure on (and offering fewer incentives to) the urban manufacturing sector to produce and to export than in the actual Korean experience. The results would probably have been in the direction of our Slow Growth 2 experiment. In this case, the poorest 60 per cent would have been much worse off than their actual experience and the impact on distribution would have been disastrous.[47]

Dispersion of industry in Taiwan Province

This is a special feature, which, all observers agree, has been conducive to labour intensity and equality. It is well described by Samuel Ho[48] and G. Ranis.[49] Its main importance has been that members of farm families could have industrial employment by commuting rather than migrating. The share of off-farm earnings in farm family income had reached 24 per cent in 1967. Moreover, these earnings were inversely related to farm size. By 1972, 47 per cent of the income of families with less than half a hectare was from off-farm services. As the

[45] The figures show increasing equality. But although they are good compared with most or all other developing countries, it is doubtful whether they are good enough for any unqualified assertion that equality has increased. See Kuznets, chapter 1 in Galenson, op. cit.

[46] See Kuo, op. cit., table 15.

[47] Adelman and Robinson, op. cit., p. 127.

[48] S. Ho, *The Rural Non-Farm Sector in Taiwan*, World Bank Studies in Employment and Rural Development, September 1976.

[49] G. Ranis, chapter 3 in Galenson, op. cit.

holding size rises to three or four hectares, the percentage fell to 13. Thus, industrial dispersion has been a very beneficial accompaniment of mini-farms which could not otherwise support a family at any reasonable standard of living. The more rural industries are also the more labour-intensive: presumably they could get cheaper labour.

This dispersion has clearly been facilitated by the good road and rail network, and by almost complete rural electrification (together with equal charges for electricity). Ribbon development along the roads from the urban areas is obvious to any casual observer. Industries have good access to ports and to demand centres, although dispersed. The government has also helped with rural industrial estates. But topography has clearly played a large role, and it is unclear how far this feature can be copied. It has not happened in Korea, although the Sae Maeul (New Community) movement is, in part, an effort to copy it.

LESSONS AND TRANSFERABILITY OF THE EXPERIENCE

Lessons

The major lesson is that labour-intensive and export-oriented policies, which amounted to almost free-trade conditions for exporters, were the prime cause of an extremely rapid and labour-intensive industrialization which revolutionized in a decade the lives of more than fifty million people, including the poorest among them.

The labour intensity of the development cannot however be attributed only to trade, although that was a very important factor, especially for the growth rate. Except for the city states, the home market dominates, especially when agriculture and services are taken into account, and production for this market should also be kept labour-intensive. The free labour markets and high interest rates, especially perhaps the former, have played a major role in maintaining labour intensity in the domestic market as well as for exports.

The equality of land ownership, the very small size of holdings together with fairly high prices for machinery, and the planned development of inputs which are complementary to labour, as well as diversification from rice and sugar into more labour-intensive crops, have sufficed to keep agricultural employment high. (These conditions and policies were beneficial for twenty years, but now the small size of holdings has become a handicap, and it will be hard to change.) Particularly in Taiwan, a great deal of effort has gone into devising and implementing strong supportive services for agriculture.

A healthy agriculture is not a precondition for very rapid industrial growth, provided exports are sufficiently buoyant. (Hong Kong and Singapore have next to no agriculture.) But in countries where, initially, agriculture employs a large part of the population, it is clear that a reasonably equitable development requires it. The high economic and social costs of excessively rapid urbanization suggest that it is worth making special efforts to bring industry within reach of the rural population.

The high level of education is notable. It is hard to believe that it has not been an important element. But concentration on education, at least at secondary and higher levels, can be counter-productive, unless the demand for skills is there. In Korea itself, around 1960, there was very high unemployment among the educated and extreme student unrest, until the economy grew fast.

I believe the above are the key elements in the success of the 'four'. Nothing else can account for it. Taiwan and Korea do not have very good capital markets. Their tax systems are not very good—perhaps the best thing about them is that taxes are low. Planning (except for agriculture in Taiwan) and the public sector have not, in my opinion, played key roles. Moreover, the non-human resources of Taiwan and Korea are notably unfavourable to high income or growth. The prior conditions for growth were very unfavourable in Korea. Luck has played little part in their development. Aid was certainly important in the early stages (though not for Hong Kong), but was not important during the high growth period. Borrowing has remained very important for Korea, but not for the others. private foreign investment has played a major role in Singapore (and possibly in Hong Kong). Elsewhere it has played a useful but only a minor role. Since the ability to borrow heavily itself depends on success, and since the attraction of foreign investment and its social value is also primarily a matter of domestic policies, I think it can be concluded that everything can be attributed to good policies and the people.

Transferability[50]

Transferability has several aspects. First, would the same policies in another country of, say, 25 million people have the same effects? Secondly, could the same policies be instituted? Thirdly, could the same success be generalized to a very large country, say India, or even to the developing world in general?

I think the answer to the first question, provided it is not a land-locked country far from any port,[51] depends essentially on the people. Entrepreneurial ability, and the responsiveness of farmers to change, surely varies. But I think all people will learn to take advantage of opportunities. I believe it is only the degree of response, and the time it takes, which is in question. This assumes of course that the developed countries would not block exports by quotas.

[50] Both Ranis, op. cit., and Thorbecke, op. cit., have written on the subject of transferability. They should also be consulted.

[51] There is no harm to be locked in by rich countries; cf. Switzerland and Austria.

Whether the policies could be initiated is more difficult. Some of the changes made in the 'four', except Hong Kong, have proved difficult and unpopular elsewhere. Strong government, not beholden to particular vested interests, may be necessary. To show this we must examine some of the main policy features separately.

Very extensive land reform, as has often been pointed out, was relatively easy in Korea and Taiwan. Japanese landlords had left. In Taiwan particularly, the authorities were not beholden to Taiwanese landlords. In Korea (as in Japan and to some extent in Taiwan also), the Americans played a key role. Political considerations are very different in most other developing countries.

As Thorbecke points out,[52] it was essential to accompany the land reform in Taiwan with strengthened services to farmers. This, and agricultural planning, was accomplished by the JCRR, which was quasi-independent of the government and was independently financed. It still pays higher salaries than regular government departments, and attracts a high level of personnel. These particular features of agricultural support may be politically difficult to copy. But the idea of a high level of attention to agriculture, with responsibility for coordination situated in a single organization and not split between many departments (agricultural research, and extension, irrigation, roads, power, etc., are generally all planned separately and with little coordination), should be transferable. Something similar has been repeatedly advocated by Professor Raanan Weitz.[53]

The industrialization and trade policies should be easier to implement.[54] But any reorientation and liberalization will be opposed by vested interests, both businessmen and bureaucrats. Hong Kong never had to reorientate: and Korea, Taiwan, and Singapore had the advantage that import substitution policies were relatively mild and had been in force for fairly short periods. Protection of certain industries can, of course, be maintained for a while, where it is needed—as has been the case in both Taiwan and Korea. Even so, the change in policy met considerable opposition in Taiwan and was probably implemented only as a result of the conviction of one or two strong characters in key positions. In some countries, the change in policy may cause a considerable, but probably short-term, shift in income distribution, which may also be troublesome.[55] I believe that free labour markets have been an important factor. Where there are strong unions, or

[52] In Galenson, op. cit.

[53] R. Weitz, *From Peasant to Farmer*, Columbia University Press, New York, 1972.

[54] Indeed, still better policies! Although the Korean and Taiwan policies fulfil the essential function of giving industrialization sufficient encouragement without discriminating against exports, simpler ways of doing the same thing can surely be devised; see e.g. I. M. D. Little, T. Scitovsky, and M. FG. Scott, *Industrialisation and Trade in Some Developing Countries*, Oxford University Press, Oxford, 1970.

[55] The history of many attempts to adopt liberal trading policies has been told at length by J. N. Bhagwati, *Anatomy and Consequences of Exchange Control Regimes*, National Bureau of Economic Research, 1988; and A. O. Krueger, *Foreign Trade Regimes and Economic Development: Liberalisation Attempts and Consequences*, National Bureau of Economic Research, 1987, and their supporting authors, in the major NBER study of this subject.

where the government itself has instituted a dualistic structure of wages, these will be very difficult to change. In Singapore, the unions were very strong, and were also communist-dominated. There was great labour unrest in the early sixties. Prime Minister Lee Kuan Yew then successfully 'rode the tiger'. Very comprehensive labour and union legislation was enacted in the late sixties. Employment conditions that were previously in the sphere of collective bargaining are now controlled by law, and the government has wide powers to settle strikes (which require a secret ballot). There appears now to be an active incomes policy, with control over wage increases as an import element in macroeconomic policy. This may often be a more possible road to travel than trying to recreate the labour market conditions of our other countries.

In the case of a very large country, like India, it is obvious that manufactured exports alone cannot revolutionize the situation. But that is no reason against liberal trading policies, and industrial decontrol. Such policies can still make a major difference to the lives of tens of millions of people, as they have in the Far East. Furthermore, we have been at pains to point out that the domestic market dominates even in a country like Korea. The rise in the capital intensity of Indian manufacturing, overwhelmingly of course for the domestic market, is terrible to behold.[56] Much greater trade in manufactures, as well as less domestic incentive to use capital and save labour, could surely have done much to help alleviate this.

Lastly, there is the question of how widely beneficial export-oriented policies can be. Here we have to contend with the evils of the new protectionism, which has grown apace in 1977 and 1978. Whether this is just a lull in the development of more liberal trading policies (in manufactures) on the part of the industrialized countries, a development promoted by the United States since 1945, or the beginning of a new mercantilist era, I do not know. Some of the portends are alarming, such as the conversion of the US trade union movement to protectionism, and the extremely restrictive approach of the EEC in the new textile agreements.

As against this, there are a number of favourable considerations. Market penetration of the labour-intensive product markets of the developed countries by developing countries is still very small. The recent World Bank *World Development Report, 1978* gives some figures. Textiles and clothing from developing countries is 8 per cent of the total supply in Germany, 6 per cent in Canada, 4 per cent in the USA and in Japan, and 2 per cent in France (which may be compared with 12 per cent penetration by Japan of the UK automobile market). It seems almost inconceivable (or anyway appalling) that, given the attractions for consumers, these proportions will not be allowed to rise. There are many other promising product lines, e.g. furniture and furnishings, where the proportion is negligible.

[56] See e.g. J. Mellor, *The New Economics of Growth*, Cornell University Press, Ithaca, NY, 1976, chapters V and VI; R. Banerji and J. Riedel, 'Industrial Employment Expansion under Alternative Development Strategies: Some Empirical Evidence', mimeographed, provide a direct comparison of industrial labour absorption in India and Taiwan.

Another favourable factor is that Japan is increasingly losing its market share of these products.[57] This is likely to permit greater penetration of North American and Western European markets by developing countries. Also, in their turn, not only are the 'four' turning to more sophisticated products, but also, the rate of growth of their exports is, quite apart from restrictions, bound to approximate to that of GDP instead of vastly exceeding it. This should leave quite a lot of room for others. The final point to make it that, even if the developed countries become increasingly protective, there is still nothing to lose, and something to gain, by more open policies. Developing countries can trade more with each other. There would *naturally* be somewhat more import substitution; but that would come about without import substitution policies.

[57] See D. C. Cole, 'Market Penetration of Asia's Super Exporters', in W. Hong and A. O. Krueger, *Trade and Development in Korea*, Korea Development Institute, Seoul, 1971.

13

Small Manufacturing Enterprises and Employment in Developing Countries (1988)

In the 1970s a number of international institutions, and development activists, became very concerned that growth in developing countries was not reaching the poor. In particular, industrial development was capital-intensive and absorbed little of the rapidly increasing labour force. An increased demand for unskilled labour was surely an essential component of any programme to alleviate poverty. This concern for employment was soon linked to the advocacy of small-scale enterprises which were widely believed to offer more employment than larger enterprises for any given amount of investment. Some international institutions, including the World Bank, tried to steer more of their loans towards small-scale enterprises; and some developing countries, especially India, intensified measures to support and protect such enterprises.

This article does not question the objectives of a more labour-demanding industrial development. Indeed, the author has long stressed the anomaly that a small minority of people in developing countries work with ever-increasing amounts of capital while the great majority continue to scratch a bare living with a few primitive tools. It does, however, suggest that supply-side interventions—subsidized loans, tax relief, industrial estates, product reservation, etc.—linked to small enterprises are of little or no use in achieving the objective of a more labour-demanding industrial development. This view is derived largely from the author's participation in a World Bank research project on the subject of small manufacturing enterprises in developing countries.[1]

This paper first appeared in the *Asian Development Review*, 6/2 (1988). Permission to reproduce is gratefully acknowledged.

[1] The principal publications resulting from this research project have been D. Anderson and F. Khambata, *Small Enterprises and Development Policy in the Philippines: A case study*, World Bank Staff Working Paper no. 468 (Washington, DC, 1981); D. Anderson, *Small Industry in Developing Countries: Some issues*, World Bank Staff Working Paper no. 518 (Washington, DC, 1982); D. Anderson, 'Small Industry in Developing Countries: A discussion of issues', *World Development*, 10 (1982), pp. 913–48; M. Cortes, A. Berry, and A. Ishaq, *Success in Small and Medium-Scale Enterprises: The evidence from Colombia* (Baltimore: Johns Hopkins University Press, 1987); S. P. S. Ho, *Small-Scale Enterprises in Korea and Taiwan*, World Bank Staff Working Paper no. 384 (Washington, DC, 1980); D. Mazumdar, *The Issue of Small versus Large in the Indian Textile Industry: An analytical and historical survey*, World Bank Staff Working Paper no. 645 (Washington, DC, 1984); J. M. Page, *Small Enterprises in African Development: A survey*, World Bank Staff Working Paper

We have seen that small-scale enterprises were believed to be labour intensive; i.e., they had a low capital–labour ratio. But this alone could not be a sufficient reason for favouring them. Value added cannot be ignored. Indeed, if only capital is scarce, capital productivity is crucial. If small enterprises have lower capital productivity than larger ones, then one should invest in the latter, since more output is obtained. Even if the larger enterprises need employ fewer workers, the employment objective can be met by making them employ workers to do nothing. This is in fact a very common practice in many developing countries; but it is not good practice, for labour almost always and everywhere has some opportunity cost. If not employed wherever it is, it would somehow earn some money and produce something elsewhere, and if possible should not therefore be used to produce nothing. There is no escaping the conclusion that the case for promoting any particular type of enterprise is that it uses factors of production more efficiently, given their social cost, than other types. Proponents of small-scale enterprises on grounds of employment and production must therefore claim that: (1) they are relatively labour-intensive; (2) they have relatively high capital productivity; and (3) these characteristics represent a more efficient use of capital and labour.

If small firms do turn out to be relatively labour-intensive, then this is probably because they face a lower price of labour relative to capital than do larger enterprises. If this relatively low wage is also closer to its relative shadow price, i.e. the relative social cost of labour, then it will follow that small-scale enterprises are employing labour and capital more efficiently from a social point of view, although it is to be expected that labour productivity will be low (but not zero) in such labour-intensive enterprises.

Clearly, the next step is to look at the facts and determine the empirical relationship between size and the three ratios, viz., capital intensity, capital productivity, and labour productivity. The expected relationship is that capital intensity and labour productivity rise with size, while capital productivity falls.

Size must next be defined. The most common measure of the size of an establishment or firm is the number of workers. In industrial countries, small-scale commonly means less than 200–300 workers. However, in developing countries, the average establishment size is smaller, and 'small' will generally be taken to mean 1–49 workers; similarly, 'medium size' will generally mean 50–199 workers. Size may also be measured by capital employed, and this may for some purposes be a more appropriate measure. It is used for policy purposes in India, but

no. 363 (Washington, DC, 1979); J. M. Page, 'Firm Size and Technical Efficiency: Applications of production frontiers to Indian survey data', *Journal of Development Economics*, 16 (1984), pp. 129–52; I. M. D. Little, D. Mazumdar, and J. M. Page, *Small Manufacturing Enterprises: A comparative study of India and other economies* (New York: Oxford University Press, 1987); and I. M. D. Little, 'Small Manufacturing Enterprises in Developing Countries', *World Bank Economic Review*, 1/2 (1987).

None of these authors, except myself, are in any way committed to the views expressed in the present article. The World Bank research project on which this article largely relies is reported at much greater length in Little, Mazumdar, and Page, op. cit.

even there size distributions by capital employed are often unobtainable. Both the availability of statistics and the fact that employment size is more easily envisaged make it the dominant measure.

Ideally, capital is measured by its replacement cost. However, this is usually unobtainable, and one has to hope that such measures as are obtainable (often simply the book value) are reasonably unbiased estimates of replacement cost. The number of workers and the amount of labour input can also present difficulties, e.g. the treatment of part-time and family workers. However, the following reported results are stark and robust enough to remain valid in the face of the manifold statistical problems encountered in the empirical research.

First, census material was investigated. For the aggregate of manufacturing, the factor proportions and productivity behaved much as expected, though with some exceptions, especially in the case of capital productivity. For instance, in the case of Japan (census of 1966) the only anomaly was that capital productivity *rose* from the smallest size class (1–9 workers) and peaked in the range 20–49 workers. Turning to developing countries, it can be said that labour productivity and capital intensity rose with size with only a few anomalies.[2] But capital productivity was highly erratic. The latest available Colombian and Korean censuses were examined under the World Bank project. In the case of Colombia (1976 census), capital productivity also behaved erratically but with a tendency to peak in the range 20–99 workers.[3] In the Republic of Korea (1968 census), capital intensity was virtually constant in the range 10–199 workers. Capital productivity was almost constant for 5–49 workers, but then *rose* dramatically before falling again for the largest size groups of 200 workers or more. Firms in the size group 100–199 dominated; i.e., they had both higher labour and higher capital productivity than the smaller size classes. Indeed, compared with the size class 10–19 workers, the larger firms achieved more than double the capital and labour productivity, while there was virtually no difference in the capital–labour ratio.[4] A very similar finding is true for Thailand, where firms in the same medium-size class (100–199 workers) also virtually dominated all smaller size classes.[5]

It already appears that there is some evidence to suggest that medium-size firms may use labour and capital more efficiently than small firms. However, thus far we have considered only manufacturing firms aggregated over all industries. But any such comparison of the economic characteristics of smaller and larger plants averaged over all industries is of very limited interest; and would still be of very limited interest even if it had been found that the expected rise in capital intensity with size, and fall in capital productivity, held good over the whole size

[2] See K. Ohkawa and M. Tajima, *Small-Medium Scale Manufacturing Industry. A comparative study of Japan and developing nations* (Tokyo: International Development Centre of Japan, 1976). This study covered nine developing countries, but excluded size classes with less than 20 workers.

[3] See Cortes, Berry, and Ishaq, op. cit., chapter 2.

[4] See Ho, op. cit.

[5] S. Tambunlertchai and C. Loohawenchit, 'Labour-Intensive and Small-Scale Manufacturing in Thailand', in R. Amjad (ed.), *The Development of Labour Intensive Industry in ASEAN Countries* (Geneva: International Labour Organisation, 1981).

range. This is because such a relationship might arise in the aggregate because some industries typically use little capital in small plants with high capital and low labour productivity, and vice versa for other industries, but with little or no regular variation between units of different sizes within industries. If this were the case, then the best way to increase the demand for labour would be to increase the demand for the products of those industries that are typically labour-intensive and have high capital productivity. The size of the establishments within each industry would be irrelevant, and supply-side intervention in favour of small enterprises would be equally irrelevant. If in contrast, within particular narrowly defined industries, small units are more labour-intensive than large units, and have higher capital productivity, while their products are closely competitive with those of large units, then supply-side intervention in favour of the small would indeed be appropriate. The moral is that disaggregation is essential if any policy conclusions are to be drawn.

The Korean census (1968) was unique in that results had been published at the four-digit and even five-digit levels of the Standard Industrial Classification. In an analysis of the census, it was found that regularities prevailing in the aggregated statistics rarely carried over to industries defined at the four-digit level.[6] For instance, monotonicity of rising capital intensity with size was found in only two of 160 industries where there were plants in at least four different size categories. More than that would occur by chance, so that it is as if there were something causing irregularity.

The figures certainly do not support the belief that small plants, as measured by numbers employed, are typically labour-intensive. The incidence of maximum labour intensity was almost even over the various size classes from 5 to 499 workers, and the highest capital intensity occurred as often in the range 5–49 workers as in the range from 50 upwards. Capital productivity peaked in the range 50–499 in two-thirds of the 160 industries in which there were units in at least four size classes. Both statistical weaknesses and reality doubtless contributed to the turbulence of the disaggregated figures. Capital measures are very unreliable. In this census, capital comprised the book value of owned tangible fixed assets but excluded rented assets. On this definition, total capital used is more likely to be understated for small enterprises than for large ones. Value added is also unreliable, most especially for the smaller size classes, many of which do not keep records. And where records are kept, value added may be falsified to deceive the tax inspector. Turbulence is also present in reality. One enterprise or even a whole size class of enterprises in a particular industry may have a good or bad year for reasons quite unconnected with production functions or normal market conditions.

Statistics for very small units are the most unreliable, and the largest size classes contained few units. For this reason comparisons were made between the size classes 20–49 and 100–199 workers. Out of 213 industries in all, 139 had

[6] See Ho, op. cit., for an analysis of the census.

entries in both these two size classes. In 67 cases, capital intensity was lower and capital productivity higher in the larger class. In 40 out of the 67 cases labour productivity was also higher. So, to this extent, the feature of the aggregate figures—non-increasing capital intensity and higher productivities—carried through to disaggregation.

It should also be noted that inter-industry variations in capital intensity were far greater than the average intra-industry variations by size group. The latter seldom varied by a figure of more than 3, while the range of the former was over 100.

A simple cost–benefit analysis using actual wages as shadow wages and a 20 per cent rate of return as the shadow price of capital was also made in the study. Out of 138 industries,[7] the peak of the benefit–cost ratio was in the range 50–499 workers in 88 cases, and was spread fairly evenly over this range. Thirty-two industries performed best in the range below 50 workers, of which seven cases were in the class 5–9 workers; 18 performed best in the range of 500 workers or more.

Under the World Bank project, in the case of India, factor ratios and productivities were first compared for the 1972 census of Small Scale Industries and the Annual Survey of Industry (averaged over the period 1974–7). The results were not very favourable to the small-scale firms.[8] Second, inspection of the 1978–9 Annual Survey of Industry showed that the size class of 200–499 workers very nearly dominated all other size classes having both higher labour and higher capital productivity. Third, a Reserve Bank of India Survey of small establishments that had been assisted by the commercial banks showed better productivity figures for the larger small (16–20 workers) than the smaller small establishments.[9]

It was also evident from this Reserve Bank of India Survey that, if one orders establishments by capital employed (especially when measured by the original value of plant and machinery) rather than the number of workers, then the capital–labour ratios and productivities behave more regularly in the expected manner than when employment is used as the size discriminator. This speaks well for the Indian formula for defining the small (which is in terms of the original value of plant and machinery), but for the fact that the Annual Survey of Industry does not publish size distributions on this basis. It should further be noted that there is other scattered evidence that the capital–labour ratios and productivities behave more closely in accordance with expectations when size is defined by capital employed rather than by employment.

The results reported thus far give little or no support to those who propose to favour small-scale enterprises on grounds of efficient employment, especially if size is measured by the number of workers. The same conclusion was reached by

[7] The number was reduced to 138 by excluding industries whose output was prima facie heterogeneous and those that did not have establishments in at least four size classes.

[8] See Little, Mazumdar, and Page, op. cit., table 7.4.

[9] Department of Statistics, Reserve Bank of India, 'Survey of Small Industrial Units 1979', *Statistical Report*, vols. 1 and 2 (Bombay, 1979).

comparing the same Reserve Bank of India Survey mentioned above with the census sector of the 1976–7 Annual Survey of Industry (which covers factories employing 50 or more workers with the aid of power, or 100 or more without power).[10] Thirty-seven three-digit industries could be compared. In 16 industries the larger Annual Survey of Industry firms dominated the smaller Reserve Bank of India Survey firms; in only one case (edible oils and fats) did the latter dominate the former. An efficiency index, weighting the relative factor productivities by their income shares (averaged over both the Reserve Bank of India Survey and Annual Survey of Industry firms), was also computed. Depending on the measurement of capital used, the Reserve Bank of India Survey firms were less 'efficient' in 34 or 35 out of the 37 industries. It was found that the relative inefficiency of small units was least where there was also little difference in the capital–labour ratio. It was concluded: 'Evidently, small-scale industries cannot be relied upon to generate a large amount of employment efficiently. Where they have substantial advantage in employment generation, they are relatively inefficient; and where they are efficient, they do not have much advantage in employment generation.'[11] Another interesting finding was that of a negative relationship between short-term bank borrowing and efficiency.[12]

It has been suggested that censuses and surveys that use employment as the size discriminator bias results against the small for the following reasons. They are snapshots of a large number of firms each of whose output and employment vary over time. At any one moment, the small size classes will include firms that are having a bad time, although they may be quite large in terms of capital or output and employment potential. Further, the small sizes will include new start-ups that have installed much of their equipment but as yet employ few people and have little output. Such firms will appear to be small, capital-intensive, and inefficient. The point is well taken. And we have seen that when some measure of capital is used as the size discriminator, then results are more in line with expectations and less damning to small units. However, as against this, there is the point that measuring by capital biases results in favour of small units. This is because censuses will normally record the written-down book value of capital, which results in an underestimate of the 'size' of older enterprises.

Partly because census figures seemed to be of doubtful reliability, and also because it was thought desirable to obtain more information than censuses give, a number of new intensive surveys of narrowly defined industries in India and Colombia were conducted under the World Bank research.[13] In India the surveys

[10] See Goldar, 'Relative Efficiency of Modern Small Scale Industries in India', in K. B. Suri (ed.), *Small Scale Enterprises in Industrial Development: The Indian Experience* (New Delhi: Sage, 1988, pp. 95–117).

[11] Ibid., p. 111.

[12] As Goldar points out, his findings are in this respect and others close to those for the Republic of Korea; see Ho, op. cit.

[13] These surveys are fully reported in Little, Mazumdar, and Page, op. cit.; and Cortes, Berry, and Ishaq, op. cit.

included printing, machine tools, soap, shoes, metal casting, powerlooms, and handlooms; and in Colombia, metal-working and food processing. These surveys support the evidence from other surveys and from censuses discussed above. In none of the industries was there a monotonic relationship between employment size and capital intensity; and when the distributions were partitioned into size groups, the intragroup variance of factor proportions and productivities was so great that intergroup differences in the means were rarely of statistical significance. Indeed, in only one industry (machine tools) was there a statistically significant difference between the factor productivities of the very small units (less than 10 workers) and those of larger-sized firms. Both labour and capital productivity were low in the small units.

When establishments were ranked by capital (undepreciated book values converted to 1980 prices), the factor proportions and productivities varied with size in a manner that was closer to expectations than when employment was used as the size discriminator. This confirms what has been found in other surveys, as already mentioned. Nevertheless, there were substantial irregularities, and the differences between size groups were frequently insignificant, intragroup variations remaining high.

Before proceeding to a more general discussion of the role of small-scale industries, and of industrial and other policies that affect the size structure of industry, it seems worthwhile drawing a few conclusions from the evidence thus far presented.

1. The size of an enterprise, as measured by the number of workers, is a poor indicator of anything of economic or social significance.
2. Nevertheless, the evidence suggests that technical and social efficiency is most likely to be found in plants in the medium or medium–large range of 50–499 workers.
3. Employment has been the most important argument in favour of supply-side interventions to promote small-scale enterprises. But employment size is a poor indicator even of labour intensity, let alone social advantage.
4. Size measured by capital employed is a better,but still unreliable, indicator of factor proportions and productivities. An enterprise that subsists with virtually no capital must have high capital productivity. Such enterprises are using traditional methods. They can be quite large in terms of employment. The important distinction between such enterprises and the small modern factory or workshop was made long ago.[14]
5. Leaving aside traditional manufacturing, which is largely confined to clothing, food processing, and the making of simple utensils, the differences in labour intensity between normally operating firms within narrowly defined industries are small compared with the differences between industries. So

[14] P. N. Dhar and H. F. Lydall, *The Role of Small Enterprises in Indian Economic Development* (Bombay: Asia Publishing House, 1961).

changes in the composition of output can do more to increase the demand for labour than interventions designed to alter the plant size structure of particular industries.

The industrial policies, and macroeconomic policies, of developing countries have certainly discriminated against small enterprises. Industrialization has been promoted in three main ways, viz. by regulating trade, by investment incentives, and by directly undertaking public sector investments. The whole strategy of import substitution encourages large-scale capital-intensive industries whether in the public or private sectors, and controls also usually favour large-scale enterprises. The same is true of investment incentives, only India in the last 10–15 years being an exception. Admittedly, most countries have adopted some measures to offset the disadvantages imposed upon small-scale enterprises by their general macroeconomic and industrialization policies. But, with the exception of India, these have been marginal.

However, our account of the facts suggests that a bias against the small is not in itself responsible for the bias against labour-intensive development. The contrasting experiences of India and the Republic of Korea strongly support this suggestion. India has done much to preserve and encourage small-scale enterprises, and its industrial development has been, and remains, highly capital-intensive. The Republic of Korea has done very little for the small enterprises, and tiny manufacturing enterprises have almost vanished. Yet its industrial development has been the most labour-intensive in the world, at least from around 1960 to the mid-1970s. In the Republic of Korea between 1963 and 1975 manufacturing employment grew by 11 per cent per annum, absorbing over one million persons, 86 per cent of which was accounted for by firms with 100 employees or more in 1963.[15]

One wonders why so many people wrongly think that large size and capital intensity invariably go together. I believe it is because they think in terms of containers—tanks and tankers, ovens, pipes, and furnaces—where the action or value added is within the container, and the few workers are outside. But there are many industries—textiles, clothing, engineering, and assemblies of all kinds—where the main container is the factory itself, and the many workers are inside. In such industries, larger size tends to result in greater labour intensity.

The negative conclusion of this article is that a policy of supply-side interventions in favour of small-scale enterprises will not promote an efficient labour-intensive development. Since the main way in which industrialization can improve the distribution of income is via increasing the demand for labour, one can also say that such interventions will do little or nothing to improve distribution or relieve poverty.

The elements of a sound policy, or policy reform, directed towards a more labour-intensive industrial development include the following.

[15] See Ho, op. cit.

1. Trade and protectionist policies should be changed to make exporting as profitable as domestic sales. At the margin, exports are more labour-intensive than import substitutes, and we have seen that there is much more mileage, so far as employment generation is concerned, in changing the composition of output than changing the size distribution of plants within particular industries.
2. Interest rates should not be subsidized. If any limit is placed on interest rates charged by banks and other institutions (and this may be advisable if the banking system is inexperienced and non-competitive), it should be quite high and intended to permit a real rate of at least 20 per cent for the riskier loans (which include those to small enterprises).
3. At present, many governments encourage, directly or indirectly, high wages in 'organized' industry. Many have also passed labour legislation making it very difficult to sack workers. Such policies strongly encourage capital intensity in the larger enterprises, and generally distort labour markets. They should be abandoned or at least modified.
4. Any supply-side industrial promotion measures should disregard and, so far as possible, be neutral between firm or establishment sizes. They should not subsidize or favour the use of capital, as so many do (e.g. low interest rates, tariff waivers on imported capital goods and accelerated depreciation).

Almost all governmental interventions in developing countries which alter prices, directly or indirectly, bias them in favour of capital intensity, and against employment. It is small wonder that policies directed towards a more labour-intensive development can be described as 'getting the prices right'. But one should add that fiscal and other policies which tend towards a more equal development probably also promote labour demand, since relatively poor persons probably demand relatively labour-intensive products. Since labour intensity is itself equalizing, there is a virtuous circle here.

14

Macroeconomic Analysis and the Developing Countries, 1970–1990 (1993)

NEGLECT OF THE MACROECONOMICS OF DEVELOPING COUNTRIES

In 1982 I wrote that 'the short and medium term macroeconomic management of LDCs was a much neglected subject until very recently, when some work began to appear'. 'But this is too recent,' I added, 'and perhaps as yet too tentative, for me to have been able to absorb it' (Little 1982).

The reasons for the neglect are clear. Until the early 1970s, there was little use of the instruments of macroeconomic policy, and little variability in such use as there was. Consider first the handling of balance of payments problems. Exchange rates were fixed, relative to the US dollar, the pound sterling, or the French franc. Of course, there were some devaluations, but they were regarded as measures of last resort. (Notable empirical studies of these measures include Díaz-Alejandro 1965, and Cooper 1971.) These studies showed that 'the most exaggerated fears of those opposing devaluation cannot be backed by substantial experience' (Díaz-Alejandro 1971). But policy-makers in developing countries preferred to control imports, and almost all development economists endorsed this policy, holding strong a priori views about the inefficiency and even perversity of changes in exchange rates. The consequent protectionism chimed in well with the belief in import-substituting industrialization.

The use of reserves and borrowing abroad can also be regarded as instruments for dealing with balance of payments problems. While, of course, these instruments were used, their use was much more constrained than it later became. Reserves were usually kept low, and were not built up when there was a favourable movement in the terms of trade. Holding large reserves was rare and widely regarded as a waste of development potential. Borrowing was, apart from trade credit, mainly concessionary and official, and was limited by the creditor countries. So there was little room for the deliberate use by a developing country of unused borrowing capacity to meet temporary balance of payments diffi-

This paper first appeared as Occasional Paper no. 41 in the series published by the International Center for Economic Growth (ICS Press, San Francisco, 1993). Permission to reproduce is gratefully acknowledged.

culties (though in some cases aid was increased for this purpose by donor agencies).

Turning to fiscal policy, we note that financial markets in many LDCs were so underdeveloped that governments could borrow little or nothing from the public. In some, however, deposit-taking banks were forced to buy government paper at low interest rates. It was recognized that this deprived the private sector of funds; but this was not a matter for deep concern where public investment was believed to be more important for development. Thus, budget deficits that could not be financed by foreign borrowing were financed mainly by borrowing from the central bank, and the increase in the quantity of money associated with a given deficit was probably fairly constant. In these circumstances fiscal policy largely consisted of deciding the size of the government deficit that would have to be financed domestically, because this would determine the increase in the quantity of money and inflation. Most countries outside Latin America were monetarist in outlook and fairly restrained in their budgetary policies. In Latin America this restraint was rare, and certain aspects of inflation were much discussed, particularly the question of whether it was an unavoidable concomitant of growth with a supposedly rigid economic structure. But it was not discussed in the context of a general macroeconomic model. Thus, the concept of inflation as a tax was not used, although it had been so christened at least as long ago as 1923.[1]

Monetary policy consisted mainly of controlling interest rates at low levels, thus ensuring an excess demand for credit, which allowed governments to influence or direct the lending of the commercial banks and development finance institutions.

The above sketch, which is not too much of a caricature, shows that the reason for the lack of studies of short- and medium term macroeconomic policy is largely that there was not much for the economic theorist to analyse. With interest rates and exchange rates (and a good many other prices) controlled, and foreign borrowing exogenously constrained, the complex interactions between the main macroeconomic magnitudes, which are now the diet of macroeconomists, were suppressed. By the same token, there was little experience on the part of economic policy-makers of how to construct coherent economic policies when there came to be more degrees of freedom.

The biggest change in the economic environment in the early 1970s was the rise in the availability of foreign finance. There was little in the recent development literature in the early 1970s, or even during most of the 1970s, about either the domestic consequences of heavy foreign borrowing or the prudent limits to such borrowing. History is studded with debt crises, but in the postwar period

[1] A subheading of chapter 2 of Keynes (1923) reads: 'inflation as a method of taxation'. Personally, I have some misgivings about the term 'inflation tax'. Although inflation resembles a tax, in that it raises resources for the government, its rate is more of an accident than a deliberate imposition. It is only in some models that the government chooses the rate of inflation. At the time of writing, Keynes thought that there was a good deal to be said for the inflation tax if it was kept low. Cooper tends to agree with Keynes (see Cooper 1991).

they were quite rare before the early 1980s. The Pertamina crisis in Indonesia was the most notorious, but this arose from the short-term borrowing of a parastatal enterprise and was atypical. Ghana was the other serious case, but this too involved overborrowing on short-term suppliers' credits. In 1970, no developing country was over the top so far as the ratio of long-term debt to gross domestic product (GDP) was concerned. A few, such as India and Pakistan, had high ratios of debt to exports (around 350 per cent) but their borrowing was concessionary, and their debt service was less than 25 per cent of exports. There was little awareness or analysis of debt traps—with the exception of Andrzej Krassowski's 1974 study—though it is also true that the state of play excused this neglect.

Other degrees of freedom were then and still are more a matter of choice by government. There were in the 1960s occasional relaxations of those controls over trade or finance that were, as we have seen, typical of the developing world. Almost all of these liberalization attempts were failures, the exceptions being those in Korea, Taiwan, and Singapore; and there followed a reversion to the trade and financial repression model. They were made in the context of balance of payments or inflationary crises without benefit of a coherent macroeconomic plan, and without surrender of the ideology of import substitution or the belief that the government should direct credit.

In *Industry and Trade in Some Developing Countries* (1970), Little, Scitovsky, and Scott (henceforth LSS) provided an analysis, based on studies of six countries, of the iniquities of import substitution and control systems.[2] Their study also contained macroeconomic analysis, especially in chapter 11 (written by M. FG. Scott), which tackled the problem of how best to traverse from a highly protected industrial system, heavily dependent on import controls, to a far less protected system, in which the balance of payments was kept in equilibrium by the traditional methods of fiscal and monetary policy and the exchange rate. The suggested steps were gradual. First, tariffs should replace quotas. Then there would be an initial large devaluation, offset by changes in tariffs and export taxes. These would be gradually reduced in a planned and announced manner to a simple, uniform low tariff. The problems of interest rates and capital movements were mentioned, but not sufficiently analysed. These latter problems were more fully considered by Mackinnon and by Shaw, whose 1973 books mounted as strong an attack on financial repression as LSS had on trade repression. Mackinnon analysed the Korean liberalization of the 1960s in particular, this perhaps constituting the first macroeconomic analysis of any liberalization process. He mainly criticized the failure to liberalize imports sufficiently, resulting in an excessive buildup of reserves, and hence monetary expansion and inflation.

[2] This whole project of the OECD Development Centre seems also to have been a model for the four much larger comparative studies initiated by the World Bank in the 1980s. The country studies that were published by Oxford University Press were *Brazil* by J. Bergsman, *India* by J. Bhagwati and P. Desai, *Mexico* by T. King, *Pakistan* by S. Lewis, the *Philippines* by G. Sicat, and *Taiwan* by M. Hsing.

So far as policy was concerned, these books were widely ignored in the 1970s, except in Chile and Korea. The Chilean liberalization of trade followed the advocacy of LSS quite closely. Perhaps this work was read in Chicago. So far as Korea is concerned, E. S. Shaw was, I believe, very influential in the later 1960s and early 1970s. When I was in Korea in the late 1970s, I asked Kim Jae-Ik, then a high official in the Economic Planning Bureau, about the trend of their policies. He said I had no need to ask him. Pulling LSS down from his shelves, he said 'these are the policies we are going to pursue'. From about 1973 to 1978, however, Korea had embarked on a drive for heavy industry which could not be said to be in the spirit of LSS (or, for that matter, of Shaw or Mackinnon).

But it is probably exceptional for a book or article to be influential in less than a decade. Normally the influence is initially only on students; one then has to wait about two decades before they are in power, even in developing countries. The economic presumptions of those in authority in the 1970s had been formed by the development economics of the 1950s and early 1960s. This impressed on them the essential role of the public sector in promoting development, the importance of industrialization through import substitution, and the need for a big push to propel the economic process on to a take-off path. Taken together, these factors clearly indicated to them a large rise in public sector investment as soon as borrowing became easy, especially as they would have read little or nothing about the need for prudence in increasing the foreign debt.

The seeds of decontrol might have fallen on less stony ground if it had not been for the new ease of borrowing. This permitted fast growth of gross national product (GNP) for the time being, despite the oil price shock of 1973–4. There was little incentive to change policies. It seems that disaster, or if not disaster at least a period of stagnation, is usually a necessary condition for successful reform. The borrowing during the years 1973–82 was disastrous for many countries, although it was accompanied by a rise in investment, mainly public investment, as a proportion of GNP. But bad policies, which the borrowing permitted to continue, resulted in the rise in investment being insufficient to prevent the increasing debt from becoming a crippling burden. A period of reform began in 1983.

A WORLD BANK PROJECT ON MACROECONOMIC MANAGEMENT IN DEVELOPING COUNTRIES

Only about two years after my published remark that macroeconomic management was a neglected subject, and despite the fact that I had paid little attention to macroeconomics since I was in the UK Treasury in the mid-1950s, I found myself designing, with the close help of Max Corden, a major research project on that subject on behalf of the World Bank. Carlos Díaz-Alejandro, who in our opinion was an almost indispensable partner in this enterprise, agreed to join.

Very sadly, before he could make much contribution, he died. Richard Cooper agreed to replace him. After the usual considerable delay, the World Bank agreed that the project should go forward under the direction of Sarath Rajapatirana, who is also co-author of the recent synthesis volume *Boom, Crisis and Adjustment: The macroeconomic experience of developing countries.*

The project was to investigate the macroeconomic policies of seventeen (later eighteen) developing countries from about 1965, to record and analyse their successes and failures in dealing with disturbances, whether internal or external, exogenous or policy induced, and to assess the effects of such short- and medium-term policies on long-run growth.[3] The countries were not selected in any scientific manner. We aimed to include all the major non-centrally planned economies, to have about equal numbers from the continents of Asia, Africa, and Latin America, and to have at least a sprinkling of small countries. Apart from the above criteria, whether or not a country was included often depended on our finding someone we trusted who was keen to do the job. The result was quite a diverse set of countries, whether diversity is measured in terms of politics, population, poverty, or previous history. Together they comprise about 60 per cent of the GDP of developing market economies.

Corden (1990, 1993) and Cooper (1991, 1992) have independently published what might be called interim reports on this research project, in particular the policy lessons to be learned. Reference should also be made to John Williamson's comment in Corden (1990). In what follows I also draw almost exclusively on this same research project. I hardly disagree with anything that Cooper and Corden have written independently, nor, of course, with the actual concluding chapter of the forthcoming book. But the stress both in the interpretation of the history of the period (1965–90, but especially 1973–90) and in the choice of lessons may differ slightly.

The whole period 1973–90 divides informatively into three periods of boom, crisis, and adjustment, as the title of the book implies. The first period, 1973–9, in which there was satisfactory growth for most countries, begins with the oil price rises of 1973–4, and ends with the second oil price shock of 1979. The second period, 1979–82, is one of rapidly developing crisis, marked by balance of payments problems and heavy borrowing, as well as recessions or stagnation, ending with the debt crisis of 1982. The last period is one of major policy reforms and a recovery of output for most countries: the debt crisis was contained, but debt remained a serious burden. Although the 1980s may be termed a lost decade for most of Africa and some countries of Central and South America, major advances were made by several Asian countries.

[3] The 17 countries were Argentina, Brazil, Cameroon, Chile, Colombia, Costa Rice, Côte d'Ivoire, India, Indonesia, Kenya, Mexico, Morocco, Nigeria, Pakistan, Sri Lanka, Thailand, and Turkey. Country studies were commissioned for all of these, usually with two authors involved. It is hoped that many of these book-length studies will be published. No country study was commissioned for Korea, but it was added because Cooper was already engaged in a Korean study and was familiar with the economy.

A PERIOD OF CHEAP AND EASY CREDIT: 1973–1979

I guess that some may think that the dominant event of this first period, for the non-oil exporters among developing countries, was the shock of the severe worsening of the terms of trade that the oil price rise caused. Although this was certainly a shock, it did not cause a recession in any of our eighteen countries, at worst a slowing down of growth.[4] During this period three of the countries benefited from the oil price rise, while for five others its importance was overshadowed by the greater importance of the price of coffee, which tripled from 1975 to 1977.[5] But even for these coffee producers, the greater ease of borrowing (itself partly caused by the oil price rise) was a major influence, while for the rest (except for India) it was the dominant influence.

Borrowing permitted countries not merely to avoid any temporary fall in consumption that might otherwise have been caused by the adverse movement in the terms of trade, but also to promote public sector investment booms. There was an investment boom between 1973 and 1978 in sixteen of our countries,[6] and in all except Chile and Kenya it was primarily a public sector boom. In most cases the boom began around the time of the oil price shock. In Colombia, Kenya, and Sri Lanka the boom began later, in 1977 or 1978. The rapidity of the rise in investment was sensational in several countries. For instance, Morocco raised the ratio of public investment to GDP from about 5 to 21 per cent from 1973 to 1977; Côte d'Ivoire from 11 to 21 per cent from 1974 to 1978; Nigeria from 5 to 17 per cent from 1974 to 1976; and Sri Lanka from 7 to 17 per cent from 1977 to 1982.

The ratio of investment to GDP was higher in the period after the oil price shock (1974–9) than it was before the shock (1970–3) for all the countries, with the exception of Colombia and Kenya. The average was about 23 per cent against 19 per cent. This of course was accompanied by a rise in borrowing. The ratio of debt to GNP rose from 1973 to 1979 for all the countries except Pakistan, Korea, India, Colombia, and Nigeria.[7] In no country, however, did debt to GNP exceed 50 per cent, exceeding 40 per cent only in Côte d'Ivoire, Costa Rica, Pakistan, and Morocco. This, combined with the fact that most of the borrowing had apparently been devoted to raising investment rather than consumption, made some influential observers complacent about the level of debt at the end of the 1970s.

It is true that there could not have been a serious debt problem if the investments made had had a good rate of return at border prices, that is, directly or

[4] Chile had a major recession in 1975. But this was only very partially and indirectly a result of the oil price rise.

[5] Indonesia and Nigeria benefited initially, and Mexico later. Cameroon benefited only at the very end of the period. Morocco gained in 1974 from a phosphate boom.

[6] Brazil and India are the exceptions.

[7] The debt figures quoted include long- and medium-term public and publicly guaranteed debt, but exclude short-term debt (less than one year), for figures that are not available for this period.

indirectly in terms of foreign currency earned or saved, greater than the rate of interest on the borrowing. Unfortunately, there are good reasons to believe that much of this investment had low or negative rates of return. Few countries if any had an adequate system of control and evaluation of public sector investments. Indeed, the extraordinary speed with which public sector investment expenditure rose was hardly compatible with such a system. Sometimes the ministry of finance did not even know what was going on. In other cases, it was powerless in the face of the president's whim, or popular support for some great project that could be plausibly dressed up in nationalistic garb. In some countries, corruption was an expensive dictating factor in both project choice and implementation. On top of all this, the value of any financial constraint was reduced by the price distortions that were so prevalent. Import substitution was still a misguiding light, and could lead to profitable projects with negative returns in terms of foreign exchange. Valid and objective cost–benefit analysis was a rarity. Manuals of cost–benefit analysis for developing countries, available by 1970, can be added to the list of useful books that were widely ignored in the developing world (though influential by the second half of the 1970s among donor or creditor agencies).[8]

The above considerations are independent of a final and more excusable reason why a litter of white elephants was conceived in the 1970s. This is the fact that expectations may be amiss. Prices had become more volatile in the 1970s, making predictions more difficult. And it can be argued that there was no good reason to anticipate the rise in interest rates in 1979 and the recession that followed. Some poor investments can be attributed to this uncertainty. But this does not alter my belief that the public decision-making processes in most developing countries were inadequate to make good use of the huge influx of funds in the 1970s, an influx that continued, as we shall see, until 1982. It must also be noted that the large rise in borrowing from 1979 to 1982 was at interest rates that were known to be high.

HEADING FOR CRISIS: 1979–1982

Our second period begins with the terms-of-trade shock of 1979, the main feature of which was a more than doubling of crude oil prices, from about $15 a barrel to over $30 a barrel. A secondary feature was the fall in beverage prices after 1977. There was also an interest rate shock at around the same time, with rates rising from the nominal rate of about 6 per cent for a three-month loan at the London interbank offer rate (LIBOR) to 15 per cent by the end of 1979. This raised the cost of servicing the existing debt, which was mostly at variable inter-

[8] See Little and Mirrlees (1990).

est rates. This shock was small, however, compared with that of the oil price.[9] Taking the two effects together over the three years from 1979 to 1981, there was an adverse effect of over 4 per cent of GDP for half of our countries. In descending order of the size of the shock, those countries were Côte d'Ivoire, Sri Lanka, Chile, Korea, Thailand, Cameroon, Brazil, Kenya, and Colombia. At the other end of the spectrum, Indonesia and Nigeria gained greatly. The effect on Mexico, by now an oil exporter, was negligible, because a positive terms-of-trade effect was offset by the rise in interest rates.

In terms of the level of debt and the current balance of payments position, most countries were less well positioned to meet the new shocks than they had been in 1973. However, the position was already seriously threatening for only a few. For instance, Chile, Costa Rica, Côte d'Ivoire, Kenya, and Morocco had reached debt–GNP ratios of over 40 per cent and also had very large current account deficits, varying from about 6 per cent in Chile to about 17 per cent in Côte d'Ivoire. In addition, Korea, Sri Lanka, and Thailand had huge current account deficits, although their debt was still moderate. All these countries, except Costa Rica and Morocco, also suffered seriously from the 1979–81 shock. As we make clear later, however, neither the initial position in 1979, in terms of indebtedness or the balance of payments, nor the size of the shocks is a good indicator of whether a country ran into a serious debt crisis in 1982, or soon after.

Eight of our countries were in deep trouble by the end of 1982.[10] These were also the 'debt-crisis' countries, meaning those whose debt was to be rescheduled in the period 1983–8. Some, for example Costa Rica, Mexico, and Nigeria, had already declared a moratorium or were in arrears on commercial debt. But the debt crisis was still in the future for others. So what do we mean by 'deep trouble'? We mean a lack of creditworthiness (or adequate reserves) combined with a severe current account deficit. This combination forces either a profound and rapid deflation in order to improve the trade balance, or a default on debt service, or both. The required improvement in the trade balance cannot normally be brought about without causing a recession or deepening already existing recession. In such a situation, a country will normally request debt rescheduling in order to avoid default, and to reduce the magnitude of the improvement in the trade account that is required.

The ratio of current account deficit to GDP in 1982 was enormous for Chile, Costa Rice, Côte d'Ivoire, and Morocco (>10 per cent) and very large for Brazil (6 per cent) and Nigeria (8 per cent). Only Argentina and Mexico had relatively modest deficits (<5 per cent). But it was Mexico that ignited the debt crisis with her extremely high debt service ratio—57 per cent—caused by a low ratio of trade to GDP and excessive use of short-term debt. The Mexican moratorium caused

[9] The increase in interest paid from 1979 to 1982 was large for several countries—notably Argentina, Chile, Côte d'Ivoire, and Mexico—but most of this increase was due to debt incurred within the period at the new high interest rates.

[10] Argentina, Brazil, Chile, Costa Rica, Côte d'Ivoire, Mexico, Morocco, and Nigeria.

many other countries to lose creditworthiness and face a need for large reductions of their deficits.

It is no accident that all the debt crisis countries except Morocco and Mexico were already in recession when the urgent need to improve the current account hit them.[11] Because such an improvement would deepen and prolong the recession, it is no wonder that they sought rescheduling. Of the other ten countries, which did not reschedule and remained more or less creditworthy, only Indonesia had a slight recession owing to bad weather in 1982, and none in 1983.

Obviously, the recessions were not initially caused by the withdrawal of foreign credit after 1982, which they preceded. In most cases the recession was caused by the government's measures to combat either inflation or a yawning current account deficit (for example in Argentina, Brazil, Chile, Costa Rica, and Côte d'Ivoire). Falls in export earnings were also important (for example in Chile, Côte d'Ivoire, and Nigeria). The withdrawal of foreign credit after 1982, however, prolonged and deepened the recessions. The pre-recession annual level of output was exceeded only after three years in Côte d'Ivoire, four years in Costa Rica and Mexico, five years in Brazil, and six in Chile. In Argentina the level of GDP in 1990 was still below that of 1980.

TABLE 1. Estimated Size of Cumulative Exogenous Shocks, 1979–1981

% of GDP	
>9	Côte d'Ivoire, Sri Lanka, Chile
5–7	Korea, Thailand, Cameroon, Brazil
3–5	Kenya, Colombia, Costa Rica, Morocco
0–3	Turkey, Argentina, Pakistan, India, Mexico
>−10	Indonesia, Nigeria

SOURCE: Little *et al.* (1993, table 4.2).

We now revert to the puzzle, already mentioned above, that neither the initial situation in 1979 nor the size of the terms of trade and interest shocks from 1979 to 1981 is a good indicator of whether countries became depressed and sought rescheduling. Table 1 classifies countries by the size of the shock. Table 2 gives our classification of countries under the headings 'bad start', 'big bad shock', and other attributes. (The definitions of these attributes are given in the notes to the table.) Of the eight debt crisis countries, only two—Chile and Côte d'Ivoire—had both a bad start and a big bad shock. But three countries—Argentina, Mexico, and Nigeria—had neither. Of the ten non-crisis countries,

[11] By 'recession' we mean a fall in annual GDP (quarterly figures are not available), with recession continuing until GDP recovers to the level of the year preceding the fall.

TABLE 2. Determinants of the Crisis of 1979–82 and Growth 1982–89

	Recession 1981–82	Bad start 1979	Big bad shock 1979–81	Policy inaction	Lack of fiscal control	Growth of GNP per capita 1982–89
Debt crisis countries						
(those rescheduling 1983–88)						
Argentina	1	0	0	1	1	−0.6
Brazil	1	0	1	1	1	2.3
Chile	1	1	1	1	0	4.0
Costa Rice	1	1	0	1	1	2.1
Côte d'Ivoire	1	1	1	1	1	−3.6
Mexico	1	0	0	1	1	−1.0
Morocco	1	1	0	1	0	1.4
Nigeria	1	0	0	1	1	−2.7
Mean						0.2
Others						
Cameroon	0	0	1	0	0	−1.1
Colombia	0	0	0	1	1	1.7
India	0	0	0	0	0	3.3
Indonesia	1	0	0	0	0	4.1
Kenya	0	1	1	1	1	0.7
Korea	0	1	1	0	0	8.9
Pakistan	0	0	0	0	0	2.8
Sri Lanka	0	1	1	0	0	2.0
Thailand	0	1	1	0	0	5.5
Turkey	0	0	0	0	0	3.1
Mean						3.1
Overall mean						1.8
Weighted mean						2.4

NOTE: 'Bad start' = current account deficit / GNP > 5.6% in 1979; 'big bad shock' = total cumulative negative terms of trade and interest shock, 1979–81 / GNP > 4.3%; for 'policy inaction' and 'lack of fiscal control', see text.
SOURCES: Little *et al.* (1993, table 4.4), and World Bank data base.

four—Kenya, Korea, Sri Lanka, and Thailand—had both a bad start and a big bad shock.

We are not, of course, suggesting that initial conditions and shocks are irrelevant. But the evidence is that other factors dominated, and overrode their influence. These other factors include the budgetary responses of governments to a deteriorating situation and their handling of the exchange rate. Official lending was also of importance in a few cases (for example Costa Rice, Kenya, and Sri Lanka).

Table 2 in effect presents a simple analysis of what separates the debt crisis countries from the rest. We have already noticed that the initial state of play and the size of the shock are not accurate discriminants. It is obvious from the table that the best discriminants are 'policy inaction' and 'lack of fiscal control'.[12]

These characteristics need some discussion, because it is a matter of judgement as to whether they should be attributed to a country or not. In so doing, we could be accused of taking a peep into the future before deciding. Policy inaction generally means a failure to reduce absorption by fiscal or monetary measures. Large deficits and heavy borrowing were allowed to continue for too long. Our ascriptions are well supported by the country studies, though it should be noted that inaction includes inadequate or very delayed action. Kenya is a borderline case. There was already a serious problem in 1979, but fiscal action was delayed until FY 1981/2. The public deficit, however, was halved from 1980/1 to 1982/3. Chile is a special case in that its inaction lay primarily in its failure to devalue, for Chile was running a public sector surplus. Of course, if no action was required there is no point in recording inaction. But, in fact, all the countries for which a zero is recorded took some deflationary fiscal or monetary action in the period, except possibly Indonesia, which experienced a large favourable shock.

Lack of fiscal control means that the finance ministry was unable to control public expenditure. This was usually because parastatal institutions or state governments could borrow, either from the central bank or abroad, without the permission, and in some cases without the knowledge, of the finance ministry. But it could be because political conditions made the finance ministry too weak to curb other central government ministries. This lack of control is ascribed where there is explicit reference to it in the World Bank project's country studies. The lack of fiscal control was clearly a contributory reason for inadequate action in the face of the huge budgetary and current account deficits that were a feature of the early 1980s. It was this prevarication and failure to act that turned a serious situation into a disaster for so many countries.

Another contributory cause was the behaviour of the real exchange rate In all the debt crisis countries, except Morocco, there was an interval of rapid appreciation during the period 1978–82, though in most countries appreciation had fallen back by the end of this period (see Table 3). These appreciations were caused by holding on to a fixed rate during the inflationary bubble that occurred after the 1979 terms-of-trade shock. They were a depressing influence on the tradable goods sector of the economies, and hence a cause of the recessions that were prevalent in this period. Although several of the non-crisis countries also experienced a significant appreciation of the real exchange rate (Colombia, India, Sri Lanka, and Thailand), only in Sri Lanka was it of the magnitude experienced in Argentina, Brazil, Chile, Mexico, or Nigeria. Sri Lanka was a special case, in

[12] It is equally obvious that 'Continent' discriminates well. There are, for example, no Asian countries in the crisis list. Unfortunately, we have no very convincing explanation of why the Asian countries handled their economies more prudently and more successfully.

that the appreciation was caused by a large inflow of concessionary funds after the reforms of 1977, which included a massive devaluation of the currency. There was probably some overvaluation of the currency by 1982, but not enough to result in a recession, especially with the high level of public investment that was maintained.

TABLE 3. Average Real Exchange Rates, 1979–1988 (1978 = 100)

	1979	1980	1981	1982	1985	1988
Debt crisis countries						
Argentina	141	184	167	93	81	69
Brazil	85	76	92	97	76	78
Chile	101	117	138	125	80	59
Costa Rica	105	115	73	84	93	69
Côte d'Ivoire	110	112	96	88	81	103
Mexico	106	119	135	97	103	82
Morocco	100	97	89	87	72	65
Nigeria	103	110	122	125	183	33
Others						
Cameroon	99	97	89	87	96	115
Colombia	103	105	113	121	96	61
India	100	111	115	111	110	79
Indonesia	76	82	89	96	74	40
Kenya	97	96	93	96	96	70
Korea	103	100	102	104	91	84
Pakistan	97	98	111	101	93	66
Sri Lanka	108	124	132	140	145	113
Thailand	101	110	113	116	106	85
Turkey	108	84	83	71	66	52

SOURCE: International Monetary Fund.

REFORM AND SLOW RECOVERY: 1983–1990

A dominant feature of this period was the change in resource flows. An inward flow of resources is measured by the current account deficit plus unrequited transfers (grants of aid and private remittances) minus interest payments on foreign debt.

From 1977 to 1982, all of our countries except Argentina and Indonesia relied on an inward transfer. This averaged over 5 per cent of GNP in the case of Costa Rica, Morocco, Kenya, Turkey, Sri Lanka, and Pakistan. From 1983 to 1988 only Morocco, Sri Lanka, and Pakistan had similarly large inflows, mainly accounted for by workers' remittances (though aid was also important for Sri Lanka). For many, the inflow changed to an outflow. The change was very large (over 7 per cent of GNP) for Côte d'Ivoire, Costa Rica, Chile, Mexico, Morocco, and Korea.

The size of the current account deficits in the early 1980s was certainly unsustainable in a number of countries. Reliance on an inflow of resources had to be reduced, whatever the state of the world capital markets. By 1983 the size and speed of the reduction was not a matter of choice. It was forced on countries by a sudden shift in lenders' perceptions of the risks involved. Korea is the outstanding exception, maintaining creditworthiness, but choosing to reduce her debt. Large current account deficits around 1980 were rapidly reduced, and became large surpluses after 1986.

Ten of our countries did continue to benefit from inflows in the 1980s, even if on a much reduced scale. But in five of these cases, the inflow was more than accounted for by remittances or aid (Costa Rica, Morocco, Kenya, Turkey, and Colombia). New borrowing exceeded interest only for India, Indonesia, Pakistan, Sri Lanka, and Thailand—all Asian countries.

We have seen that neither initial conditions of debt and current account deficits in 1979, nor the size of the exogenous shock experienced in the period 1979–81, was a good indicator of whether or not countries succumbed to recession or became unviably indebted in the next few years. Rather similarly, neither the initial conditions in 1982, nor the shock of the virtual elimination of commercial credit that we have just described, were good indicators of the growth in GNP per capita from 1982 to 1989.

Let us elaborate on the above paradox. Simple regressions were calculated of the growth of GNP per capita on various measures of initial debt, on the current account deficit, as well as on a dummy variable for whether the economy was in recession. Although the coefficients all had the expected signs, none was significant at the 10 per cent level. The statistical insignificance of debt may surprise readers. It can be explained by a few outliers. Costa Rica had a huge debt, but grew faster than the mean rate. Korea was quite highly indebted, but grew famously. Nigeria had negligible debt, but its GNP per capita fell faster than that of any other country except Côte d'Ivoire. This does not show that debt was irrelevant; high debt surely handicapped growth. What it perhaps shows is that cross-country regressions are of questionable value, especially when countries as fundamentally different as Korea and Nigeria are included.

But what about the change in transfers? The eight debt crisis countries suffered the largest falls in inward transfers. On average, the change was −6.6 per cent of GNP, comparing (as before) 1983–8 with 1977–82. For the other ten the average change was −1.9 per cent of GNP. So there was a strong association of debt crisis, that is, rescheduling, with the change in transfers. The debt crisis countries also grew much more slowly in GNP per capita from 1982 to 1989. Four of them suffered a fall—namely, Argentina, Côte d'Ivoire, Mexico, and Nigeria—and the (unweighted) average growth rate was 0.2 per cent per annum.

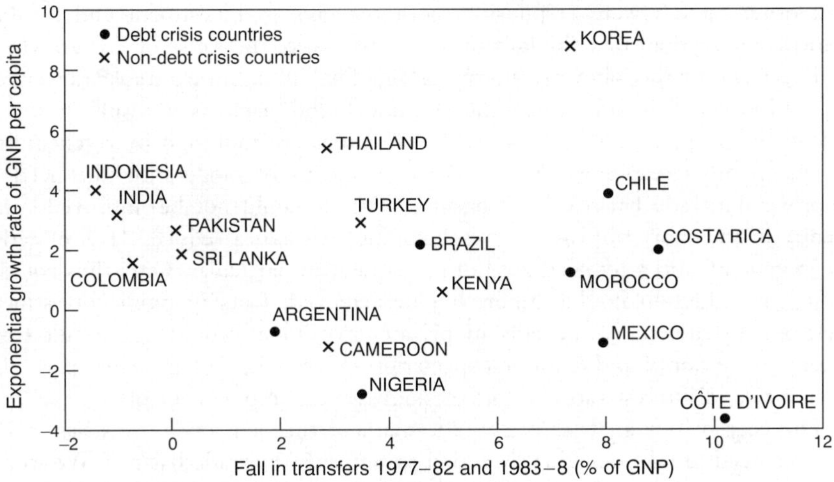

FIGURE 1. Growth and the Change in Transfers, 1982–1989
Sources: Exponential growth rate of GNP per capita from Table 2; fall in transfers from Little *et al.* 1993, table 5.1.

The average growth rate for the others was a satisfactory 3.1 per cent per annum (see Table 2).

But despite the strong association of debt crisis with both low growth and a large fall in inward transfers, there was no significant correlation between the latter two, as Figure 1 illustrates. The debt crisis countries are marked with bullets, and the rest with crosses. With the exception of Cameroon and Kenya, the bullets and the crosses form distinct groups.[13] The bullets tend to correspond to low growth and a large fall in transfers, and vice versa for the crosses. Regressing growth on the change in transfers and a dummy variable for rescheduling showed the latter to be significant. One might have expected a close relationship between the fall in transfers and growth, via investment. Thus,

Fall in inward transfers → Fall in investment
→ Low ratio of investment to GNP → Low growth.

Of the three links in the chain, the second and third were elastic ($R^2 \cong 0.50$), but the first was virtually non-existent ($R^2 = 0.14$), as was the simple correlation between the change in transfers and growth. Thus, the significant positive relationship between falls in investment and growth is not a satisfactory explanation of the relationship between the debt crisis and low growth. It seems likely

[13] It would have been neater if Kenya had asked for her quite heavy debt to be rescheduled. That she did not was probably because of a high proportion of official debt. Cameroon also became a debt crisis country in 1989, but this was the result of the oil shock of 1986, not those of 1979–82.

that other factors were responsible both for falls in investment and for low growth, rather than that the falls in investment were the cause of low growth.

This suggests the following interpretation. The fall in inward transfers resulted in reduced growth only when the country found itself as a result in severe balance of payments difficulties. Such difficulties are indicated by rescheduling (or payments arrears), which was the only means of moderating the need to improve the trade balance. The balance of trade could not be improved sufficiently in the short run (despite rescheduling) without a reduced level of activity in general, and a reduced level of investment in particular. Only thus could a sufficient reduction in the import bill be achieved. Cuts in public investment were an instrument, while falls in private investment would also result from greater uncertainty and a lower expectation of growth, and in some cases also from a rise in interest rates and increasingly severe import controls.

The core of our analysis of the aftermath of the debt crisis thus lies in the varying need to take deflationary action to improve the trade balance. We would therefore expect a strong positive correlation between exports receipts and growth. This expectation is not disappointed. We have already seen that simple correlations between growth in GNP per capita during 1982–9 on the one hand, and on the other hand initial conditions of debt, the current account balance, and the change in average transfers between 1977–82 and 1983–8 were insignificant. But the average ratio of investment is significant ($R^2 = 0.45$), and so also is the growth in the value of exports ($R^2 = 0.52$). Together these explain 63 per cent of the variance, as in the equation

$$G = -4.4 + 0.22\, INV + 0.19\, GVALEX,$$

$$R^2 = 0.63 \quad F = 13.00 \quad DW = 2.50,$$

where G = exponential growth rate of GNP per capita, 1982–9, and INV = average ratio of investment to GNP, 1983–8.
where $GVALEX$ is the exponential growth rate of the f.o.b. value of imports into industrialized countries, 1982–8, UN sources. (This is believed to be a more reliable indication of export success than one derived from the export statistics of the developing countries.)

Rising export receipts might be a matter of luck (for example, improved terms of trade), or might result from changes in trade policies, variables that we have thus far neglected.

Changes in the terms of trade were minor until early 1986 when the price of oil collapsed. Coffee, tea, and cocoa prices were also weak. Cameroon, Colombia, Côte d'Ivoire, Indonesia, Mexico, and Nigeria were adversely affected. All of these except Colombia and Indonesia experienced recessions. Those most dependent on oil imports, for example Brazil and Chile, gained. However, the very wide variance of the growth rate of the dollar value of exports (with a range from

−12.0 per cent per annum in Nigeria to 21 per cent per annum in Korea) closely matches that of the growth rate of the volume of exports. The main exceptions were some of the oil producers. Thus, Nigeria's large fall in value was accompanied by a (small) rise in volume. Indonesia and Cameroon also experienced a fall in value despite a rise in volume. Chile was luckier; a small rise in volume translated into a large rise in value as the price of copper rose.

To what extent was the varying success with export volume a consequence of changing trade policies? A feature of the 1980s was a more flexible use of nominal exchange rates. Most countries for most of the time managed the exchange rate with a view to making exports more competitive, and keeping them competitive. They were successful in bringing about a depreciation of the real exchange rate, which is a measure of competitiveness (see Table 3). For all countries except Cameroon and Côte d'Ivoire, whose currencies were pegged to the French franc, there was an important real depreciation over the period 1982–8. The mean depreciation was about 25 per cent. This shows that substantial real depreciations could be and were brought about by nominal changes in the exchange rate. In other words, nominal devaluation was not immediately or very quickly offset by increased inflation. Ignoring the two near-hyperinflation countries, figures for which would distort the averages, and also the two franc zone countries that experienced a rise in the real exchange rate, the mean inflation rate for the other fourteen was 21 per cent in 1982, 26 per cent in 1988, and 18 per cent in 1990.

There is no correlation between the extent of the depreciation from 1982 to 1988 and the rate of growth of total export volume. This was hardly to be expected in view *inter alia* of the widely different commodity composition of exports (oil and coffee volumes were not responsive to price for institutional reasons), the varying extent of the initial overvaluation of the currency, and the fact that the main depreciation came only towards the end of the period in a number of cases. Manufacturers may be expected to be the most responsive to changes in exchange rates, and there was indeed a significant correlation between the growth rate of imports of manufactures by the industrialized countries in the period 1986–9 and the size of the depreciation in the period 1985–8. In several countries the growth of manufactured and other non-traditional exports was a major factor in their successful recovery in the 1980s. From 1986 to 1989, the growth rate of the value of manufactured imports into industrialized countries from the world as a whole was 14 per cent, and 20 per cent from developing countries. The star performers among our countries, with growth rates of over 30 per cent per annum, were Chile, Indonesia, Thailand, and Turkey. In all of these there was a real depreciation of 20 per cent or more. There can be little doubt that the conversion of most developing countries to flexible exchange rates was a necessary element in recovery. Cameroon and Côte d'Ivoire have suffered grievously in recent years from their adherence to a fixed rate relative to the French franc.

The oil exporters suffered a new shock in 1986. All except Colombia (a new fuel exporter) suffered large losses of export income from oil. As a result, Cameroon, Nigeria, and Mexico fell into recession in 1986 or 1987. (Cameroon's recession later deepened, and she joined the ranks of the debt crisis countries.) Colombia escaped partly by luck (new oil discoveries), but also because of a surge in coal and manufactured exports. (The real exchange rate fell by 36 per cent.) Indonesia also escaped recession, and indeed grew rapidly from 1985 to 1990 (by over 6 per cent per annum) despite a 23 per cent fall in the dollar value of exports in 1986. She devalued by 45 per cent in 1986, took other export promotion measures, and liberalized imports. The result was a quadrupling of manufactured exports from 1985 to 1989, which completely offset the fall in oil export revenues.

A comparison with Mexico is interesting. Mexico suffered a similar loss of export revenue in 1986, but also achieved similar success with non-oil exports from 1985 to 1989. However, Mexico had to combat 100 per cent inflation in 1986, after suffering a major earthquake in December 1985. Unlike Indonesia, she had lost creditworthiness and suffered from capital flight. Debt service was a larger burden, and she could not run large current account deficits as did Indonesia. Investment cuts and slow growth were required to reduce imports, despite the export successes.

Much has been written about the merits of a trading policy that is unbiased against exports. Comparative advantage has at last ceased to be ridiculed as it was until about fifteen years ago. On top of the simple static efficiency benefits, a good many dynamic advantages have been discerned. Keeping production in line with comparative advantage yields both higher social profits (and hence national savings), and greater equality in most countries. A more open and high trading economy generally permits a faster absorption of technology as well as the ability to borrow more abroad without the danger of a debt crisis. Although I am convinced of the validity of these and other supporting arguments (and have been for about twenty-five years), the present contention that successful growth in the 1980s, and recovery from the 1982 crisis, was largely dependent on export growth (itself largely dependent on a reform of trading policies and more flexible exchange rates) is quite different. Rapid export growth reduced the need for recession, or reduced activity, to restrain imports to a level that could be financed.

OTHER FEATURES OF BOOM, CRISIS, AND ADJUSTMENT

The above mainly historical account does not do justice to much of the forthcoming book[14]—in particular, those parts to which my colleagues devoted the most attention.

[14] i.e., Little *et al.* (1993).

I have scarcely mentioned the problem of inflation. But its causes, effects, and cures are discussed at length in two chapters that distinguish moderate chronic inflation from very high inflation and the stabilization attempts that the latter demands. Two chapters are also devoted to trade policies, both the exchange rate regime and controls over capital movements and imports.

My own analysis in this paper has run mainly in terms of current account deficits and international borrowing and debt. Deflationary action through fiscal and monetary policy was mentioned *en passant*. But, of course, current account deficits are usually matched by budgetary deficits; and we saw that inaction on the fiscal front was the main reason why nearly half our countries ran into deep trouble in the early 1980s. The countries' fiscal and monetary policies, and some of the political economy reasons for their differences, are discussed in two further chapters. Finally, there is a chapter discussing the relationship between short- and medium-run macroeconomic policy and long-run growth.

SOME CONCLUSIONS AND POLICY ADVICE

The following conclusions are not fully supported by this particular paper, but are, I believe, supported by the research described. Readers can verify this only by reading the full published results, especially Little *et al.* (1993).

Firm central budgetary control, meaning control of the access of all public spending agencies to loan finance, domestic or foreign, is essential. Public sector deficits should be planned with an eye on the long-run consequences for the public debt, both internal and external, and the cost of servicing it. Provided only that debt has not already become excessive, deficit finance may be used to help stabilize the real non-agricultural economy in the face of exogenous fluctuations. (Surpluses may be in order if the private sector becomes unduly euphoric, which can happen.) But adaptation to adverse exogenous events must not be delayed for long if no reversal is in sight. Current account deficits and debt can be built up rapidly and lead to a loss of creditworthiness, which forces a much more disruptive adaptation than if policy response had not been delayed.

Public investment must be coordinated to avoid the common situation whereby decentralized agencies embark on projects that together will require more public investment than is likely to be financially possible in the future. Further to this, all large projects should be subject to a system of agreed cost–benefit analysis, and serious heed should be paid to its findings. Windfalls arising from favourable changes in the terms of trade or mineral finds should not be allowed to result in an immediate investment boom. Even if the favourable change is expected to last, sudden rises in expenditure are unlikely to be efficient in achieving their objectives. If the favourable change does not last, rises in expenditure are difficult to reverse. Increases in reserves, invested abroad, can later be used whether the favourable circumstances continue or are reversed.

The exchange rate regime cannot be considered independently of inflation. It is obvious that an economy that is inflating at a significantly higher rate than its trading partners must devalue from time to time, or almost continuously, if it is to enjoy the full (and major) benefits of trade. An overvalued exchange rate necessitates the repression of imports by controls, a highly inflexible and inefficient method of balancing a country's foreign accounts. I believe that a flexible exchange rate is better than intermittent devaluations, which often get delayed and hence lead to undesirable overvaluation and recession, and to adverse speculation and destabilizing uncertainty. Not devaluing frequently when inflation is high amounts to an attempt to control inflation by fixing a price. This may or may not be part of a package of decrees that make rises in other prices, and wages, illegal. In certain (rare) circumstances a brief resort to such price controls may be helpful; such as where the expectation of inflation has become embedded and needs to be broken as part of a drive to stop inflation, or reduce it to very low levels. But the emphasis must be on 'brief', because the inefficiencies that result if inflation is not in fact stopped rapidly become intolerable. A corollary is that a fixed rate of exchange should not be maintained for fear of inflation: a devaluation is an essential adjustment to inflation, not a cause of it.

Inflation presents the authorities with many problems. It also has many disadvantages for private persons and institutions. It has only one, albeit important, countervailing merit. It permits the authorities to spend without taxing. Where taxing is very difficult for institutional or political reasons, this may be a social advantage. But there are grave dangers. The disadvantages of inflation lead to indexing, which reduces its value for the authorities. For this and other reasons, the rate of inflation tends to accelerate. When inflation becomes very high, action has to be taken. Both it and its cure become very costly in economic and social terms. I believe that the authorities should become alarmed if inflation rises to 10 per cent or more. The long-run control of inflation must lie with fiscal and monetary conservatism. But if the cause is a supply-side shock, such as a blip in world prices, a revaluation of the currency may be more appropriate than any deflationary, monetary or fiscal, action. If the prime cause of a price rise is a harvest failure, deflationary action may also be inappropriate. Prices will stop rising and may fall as agricultural output recovers.

Finally, our research suggests that stability of growth, and especially stability of the investment ratio, is good for growth. This may not be quite as obvious as it sounds, for one has often heard the suggestion that living dangerously by boom and bust may be better than steady progress. While the average level of investment over the years was positively significant, a simple cross-country correlation explained only 29 per cent of the variance of growth in income per capita from 1970 to 1989. The apparent productivity of investment (the growth rate of income per capita divided by the investment ratio) varied enormously, from over

20 per cent to less than zero. What determines the efficiency of investment is still a neglected subject.

References

Cooper, R. N. (1981), 'Currency Devaluation in Developing Countries', in G. Ranis (ed.), *Government and Economic Development*. New Haven: Yale University Press.

——(1991), 'Economic Stabilization in Developing Countries', International Center for Economic Growth Occasional Paper no. 14. San Francisco: ICS Press.

——(1992), *Economic Stabilization and Debt in Developing Countries* (the Ohlin Lectures). Boston, Mass.: MIT Press.

Corden, W. M. (1990), 'Macroeconomic Policy and Growth: Some lessons of experience', in *Proceedings of the World Bank Annual Conference on Development Economics*. Washington: World Bank.

——(1993), 'Exchange Rate Policies for Developing Countries', *Economic Journal*, 103 (Jan.).

Díaz-Alejandro, C. F. (1965), *Exchange Rate Devaluation in a Semi-Industrialized Country*. Boston, Mass.: MIT Press.

——(1971), 'Comments on Cooper', in G. Ranis (ed.), *Government and Economic Development*. New Haven: Yale University Press.

Keynes, J. M. (1923), *A Tract on Monetary Reform*. London: Macmillan.

Krassowski, A. (1974), *Development and the Debt Trap: Economic planning and external borrowing in Ghana*. London: Croom Helm for the Overseas Development Institute.

Little, I. M. D. (1982), *Economic Development: Theory, policy and international relations*. New York: Basic Books.

——and Mirrlees, J. A. (1990), 'Project Appraisal and Planning Twenty Years On', in *Proceedings of the World Bank Conference on Development Economics*. Washington: World Bank.

——Cooper, R. N., Corden, W. M., and Rajapatirana, S. (1993), *Boom, Crisis and Adjustment: The macroeconomic experience of developing countries*. Oxford: Oxford University Press, for the World Bank.

——Scitovsky, T., and Scott, M. FG. (1970), *Industry and Trade in Some Developing Countries*. Oxford: Oxford University Press.

McKinnon, R. I. (1973), *Money and Capital in Economic Development*. Washington: Brookings Institution.

Ranis, G. (1971), *Government and Economic Development*. New Haven: Yale University Press.

Shaw, E. S. (1973), *Financial Deepening in Economic Development*. New York: Oxford University Press.

Williamson, J. (1990), 'Comment on Corden', in *Proceedings of the World Bank Annual Conference on Development Economics*. Washington: World Bank.

15

India's Economic Reforms, 1991–1996 (1996)

1. INTRODUCTION

I am honoured to have been asked to talk about India's reforms to this gathering. Like me, you may well wonder why, when there are many highly qualified Indians with more intimate knowledge than I of the reforms, and of the political context in which they are embedded. It is sometimes asked what a Martian—presumably unprejudiced—would say if he dropped in. I cannot even qualify as a proper Martian, for I do drop in from time to time, and I may be prejudiced by some knowledge of terrestrial economic systems.

The occasion is for me not only honorific but also embarrassing. I am going to talk about the reforms, at a conference opened by their chief architect, Dr Manmohan Singh. What makes this confrontation unusual, perhaps unique, is that I was one of Dr Manmohan Singh's supervisors in the early 1960s when he was reading for his Oxford doctorate.

Our long friendship since those days is not going to inhibit me from re-adopting the critical stance appropriate to a supervisor—a stance, however, that is consistent with profound admiration. My task of commenting on the reforms would have been too daunting to undertake if Vijay Joshi and I had not finished a book on the subject.[1] This book is itself a follow-up of our book on India's macroeconomic policies from 1964 to 1991.[2] That period of study ended just as the period of major reform began. The temptation to write another book on the reforms was irresistible. In what follows, when I say 'I', I often mean Joshi and I.

I shall not be evaluating the reforms from the point of view of their economic outcomes. There are two reasons for this. First, I believe it is too early to assess their lasting effects. Secondly, I think it can be misleading to analyse the effects of incomplete reforms. So I shall be evaluating the reforms from the point of view of how far they have progressed towards creating a new economic system, one

This paper, which was presented at a conference on 'India's New Economic Policy' on 11–14 March 1996, first appeared in the *Journal of Asian Economics*, 7 (1996). JAI Press Inc., Stamford, Connecticut, and London, 1996. Permission to reproduce is gratefully acknowledged.

[1] V. Joshi and I. M. D. Little, *India's Economic Reforms 1991–2001*. Oxford University Press, Delhi and Clarendon Press, Oxford, 1996.

[2] V. Joshi and I. M. D. Little, *India: Macroeconomics and Political Economy 1964–1991*. Washington: World Bank and Oxford University Press, Delhi, 1994.

that is likely to serve India well. I believe there was in 1991, and still is, a wide consensus that the Indian Economic Model that prevailed from 1947 to 1991 did not well serve the objective of a rapid rate of growth in which all, especially the poor, would share. To put it crudely, the regime was too *dirigiste* and too autarkic. So we know the direction of change. But we also need to know the end product if we are to judge how much progress has been made towards that end.

Reformers themselves may have no very clear idea of the system or regime they are trying to achieve. Or, even if they have, they may prefer for political reasons to leave it obscure or undefined. This is certainly the case in India. Goals are expressed in terms of desired oucomes such as 'a high rate of labour-demanding growth in which all will share', rather than a description of the economic system that will achieve such desirable results. This vagueness must, I think, make it difficult to build a constituency for reform. Several observers, notably Jagdish Bhagwati and T. N. Srinivasan,[3] have urged the Government to use every available occasion to put the rationale and importance of the reforms before the public. This cannot be convincingly done if the process of reform seems to be piecemeal. As against this, it can be argued that the electorate would have been scared silly by being presented with a more explicit and comprehensive programme: and the great achievements of the past five years would have been aborted. I guess this is what the Prime Minister thinks, and he is in a rather better position to judge than I am!

However, to assess how far there is still to go, I must as a critic describe the economic system towards which I believe the reforms should be leading:

1. There is virtual free trade, and freedom of foreigners to invest in India, and Indians to invest abroad.
2. Private ownership is predominant. The State produces goods or services only where external economies make private sector production impossible or very inefficient.
3. The State produces the normal range of public goods—defence, law and order, and a reasonably stable currency. It regulates private activities that are harmful to others; this includes the regulation of natural monopolies. It supervises and creates pro-market institutions which encourage competition and fair trading.
4. The State also relieves extreme poverty, and ensures that the poor have access to primary health and educational services. This does not imply that the State must itself produce such services, for they are not public goods.

This is not an extreme model. It is closely approximated by all the OECD countries, and by several Eastern European countries. I think by now the great majority of developing countries come much closer to it than India does. This is certainly true of East and South-East Asia and Latin America. Of course, there

[3] J. Bhagwati and T. N. Srinivasan, *India's Economic Reforms*. Delhi: Finance Ministry Government of India, July 1993.

are deviations everywhere, and countries differ a good deal in the extent to which they provide for the poor. But it is nevertheless a recognizable model, now almost a world model, from which it is informative to measure deviations. In India's case it would result in both faster and more equitable growth than the old Indian regime which concentrated benefits on a small minority of the population. The idea that there is some alternative model which is better for developing countries has been largely abandoned, except by a few conservatives, some of whom are still teaching in Oxford, a famous home of lost causes.

2. A REVIEW OF PROGRESS

I review progress in four areas: (1) macroeconomic balance; (2) trade and taxation; (3) industrial policy; and (4) the social sectors. Lack of progress towards particular features of my 'world' model may stem either from disagreement as to its merits, or from the political judgement that its merits are not yet sufficiently recognized for reform to be vote-winning, or from lack of resources and skills to design the details of reform, or from inertia, or even simply from exhaustion on the part of the chief proponents of reform. After reviewing progress, I shall try to indicate what seem to be the impediments.

Macroeconomic balance

Paradoxically, this has nothing to do with reform. No matter what the system, macroeconomic balance has to be achieved. In 1991 short-term stabilization was achieved in an orthodox manner, by cuts in expenditure, and by devaluation and tightening import controls. Many critics wrongly attributed the increase in poverty in 1991/2 and 1992/3 to reform. It was caused, at least partly, by the cuts in expenditure. But obviously, these cuts were not part of the process of structural reform: they were quickly reversed, and poverty has fallen.

Since the measures of 1991 the economy has been reasonably stable, and creditworthiness has been regained. The exchange rate has been well handled, and the current account is not a serious problem. But *long-run* stability has *not* been achieved. There is a time-bomb ticking away, since borrowing is at unsustainably high levels. India is heading for another crisis. Dr Singh is well aware of this, and would agree that he has not yet been able to reduce the central government's fiscal deficit to the extent he believes is necessary. Other politicians, including opposition leaders, must also be aware that the present levels of deficits, both at the Centre and in the States, are unsustainable.

It is obviously only the nature of the political system, and its present balance of forces, that prevents India from regaining the fiscal discipline which was taken for granted until the 1980s. I do not know by what combination of political forces this deadlock is to be broken. It may need another crisis. The future of reform in any of the other dimensions that I now turn to examine will be endangered, or even brought to nought, by continuing failure to face up to the macroeconomic disequilibrium that prevails.

Trade and taxation

Why do I take these together? Many years ago, Jagdish Bhagwati and V. K. Ramaswami[4] showed that any domestic activity that deserves protection should be protected by subsidy, and not by restricting trade by quotas, tariffs, or export taxes. Once this is accepted, the trade regime becomes an adjunct of the tax regime. Imports and exports should in general be taxed no differently from domestically produced goods. There are two exceptions. The first is when a country can exercise some monopoly or monopsony power. This applies only to one or two Indian exports. The second is when a good is more easily taxable at the border than at the point of production. This arises in the case of very small firms when the cost of collecting excise would be too great. They are thus protected both from larger firms and from imports when there is excise taxation or tariffs.

This is the area where greatest progress has been made. Trade controls have been largely eliminated, except on imports of most consumer goods, and on agricultural products. That consumer good industries should be especially protected by import bans (or the highest tariff rate of 50 per cent) is a strange anomaly which can persist only for historical xenophobic reasons. It defies economic logic, and runs counter to the whole idea of an open internationally competitive economy. If Mahalanobis had not been a Hindu, he would be turning in his grave knowing that drink is more protected than heavy machinery. The primary reason why exports of agricultural products, especially cotton, are still controlled is protection of domestic industry, especially handloom weaving. A case can probably still be made for protecting handloom weaving, but it should be by direct subsidy, not by reducing the output and export of cotton.

Tariff reduction is certainly one of the most important achievements since 1991. It seems to have aroused surprisingly little opposition. This is probably because the large devaluations of 1991 more than compensated most producers of traded goods for the reduction in protection. This suggests that tariff reduction could have gone faster. More seriously, the targets apparently still fixed for the end of the reform period are faulty. Too many rates (seven) are proposed, and the levels are far too high (up to 50 per cent). India would emerge after ten years of reform as one of the most highly protected economies in the world. I

[4] J. Bhagwati and V. K. Ramaswami, 'Domestic Distortions, Tariffs and the Theory of Optimum Subsidy', *Journal of Political Economy* (Feb. 1963).

have preached the merits of a low uniform tariff for twenty-five years. Uniformity is not theoretically correct, but it eliminates lobbying, 'boundary' disputes, and constant opportunities for corruption. Any change in a multiple rate system results in changes in effective protection everywhere. Dr Singh must have spent many hours in the past four and a half years listening to evidence of anomalies, and making complex calculations to prevent them arising (unsuccessfully!).

Although there has been excellent work on the subject, especially at the National Council of Applied Economic Research, there seems to be no official policy for agricultural trade. There are several reasons for this. Freeing trade with the low uniform tariff of say 10 per cent that I advocate would result in a large overall rise in agricultural profits, though some crops, oil seeds and sugar, would become less profitable. This should be the occasion for the elimination of the huge input subsidies on water, power, fertilizers, and credit (except perhaps for small farmers). But there would be a rise in the price of cereals which would hurt the poor. This in turn would necessitate reform of the public distribution system, together with other approaches to the relief of poverty. A further complication is that agriculture and the social sectors (which should be involved in poverty relief) are state subjects. Thus, planning for reform should ideally involve, with the assistance of the States, simultaneous reform of the extensive nexus involving agricultural trade, agricultural subsidies, the price of food, and poverty relief. Thus, the complications are great. However, the benefits would be huge in terms of increased value of output and fiscal economy. Unfortunately, after nearly five years there is little to report, only some very cautious trade liberalization. The main political reason is, no doubt, fear of the farming lobby. It may be very difficult to convince farmers that free trade in agricultural products (except for a low tariff) would more than compensate for the loss of subsidies.

Customs duties constitute a minor part of the total indirect taxation in India. The major parts are central excises and state sales taxes, which together account for almost half of the total tax revenue. Both are levied on essentially the same base—the first point of sale of industrial products. There is no disagreement that these taxes are highly distortionary and their incidence opaque and irrational. The same has been true of the manner in which central taxes are redirected to the States. Excellent work has been done on planning a rational reform of the system, involving the best way in which a value added tax can be introduced into a federal political system. I have no quarrel with the targets suggested by the National Institute of Public Finance and Policy, except that I would prefer a single VAT rate to the three suggested.

Significant progress has been made with the simplification and reform of central excise duties. Getting agreement of the States to substitute VATs (with extra-state sales zero rated) for sales tax will inevitably be slow. Considerable education and retraining of staff is required. But I am not aware of any fundamental conflicts of interest. Since all States can be expected to benefit in the end from a more rational system, the seeming lack of political pressure from the Centre is to be regretted.

The share of *direct taxation* in total revenue, and as a proportion of GDP, is very low, even compared with many other poor countries. It is well known that this is largely due to poor administration, the soft treatment of evaders, and official corruption. There has been some recent improvement which will hopefully continue.

The financial system

There can be no disagreement about the need for banks and other financial institutions which (*a*) well serve the transactions needs of the community, and (*b*) efficiently channel savings into socially productive investments. But after the bank nationalization of 1969, the banks had by 1991 so degenerated that they served neither purpose. They were forced to lend to the Government and to certain priority sectors at low controlled interest rates. By 1991 many were so ridden with bad debts that they were effectively bankrupt. A traditional and essential bankers' skill—how to make good loans—had perforce been forgotten. Lastly, trade unions have become powerful, and they continue to hamper the development of an efficient transactions service for the public at large.

The banks have now been rescued by an infusion of public capital, and the Government has agreed to pay market rates of interest. The direction of credit to 'priority' sectors remains, but this has been somewhat reduced. Although interest rates have largely been decontrolled, this is not true of priority sector loans which continue to be heavily subsidized. Useful reforms concerning the prudential regulation of banks and other financial instructions have been made, but there needs to be a further reduction in priority lending, and subsidization. Further stock market reforms are also needed if portfolio investment is not to be discouraged.

Agricultural credit is a special problem. Most agricultural credit institutions are insolvent. A high proportion of the subsidized loans go to medium and large farmers. The servicing and repayment record is abysmal. Indeed, debtors have been encouraged not to repay by a series of governmental debt write-offs. Small farmers continue to rely mainly on family savings and money lenders. There is no good case for interest rate subsidization or periodic forgiveness; and effective directed credit requires subsidization. However, there is a case for banks or other institutions, specializing in agricultural lending on commercial lines, to take the place of the existing maze of insolvent institutions. I cannot formulate a reform plan, but one is certainly needed.

Perhaps the most serious concern is whether there is sufficient guarantee against the recurrence of short-term exploitation of the banks by the Government, and the use of concealed credit subsidies on a damaging scale—that is, a reversion to the policies of the 1970s and 1980s. Such misuse of the financial system is very easy when the banks are predominantly public and fiscal deficits are large.

I believe that privatization of the banks, or most of them (and other financial institutions, including the insurance companies) is needed for the development of an independent and efficient financial system. But there is no sign that privatization is on the Government's agenda. Privatization is also not in sight for the industrial sector, to which I now turn.

Industrial policy

There is no need for me to describe the almost incredible restrictions under which private enterprise operated under the *ancien regime*. Most controls over production and investment by domestic enterprises have now gone, and private enterprises can in principle compete in nearly all industrial sectors. Foreign direct investment has been made much more welcome, though it is still restricted and controlled. This all adds up to an important change of regime and outlook. The combination of increased competition and reduction of controls will certainly make Indian industry more efficient and more enterprising. So far so good. But there is still a great deal that is wrong. It stems largely from the continued importance of public industry, and its dominance of the non-tradable goods or infrastructural sectors.

There has been a great wave of privatization in the world in the past fifteen years, a wave that has not broken upon India's shores. What has caused this wave? State ownership of the means of production was ideological, but its reversal has not been for ideological reasons. It has resulted simply from the inefficiency of public enterprises. The tendency to inefficiency is innate. The ultimate shareholder is the nation. But the national interest is interpreted by the responsible minister. He may intrude his *personal* interests. In turn, he is constrained by the government of which he is part: but then, the government has *political* interests. The public sector manager is thus faced with conflicting objectives, and many constraints on his freedom to manage. There is an insoluble problem of reconciling managerial autonomy and public accountability. Some countries massage this problem better than others. It depends on the political system. India seems to be among the worst.

The inefficiency of public enterprises goes beyond low productivity. It has a serious fiscal impact. Public money is always scarce, but becomes scarcer when the losses of public enterprises have to be funded. This has been the most important reason for privatization in many countries. In some cases also, the inefficiency combined with the shortage of public money has caused underinvestment. This has been an important cause of India's present serious infrastructural deficiency.

Privatization is most desirable when adequate competition can be assured. This is always so in the case of tradable goods. If economic techniques and the market are such that only a few domestic producers would be viable, competition can still be assured by free trade. In the case of non-tradable goods, competition may sometimes be impossible to organize, in which case either regulation or continued public monopoly may be socially necessary. One should therefore look at the public production of tradables and non-tradables separately.

Public sector non-departmental enterprises produce mainly tradables. They are important if not dominant in steel and other metals, the oil industry, heavy machinery, and fertilizers. Many make losses, and the return on most others is poor (apart from the oil industry). They will be facing increasing competition not only from new private investors, but also from imports. There is little hope of increasing efficiency, for the reasons I have already given. Managers are impeded by ministerial interference, by confusion of objectives, by lack of incentives for cost reduction, and by the regulations on pay and hiring and firing, which prevent the creation of an efficient managerial structure. All this has been known for thirty years, but nothing effective has been done. With increasing competition, these public enterprises will need increasing subsidies. But this cannot be allowed, and 'hard' budgeting is promised. Long drawn-out decay, involving a serious waste of resources is a real possibility. This implies a growth of 'sick' industries, the peculiarly Indian phenomenon of bankrupt firms that are not allowed to die. Privatization is an urgent need. But it is not on the agenda, not even being seriously studied. The sale of minority shares in public enterprises is not, of course, privatization: and there is little to be said in its favour.

Departmental enterprises

These provide mostly non-traded infrastructural services—transport, telecommunications, power, and water. India's infrastructure is in poor shape. Rail freight services are inadequate, and many main roads are highly congested. Ports are also congested, and delays endemic. Telephones are scarce, and connections erratic. Parts of the irrigation system are falling into disrepair. However, power shortages are probably the most threatening for economic growth. All this results from a sorry history of undercharging and underinvestment. The undercharging comes from political control of pricing, and the fact that politicians both at the Centre and in the States are unable to resist the short-term popularity of subsidizing rail and bus travel, and giving farmers subsidized, even free, electricity and irrigation water. Looking after the really poor takes second or third place.

The undercharging implies that the extent of underinvestment is difficult to estimate; but there is little doubt that, even with economic prices that cover long-term marginal costs, massive investment is needed, now far beyond the possibility of public sector finance. The underinvestment in infrastructure stems in turn from the waste of public revenue on subsidies, and on investment in manufacturing projects with very low returns.

The urgent need to intrude private investment, both domestic and foreign, into infrastructural projects on a large scale is accepted in principle. In practice, the modalities for doing so, thus permitting competition with the public sector, do not seem to have been fully researched, let alone settled. The same is true of the problem of regulating natural monopolies where adequate competition cannot be ensured.

Redundancy

Overstaffing is a common feature of public sector enterprises in both the tradable goods and infrastructural areas. Not only that, it extends to government in general. Decontrol makes many controllers redundant. Thus, reform, whether or not it includes widespread privatization, entails redundancy. And it is the fear of redundancy that is a major factor, perhaps *the* major factor, in inhibiting public sector reform.

A major reason for excessive employment in the public sector is that Indian industry has been far too capital-intensive, for many well-known reasons—import substitutes being preferred to exports, excessive investment in heavy industry, labour laws that discourage employment, and low real interest rates, among others. With disappointingly little productive employment being generated, governments have felt unable to resist unproductive employment in the public sector, at relatively high wages.

The government now naturally fears making large numbers redundant. This is not primarily a concern for poverty. Indeed, paying (directly and indirectly) large numbers of workers relatively high wages to do nothing useful prevents the Government from promoting schemes (including employment guarantee schemes at low wages) which target the very poor. Yet it is true that the loss of a job, involving both reduced circumstances, even absolute poverty, and loss of status, is worse than just being poor. The Government's concern is thus not merely political, but also humanitarian.

The solution to this daunting problem is easier than it might seem at first sight. Consider the case of a fully redundant man in a public industrial enterprise. He is producing nothing; indeed, he has negative productivity, for he takes up space, absorbs some administrative time, and may well cause trouble. The enterprise pays him directly, but the government (ultimately the taxpayer) pays him indirectly—obviously so if the government has to cover the losses of the enterprise, but also even if the enterprise makes a profit, for the profit which belongs to the government is thereby reduced. In the case of negative productivity, which may not be uncommon, it would actually improve the public finances as well as output if the government paid full wages until retirement age on condition that the excess labour walked away. I do not suggest anything so extreme.

The point I want to make is that it is possible to arrive at a scheme which would make the shedding of surplus labour advantageous to all parties. But it should be noted that the terms arrived at for existing public sector employees with expectations of permanent employment would be too generous for *new* contracts, whether public or private, since redundancy payment liabilities discourage employment. The National Renewal Fund, instituted to deal with redundancy, is tiny relative to the magnitude of the problem. There are probably 2 million workers redundant in the public sector. It is reported that 75,000 workers, mostly in textiles, had been voluntarily retired by March 1994. So there is a long way to go. Even if one allows a ten-year horizon, the release of redundant labour needs to be accelerated.

POLICY FOR THE PRIVATE INDUSTRIAL SECTOR

Privatization, and introducing private competition into infrastructural services, should be the most burning issues in industrial policy. But there are also a good many legal impediments to the efficient private use of productive resources. Indian businessmen have long been harassed by restrictive regulations, but also protected from competition. These features have been reduced, but not eliminated. Company law, labour laws, and urban land law have combined to create the Indian phenomenon of sick industries—firms that are bankrupt but cannot be closed down. Creditors cannot sell the assets, and labour is unpaid. The waste of assets that should be redeployed is considerable. These laws are enacted with good intentions, but no understanding of economics. Civil servants and legislators seldom understand, or refuse to recognize, that protection of incumbent workers in larger firms reduces their demand for labour, and thus by exclusion harms the poor outsiders; nor that company laws which protect incumbent management often preserve an inefficient use of assets.

Another interference with the free working and efficiency of manufacturing industry is the reservation of many products for exclusive production by small firms. This, together with excessive fiscal favours, distorts the natural growth of firms, and impedes technical progress and exports. No doubt this legislation was intended to promote employment. But research has shown that small firms are not reliably labour-intensive or efficient.

A thorough revision of all the legislation that affects the ownership and use of industrial assets is needed. Labour legislation that favours only a tiny minority of the workforce must be looked at askance. The scope for appeal to the law also needs to be reduced. The courts are too overburdened, and delays too long, for justice to be dispensed. More generally, some critics have maintained that the once proud Indian legal system has degenerated to the point that it can no longer fulfil its essential commercial role of impartially administering property laws and enforcing contracts.

Social sectors

I consider the social sectors in so far as stabilization policies and the structural changes that I advocate might have worrying distributional consequences. The only major consequence that one can reliably predict is a rise in the price of cereals, if and when Indian farm prices are linked to world prices. Over the years, world prices have usually been higher than domestic prices. A rise in the price of food would hurt the poor. But the best counter would not be to increase food subsidies via the present Public Distribution System. There is too much evidence that the Public Distribution System is highly inefficient, and mainly benefits those who are relatively well off. Furthermore, increased food subsidies would moderate a rise in agricultural wages that would otherwise partly compensate farm labourers. The rise in farm output prices would more than compensate the farming community as a whole for the reduction in subsidies, which would be an essential and highly desirable accompaniment of the liberalization of prices: but it would not compensate the poorest farmers who have little or nothing to sell, and some way of helping them would need to be found.

If food subsidies are not increased, whether by food stamps or a reformed Public Distribution System, then further reliance needs to be placed on public employment schemes, and on direct welfare benefits for those who cannot or should not work. Despite a good many enquiries, there is still considerable ignorance and disagreement about how well targeted and cost-effective the various schemes are, and how they can be improved. More research is certainly needed. But such evidence as there is favours these modes of poverty alleviation to food subsidies. Higher spending on primary education and primary health care is also a high priority, as has been recently emphasized by Jean Dreze and Amartya Sen.[5] When cuts in expenditure are essential for stabilization reasons, the social sectors should so far as possible be protected.

3. REASONS FOR SUCCESS AND CAUSES OF FAILURE

The macroeconomic crisis of 1991 was the occasion for reform. But while adjustment, in the sense of a large reduction in the domestic absorption of resources, was forced by the crisis, this was not wholly true of the accompanying programme of structural reform. A realization that a major change of economic system was needed had been slowly gaining ground in policy-making circles over the previous decade. The crisis permitted the new prime minister to take advantage of this change of outlook, and initiate a wide-ranging programme of reform with devastating speed.

[5] J. Dreze and A. Sen, *India: Economic Development and Social Opportunity*. Delhi: Oxford University Press, 1995.

It is amazing how much has been achieved, given the tiny base from which the reforms have sprung. There were in the beginning, to all intends and purposes, only two politically active reformers, the Prime Minister and his Finance Minister, Dr Manmohan Singh. They were supported by a small select band of like-minded economic advisers, nearly all in the Ministry of Finance. Mr Rangarajan, the Governor of the Reserve Bank, has also played a strong supportive role; and in the past year Mr Chidambaram, the Minister of Commerce, has also shown himself to be an enthusiastic reformer. But unfortunately, the Prime Minister seems to have decided, after the state electoral set-backs for the Congress Party at the end of 1994, that any change would lose votes in the forthcoming national election. Moreover, the Congress Party is not a party of reform, and many ministers were probably quite reluctant to agree to some of the changes they approved. The Finance Minister has continued to argue strongly for reform, but his wings have clearly been clipped. Almost nothing was achieved in 1995, although the economy was booming. The momentum of reform has been lost.

Given the base of the reforms, it is not surprising that most was achieved in areas that were the direct responsibility of the Prime Minister or the Minister of Finance. The Prime Minister held in 1991 the Ministry of Industry portfolio from which sprang the decontrol of industrial investment and production. The other major achievements are almost in the purview of the Finance Ministry—the reduction of protection, the reforms of the domestic indirect tax system, and the reforms of the financial system including exchange controls, though here the Reserve Bank also had a large role to play. The encouragement of foreign investment was presumably promoted by both the Prime Minister and the Finance Minister.

Despite his very remarkable achievements, far greater than any other finance minister since independence, my plaudits for Dr Singh are not unqualified. The principal failure lies with expenditure control. Most important are the fertilizer and food subsidies (export subsidies went out quite easily with devaluation); but pay and employment in the public sector have also not been adequately curbed. The loss of revenue from favours to small-scale industries (excise tax reductions and interest rate subsidies) is not negligible either. Explanation of failure in all cases lies with the reluctance to confront a powerful interest group—the farmers, the bureaucracy, public sector trade unions, and the small-scale industry lobby. I suspect that Dr Singh has lacked support from the Prime Minister and the Cabinet (not to speak of the particular ministers involved).

The two main areas of darkness are public sector reform and agriculture. Public sector reform cries out for the privatization of banking and other financial institutions, and many industrial enterprises. While private competition in most sectors has been welcomed, if only because sufficient investment by the public sector has become impossible, the authorities have baulked at privatization. It seems unlikely that the electorate at large would be concerned, and so the political barriers to privatization must be the bureaucracy and the public sector unions. It has also been suggested that the issues involved in public enterprise reform are too complex to be solved within the present institutional framework of highly disseminated administrative responsibility, and lack of expertise in the modalities of industrial restructuring. A kind of super-ministry for reform might be needed, which could perhaps also promote reform in company law and other matters affecting corporate governance. However, it is also possible that the reformers themselves have not been convinced of the necessity for privatization. Lastly, one should note that the States have in this respect been more reformist than the Centre. Several have embarked on a programme of privatization. Even the Marxist government of West Bengal has been actively courting the multinationals.

I have indicated that agricultural reform is very complex, necessarily involving reforms in other policies and the cooperation of the States. But it is not clear that there should be any long-run insuperable opposition, since the opening of trade would more than compensate most farmers for loss of subsidies, and the poor could be compensated in various ways for a rise in cereal prices. Nevertheless, careful phasing and coordination involving several different ministries as well as the States would be desirable. But there is no over-arching institution to steer the process of reform. I have mentioned the same lack in connection with industrial restructuring and privatization. It is ironical that reforms leading to an unplanned economy need planning: and one must bear in mind the danger that institutions which should quickly make themselves redundant would actually survive.

4. REFORM PRIORITIES

Although almost everything needs reforming, some things are more urgent than others. The most urgent are reforms needed to ensure fairly rapid growth of GDP—say 6 per cent—in the next few years. Given that, many difficulties in the way of further reform, poverty alleviation, and growth will be eased.

Government deficits

One must first single out the central government fiscal and current deficits. Vijay Joshi and I, among others, have shown that present levels are unsustainable. Unsustainability of deficits might be thought of as a problem only for the long term. But this is not so. Present fiscal deficits will very soon bring debt to levels that threaten stability and a loss of creditworthiness. Not only that, they are currently threatening growth. In order to contain inflation, the Government is borrowing heavily on the market rather than 'printing money'. This forces up interest rates to levels which must reduce investment. There is too much monetary restraint because there is not enough fiscal constraint.

There is no doubt that government expenditure on infrastructure investment should rise. The small curtailing of the fiscal deficit has been achieved by restricting public investment, not current expenditure. There is little or no possibility of rapidly rising revenue (as a percentage of GDP). This implies that it is the current revenue deficit that is the villain of the piece, and that this deficit must be reduced (in other words, government savings must be increased from the present negative level) by reducing current expenditure (as a percentage of GDP). This in turn implies reducing the subsidies, reducing public employment, and restraining public pay levels. Public enterprise losses must also be reduced, by privatization where necessary. Expenditure on poverty alleviation, and those social services which relate primarily to the poor, should remain sacrosanct. The States also run deficits. In theory, the Centre can control these deficits. In practice this is far from easy, and the States must play their part in fiscal adjustment, especially through greater cost recovery.

The infrastructure

Shortages of power and transport services are even now holding back industrial production. Power is the most serious. The roots of the problem are in the State Electricity Boards. They heavily subsidize, even give away, this vital scarce resource, and are otherwise mismanaged and corrupt. Consequently they are insolvent, and cannot be trusted to pay for electricity bought from independent generators.

To satisfy the present rate of increase of demand, projected over the next decade, would require an investment over the next five or six years that is far beyond not only the means of the public sector, but of the Indian private sector as well. Massive foreign investment is required. This has been recognized since 1992. The new Maharashtra Government, elected in 1994, repudiated its predecessor's agreement with Enron to build the very large Dabhol power project. This was the first of a number of 'fast-track' foreign-backed projects to be agreed. Fast-track indeed! After protracted renegotiation, it is reported that agreement has again been reached. The Maharashtra Government may have secured some cost reduction, but at a high cost for India. The politicization of the issues will cause other States to seek to renegotiate and will have made foreign investors even more wary than they already were.

The way forward can come only via an urgent and drastic reform of the State Electricity Boards that requires them to adopt commercial standards and practices in general, and in particular to charge economic tariffs to all customers. Power supply has to be primarily a state responsibility. The Centre should give expert technical assistance in negotiations with foreign suppliers, and on the tariffs and conditions of purchase of power from any source by State Electricity Boards that will best economize in both capacity and fuel; and similarly for sales. Unfortunately, the guidelines laid down by the Ministry of Power (advised by the Central Electricity Board) in 1992 for 'Widening the scope for private participation' do not inspire confidence that the economic expertise available to the Ministry was adequate. It seems that these guidelines may have contributed to the Dabhol debacle. Finally, the Centre must never provide 'counter-guarantees' of payment by State Electricity Boards unless and until they have been fully reformed. As in other areas, privatization may be an essential part of the reform. It is reported that Orissa has grasped the nettle of privatizing the State Electricity Board and installing independent regulators to see that economic non-political tariffs are set. Other States must be encouraged to follow suit.

Transport is the other part of the infrastructure where the need for improvement is both difficult and urgent. The railways should play a larger part in freight transport, which requires not only investment but also, like power, a reform of the tariff structure which has been heavily politicized. More investment in both ports and roads is needed. Both the urgency of the problems and the means of solving them are fully appreciated by the central Government and its bureaucracy. Unfortunately, in India it does not follow that anything much is done.

5. THE FUTURE OF REFORM, 1996–2000

Even in the unlikely event that the Congress Party can form a majority government or a very strong minority government, after the national elections next month it cannot be presumed that there would be rapid progress towards the model of the economy that I have espoused. Some features of the model cannot be assumed to be fully and widely accepted. Examples are full freedom for foreign corporate ownership; extensive privatization; a low uniform tariff and no import controls even on consumer goods; virtual free trade in agricultural products; and the reform of company and labour laws. Moreover, as I have said, the momentum of reform has been lost.

However, progress on certain fronts would probably continue, e.g. tax and tariff reform and simplification, and further liberalization in the financial sector, e.g. insurance. Gradual improvement of the public finances might also be expected, together with stronger efforts to improve the infrastructure. These latter moves may almost be forced by economic circumstances. But we have seen that the Government has balked at tackling the more politically difficult reforms, such as privatization and agricultural trade: and there is no obvious reason to hope for greater resolve on the part of a new Congress-led government. If the reforms are stalled, there will remain enough inconsistencies and impediments in the Indian economy to prevent it achieving the very high rates of growth which I believe to be possible.

What happens if some other party or a coalition forms a government? This is difficult to predict because parties in India do not proclaim economic programmes, and do not stand for any clear model of society. Thus, elections are not mainly about economic issues. However, all parties claim that they are in favour of economic reform, and almost all observers agree that there will be no going back on reform. However, I suspect that this means only that there will be no going back to the 'permit raj' or 'licence raj' that is so widely discredited. In other words, comprehensive controls over domestic production and investment will not be resorted to. But I am not confident that import restrictions would not be reimposed in the event of balance of payments difficulties that might arise from populist policies. This has happened in many other developing countries. Exchange controls could also be tightened, and foreign investment restricted to sectors where the government believes the need is manifest. In short, the conviction of the benefits of a very open competitive economy may not be sufficiently deep in India to prevent resort to such policies. There is still enough xenophobic nationalist sentiment to confer popularity on measures to restrict foreign trade and capital inflows. Even if there is no backsliding, there seem to be no very good grounds for hoping that a BJP or National-Front-led government would pursue reform with greater resolve than a Congress-led government, though this is a possibility.

Some observers believe that there will be an increase in the power of the States whatever the result of the national elections. A few States have shown themselves to be more aggressive in reform than the Centre, especially in privatization and inviting foreign investment: and other States may copy them. But the States cannot do a great deal independently of the Centre.

India is beset by an extraordinary diversity of economic, regional, communal, and caste interests. The Congress party effectively managed a wide range of conflict for a long time, but it was not a party of reform. Its dominance has now been overtaken by the rise of many parties with narrower interests, which are weak at the national level. This, and the continuing growth of pervasive corruption, casts doubt on the ability of the Indian political system to deliver governments which are strong and cohesive enough to avoid fiscal excesses and promote difficult reforms.

I end therefore on a mildly pessimistic note. The achievements of the past four and a half years are impressive, and will lead to higher growth for the Indian economy. But the many further reforms which would enable India to achieve its full potential are not likely to be quickly made. I believe that the best hope is that Manmohan Singh is still finance minister this time next year, and for as long thereafter as he can stand the strain, and is allowed to do what he wants.

PART IV

Loose Ends

Not all my professional activities are covered by the concepts of welfare theory and development economics. As already noted in the chapter dealing with my years at the Treasury, I thought about fiscal and monetary policy in the late 1950s and early 1960s. Although I had worked mainly on foreign economic policy when in the Economic Section of the Treasury, I clearly absorbed some of its thinking on domestic policy even if I did not contribute to it. In the 1960s a good deal of time was devoted to managing Nuffield College investments. Other interests from time to time included airports and airport pricing, a possible wealth tax, and international justice. These are commented on in the following chapter. The final chapter contains some afterthoughts.

Miscellaneous Activities

FISCAL POLICY

From about the mid-1950s, the Economic Section became increasingly worried by the exaggerated role that, it believed, ministers were beginning to give to monetary policy, and by the confused mystique apparent in some of their pronouncements, particularly those of Mr Thornecroft, concerning money and inflation. It was apparently believed that monetary measures could reduce inflation without reducing demand. Ever since the revival of monetary policy, chancellors have been extremely reluctant to raise taxes, preferring to raise interest rates or restrict credit. This may well have destabilized the economy.

The above worry is reflected in the excerpts from chapter 8 of G. D. N. Worswick and P. H. Ady's *British Economy in the 1950s* (1962), which form Paper 16. The main thesis of the paper is that stabilization should consist primarily of smoothing the growth of consumption by fiscal means. It is argued that consumption is more predictable, and more predictably influenced, than investment, and that fluctuations in investment would anyway be reduced if consumption grew smoothly.

Monetary policy influences investment more than consumption, but with uncertain lags and strength. This reduces the desirable role of monetary policy. But if investment (and purchases of consumer durables) must occasionally be restrained or encouraged, fiscal policy can be much more powerful than monetary policy. This contention took account of fiscal devices such as initial allowances and investment allowances. Varying the taxation of mortgage payments might also have been mentioned. This left little for monetary policy to do.[1] The main role left was to influence international capital movements.

This thesis probably underestimated the influence of monetary policy on consumption. It can influence it through asset prices, through the cash flows of debtors, and through interest rates on overdrafts, credit cards, and hire purchase contracts. But I still believe that these effects, though important, are more

[1] The chapter on monetary policy in the Worswick–Ady book, by Charles Kennedy, took the same view. He reached the conclusion that 'the use of monetary policy as a *major* instrument of control over the economy' should be abandoned (p. 322). More recently, with his wealth of experience in the Treasury and the Bank of England, Christopher Dow accords monetary policy only a secondary role; see Dow and Saville, *A Critique of Monetary Policy*.

uncertain in both their size and timing than the effects of, for instance, a change in the rates of income tax or VAT. This is not to argue that demand can be fine-tuned by fiscal policy, either. Changes in the current account, that is in foreign borrowing or lending, can accommodate a good deal of fluctuation. But when it becomes clear that consumption expenditure is growing too fast or too slowly for long-run equilibrium, taxes should be varied. The chronic unwillingness of politicians to raise taxes has resulted in excessive public indebtedness in many countries. When demand is very strong, the national debt should be reduced; this permits it to be increased when demand is weak and stagnation threatens.

In 1962, when I wrote the chapter for the Worswick–Ady book, the exchange rate was fixed. Now one would add that influencing capital movements also implies influencing the exchange rate. This may be one of the main transmission belts through which monetary policy affects demand. Thus, a rise in interest rates will cause a rise in the exchange rate, which will reduce exports and probably also investment in creating export capacity.

The desirability of raising interest rates was hotly debated in the summer of 1997, when many economists and businessmen took the view that the threatening consumption boom would better have been restrained by taxation than by raising interest rates, which reduced the profitability of exporting. I thought so too, consistently with the analysis of Paper 16. Politicians also still run true to form, avoiding tax rate increases if at all possible.

A new consideration has been added in the UK to the debate on monetary versus fiscal policy. Monetary policy has been handed over to the Bank of England, which seems implicitly to presage a leading role for monetary policy in restraining demand when need be. This is clearly at variance with the views that I have expressed in Paper 16, and still hold. Ideally, fiscal and monetary policy should be closely coordinated. A division of responsibility cannot be the best way to achieve this, and is in this respect irrational. But if the government cannot be trusted *not* to abuse monetary policy, this prima facie irrational separation of powers may become rational. But then it becomes pertinent to ask whether the government should be trusted with fiscal policy, either. Indeed, more than one country has tried to limit constitutionally the government's recourse to borrowing. This is difficult in the UK as there is no constitution.

Perhaps finally I should add that I have not kept up with the massive literature on these difficult matters. No doubt I might think differently if I had.

FUND MANAGEMENT

I was for many years one of the two investment bursars of Nuffield College. Investing money might not be considered an intellectual activity, at least not a respectable one for an academic economist. But it did lead to some economic research, as a result of which I was for a while quite famous in the City of London.

In 1958 Nuffield College ceased to be a department of the University, and acquired control over its own investments. From 1958 to 1961 Sir Donald Macdougall was First Bursar, and I was Second Bursar. This distinction arose because the Warden, Norman Chester, did not at first quite trust me. He did later,but initially he felt safer with Donald Macdougall, who projected a greater impression of gravitas than I have ever managed. The distinction was not operational in any way, for Donald and I simply took it in turns to manage the portfolio. We used only one broker, Vickers da Costa, and the mode of operation was a daily talk with Ralph Vickers, the senior partner, who became a personal friend. When Donald Macdougall left in 1962 to be the Economic Director of the National Economic Development Office (popularly known as NEDDY), Uwe Kitzinger became joint-bursar. Peter Oppenheimer took my place in 1965–7 when I was at the OECD. I finally gave up when I became a professor in 1970.

The performance in the first few years was sensational. The accompanying table gives the total return (income plus capital gains) for the first four years, the next six up to 1968, and the twenty-two years from 1968 to 1990, for the College's non-property portfolio, its holdings of UK equities, and the FTA all-share index.

Total Money Returns and the Retail Price Index, per annum

	All non-property	UK equities	FTA All Share	RPI
1958–62	31.4	38.6	21.0	3.0
1962–8	12.6	16.3	11.2	4.4
1968–90	14.7	15.1	15.4	9.7

It must be noted that the comparison for the first four years is mainly with the FT30 index not the FTA All Share Index, which did not exist. The FT30 Index was easier to beat than the FTA Index. Nevertheless, the fact that the College's UK equities outperformed by 17.6 per cent annum was extraordinary. I cannot give a better explanation than I gave in a special report to the College's Investment Committee in May 1963.[2] So I quote from it at some length.

The Bursars in earlier years acquired much credit from the fact that they fell in with the start of a highly successful policy operated by Vickers da Costa generally, but one later associated particularly with the formation of the trust 'Investing in Success'. Both 'Investing in Success' and the Bursars made their particular choices from stocks with a consistently good record, and other stocks were seldom put forward for consideration by the brokers or suggested by ourselves. The Bursars and the directors of 'Investing in

[2] Of course such a report was highly confidential. But I am now assuming that a notional 30-year old rule protects me from any accusations of impropriety.

Success' would on occasion make different detailed decisions and the opportunities for purchase were not always identical. Nevertheless the portfolios showed considerable overlap, and their similarity as to the kind of share held was even more marked than the overlap suggested. The performance, not surprisingly, was very similar. The main reason for the great success of this joint policy was a shift of market opinion in favour of so-called growth stocks. This shift was at least partly initiated by Vickers da Costa themselves. It had the effect not only of causing a relative revaluation of well known stocks with a fine past record, but also led to a search for smaller and less-known companies with equally good records. We were early starters in this hunt, and thereby profited greatly. But rather over a year ago it was clear that it was becoming very difficult to find shares which looked under-valued when considered as growth stocks. It seemed that the halcyon days were over. It was for this reason that I rightly warned the Stated General meeting last year that I thought it most unlikely that we could continue to 'beat the index' at anything like the rate we had done in the past.

The reason for the success was *not* that shares with a good past record have on average any better expectation of future success than other shares. I claim to have established this in an article I published last December, called 'Higgledy-Piggledy Growth'. I had convinced myself of it early in 1962. But, in any case, even if it *were* true, the market would eventually adjust the values of such shares so that their future would be fully or more than fully discounted. Given that it is not true, growth stock prices probably overdiscounted the future, and about a year ago the market fashion in favour of such stocks reversed itself. This happened most dramatically in the USA, where the prices of such shares fell very steeply, and have still largely failed to recover. We were involved in this crash, though not fortunately to a very important extent. More important to us, the same relative downward valuation of 'growth' stocks, which very broadly speaking coincide with low yielders, has happened here.

A few postscripts are in order. First, the non-UK equity non-property portfolio has performed worse than UK equities. In the beginning this consisted largely of fixed-interest stocks, but later it included much foreign equity. Some have thought that the College's early entry into the Japanese market explained much of the success. This seems not to have been the case. Second, despite the demise of the growth stock fashion in 1962, the College continued to invest mainly in low-yielding equities, and continued to beat the index until about 1968. So the 'bandwagon' element I have underlined was not quite the whole story. But I am not sure what *was* the whole story.

The 'Higgledy Piggledy Growth' article mentioned in my report is included here as Paper 17. Despite its publication in a rather obscure journal, it created quite a sensation in the City. It upset Charles Gifford, the chairman of Investing in Success, of which I was a director. He thought I was being perfidious in publicly disproving the theory on which Investing in Success was founded.[3] I did not see it that way, as I did not believe that success could continue for long if based

[3] The idea that past growth was a good indicator of future growth was, I believe, due to Nicholas Kaldor. I remember him assiduously calculating growth rates on a slide-rule. He taught me how to do this, a bit of know-how that was soon to become obsolete. I no longer know how!

on error. In fact, the fashion for 'growth' stocks was already turning. Investing in Success and the College continued to invest very successfully in low-yielding equities, but the appraisal of what constituted a *future* growth stock became more sophisticated. However, I resigned from Investing in Success. But Ralph Vickers did not seem to share Gifford's opinion, for he soon made me a director of Vickers da Costa's other big trust, General Funds.[4]

Twenty years later, in 1990, I again became Investment Bursar for the best part of two years when my friend Maurice Scott was Chairman of the Investment Committee. I took over on the day before Saddam Hussein attacked Kuwait. I found the College had nearly 30 per cent in bonds and cash, a position which I thought to be inconsistent with its long-term investment philosophy. I very soon started going back into the market. But I cautiously took over six months to get back to a position of nearly 90 per cent in equities. This was too slow, as the market was booming in the autumn and early in 1991. But from conversations with colleagues and members of the Investment Committee, it was very evident that no one else who might have been acting bursar would have been as 'bold'. Largely as a result, I believe I made the College a lot of money.

The Warden, Sir David Cox, took over as Chairman of the Investment Committee in 1991. It appeared that he could hardly wait to be rid of me for he mistakenly predated the end of the term of my appointment. He apparently thought that I was a dangerous gambler. Sir David was very risk-averse. I believe he thought the College should always have a significant proportion in cash and fixed-interest securities. In my opinion he feared the wrong risk, i.e. that a fall in the market would endanger the College's activities. I thought the College could easily weather any such temporary storm, and that the real risk was that of failing to keep up with the costs of teaching and research in the long run. A yachtsman will not win a long-distance race if his mainsail is always reefed. I tried but failed to arrive at any meeting of minds on this subject.

AIRPORTS AND AIRPORT PRICING

Another miscellaneous activity was being a member of the board of the British Airports Authority from 1969 to 1974. I owed this appointment to my friend Tony Crosland. I managed to reform the pricing policy of the Authority, introducing a time-of-day (and year) tariff for Heathrow. This is described in an article I wrote in 1972 with the Finance Director K. M. McLeod, 'The New Pricing Policy of the British Airports Authority'. The most important general point it makes is that the long-run marginal cost principle, endorsed in official publications, and still very

[4] Donald Macdougall gives an account of our joint-bursarship in *Don and Mandarin*, and refers, I am sorry to say, to the publication of 'Higgledy Piggledy Growth' as 'Rather letting the side down one might think'.

much alive, was inappropriate in the case of very lumpy investments such as airports. It was also argued that the Roskill Commission[5] had greatly overestimated the benefits of a new Third London Airport by failing to consider the use of optimal peak load pricing at existing airports: and consequentially the 'timing of the need' for a new airport was too soon (1980). The proposed huge four-runway Third London Airport (Stansted did not count) was out in the North Sea, and was known first as Foulness and then as Maplin. Sometime early in 1974, I had a telephone call quite late at night from Tony Crosland, then Minister for the Department of the Environment, to ask what he should do about Maplin. I said 'ditch it'. He did. I had in fact already briefed him on the subject when in opposition, telling him that only one new runway was needed in this century in the London area. I was exaggerating, to be safe. If I had any decisive influence on this issue, I earned my £1,000 salary as a board member of the BAA tens of thousands of times over.

WEALTH TAXATION

Another miscellaneous venture was writing a pamphlet in 1974 with J. S. Flemming, entitled *Why We Need A Wealth Tax*. The title was misleading and was not our choice. The Chancellor had announced an annual wealth tax, and a Green Paper thereon. I was afraid that this would be just another tax, at a low rate. I thought that there was much to be said for a wealth tax, on grounds of both equity and efficiency, but only if it took the place of many other taxes, and so led to a great simplification of the tax system, making tax returns much less of an administrative chore. So John Flemming and I made proposals to abolish all taxation of property incomes, property transfers, and capital gains. A progressive wealth tax would take their place. This annual tax would rise to a rate that would make it almost impossible to maintain a wealth of over £350,000, which in today's monetary values would be about £2 million. I sometimes wonder why I am widely regarded as right-wing. I know of no accredited left-wing, supposedly egalitarian, economist or politician who would dare today to suggest anything so egalitarian. I have also wondered whether such irresponsible proposals had anything to do with the Establishment's distrust of me. But the subsequent career of John Flemming seems to be evidence to the contrary.

[5] A Commission appointed to choose a site for a third London airport, and the date by which it should be operational.

INTERNATIONAL JUSTICE

Finally, I wrote two articles in 1978 and 1989 about international justice, one with reference mainly to aid and the so called 'New International Economic Order', and the other with reference mainly to migration and capital monuments. International justice has been a rather neglected subject, so these invited contributions to conference volumes are reproduced here as Papers 18 and 19. The first is concerned partly with the validity of the claims made by developing countries in the name of justice as part of the demands for a 'New International Economic Order' in the 1970s. It invoked Rawls's and Nozick's recent theories of justice, noting that neither could be applied internationally, whether to states or individuals. When writing this paper, I did not have access to the already weighty mass of articles about their theories. Subsequent dipping, however, seems to confirm that these eminent philosophers had nothing useful to say about international justice.

The movement for a new international order died with the 1970s and the onset of the debt crisis.[6] However, similar demands will arise again, and Paper 18 is also relevant to international aid which was discussed in the chapter above dealing with India. Its conclusions concerning aid still seem acceptable to me. The second paper is concerned mainly with the ethics of migration, and the obligations that a state has to aliens. I commend it, together with the other papers on a relatively neglected subject in the same book—*Free Movement*, edited by Barry and Goodin.

[6] I considered most of its demands in detail in *Economic Development. Theory, Policy, and International Relations* (1982). In my opinion it did not serve the best interests of the developing world, and its death was to be welcomed.

Reflections

Despite a late start, owing to the War, I have been an active economist for fifty years. What, apart from earning a living, have I achieved thereby?

I make two claims, one minor and one major. The minor claim is that I made some contribution to the philosophy of welfare economics, which served to undermine its excessive pretensions while preserving its essential validity.

The major claim is that, a little more than any other economist, I was responsible for the renaissance of orthodox mainstream economics for the developing world, after twenty-five years of preaching by development economists that conventional Western economic thinking was inappropriate and inapplicable. This renaissance has in turn contributed to the dramatic changes in policy that occurred in most developing economies in the 1980s and 1990s. I believe that these changes have assisted economic growth and the relief of poverty in much of the developing world.

This claim is based mainly on the research that I initiated at the OECD Development Centre in 1966, which culminated in *Industry and Trade in Some Developing Countries* (with Scitovsky and Scott, 1970). The simultaneous work on project appraisal culminating in the OECD *Manual of Industrial Project Analysis* and *Project Appraisal and Planning for Developing Countries* (both with Mirrlees, 1969 and 1974) was complementary. Both were followed up by many articles that pointed to the value of openness for growth, employment, and poverty alleviation.

Economists have become more specialized, and most now use more sophisticated mathematical techniques than erstwhile. The papers in this volume show that I am not at all specialized. I have written on both macro and micro levels. I am not a specialist in international trade, industrial economics, foreign investment, collective choice, taxation, growth, cost–benefit analysis, or fund management; but I have written about them all, and much else. I am a development economist, but only in the sense that I have worked for many years mainly on developing economies, and not in the sense that I claim my special expertise relevant to these countries.

This diversity has come partly from the fact that, after the early writing on welfare economics and collective choice, my work has been inspired by problems that were apparent in the real world. In contrast, with honourable exceptions, most theorists are inspired by what already exists in the journals, which they think they can improve on, or pull apart. In this way I think they also tend to specialize. But I am no theorist. Furthermore, my work has been largely other-directed in that I have responded to demands coming from the institutions I joined, or to attractive invitations such as joining the MIT mission in India in 1958.

Apart from its diversity, my work is unusual in appearing as much in books as in journal articles. But of the twenty or so books or pamphlets (excluding translations and editorships), all but six were of joint authorship. I could not have authored so much without collaboration. Empirical work requires collaboration unless one is a person of outstanding energy and application. I am fortunate in having been a member of or associated with institutions where such collaboration was easy to come by. My fourteen co-authors range from research assistants to a Nobel Prize winner. However, to do myself justice, I should add that with one exception I was the originator, or chief architect, of the research that underlay the book.[1]

Nowadays few well-known academic economists write books, and I guess that it is rare for any young economist to plan to write one.[2] This is understandable, for when he or she is assessed for a job or promotion their articles, especially those that appear in refereed journals, will carry, page for page, several times the weight of a book. This is a big change. Right up to Keynes's *General Theory* and the Second World War, the major treatise remained the dominant mode of expression. Since the war such famous economists as Hicks, Meade, and Milton Friedman have largely expressed themselves in books, but their careers were rooted in the 1930s.

The dominance of the journal article has probably resulted largely from increasing specialization on narrow issues, the exploration of which could hardly justify a book. The greatly increased use of mathematics has also probably contributed, not only by permitting a more concise treatment but also by reducing the number of readers. The subject as it thrives in academic circles is in danger of becoming undesirably remote: undesirably so because there are many intelligent laymen properly interested in economic policy who do not read journal articles and cannot read mathematics. They must rely on economic journalists. Fortunately, the quality of economic journalism has, I think greatly improved in recent years, at least in the UK.

I have employed no sophisticated techniques. My mathematics is limited to elementary calculus, and my econometrics to the simplest regression. When I returned to academe after six years in the RAF, I was too impatient to invest much in acquiring skills of uncertain value. In the event, would more equipment have made me a better economist? I think not, given the work I undertook. With

[1] The exception is Joshi and Little's *India's Economic Reforms 1991-2001*, which was joint in every respect.

[2] But a few may try to hit the jackpot with a popular textbook.

more mathematics I might have done more theory. But I do not know who would have benefited from that! With more econometrics I might have produced results which, a few years later, would have been demolished by the latest advances in the subject. One cannot be against econometric striving, but it is sad that useful estimates of the most important economic relations such as the determinants of saving and investment still do not exist. I hazard the prediction that they never will.

It is common for old economists to complain that economics has become excessively mathematical. Should I join the chorus? I think that to say that economics has become too mathematical is much the same as to say that there is too much theorizing that feeds on itself and is only very remotely, if at all, related to real problems. I suspect this is true. A corollary is that there is a great deal of useful economics that can be well done without much mathematics, and that important problems can be approached by means other than making models. A danger is that young, potentially good, economists may be put off the subject by the heavy training required, or by a lack of mathematical talent and the fear that publications and promotion will be difficult if ideas are not expressed in equations. I am not the first to express this fear. But when I contemplate the vast array of economic journals, many unreadable, I wonder whether there are not too many economists anyway!

16

Fiscal Policy (1952)

I. THE RELATION OF FISCAL TO MONETARY POLICY

It has been seen that the removal of quantitative restrictions has reduced the means of control without reducing the ends. But to what extent is monetary policy an additional weapon? Are monetary and fiscal policy taken together sufficient in principle to achieve the Government's aims? These questions cannot be fully answered here. But some comparison of the two is essential to a discussion of fiscal policy.

The relative effects on demand

Monetary policy acts initially on demands which are largely financed either by borrowing or by the sale of other assets, whereas most taxes act initially on demands financed from current incomes.[1] These categories of demand shade into each other, but the distinction is still worth making. Both act by influencing demand. Since, for the most part, investment is financed by borrowing (or the sale of financial assets), and consumption by current income, it is obvious enough that the initial impact of monetary policy must be primarily on investment in stocks or fixed capital, including houses, and that of taxation on consumption. But, since consumption and investment demand are connected, monetary policy has, after some possibly long lag, induced effects on consumption; and similarly for taxes and investment. Finally, fiscal policy, in the wider sense which includes expenditure control, can not only alter private incomes, but also acts directly on government consumption and on the 40 per cent or more of investment subject to such control.

This paper contains two excerpts from a chapter in G. D. N. Worswick and P. H. Ady (eds.), *The British Economy in the 1950s* (Oxford University Press, 1962). Permission to reproduce is gratefully acknowledged.

[1] In pure theory, with perfect capital markets, the source of investment finance is irrelevant: even if an investment is financed from current income, the same effect should result from a tighter monetary policy, since the savings could be lent on better terms. In practice it is far from irrelevant, partly because of imperfect capital markets, and partly because of inertia.

Some of the above statements are, of course, only approximately true. Monetary policy may also affect consumption directly, mostly because durable consumption goods are bought on credit to a significant and growing extent. Thus, hire-purchase control is the most obvious and dramatic way in which monetary policy affects consumption, although it also tends to be reduced by a reduction in personal advances. (It should be noted that with hire purchase control consumption in total may be a little less affected in absolute terms than the output of particular durable goods, since the deposit money is partly switched to other things.)

Of potentially greater importance is the fact that, since the introduction of initial and investment allowances, taxation has been capable of influencing private investment in a very similar manner to monetary policy. Thus, the initial allowance operates as a government loan at zero interest covering part of the cost of equipment, and to be paid back over its life.[2] But this loan amounts only to the saving in tax in the first year, which, with a 20 per cent initial allowance, is about 10 per cent of the cost of the equipment. To get this amount interest free represents a small (10 per cent) reduction in the effective rate of interest paid on the whole cost of the equipment. If it is difficult to get loans at all, there is also the additional consideration that a company's current cash flow is increased in relation to its capital commitments. It can thus be seen how extremely alike fiscal and financial policy can be in their potential effects on private fixed investment.

It cannot be expected that at the levels at which they have been used (no more than 30 per cent except for mining equipment and shipping), initial allowances could have a large effect on fixed investment in plant and machinery. Roughly speaking, a 20 per cent initial allowance is equivalent to a reduction in the interest rate from 5 to 4½ per cent. A 100 per cent initial allowance would be roughly equivalent to halving the rate of interest.

Investment allowances, so similar in name, are different in principle, and potentially far more powerful than monetary policy. The tax remission in the first year is unconditional, and does not increase subsequent tax liability. A 20 per cent investment allowance is roughly a 10 per cent subsidy to investment[3] (exactly 10 per cent if profits tax plus the standard rate of income tax were 50 per cent). This is far more powerful than the initial allowance, especially for

[2] The analogy is not quite complete, but corresponds with accountancy treatment of initial allowances, which is what probably matters in practice. It is also not inconsistent with the fact that, if the firm invests the same amount continuously, it never pays back the tax remission, and gets ever-increasing tax remissions if its investment increases continuously. These cases can be equated to continuously renewed, or increased, interest-free loans. The yield on each individual investment parcel will be calculated on the basis that the loan is repayable.

[3] It differs from a direct subsidy only in that the firm must make some profit to get the subsidy. The investment allowance has found wide favour with both parties. Any academic or other economist who had suggested subsidizing investment in 1954 would have been regarded as dangerously silly. But some Treasury economists had the subtle idea of presenting the subsidy as a mild logical development of the initial allowance.

short-lived equipment, since it reduces the minimum earnings required to write off the investment by 20 per cent. For instance, for equipment which is written off in five years, the 20 per cent initial allowance (or a 10 per cent fall in interest rates) reduces the gross break-even yield of an investment by only about 1 per cent, the investment allowance by almost 20 per cent. No fall in interest rates could be so powerful.[4] For longer-lived equipment the differences are less startling. For equipment written off in 20 years, a 20 per cent investment allowance is roughly equivalent to reducing interest rates from 5 to 2½ per cent.

If some level of investment allowance (say 20 per cent) comes to be regarded as normal, variations round that rate can thus be far more powerful than any practicable monetary policy as a deterrent or encouragement to fixed investment (except where credit is rationed so effectively that some firms—and this is usually only likely to apply to very small firms—cannot obtain finance at all). Even if the normal investment allowance is zero, the system could be used to discourage investment if need be, since there is nothing in principle against a negative investment allowance, in effect an investment tax. Moreover, investment allowances can be, and are, made selective. They do not apply to houses or cars, and apply at a lower rate to buildings, and at a higher rate to mining equipment and ships. Thus, investment allowances can be used in a fairly rational manner to help achieve specific ends, e.g. to encourage private investment in those parts of the economy whose development is likely to strengthen the United Kingdom's trade balance.

Monetary policy is also highly directional. It hits (when it hits at all) at illiquid firms with little pull with the banks—that is, usually small firms. Attempts have been made from time to time to make it rationally selective by giving bank managers and the Capital Issues Committee (often bypassed by legally ingenious devices) instructions about national priorities. But it must be an impossible task in very many cases to apply the Treasury's vague criteria,[5] and neither bank managers nor the Capital Issues Committee themselves are particularly qualified to judge what is in the national interest, being more experienced in judging creditworthiness than matters connected with the balance and structure of the economy.

So far as I know, the possibility of using taxation directly to influence stock-holding has never been investigated. This is an important field in which

[4] Roughly speaking, equipment costing £100 with a life of 5 years, with interest of 5 per cent, must earn £22½ per annum to break even (£20 for depreciation and £2½ for servicing the average outstanding loan of £50). A 20 per cent initial allowance reduces the average outstanding loan to £45. Hence required earnings are £22¼. A reduction in the rate of interest to 4½ per cent would have the same effect. A 20 per cent investment allowance reduces the annual earnings required to write off the equipment to £16, making £80 in five years. But since depreciation allowances total £120, this produces a taxable income loss of £40, with a tax saving of £20, which taken together with the £80 suffices to write off the equipment. The interest charge falls to £2¼, and hence break-even earnings to £18¼. This is better than a zero rate of interest.

[5] Cf. Radcliffe *Report*, 1900, paras. 965–77. These paragraphs are a forceful exposure of the futility of the qualitative capital issues control, but do not rule out quantitative control in all circumstances.

monetary policy may have a role which taxation policy cannot emulate; although it must be noted that its effects are highly uncertain. Corresponding to the possibility of its influencing stocks, there may also be a role for monetary policy in smoothing short-term fluctuations in the balance of trade (via its influence on private imported stocks), though here again its effectiveness is in serious doubt. The danger that its short-term use to try to influence stocks (or to cause a capital inflow to lend temporary support to the reserves, or to scare potential speculators against sterling) will cause unwanted cancellations of or delays in fixed capital formation could be minimized by assurances that this was not the intention, by making short-term credit very expensive rather than rationing it, and by using an increase in initial allowances to offset any effect of monetary policy on fixed investment.[6]

Finally, monetary measures have been thought more appropriate than fiscal measures if it is desired to influence private house building. This is a field in which monetary policy has a far more reliable effect than elsewhere, but there is also no reason why fiscal measures should not be used.

Thus, monetary policy has some functions distinct from fiscal policy. But they overlap so far as both fixed private industrial and commercial investment and the consumption of durables are concerned. In so far as monetary policy acts on business decisions by altering the rational calculation of net yields by altering interest rates, there is no doubt that taxation is potentially a much more powerful weapon. In so far as monetary policy acts by credit rationing, its selective effect is unplanned and may be deleterious; and the selective effects of taxation can certainly be more rationally controlled. The levers of monetary policy can be shifted more rapidly, but both methods of trying to influence fixed investment are very uncertain in the magnitude and rapidity of their effects. In this connection it is relevant that there is very long experience of the incapacity of monetary policy to stabilize investment; and that more experience of fiscal policy might clearly show it to be decisively superior.

So far as consumption is concerned (and remembering that we are not considering induced effects on consumption), monetary policy must act almost entirely on durable goods,[7] partly by limiting personal loans but mainly by hire-purchase control. The results are more difficult to predict than in the case of more general fiscal measures, and there is also the strong disadvantage that its use must cause severe fluctuations in home demand for the products of a few particular industries; fluctuations which make sense only if there is unsatisfied demand for these products abroad.

[6] Since high interest rates are a weak deterrent to fixed investment, only the weak offset of increased initial allowances would be called for.

[7] It is possible that restraining stock market prices may have some dampening effect on consumption. If it does, this too is likely to fall on durables, which are the marginal element in the expenditure of the richer classes who may be influenced by stock market prices.

Thus, in almost all respects, taxation (or, more generally, fiscal policy) is superior to monetary policy. The main exception is that higher indirect taxes may raise the rate of wage increase. The corollary of this is that it is in some ways better to *induce* people to save and hence consume less. Unfortunately, there is no quick or sure means of rapidly changing the rate of private saving.

Are fiscal and monetary controls sufficient?

Finally, let us revert to the question asked at the beginning of this section: are monetary and fiscal policy together sufficient means of control to achieve governmental aims? The active use of monetary policy adds nothing to fiscal policy so far as long-run equilibrium in the labour and foreign exchange markets are concerned—since what matters here is the general level of home demand, and the problem is that a sufficient level of demand for full employment and optimum growth may well be inconsistent with balance in these markets (in the absence of other controls or influence). But monetary policy can help to solve temporary balance of payments difficulties, and the fact that it has no immediate effect on the cost of living may sometimes be important.

Abstracting from the above two markets, means of stabilizing consumption and investment, and means of influencing them independently (or, rather, of modifying their interdependence, since it cannot be eliminated) are required for the purpose of achieving steady growth with a sufficiently high level of investment. There is no doubt that fiscal policy can act sufficiently powerfully to ensure the steady growth of consumption, provided that potential deviations can be adequately foreseen. Some 40 per cent of investment is subject to controls, which to some extent can be used to help stabilize total investment. It should also be noted that if consumption is successfully stabilized, then the most intransigent sector, private investment, should tend to behave much less erratically than has been the case in the past. Nevertheless, it may be necessary to take steps to influence private investment, in both fixed equipment and stocks, from time to time. In principle, fiscal policy can act sufficiently powerfully on private fixed investment in either direction. The problem is not lack of weapons, but the difficulty of foreseeing changes in private investment, and even more the difficulty that little is known of the magnitude and timing of the effects of policy measures (whether fiscal or monetary). Investment in stocks is even more difficult to influence, for here fiscal policy is apparently impotent, and the effects of monetary policy are highly debatable.

It is for the above reasons that many favour some controls over private investment (and over imports primarily as a means of influencing investment in stocks) to act as a long stop in the event of stimulating measures overshooting the mark. Without such long stops it can be argued that a wide-open economy, such as that of the United Kingdom, short of reserves, is in too precarious a situation to pursue a sufficiently progressive policy. But the effectiveness of controls as means to this end is also uncertain, and cannot be discussed here.[8]

2. FISCAL POLICY AND STABILIZATION: CONCLUSIONS AND LESSONS

Price stability and the balance of payments have from time to time overridden the aim of steady expansion with full employment. The means of achieving the latter aim will first be discussed on the assumption that the former two will not stand in its way.

Price stability apart, the economic freedom achieved in the 1950s has made central economic management a matter of modifying, and if possible eliminating, fluctuations in economic activity without the use of physical controls, while doing so with an average level of investment sufficiently high to secure the growth desired.

At the same time, there has been a retreat from the use of fiscal policy to restrain consumption. To this extent, the main method of ensuring adequate full employment without excessive demand has become one of encouraging or discouraging investment (and to a lesser extent the consumption of durables), together with tax reductions whenever any slack could be envisaged.

So long as this policy continues, there is little or no prospect of steady growth, although the aim of full employment may be achieved (in the absence of a severe disturbance originating abroad), if only because the authorities show no signs of being unwilling to *reduce* taxes. The reason for this is that trying to control the economy by controlling investment is like controlling a dog by its tail, when you are not even sure how much and how soon you can make the tail move.

Investment is much less predictable than consumption, and the measures which can be taken to influence it are inevitably highly uncertain in their operation, both as to magnitude and speed.[9] The most important fluctuations of general economic activity result from the interaction of consumption and investment. If the one can be made to grow smoothly, there is every reason to suppose that fluctuations in the other will be greatly moderated. Because investment fluctuates most, some may think that this is the nettle to grasp. This is false, because there is little prospect of the authorities being able to smooth investment adequately

[8] The above section leaves rather little for monetary policy. Obviously one must have some monetary policy. But the author's view is that its active short-run use should be chiefly to influence capital movements, and possibly to influence stock-holding (although this latter is much more open to doubt).

[9] See R. R. Neild and E. A. Shirley, 'An Assessment of Forecasts, 1959–60', *Economic Review*, May 1961, for a discussion of the reliability of forecasts which are made in very much the same way as are the Treasury forecasts.

by measures which act directly on it rather than on consumption. There is even a significant risk that the authorities will produce worse fluctuations.

On the other hand, it should not be difficult to make consumption grow at a considerably steadier rate than it has since 1952. Not only is consumption much more predictable, but fiscal measures operate within the period within which reasonably accurate predictions can be made. If a steady growth of consumption (including export) demand could be achieved, it is probable that fluctuations in investment would be greatly reduced.

As Sir Roy Harrod has recently argued, the key to a more modern and successful approach to smooth progress is for the authorities to think in terms of rates of growth, rather than in terms of *ad hoc* short-term adjustments of demand to supply. Such thinking would reduce the temptation to let things slide and then do too much too late, which has been clearly apparent since 1954. More fundamentally, thinking in terms of correcting deviations of the rate of growth of consumption from some long-run target level is the most hopeful approach to the desirable end of virtually eliminating fluctuations in general economic activity. An Harrodian revolution is now needed to supplant the Keynesian revolution. This does not mean that one would expect investment to grow steadily, even if consumption grew steadily. For many reasons this would be too much to expect. But the fluctuations in private investment might be so reduced that the use of public investment as an offset, to whatever degree possible consistent with reasonable efficiency, would make the need to use short-term fiscal or financial measures to stimulate or restrain private investment a rarity.

Such a programme requires, in broad outline, a long-term plan. With the experience of the fifties it is not too difficult to predict what the economy is capable of, and to produce target rates of growth for the major categories of demand, which will 'add up' in the sense that they will suffice to keep resources reasonably fully employed. Within the public sphere, more detailed and coordinated plans are needed, permitting the Government to oversee the future role of public expenditure as a whole. Any efficient rephasing of public expenditure in the interests of stable growth can be achieved only if the longer-term programme, from which deviations may become expedient, is known. Moreover, rational choice between conflicting demands on the public services, that is, a modern system of expenditure control, also requires long-term plans which as yet exist only over parts of the field.

I believe that work on long-run economic plans is carried on, at least to some extent, in Whitehall. But there is as yet little sign of this work entering into the thinking of ministers.[10] Nor will it do so if they do not publicly embrace the results of this long-term thinking.

[10] Mr Heathcoat-Amory was the first chancellor to predict demand in percentages, in his 1960 Budget speech. More recently Mr Selwyn Lloyd has said, 'I believe it to be well within our power to expand at the rate of 3 per cent per annum over the next five years, but to do this our exports will have to rise at approximately double that rate' (*Hansard*, 6 February 1961). Let us hope these are straws in the wind of change.

It is always possible that the chosen rate of growth of consumption will not be sufficient to support the chosen (one hopes greater) rate of growth of investment. This is where initial and investment allowances come in. They should be regarded as long-term methods capable of altering the rate of growth of investment which any given rate of growth of consumption would otherwise produce. Investment is tied to consumption growth to varying extents—the relatively autonomous is most likely to be affected by investment allowances. If market demand flags a little when consumption is on the proper path of growth, the authorities should not be in a hurry to step in. They may interfere just when sufficient recovery was about to begin anyway. If both consumption and investment are flagging or growing excessively, the best way of getting investment right without underwriting further fluctuations is probably to try to get consumption back on to its proper path.

Variations in export demand may make steady growth difficult. There is no final answer to this problem. To a limited extent it should be possible to compensate by variations in home consumption demand—so that the total growth of demand for consumer goods is smoothed. But, of course, variations in export demand affect the investment-goods industry most. This is a more difficult problem, for compensatory movements in domestic orders and deliveries of capital goods are probably impossible to organize by fiscal or monetary means. To some extent it may be possible to use public investment in a compensatory manner. But we have seen that this is not altogether easy. *A fortiori*, direct control of private investment would be very difficult to use successfully. Perhaps one should not be too worried by some excess capacity in the investment goods industries when export demand is slack. Some, even considerable, excess capacity seems to be quite consistent with full employment.

With any given value of the currency, the balance of payments may be too weak to permit the growth of which the economy is capable. Wage inflation may also interrupt growth, and cause subsequent fluctuations, if the authorities are minded to counter it by depressing demand so that the economy falls below the rate of growth it can sustain. If these inconsistencies arise, the authorities are faced with the choice of abandoning the path of progress, or introducing and using extra means of control besides influencing the levels of demand for investment and consumption goods. There is little doubt what the choice would be in the long run, for finally full employment would be threatened. But stagnation could intervene for quite a long time before excessive unemployment forced the authorities to act. However, stagnation cannot be a rational policy. In the short run it is a grossly expensive substitute for reserves. In the long run it is intolerable and other measures must be resorted to.

But the possible inconsistencies are much less likely to arise under steady progress than if the economy veers constantly between excess capacity and excess demand. This is for several reasons:

1. Excess demand appears to accelerate wage increases.
2. Excess demand probably worsens the balance of payments in the years when it occurs, more than excess capacity improves it. The average level of imports over a period of years may not be significantly affected, but exports suffer and good will is lost when home demand is excessive, and they gain little or nothing when over-capacity gets beyond a certain point.
3. Steady growth should imply a greater average rate of growth. This is because investment can be better planned if the future is more clearly foreseen; because it is expensive to interrupt investment; because the most productive investment may be relatively unprofitable if there is a risk of fluctuation;[11] and because the average amount of over-capacity in the economy should be less.[12] In turn, greater growth for any given average level of unemployment reduces the rate of increase of wage costs.

For these reasons, the strain which steady growth may put on the price level and the balance of payments should be less than with periodic growth.

The shift of emphasis in the philosophy of central economic management, sketched out above, cannot be reconciled with the retreat from fiscal policy which has been apparent. For it is only fiscal policy which can be used to steer consumption within the narrow limiting growth rates which are required for stabilization. It also cannot be reconciled with any practice of giving large tax reductions in election years.

Of course, the programme sketched strains at the economists' and statisticians' expertise. As always, more officially supported research is required. But there have been great improvements, particularly in statistics, in the last five years. The professional inadequacy of economists should not now be a barrier to some improvement in the central direction of the economy. But if politicians feel called upon to wrench the steering only when unemployment and the balance of payments scares them, then progress will continue to be erratic.

[11] Because high overheads are dangerous if there are risks of fluctuation.

[12] A boom in demand tends to be concentrated on particular lines, and may result in excessive optimism on the part of the producers of those goods, with resultant over-capacity.

17

Higgledy Piggledy Growth (1962)

1. INTRODUCTION

This article originated in my belief that the information provided by Moodies Services, Ltd, had not been adequately exploited for academic purposes. The corrections which must be made to earnings and dividends for capital changes are very laborious, and could hardly have been done without the cooperation of Moodies Services, for which I am most grateful.

Being but an amateur statistician, I apologize in advance for the elementary and probably inefficient methods used,[1] and also for the fact that time has prevented me tying up a number of loose ends, and a really full exploitation of the figures collected. I have, however, at least convinced myself of the truth of the results arrived at. Furthermore, the raw figures are now available to anyone who sees further possibilities of analysis. In spite of the free use made of the Oxford computer,[2] a great deal of laborious calculation was required which was undertaken by Mr Liaquat Ali.[3]

2. COMPANY EARNINGS AND DIVIDEND GROWTH, 1951–1959

The figures given in this section are a by-product of the attempt, described in later parts of this article, to find some laws of growth of company earnings. As far as I know, such broadly based figures for changes in earnings and dividends, which have been corrected for capital changes, have not previously been compiled and published.

The main sample was taken from the companies charted by Moodies in their 'Security Indices and Chart Service'. This service covers UK companies which Moodies consider to be of sufficient general investment interest. All large com-

This article first appeared in the *Oxford Institute of Statistics Bulletin*, 24 (Nov. 1962). Permission to reproduce is gratefully acknowledged.

[1] It was only late in the day that I had some advice from Professor Gorman. I am also indebted to Mr J. Wright for comment.

[2] I am much indebted to Mr Peter Vandome for programming the computer for me.

[3] I am also indebted to Mrs S. M. Pugh and Mr Frank Souch for same calculations.

panies are included, and many of moderate size. No very small companies are included.

For the purpose of this section, companies were excluded which did not have a complete record from 1951 to 1959, that is companies which were born into Moodies Service after 1951, and those which died by merger or bankruptcy. Otherwise the sample consists of all companies charted by Moodies belonging to the following groups:[4]

Breweries
*Building (including materials but excluding the sub-industries 'contractors' and 'road making materials')
*Chemicals and Pharmaceuticals
Cotton Textiles
*Electrical Engineering, Radio, and Television
Food
*Motors (including components and distributors)
*Mechanical Engineering and Shipbuilding
Miscellaneous
*Paper and Printing, Newspapers and Publishers
Stores
*Wool, Silk, and Rayon.

Other groups were excluded either because I did not want them (Banks, Hire Purchase, Investment Trusts, Oil, Mining, Plantations), or because there were less than twenty firms in the group *and* it could not be plausibly amalgamated with another (e.g. Steel).[5] The miscellaneous group was already large enough without adding such firms to it. The total number of firms in the sample for this part of the paper was 441.

A second sample consisting of public companies of small size has also been used. This was selected at random from Moodies Index of Public Companies. Companies without a continuous record from 1951 to 1959 were again rejected, and also those with trading profits of over £250,000 in 1951. This limit was low enough to ensure that there was in fact no overlap between the samples.

The figures used are throughout corrected for scrip and rights issues. This task was undertaken by Moodies Services, Ltd.[6]

The figures from which the growth rates produced below are derived are in respect of three magnitudes:

[4] Those marked with an asterisk are amalgamations of different sections published by Moodies, the purpose of amalgamating being to obtain a reasonably large number of companies in each group.

[5] Financial and commodity companies were excluded because I thought it unlikely that they would exhibit similar laws of growth (if any existed) to those of industrial and commercial companies.

[6] The formula used is as follows: suppose the issue is 1 for n new shares at a price of pr per share. Suppose the last cum rights price is pc. Then the correction applied to pre-issue dividends, earnings, etc., is $(n + 1)/(n + pr/pc)$.

1. dividends expressed as a percentage of equity capital;
2. earnings, net of interest, taxation, minority interests, and preference dividends (i.e. 'earned for ordinary'), expressed as a percentage of equity capital;
3. pre-tax earnings per £1 nominal of equity capital: in effect this differs from 'earned for ordinary' only in that it is before tax, and before preference dividends.

The latter magnitude is, perhaps, a slightly illogical one. It would have been better to have subtracted preference dividends, in order to work with pre-tax earnings attributable to the ordinary shares. This was not done, because Moodies Services already had the figures actually used recorded, and because preference dividends are very seldom large enough to distort the recorded growth significantly.

TABLE 1. Average Annual Compound Percentage Growth, 1951–1959

	Pre-tax earnings	Earned for ordinary	Dividends	Retail prices	Income from employment
441 large firms	5.1	7.1	11.5	3.8	6.5
81 small firms	5.8	8.1	7.9		

Table 1 gives the summarized results. The figures are obtained by striking an arithmetic average of the ratios of the relevant magnitudes in 1959 to those of 1951, and then reducing this average to an annual compound rate. But a convention had to be adopted to limit the size of the ratios since these can approach infinity where, e.g., a company makes zero or near-zero earnings in the base year. The convention adopted was to limit the size of any ratio to 10; that is, a company was not permitted to multiply its earnings or dividends by more than ten times over the course of the eight years.[7] Subject to this convention, the significance of, for example, the dividend growth rate is that someone who invested in the large companies so as to obtain an equal income from each in 1951, and left his holding undisturbed until 1959, would have seen his money income grow at an average annual geometric rate of 11.5 per cent per annum (and similarly at 7.9 per cent per annum for the small companies).

The most notable feature of the table is that pre-tax earnings, which are the ultimate long-run prop supporting equity share prices, grew rather slowly for large companies. In real terms, they grew by only 1.3 per cent per annum in spite of the fact that the equity shareholder was, as an average over the whole period,

[7] In the first column of the table this convention affected 5 large firms and 4 small firms. In the second column the corresponding figures were 5 and 5: and in the third column 9 and 3.

having roughly two-thirds of the earnings to which he was entitled ploughed back for him. Neglecting tax changes, these savings were, in effect, yielding him only about 2 per cent (tax free).[8] Since a 2 per cent yield on marginal capital seems too low to be plausible, it is likely that the earning power of old assets fell during the period.

'Earned for ordinary' rose rather faster. To a small extent this was due to the gearing element introduced by preference dividends, but mainly it must have been a result of reduced taxation. (In 1951 the rate of tax, excluding allowances, for a company which distributed an average proportion of its profits was 55 per cent; in 1959 the rate was 47.5 per cent, and was not dependent on the proportion distributed.) However, the rise in equity shares between these dates (the FT index, well known to be a rather sluggish indicator, rose from 30 December 1952 to 30 December 1960 by 164 per cent, an annual compound rate of 12.9 per cent per annum[9] which is very close to the dividend increase) was due mainly to the relaxation of dividends (the average cover fell from 3.9 times in 1951 to 2.3 times in 1959) and partly to a general market revaluation of the prospects of equity shares in a period of inflation. In fact, if equity share prices had moved with earnings, and there had been no tax reductions, they would barely have kept pace with inflation in spite of the savings being ploughed back.

The experience of the smaller quoted firms was rather different. Dividends rose by 7.9 per cent per annum, slightly more slowly than earned for ordinary (post-tax); while pre-tax earnings and 'earned for ordinary' rose a little faster than those of larger companies. Although dividends rose slightly more slowly than 'earned for ordinary' in the case of small companies, the mean dividend cover fell from 3.1 to 2.0. This is superficially paradoxical, but of course quite possible, even apart from the need to introduce conventions when 'earned for ordinary' or the dividend is zero.[10] Table 2 gives the performance of the large firms by groups.[11]

Ignoring Wool and Cotton, whose growth rates are peculiarly sensitive to the particular years chosen, it is noticeable that the non-durable consumer goods and stores are at the top of the list. Apart from paper, those sectors most concerned with investment and exports are at the bottom of the table. Investors are, of

[8] 66⅔ per cent of net earnings ploughed back can be roughly associated with a growth in gross real earnings from £100 to £101 6*s*.—a tax-free yield of approximately 2 per cent. Abstracting from tax changes and preference dividends, net earnings attributable to the equity would grow at the same rate as gross earnings.

[9] These dates are selected as ones by which 1951 and 1959 earnings and dividends were known. A company's results are ascribed to, e.g., 1951 if the year to which they relate coincides more with the calendar year 1951 than any other. Hence the so-called 1951 results might not be known until late in 1952; but few 1952 results would be known by then.

[10] The convention adopted was to write the cover as zero if 'earned for ordinary' was zero or negative—even if the dividend was zero. If 'earned for ordinary' was positive but no dividend was paid, the cover was written as 10, which was also used as the limiting value in other cases.

[11] For slightly more detail on the groups, see the remarks on the sample at the beginning of Section 2.

TABLE 2. Annual Compound Growth Rates, 1951–1959

Group	No. of companies in group	Pre-tax earnings (%)	Earned for ordinary (%)	Dividends (%)
Wool	28	13.2	14.9	7.4
Food	32	10.3	12.6	14.7
Stores	29	6.9	11.1	14.4
Breweries	25	6.0	8.2	7.7
Motors	44	5.5	7.4	12.6
Miscellaneous	48	4.6	6.2	12.8
Building	35	4.3	7.1	10.2
Chemicals	23	4.1	5.3	12.2
Electrical eng.	39	3.8	6.9	11.7
Paper	23	3.0	4.5	10.1
Mechanical eng.	91	2.1	3.3	11.4
Cotton	24	−0.7	−0.9	4.7
		5.1	7.1	11.5

course, well aware of this. Food and Stores shares have much lower yields than other sectors, with Breweries next in spite of their sluggish dividend behaviour. Paper, Mechanical Engineering, and Cotton's pre-tax earnings failed to keep pace with the cost of living. Only in Wool, Food, and Stores did pre-tax earnings growth exceed the growth in income from employment (6.5 per cent per annum).

Table 3 gives the year-to-year percentage changes of pre-tax earnings by groups for the same 441 firms, together with the geometric means for the whole period. Table 4 gives the same figures for dividends.

It is to be noted that the geometric means of the average annual percentage changes differ from the mean compound annual growth rates as given in Table 2. The difference is essentially one of weighting. The figures of Table 2 are base-weighted—that is, the weight of each firm is unity in 1951—while those of Tables 3 and 4 are chain-weighted; that is, each firm's percentage growth has unit weight in each year. In terms of dividends, Table 4 shows what would have happened to someone's income who costlessly rearranged his investments to maintain an equal income from each firm. The resultant rate for the whole group is 10.4 per cent per annum—slightly slower than under a no-change policy. The earnings growth for the whole group is 5.0 per cent in Table 3 against 5.1 per cent in Table 2.

For most individual groups, the dividend growth shown in Table 4 is less than that in Table 2, but the reverse is true for earnings. One would expect to find that Tables 3 and 4 would show lower figures if the changes in successive years were positively correlated, since the effective weight of a successful firm is not

TABLE 3. Average Year-to-Year Pre-tax Earnings Growth for Large Companies (%)

	Breweries	Building	Chemicals	Cotton	Elect. Eng.	Food	Mech. Eng.	Misc.	Motors	Paper	Stores	Wool	Weighted arithmetic mean
1952–1	4	−3	−23	−55	6	3	8	−9	8	−22	8	−6	−3.0
1953–2	12	15	33	26	4	19	−1	7	4	22	18	36	12.3
1954–3	4	15	17	19	14	19	11	3	18	19	16	10	13.0
1955–4	9	3	2	−23	5	9	13	16	5	1	10	−13	5.5
1956–5	5	2	−1	4	−2	15	3	4	−13	3	6	12	2.3
1957–6	11	−3	9	14	7	2	2	7	0	6	−1	−8	3.3
1958–7	0	−2	−5	−5[illegible]	−0	7	−8	−3	11	5	−4	−19	−4.8
1959–8	7	17	25	26	−2	12	1	16	25	−4	0	61	13.3
Geometric mean	6.4	5.2	5.7	−11.4	4.0	10.7	3.4	4.7	6.5	2.1	6.4	6.5	5.0

TABLE 4. Average Year-to-Year Dividend Growth for Large Companies (%)

	Breweries	Building	Chemicals	Cotton	Elect. Eng.	Food	Mech. Eng.	Misc.	Motors	Paper	Stores	Wool	Weighted arithmetic mean
1952–1	2	13	2	−1	10	11	11	7	8	3	12	8	8.1
1953–2	7	18	24	21	15	16	15	15	12	18	25	19	16.4
1954–3	6	23	20	14	25	19	23	19	27	29	34	13	22.0
1955–4	4	5	6	−2	5	15	12	7	8	11	6	−2	7.3
1956–5	4	3	3	0	4	11	1	5	−9	2	4	−6	2.0
1957–6	7	−2	9	−3	2	8	8	6	2	0	2	−6	3.6
1958–7	6	11	9	−13	13	12	8	8	18	10	2	−1	7.9
1959–8	17	16	25	15	10	22	13	21	24	7	13	31	17.3
Geometric mean	6.5	10.6	11.9	3.3	10.3	14.1	11.2	10.9	10.7	9.6	11.8	6.3	10.4

allowed to increase. The results therefore indicate, so far as earnings go, that there is on balance a slight negative correlation between successive changes. On the other hand the fact that one would have done better on income by staying put indicates that there is some slight positive correlation between successive dividend changes. The connection between changes in earnings from one period to another is examined at length below.

3. DOES GROWTH BREED GROWTH?

As a prelude to attempting any statistical explanation of growth on the basis of the figures obtained from the sample discussed in Section 2, it was desired to establish whether there was any correlation of growth in one period with growth in another. My impression is that many stockbrokers, financial journalists, economists, and investors believe that past growth behaviour is some sort of a guide to future growth. This belief seems to have developed especially in the last few years. The figures for adjusted pre-tax earnings, discussed in the previous section, were selected for this purpose.

Earnings were taken pre-tax because (1) it was considered that the tax which a company pays in a particular year bears only a loose relation to its liability on current earnings, owing to adjustments in respect of past periods, and this variability would introduce an irrelevant and disturbing influence; and (2) with a possibly uneven capital development programme, investment and initial allowances would also introduce variations which would be irrelevant so far as longer-term trends were concerned.

Earnings were adjusted for capital changes because (1) variations in earnings caused by the issue of new shares—whether to present shareholders or to others in payment for assets acquired—would also cause haphazard variations in earnings; and more fundamentally because (2) earnings for existing shareholders seem more relevant to an assessment of a firm's success, not only from the point of view of the investor, but also, on general grounds of economic theory, from the point of view of society.[12]

The whole sample of the larger companies (462 firms in all) was divided into the same groups as those of Tables 3 and 4, except that the large mechanical engineering group was split into two groups—those with accounting dates ending 31 December, and the rest. This was done because the variability of accounting dates means that nominal years do not in fact cover the same period; and, since this

[12] This is not meant to imply that the interests of society and existing shareholders coincide. For instance, it may well benefit society if a good management buys another business by issuing shares, and thereby improves the use of its assets, even at a price which reduces earnings per share. On the other hand, if earnings were not adjusted, a firm could appear remarkably successful merely as a result of acquiring other firms, even if no improvement resulted.

was an obvious imperfection in the data, it was desired to have one group in which this possibly disturbing element was not present. Firms that did not have a continuous record were not for this purpose eliminated—although of course, if a firm was not operating within one of the periods between which correlations were established or was not in Moodies Service, it does not enter the calculations.

Annual compound growth rates were then calculated for each firm for every period 1951–2, 1951–3 and so on up to 1951–9; also 1952–3, 1952–4 up to 1952–9; also for 1953–4, and so on. It was necessary to adopt some convention when the change was from positive to negative, negative to negative, or negative to positive. In these cases the annual compound growth rate was deemed to be, respectively, −100 per cent, 0 per cent, and +100 per cent. Growth greater than 100 per cent per annum was scaled down to 100 per cent.

Correlation coefficients were then calculated for each group as follows: all possible combinations of single-year growth periods with all previous contiguous growth periods; all possible combinations of two-year growth periods with all previous contiguous growth periods of two years or more; and similarly for three-year and four-year growth periods.

This gave, for each group, seven correlations of one year's growth on that of the previous year; six correlations of one year's growth on the previous two years' growth, and so on; similarly, it gave six correlations of two years' growth on the previous two years' growth, and so on.

The intention, apart from establishing the facts, had been to select the most apparently reliable growth periods for inclusion in a multiple regression analysis. It had been rather expected that continuing good and bad management would tend to establish positive correlations. This was partly why the sample was divided into groups (however rough an 'industry' the group made), since a management which produced above-average results in a particular 'industry' for some years might not at the same time produce above-average results so far as the whole sample was concerned, in view of some tendency for industries to have non-coincidental good and bad periods.

Inspection of the first results suggested that firms' successes and failures were irregular (see Table 5), albeit with some tendency to negative correlation. This tendency to negative correlation might be explained by the fact that what was being correlated was, for example 1953/1952 with 1952/1951.[13] A random element would then tend to produce a negative correlation by virtue of the fact that 1952 was the denominator of one growth period and the numerator of the other. The longer the two periods, the less would this tendency to negative bias be operative. In fact, it did seem (see Table 5) that the tendency to negative correlation was dying out a little as the periods lengthened (without any systematic tendency to positive correlation appearing).

[13] I am indebted to Mr Maurice Scott for drawing my attention to this point, which I had overlooked.

TABLE 5. Unlagged Correlations of Growth on Growth—Large Companies

No. of years in earlier period	No. of years in later period	No. of correlations	No. positive	No. negative	Mean
1	1	33	19	36	−0.11
2	1	47	14	33	−0.18
3	1	39	8	31	−0.17
4	1	31	6	25	−0.11
5	1	23	9	14	−0.06
6	1	15	5	10	−0.05
7	1	8	1	7	−0.15
8	1	1	0	1	−0.31
2	2	40	7	33	−0.22
3	2	33	10	23	−0.14
4	2	24	14	10	−0.05
5	2	16	10	6	−0.05
6	2	9	3	6	−0.08
7	2	1	0	1	−0.59
3	3	24	8	16	−0.06
4	3	16	7	9	0.00
5	3	9	5	4	−0.01
6	3	1	0	1	−0.42
4	4	9	5	4	0.02
5	4	1	0	12	−0.37
Totals		402	131	271	−0.12

NOTE: The sample size of the above results varied from 22 to 55 with a mean of 39.

The programme was stopped after eight groups had been through the computer, and adjusted to produce in addition similar correlations lagged by one period. Thus, for example, 1959/1958 was now correlated with 1957/1956, 1957/1955 etc. The tendency to negative results was reduced, but by no means eliminated, by introducing this lag (see Table 6).[14] The results still seemed so unsatisfactory that the remaining five industries were not investigated on either basis.

In Figure 1, the 55 calculated unlagged, and the 47 calculated lagged correlation coefficients of one year on one year are charted. The slight negative mean and skewness of the unlagged results is apparent. The negative tendency of the

[14] In his article 'Relative Share Prices and Yields', *Oxford Economic Papers* (Oct. 1952), M. F. G. Scott obtained a near-zero correlation coefficient between two contiguous periods. In the appendix to that article he has an a priori argument to suggest that positive correlations might be obtained for non-contiguous periods. This is not in general borne out by my results.

TABLE 6. Lagged Correlations of Growth on Growth—Large Companies

No. of years in earlier period	No. of years in later period	No. of correlations	No. positive	No. negative	Mean
1	1	47	11	36	−0.13
2	1	39	13	33	−0.11
3	1	31	13	18	−0.05
4	1	23	14	9	0.02
5	1	15	8	7	−0.02
6	1	8	3	5	−0.10
7	1	1	0	1	−0.34
2	2	33	12	21	−0.06
3	2	24	13	21	0.00
4	2	16	10	6	0.02
5	2	9	4	5	0.00
6	2	1	0	1	−0.43
3	3	16	10	6	0.09
4	3	9	5	4	0.08
5	3	1	0	1	−0.28
4	4	1	0	1	−0.31
Totals		274	116	158	−0.05

lagged results is rather less, but still visible. No conclusion can be drawn except that there has been a slight tendency for above-average growth to be followed by below-average growth, which tends to die away to insignificance as the periods lengthen.

Inspection of the results for each 'industry' separately did not suggest that any reliable conclusion could be drawn, either. Mechanical Engineering (31 December) appeared to yield as hopeless results, in spite of the uniformity of the period covered by the accounts, as any other 'industry'.

Further to the above correlations, a visual demonstration of the lack of connection between past and future growth was made. For this purpose a predictor or base period of four years was selected as apparently the least bad. Regardless of 'industry', the firms[15] were then divided as near as possible into ten equal sets in order of their growth-rate ranking in the base periods 1951–5, 1952–6, and 1953–7. The arithmetic mean growth rate for each set was then calculated, and plotted as a deviation from the arithmetic mean growth rate of the whole sample on semi-log paper, together with the subsequent performance of each of the ten sets of firms (also taken as deviations from the mean of all firms). The subsequent dividend growth performance was plotted as well as the subsequent pre-

[15] In this case the 441 firms with a continuous record, which were discussed in Section 2.

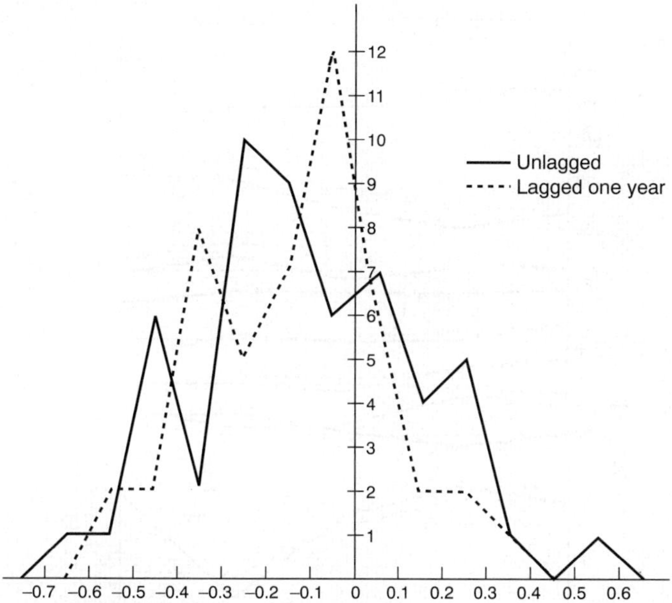

FIGURE 1. Distribution of Correlation Coefficients of One Year's Growth with Another

tax earnings. Finally, a longer base period consisting of the six years 1951–7 was used, and a similar chart made. The four resultant charts are numbered 2, 3, 4, and 5. The slopes of the lines register the mean growth rate of earnings and dividends in the sets.

Figures 2 (1951–5 base) and 3 (1952–6 base) show a tendency for the growth performance of earnings to reverse itself in the following year. In Figure 4 (1953–7) there is a slight tendency for the previous growth performance to continue (at a much more moderate rate) for one year. This is not confirmed by the corresponding correlation coefficients calculated for seven of the thirteen individual groups, six of which were negative. The tendency referred to is thus probably the result of some positive correlation for the groups rather than the firms. In Figure 5 (1951–7 base) there is a marked tendency for past earnings performance to continue for one year. In spite of a reversal of this trend in the second year, the good past-growers tend to show above-average performance over the subsequent two-year period as a whole. However, five out of the seven correlation coefficients of 1957–8 with 1951–7, calculated for the individual groups, were negative. Only two individual group correlation coefficients were calculated for 1957–9 with 1951–7, and both were negative. Again, therefore, it appears that the tendency in these two cases for past growth performance to continue is due more to positive 'industry' correlation than to positive firm correlation within 'industries'.

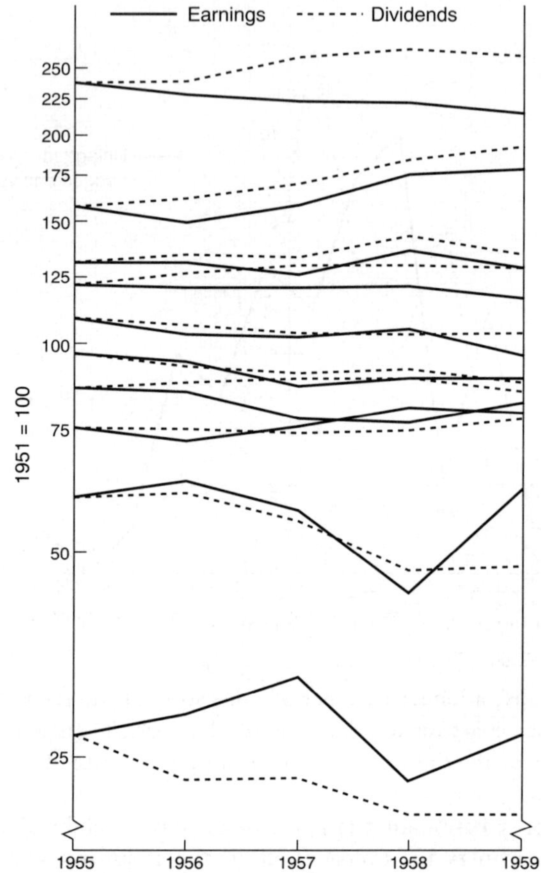

FIGURE 2. Indices of Subsequent Growth of Mean Earnings and Dividends of the Fastest Growing Tenth, Second Tenth, and so on, of Large Firms in the Period 1951–1955

In each of the three cases of a base period of four years, the subsequent performance of earnings for periods of two years or more seems remarkably random.

Finally, as far as dividends are concerned, there is a clear tendency, shown in all four charts, for future dividend growth to be correlated with past earnings growth. There is an obvious explanation for this. Dividend changes are more sluggish than earnings changes. Among rapidly growing firms, the dividend cover rises. When growth reverts to the average, further dividend increases for a year or two are required to re-establish a more normal relationship between the two—and similarly for declining firms.[16]

[16] This result confirms that of Scott, op. cit.

Similar operations to those described above were performed for the sample of small firms. Table 7 shows the means of the correlation coefficients between the various periods, both lagged and unlagged. The tendency to negative correlation is even more marked than in the case of the large firms, and is similarly reduced by lagging.

Similar charts for the small firms as for the large were prepared (Figures 6, 7, 8, and 9). In this case only four sets were used (so as to preserve enough firms in each set). Very similar remarks apply as to the larger firms. With base periods of 1951–5 and 1952–6, there was a tendency for growth to reverse itself in the subsequent year; but for a subsequent period of three or four years' growth the results for each set seem to fluctuate randomly around the mean growth (i.e., roughly zero growth is shown). But, as for the larger firms, when the base was

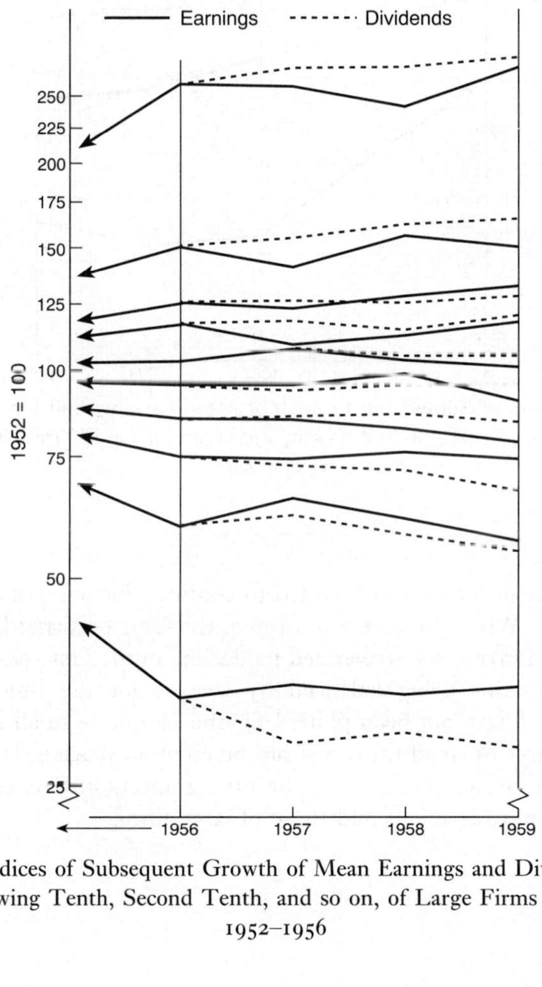

FIGURE 3. Indices of Subsequent Growth of Mean Earnings and Dividends of the Fastest Growing Tenth, Second Tenth, and so on, of Large Firms in the Period 1952–1956

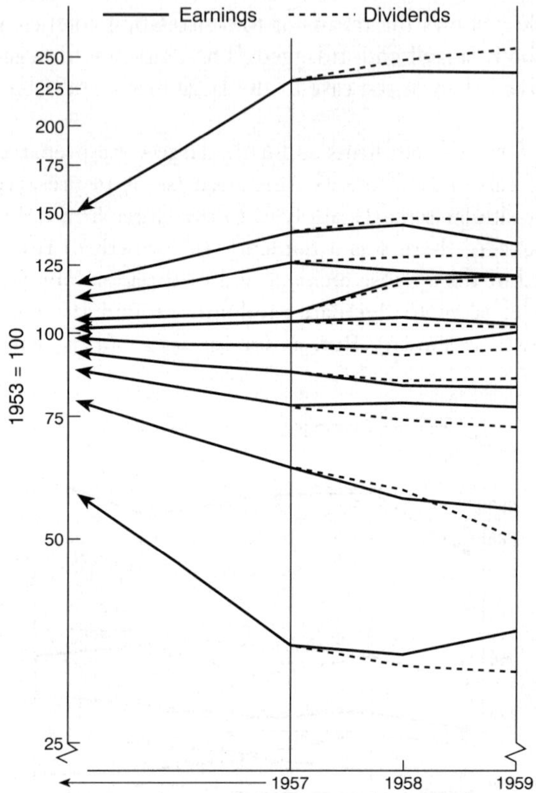

FIGURE 4. Indices of Subsequent Growth of Mean Earnings and Dividends of the Fastest Growing Tenth, Second Tenth, and so on, of Large Firms in the Period 1953–1957

1953–7, past growth for each set tended to continue for one year before reversing itself sharply. When the base was 1951–7, the same occurred (except that the fourth or lowest ranking set accelerated its decline in the first year subsequent to the base period—this being balanced by success for the third-ranking set). Dividend changes have not been plotted for the sample of small firms.

Since the sample of small firms will not be mentioned again, it may be said at this point that there does not appear to be any significant difference between their patterns of earnings behaviour and those of large firms.

TABLE 7. Correlations of Growth on Growth—Small Companies

No. of years in earlier period	No. of years in later period	No. of correlations	Mean of the correlation coefficients	No. of correlations	Mean of the correlation coefficients
1	1	8	−0.18	7	−0.20
2	1	7	−0.23	6	−0.09
3	1	6	−0.21	5	0.01
4	1	5	−0.14	4	−0.08
5	1	4	−0.24	3	−0.10
6	1	3	−0.25	2	−0.41
7	1	2	−0.43	1	−0.26
8	1	1	−0.31	0	—
2	2	6	−0.32	3	0.03
3	2	5	−0.24	4	0.05
4	2	4	−0.25	3	−0.01
5	2	3	−0.22	3	−0.13
6	2	2	−0.41	1	−0.52
7	2	1	−0.46	0	—
3	3	4	−0.33	3	−0.04
4	3	3	−0.34	2	−0.22
5	3	2	−0.32	1	0.14
6	3	1	−0.27	0	—
4	4	2	−0.35	1	−0.18
5	4	1	−0.02	0	—
		70	−0.26	50	−0.09

4. DO COMPANIES GROW OR DECLINE BY CHANCE?

The obvious tendency to randomness of growth recalled the work of P. E. Hart and S. J. Prais,[17] who claimed that the size distribution of firms tended to log-normality, and hence that growth rates would also form a log-normal distribution.

A number of distributions, both for individual groups and for the whole sample, of the logs of the deviations of the growth rates relative to the mean growth rate for different periods were plotted. These all showed little sign of skewness, but all had a high degree of leptokurtosis—that is, the curves had much steeper and higher peaks, and longer tails, than normal curves of the same area. These

[17] P. E. Hart and S. J. Prais, 'The Analysis of Business Concentration: A Statistical Approach' *Journal of the Royal Statistical Society*, A, 119/2 (1956). Their growth periods were much longer than mine, and the firms' growth was measured by its stock market valuation. Thus, their results cannot be at all closely compared with mine, though there is an obvious rough general resemblance.

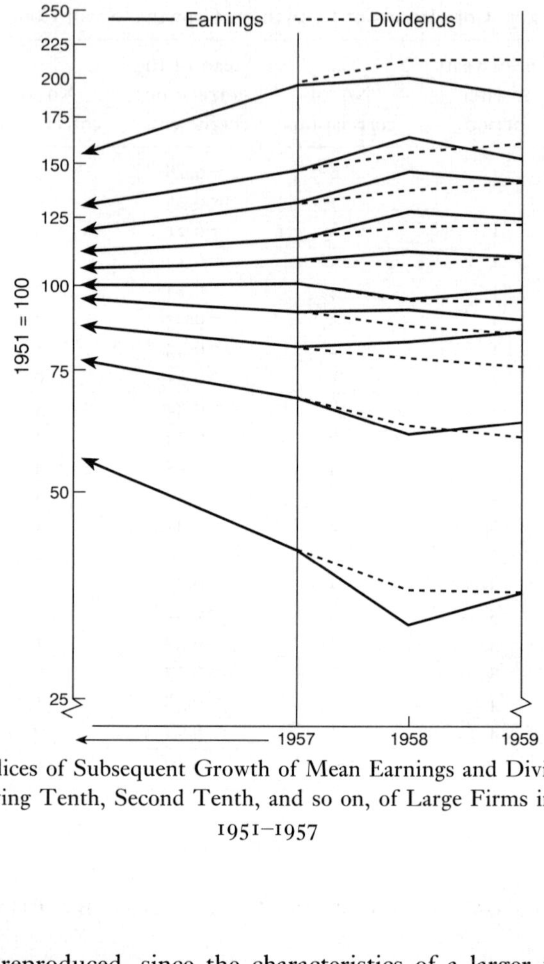

FIGURE 5. Indices of Subsequent Growth of Mean Earnings and Dividends of the Fastest Growing Tenth, Second Tenth, and so on, of Large Firms in the Period 1951–1957

curves are not reproduced, since the characteristics of a larger family of such curves are given below.

It was investigated how the variance of the growth distributions grew through time, and how the skewness and kurtosis changed. Table 8 shows the results. The population is the same set of 441 firms referred to in Section 2. The convention adopted here was to limit the log of the annual average growth or decline of firms to $\pm t^{-\frac{1}{2}}$ where t is the number of years in the growth period. These limits would cut off the same proportion of each distribution on the assumption that the law governing the growth of companies is 'the law of the log-random walk'—i.e., that the frequency distribution of the logs of each single year's growth has equal variance, and is uncorrelated with that of the previous year. Since the figures are the logs of annual compound growth rates, i.e. $1/t$ times the log of the growth factor, it follows that the variance of a period of t years should be V_1/t where V_1 is the variance of a single year's frequency.[18] Consequently, in column (4) of Table 8 the variances have been multiplied by *t*. If the table were the product of a log-random walk, the figures in column (4) should be invariant. Actually, between 1951–2 and 1951–3 there is a sharp fall, and an almost equal sharp rise between 1951–7 and 1951–8. This feature of Table 8 was investigated further by deriving the variances of the logs of the growth factors in the individual one-year periods, and the correlation coefficients between them. The results were as shown in Table 9.

From Table 9 it can be seen that the variance fell from 1951–2 to 1953–4, but grew from 1953–4 to 1958–9. Indeed, during this period the variance increased eight times, and thus the standard deviation by nearly three times. The correlation coefficients, where not extremely small, are negative and have thus tended

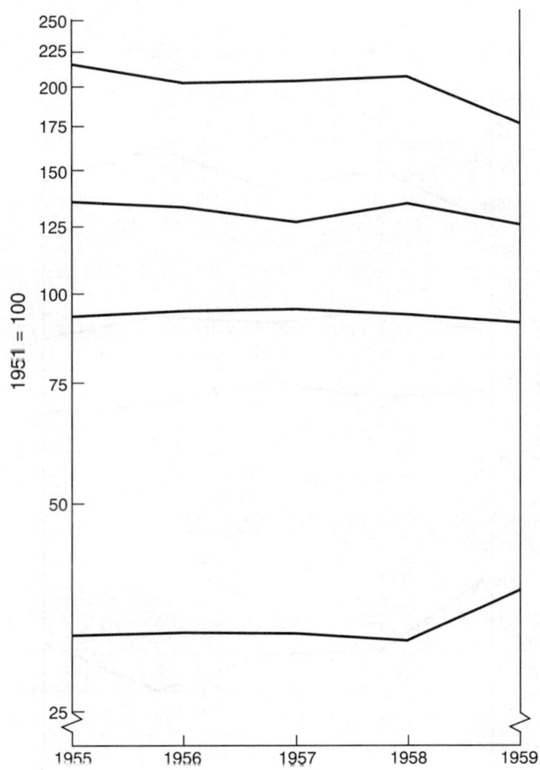

FIGURE 6. Indices of Subsequent Growth of Mean Earnings of the Fastest Growing Quarter, Second Quarter, and so on, of Small Firms in the Period 1951–1955

[18] The variance of the logs of the growth factors of a period of *t* years should be V_1t—but since each such log has been pre-multiplied by $1/t$, the variance becomes $V_1t/t^2 = V_1/t$.

TABLE 8. Characteristics of the Frequency Distribution of the Logs of Annual Compound Growth Rates

t	Growth period	Variance	$V_{1}t$	Skewness	Kurtosis
1	1951–2	0.307	0.307	0.064	5.99
2	1951–3	0.095	0.191	0.107	9.64
3	1951–4	0.059	0.176	0.060	13.86
4	1951–5	0.048	0.192	0.028	14.48
5	1951–6	0.040	0.202	0.073	14.34
6	1951–7	0.035	0.209	0.157	14.35
7	1951–8	0.043	0.301	0.365	9.85
8	1951–9	0.039	0.303	0.274	10.25

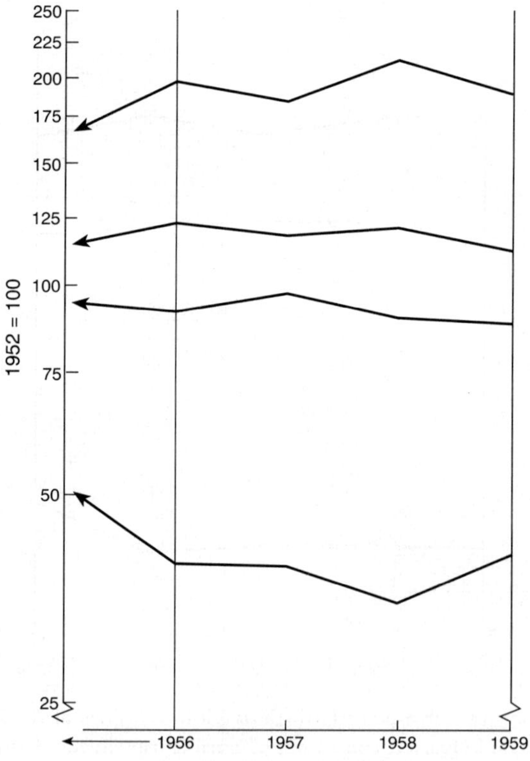

FIGURE 7. Indices of Subsequent Growth of Mean Earnings of the Fastest Growing Quarter, Second Quarter, and so on, of Small Firms in the Period 1952–1956

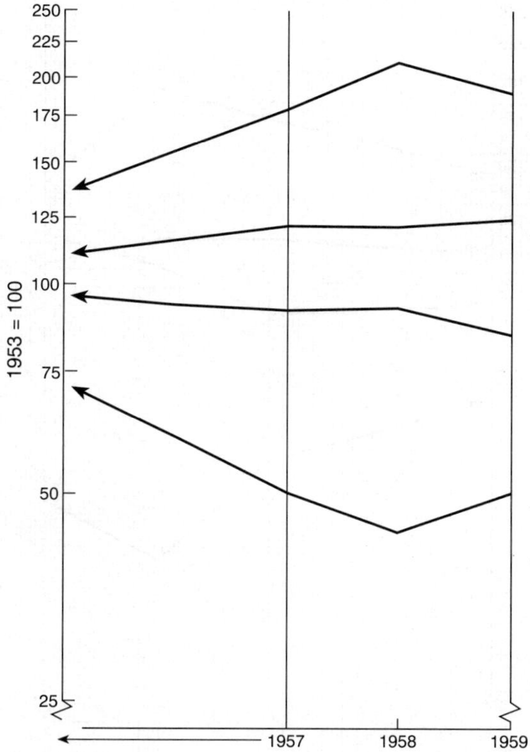

FIGURE 8. Indices of Subsequent Growth of Mean Earnings of the Fastest Growing Quarter, Second Quarter, and so on, of Small Firms in the Period 1953–1957

Table 9. Variances of the Logs of the Growth Factors of Individual Years and the Correlation-Coefficients Between Them

Growth period	Variance	Correlation coefficient w.r.t. the previous year
1951–2	0.307	
1952–3	0.181	−0.23
1953–4	0.175	−0.05
1954–5	0.182	+0.09
1955–6	0.306	−0.07
1956–7	0.736	−0.29
1957–8	1.118	−0.11
1958–9	1.401	−0.32

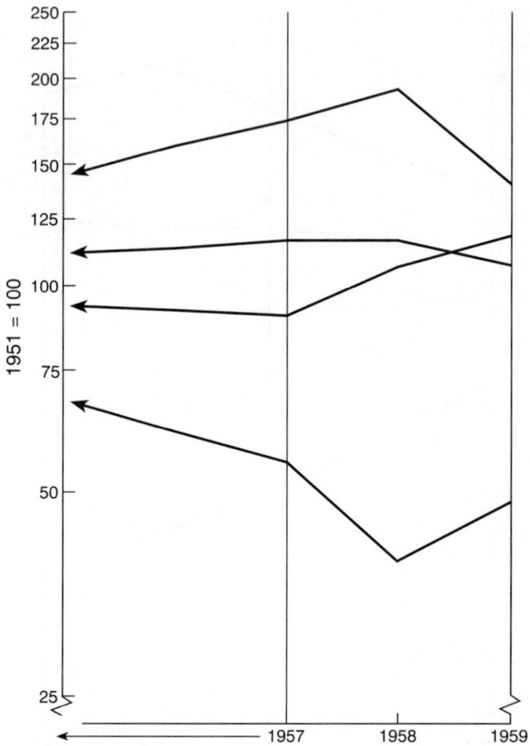

FIGURE 9. Indices of Subsequent Growth of Mean Earnings of the Fastest Growing Quarter, Second Quarter, and so on, of Small Firms in the Period 1951–1957

to reduce the variance of the logs of the cumulative growth factors: but nevertheless, the latter variance has grown much faster than the log-random walk hypothesis would have led one to expect, as a result of the increasing variance of the individual year's growths. It is difficult to interpret these results, although one might suggest that it was the result of increasing competitiveness beginning in 1955.

Turning back to Table 8, one notes that the skewness remains small throughout, though possibly with some tendency to increase. The kurtosis is positive and very marked throughout, with no obvious tendency to increase.

To sum up on the log-random walk hypothesis, first, it is broadly true that adjusted pre-tax earnings per share are as likely to be multiplied by any factor xm (where m is the mean growth) as they are to be multiplied by m/x. In other words, the distributions are roughly log-symmetrical. But there is no doubt that the 'shocks' to which the firms are subject are not of constant force, but have been growing. Furthermore, they do not tend to result in distributions which could be described as close to log-normal; nor is there any apparent tendency for the growth distributions to become more log-normal as time marches on. I do not know what plausible hypothesis explains the highly leptokurtic nature of the distributions.

5. DOES THE SIZE OF A FIRM, OR THE AMOUNT IT PLOUGHS BACK, INFLUENCE ITS GROWTH?

The work done of correlating past and future growth had so strongly suggested that the true relationship was rather random that it was at first decided not to introduce past growth as a variable into this analysis. It was felt that particular (chance) values that the correlation between past and future growth might take might do more to disturb the estimates of the other relationships than improve them.

Two possible size variables were available: the market value of the equity, and the book value of assets. Since asset value is much less sensitive to past growth, changing slowly and fluctuating less (so that the choice of time at which the size measure is taken is not critical), it was preferred to market value of the equity in spite of its well-known defects.

How in theory should growth be related to the amount ploughed back? Where e is the percentage 'earned for ordinary' and g the rate of growth of earnings, d the dividend percentage, t the rate of tax, and p the rate of profit on money ploughed back, the following formula holds, provided that there is no change in the profitability of already existing assets:

$$g = p(1-t)\left(\frac{e-d}{e}\right);$$

$(e-d)/e$ was therefore chosen as the 'ploughback' variable.

The problem of lags presented itself, especially for this latter variable. If some firms have typically high dividend covers, the choice of lag would not matter. For one group (Stores) a calculation was made to see how much of the sum of the squares of the deviations of the dividend cover[19] was accounted for by the deviations of particular firms about their own mean cover for the period 1951–9, and how much was accounted for by the deviations of these means from the mean of the set. We have:

$$\begin{aligned}(\text{Deviations})^2 \text{ from own means} &= 16.15\\ (\text{Deviations of own means})^2 &= 12.52.\end{aligned}$$

[19] Where c stands for the dividend cover, $(e-d)/e \equiv 1 - 1/c$.

Rather a large part is thus accounted for by the year-to-year variability of each firm. But the time available to me prevented any elaborate attempt to discover the best lag to take. I decided to do trial regressions as follows:

$$X_1 = \frac{1959}{1958} \text{(pre-tax earnings)}$$

$$X_2 = \left(\frac{e-d}{e}\right) \text{in } 1957$$

$$X_3 = \text{asset size } 1956 \text{ (£'000)}.$$

There was no particular reason for choosing 1957; 1956 was chosen as the latest asset value which could not be affected by the ploughback. The regression equations were calculated for each 'industry', and for the entire sample.

Results were as follows:

1. *Ploughback variable* (X_2)
   (*a*) Of 13 groups, the regression coefficient had the wrong sign in 8 cases, but the coefficient was significant in none.[20]
   (*b*) Of the 5 groups with the proper sign, only one was significant (Electrical Engineering)—probably a freak result.
   (*c*) For the whole sample of large firms, the sign was both wrong and significant.
   (*d*) For small firms, the sign was wrong but insignificant.
2. *Size variable* (X_3)
   (*a*) Among the 12 groups (excluding the small-firm group), the sign was positive in 7 cases and negative in 6—but significant in none. Indeed, in 10 out of 13 cases the standard error exceeded the value of the coefficient.
   (*b*) For the whole sample of large firms, the coefficient was positive—but smaller than its standard error.
   (*c*) Curiously enough, the coefficient was negative and significant (with a statistical probability of about 98 per cent) in the small group case. On the other hand, it was very small.[21]
3. *Multiple correlation coefficient for the whole sample*
   Variance of $X_1 = 0.171597$
   Residual variance $= 0.171152$
   Variance explained $= 0.000445$
   Percentage of variance explained $= 0.25$ per cent.

Is this a record?

The fact that size has no apparent influence on growth is not very surprising, and confirms the work of Hart and Prais.[22] That ploughback has no apparent

[20] That is, within two standard errors.

[21] The equation was $X_1 = 1.421 - 0.184X_2 - 0.000189X_3$.

[22] Hart and Prais, op. cit.

influence is rather more difficult to accept, and certainly more shocking. So further attempts were made to investigate this.

It seemed possible that, in some cases, the influence of ploughback on future growth might have been masked by a chance negative correlation of growth on growth, combined with the probability that high past growth would be associated, because of a lag in dividend adjustment, with high ploughback. For this reason, it was decided that a partial regression analysis of growth on ploughback and past growth should be undertaken.

It is worth noting also that partial regression analysis aims to eliminate the possibly causative sequence, past growth → past ploughback → future growth, as well as the effect mentioned above. To this extent the partial regression may measure the influence of 'normal ploughback', that is ploughback which was not the result of a recent period of rapid growth. It seemed possible that 'normal ploughback' might be better related to future growth. Finally, the choice of a single year's growth, and a single year's ploughback, may have been unfortunate in the multiple regression of growth on size and ploughback.

Accordingly, for two groups (Mechanical Engineering, 31 Dec., and Mechanical Engineering, Others) growth for two years was related both to ploughback and to past growth.[23] The growth period chosen was (1959/1957) (X_1), the ploughback taken was the mean for the three years 1955–7 (X_2), and the past growth period chosen was 1954–7 (X_3), since growth in these years might well influence the ploughback in 1955–7.

For Mechanical Engineering, 31 Dec., the correlation coefficients were:

$$
\begin{aligned}
r_{12} &= -0.05 \\
r_{13} &= -0.08 \\
r_{23} &= +0.24 \\
r_{12.3} &= -0.02.
\end{aligned}
$$

The partial regression coefficients were also, of course, negligible. For Mechanical Engineering, Others, the correlation coefficients were:

$$
\begin{aligned}
r_{12} &= 0.17 \\
r_{13} &= 0.16 \\
r_{23} &= 0.33 \\
r_{12.3} &= 0.13.
\end{aligned}
$$

In this case $b_{12.3}$ was positive and equal to 0.28 (expressing ploughback as a percentage); i.e., other things being equal, an increase of 10 percentage points in the percentage of earnings ploughed back would raise the growth of earnings by 2.8

[23] For two groups (Breweries and Mechanical Engineering, 31 Dec.) the simple correlation coefficient between growth in 1952–9, and ploughback in 1951–8 was also calculated, to see whether over this long period any relationship existed. The relationship in each case was positive but weak. The correlation coefficient for Breweries was 0.24, and for Mechanical Engineering, 31 Dec., 0.18. In view of the long period of overlap, these figures could easily be the result of dividend lag, and not arise at all from any real influence of ploughback on growth.

per cent. However, regarded as a random sample, this is not significant, for the standard error of $b_{12.3}$ was 0.27. Our tentative conclusion from these two results is that there is no relation between ploughback and growth, even after making allowance for the independent influence of past growth on past ploughback and future growth. Obviously, however, this relation has not been exhaustively analysed. I was prevented by other commitments from trying other lags. The figures are available to anyone who wishes to make more complete tests.

6. CONCLUSIONS

Mainly for investors

1. In spite of the heavy ploughing back of profits, the growth of adjusted pre-tax earnings per share has lagged behind earned incomes, especially in industries most concerned with exports and investment. That the growth of dividends, except in textiles, has been fast is better known. If the figures had been more up to date, the growth of pre-tax earnings would undoubtedly have been much slower still. Unless there is some fundamental change in the economy making for greater profitability of capital, the prospect for equities is worse than past performance suggests. Equity values cannot continue to ride the surf of reduced taxation and dividend regulation. This is certainly not, however, to say that present prices (June 1962) are too high in relation to fixed interest investments.

Since even the smallest investor can avoid the risks attaching to a particular share, or small selection of shares, all that is needed to justify a reverse yield gap is the confident expectation that the sum of the dividend yield and its rate of growth should exceed the redemption yield of fixed-interest investments. There is certainly nothing in the past to suggest that equity shares are overvalued, in spite of the relatively sluggish performance of earnings, and the very low apparent rate of return on money ploughed back.

2. It is useless to try to predict future earnings from any single past earnings growth ratio, or from dividend cover, or from asset size. None of these factors should influence the price of a share except in so far as a high dividend cover probably on average results in a higher-than-average future dividend performance. But a share's price is only loosely tied to its earnings. Mr Scott has found a correlation between past earnings and the future share price (for up to a year after the last results).[24] This is explicable in so far as future dividends and past earnings growth *are* related; but, probably, the main reason is a naive belief that past growth tends to continue.

[24] Scott, op. cit.

Mainly for economists

1. I wrongly expected that I would be able to find some correlation of future and past growth (in relation to the average for the 'industry'), primarily on the view that some continuity of good and bad management would establish such a correlation. If a good management is one that earns a higher rate of profit on equity capital than the average for the 'industry', and which maintains this rate on new money for a period of, say, 5–8 years or more, then good and bad management are extremely rare. Statistically speaking, Marks and Spencer does not exist. Evidently, much too high a standard was being expected. Not only may luck play so big a part that steady success or failure is most improbable, but also the forces of competition may operate to prevent above-average returns being maintained.

2. It was noted that the variance of the growth distributions had greatly increased since 1955. This can be equated with an increase in uncertainty, which may be associated with a growth in the freedom and competitiveness of markets.

3. The tentative conclusion of the lack of significant correlation between ploughback and growth is disturbing. It shows that, among those firms which plough back relatively heavily, about as many decline in relation to the average as grow. It is, of course, possible that the new investments of those which decline are just as profitable as those of the rest, the whole of their relative failure being accounted for by the declining profitability of old assets. Even so, if the heavy 'ploughers-back' contained only their fair share of declining profitability of old assets, one would still expect the group as a whole to grow faster than the average. The lack of correlation could be accounted for by the hypothesis that firms with declining profitability tend to plough back more as a kind of insurance (possibly buying mainly financial assets). But this we know to be in general false, since it is a fact that rapid growth induces a relatively high ploughback. One seems to be left with the conclusion that those which retain a relatively high proportion of profits select relatively unprofitable investments. The present results therefore seem to lend some weak support to the view that institutional or fiscal arrangements which limit dividends are a relatively inefficient method of increasing investment. But, as has already been emphasized, a more complete investigation of the relationship might be made.

18

Distributive Justice and the New International Order (1980)

1. INTRODUCTION

I believe that equality of rights, and freedom from coercion, is of value even to the poorest people, if they have ever experienced them. But many socialists have argued that economic equality is a condition of equality of rights, thus linking distributive or social justice to political and legal justice. Nevertheless, so far as I am aware, a full theory of distributive justice—ironically, a theory which might in principle justify great inequality—has been only recently elaborated by John Rawls. He states: 'a conception of social justice, then, is to be regarded as providing in the first instance a standard whereby the distributive aspects of the basic structure of society are to be assessed' (Rawls 1972, p. 9). A still more recent work by Robert Nozick (1974) challenges the view that justice has anything to do with the size distribution of income or wealth.[1] These works relate essentially to justice as between members of a state. But the New International Economic Order (NIEO) also bases its claims largely on the concept of distributive justice. Before examining these claims, I thought it of interest to consider the theories of Rawls and Nozick, and see how far they carry over to the international sphere.

2. JUSTICE AND EGALITARIANISM WITHIN STATES AND SOCIETIES

Both Rawls and Nozick start from the inviolability of human rights. Rawls makes liberty, and equality of liberty, lexicographically prior to anything else. But his conclusions imply that it is just for the state to coerce some to aid others. Nozick

This paper first appeared as a chapter in P. Oppenheimer (ed.), *Issues in International Economics* (Oriel Press, London, 1980). Permission to reproduce is gratefully acknowledged.

I am indebted to Robert Skidelsky, A. K. Sen, and P. M. Oppenheimer for some valuable comments. Many of the issues addressed in this paper are also considered by Sen (1978), a paper I saw only after writing this. Sen provides a far more extensive bibliography than I do.

[1] I recall that Harry Johnson once asked me to join a seminar to discuss this work, which he believed to be very important. Unfortunately I could not find the time.

denies that the state has a right to do so. It is therefore important to understand how redistributive taxation, or other restrictions on a person's liberty to do what he will with what he has or earns, can be justified within the framework of Rawlsian theory.

Rawls's first principle of justice is that 'Each person is to have an equal right to the most extensive total system of equal, basic liberties compatible with a similar system of liberty for all', and there is a 'priority rule' such that

> the principles of justice are to be ranked in lexical [= lexicographic] order and therefore liberty can be restricted only for the sake of liberty. There are two cases: (*a*) a less extensive liberty must strengthen the total system of liberty shared by all, and (*b*) a less than equal liberty must be acceptable to those citizens with the lesser liberty.

Rawls's second principle is that social and economic inequalities are to be arranged so that they are to the greatest benefit of the least advantaged (p. 83). This is called the difference principle. (There is also a second part to the principle not relevant to my argument.)

These principles are claimed to result from the 'original position' in which the parties are rational, self-interested, people called upon to produce the principles of justice. They operate behind 'a veil of ignorance', which means that they do not know their own position in society, nor their own preferences or abilities. I shall refer to them as the 'veiled participants'. Each is assumed to try to maximize the minimum outcome for himself, in accordance with the maximin principle of game theory choice under uncertainty. I shall not add to the considerable criticism which has been directed at this assumption about how rational people would actually behave if put into a situation which would make them perfectly impartial. Given this assumption, Rawls can derive principles which he claims to be normative, since he regards them as rules for the design of just social institutions.

The first principle of justice makes it clear that basic liberties cannot be arbitrarily circumscribed. But are property rights, including the right not to have property (which includes earnings) removed for the benefit of others, among the basic liberties? Rawls lists the basic liberties as 'political liberty (the right to vote and be eligible for public office) together with the freedom of speech and assembly; liberty of conscience and freedom of thought; freedom of the person along with the right to hold (personal) property; and freedom from arbitrary arrest and seizure as defined by the rule of law' (p. 61). But evidently this right to hold personal property does not exclude the state's right to take some of it away to give to others. For Rawls's 'distributive branch' of government is there 'to preserve approximate justice in distributive shares by means of taxation and the necessary adjustments in the rights of property' (p. 277). For many people, there may seem to be no difficulty in arguing that the state is justified in restricting some persons' rights for the sake of material benefits to others. But Rawls's lexicographic principle puts him into the position of either defining some rights as non-basic and therefore tradable in the above sense, or else of justifying restrictions of property rights by the priority rule.

Property rights are fundamental to the proper working of any state. But it might be argued that they are created by the state, and are not 'basic', i.e. 'natural'. As against this, it seems that they are fundamental to any known society; people generally have some belongings even in the most communist communes, and also in the most natural of all social units, the family. Furthermore, it is difficult to draw a clear line between personal rights and property rights. My right to my hand is not morally very different from another man's right to his artificial hand. And what about a pacemaker? As against this, the difficulty of defining boundaries cannot be taken as a compelling argument against drawing distinctions.

I have found no guidance from Rawls on this point. I shall assume that restriction of property rights must be justified by the priority rule, and therefore ask whether either case of the priority rule can be held to justify redistributive taxation.

Under the first case, the total system of liberty must be strengthened. In defining liberty, Rawls does not count poverty as a constraint. A person's liberty is not constrained by his purchasing power; although the value of his liberty is (p. 204). Where then do we find the increase in liberty which offsets the various restrictions on spending their gross income (or dealing with their gross wealth) which are placed on the rich?

It might be argued that redistributive taxation is necessary to hold society together, and the system of liberty would certainly suffer if it broke down. Rawls does indeed justify his principles on grounds of stability. He connects stability with 'publicity' (p. 177). Publicity is one of the 'constraints of the concept of right' (p. 130f.). The concept of right is prior to the original position in that it constrains the deliberations of the veiled participants. They must choose principles for a *public* conception of justice. 'They suppose that everyone will know about these principles all that he would know if their acceptance were the result of an agreement. Thus the general awareness of their universal acceptance should have desirable effects and support the stability of social co-operation' (p. 133). One could read this as saying that the desirability of designing cohesive principles does not spring from veiled maximin logic, but is an imposed injunction. But this may be an incorrect reading. Knowing, despite his veil, the laws of social psychology, each participant may alternatively argue that anyone who is going to be rich in the society he votes for must be coerced to aid the poor, because otherwise the poor may upset the applecart, thus reducing the total system of basic liberties, and he would not choose to be an apple in so unstable a cart. This sounds to me more like expediency than justice.

Under the second case of the priority rule, we have to suppose that all the veiled participants accept the restriction of property rights, and that the subsequent actual rich are therefore deemed to have contracted in. Thus, Rawls writes:

then having chosen a conception of justice, we can suppose that they are to choose a constitution and a legislature to enact laws, and so on, all in accordance with the principles of justice initially agreed upon. Our social situation is such that by this sequence of hypothetical agreements we would have contracted into the general system of rules which defines it. (p. 13)

This, which recalls Rousseau, might seem to be a recipe for an overbearing state to those lovers of liberty who would find the notion of a hypothetical 'contracting in' a monstrous pretence.

This brings one to Nozick. His preface begins with the resounding sentence: 'Individuals have rights, and there are things no person or group may do to them (without violating their rights). So strong and far reaching are these rights that they raise the question of what, if anything, the State and its officials may do' (Nozick 1974, p. ix). His answer to that question is 'very little', and this very little certainly excludes redistributive taxation, or any interference with property rights. He rejects the idea that different patterns of distribution can or need be justified. Any end-state is just if it is arrived at by just historical processes. These include taking possession of anything that was not scarce, and transfers by gift or exchange contract. Only holdings thus acquired are entitled. A distribution is just if everyone is entitled to their holdings under it. Unjust distributions can arise only by unjust acquisition of holdings. Redistribution is just only if it 'rectifies' such unjust distributions, e.g. undoes the results of aggressive acquisition in the past (p. 151).

This constructive theory is accompanied by a destructive attack on any end-state conception of justice, including that of Rawls. One of Nozick's powerful arguments is that any just distribution, as perceived by any end-state theory, can and will be upset by transactions which the parties are entitled to make, that is by just transactions. The preservation of the particular pattern of a just end-state distribution (supposing that such a concept makes sense) requires continuous intervention by the state, and a continuous infringement of people's rights. In principle, any gift, except to the most disadvantaged, made in a state which is just by Rawlsian standards is necessarily unjust. Gifts, I suppose then should be outlawed, if that were possible.

With Nozick, gifts present no problem. Anyone is entitled to make a gift. Furthermore, in certain circumstances, people ought to give. There is no reason in Nozick's philosophy why a person should not regard one distribution as better than another, although neither is unjust. If so, it could certainly be argued that he ought to bring about an appropriate redistribution in so far as he can. The obligation may be especially strong where there is a special relationship, e.g. a family relationship, between the donor and potential recipient. There is also no reason why non-familial redistributive communities should not be formed within a state, such as kibbutzim, provided persons are not coerced to join them and are free to leave them. (It is too difficult to leave a state—even one without a wall, or exchange controls.) Such a community could establish a right for its members to receive their basic needs.

I think I have said enough to show the essential similarities and differences between Nozick and Rawls. While both proclaim the priority of rights, Rawls theorizes that the concept of justice requires the supposition that people have traded away many rights for the sake of not risking relative or perhaps absolute deprivation; all, in fact, except the basic rights (and here I have failed to find the principle which separates basic rights from others). Nozick stands much firmer on rights. These are the natural rights of Locke—' "no one ought to harm another in his life, health, liberty or possessions". Some persons transgress these bounds "invading others' rights and . . . doing hurt to one another" and in response people may defend themselves or others against such invaders of rights' (p. 10). For the sake of security, people transfer to a minimum state most of their rights of defence and punishment. There is nothing else they can transfer. The state is a protective association with monopoly powers, but these powers 'are merely the sum of the individual rights that its members or clients transfer' (p. 89). Thus, people cannot, it appears, create new rights for the state when they create a constitution. This would inevitably transgress against the rights of members. The state is being created to protect people against immoral aggression against their rights. A state with powers to transgress the rights of innocent people would be perpetrating the moral crime it is being created to prevent. Everything in Nozick follows, I think, from this.

Rawls and Nozick are, however, united in opposition to utilitarianism. I suppose most economists are rather unthinking utilitarians. When pressed, they would perhaps admit that some rights are inviolable, and that it is unsatisfactory and implausible to derive the inviolability of all rights from utilitarianism itself. But then, why not maximize (average?) utility subject to some moral side-constraints? Unless combined with the assumption that all persons have the same utility functions, this still produces inegalitarian and possibly unacceptable results, as A. K. Sen has emphasized (Sen 1973, pp. 15–18). Thus, imagine two persons with equal real wealth, but one is physically or mentally handicapped in such a way that the marginal utility of money is lower for him.[2] Then the utilitarian takes money from the cripple and gives it to the robust fellow, which is anti-egalitarian and possibly wrong. Perhaps economists slide over this difficulty, tending to forget it, because they think in terms of representative men, who do have the same utility functions. But this will not do either, at least in rich societies, because the poor are precisely the old and the sick, or have other atypical disadvantages. In other words, the above 'difficult' case may be typical.

Brian Barry makes the same point forcibly against Rawls, whose maximin principle is made to apply to a representative person of the most disadvantaged class,

[2] It could perhaps be argued that this sentence is self-contradictory, and that equality of marginal utility of money is a sufficient condition of equality of real wealth. It is difficult indeed to define 'equal real wealth', but I do not think it is quite the same as 'equality of marginal utility of money', although this is a position one might want to take up if one regarded marginal but not total utility to be interpersonally comparable (see Little 1957, ch. IV; and Sen 1973, pp. 44–6).

somehow but quite broadly defined (Barry 1973, pp. 49–51). Why should not the veiled participant want to guard against his turning out to be a manic–depressive cripple? Rawls does not seem to see this as a problem, since he regards the laws of justice as applying only to the basic structure of society. A counter-view is that justice is essentially a matter of human detail, and that a theory of justice must be able to deal with these atypical cases which nevertheless abound.

Even in cases where it seems legitimate to think in terms of averages—the general shape of the distribution—it may be asked (as Nozick does—pp. 204 ff.) whether one can be comfortable with a macro theory which produces nonsense at the micro level. In other words, can one be comfortable with a theory that produces institutions which are fair as between similar people, but which also produce unacceptable guidance in dealing with particular cases? If one does not see this as an objection, then the case of the cripple is also no objection to utilitarianism. Moreover, given a broad sweep—and rough justice—utilitarianism by quantitative aggregation produces more plausible results than Rawls. Who would not want to benefit 99 per cent of Indians by 100 Rs a year per head, at the cost of further impoverishing the poorest 1 per cent by 1 rupee?

I can only conclude from all this that there is no acceptable theory of justice. It seems to me that Rawls's theory has been seriously undermined. The entitlement theory of Nozick (which he admits is underdeveloped) is very appealing in many ways; but for most people it produces, I think, unacceptable results. Most people would probably think that some liberties can be *justly* curtailed if the material gain for the poor is great enough. Or am I wrong about this? Those in doubt should read his Chapter 10, entitled (to use the *mot juste*) 'A Framework for Utopia'.

3. INTER-STATE AND WORLD DISTRIBUTIVE JUSTICE

The applicability of political philosophy

Despite the doubts about Rawlsian theory, it is worth asking whether it could be applied beyond the state. His veiled participants are already members of some society. Provided one can conceive of a society of states, there is no reason why one should not imagine that the veiled participants represent states, without knowing, of course, which state. Rawls does indeed adopt this device and argues that 'justice between states is determined by the principles that would be chosen in the original position so interpreted' (p. 378). Without further argument, he simply goes on to say that the principles of self-determination, self-defence, forming defensive alliances, and respecting treaties would emerge. He makes no attempt to apply the difference principle. Why not? A veiled participant would know that he might be an Indian. Since he is assumed to want to apply the maximin principle within a state, why not also between states? Brian Barry asks the same question, again forcibly (Barry 1973, ch. 12). I suppose Rawls assumed that international society has insufficient institutions with insufficient powers for it to make sense to talk about *distributive* justice between just states. (Justice, he says, is the first virtue of social institutions.) The veiled participants are not allowed to start designing a world state which would impose an international income tax. Justice presupposes a society. There is, as it were, enough of an international society for some rules of justice, but not enough for rules of distributive justice. It is also worth noting that it appears to be impossible to apply Rawls's priority rule internationally. This implies that property rights cannot be regarded as 'basic' if the Rawlsian system is to work internationally, since the restriction of basic liberties can be justified only by application of the priority rule.

We could also imagine that the veiled participants were designing the world, without it being presupposed that they were representatives of states. The whole world order would then be in question. Perhaps they would opt for empires, not nation-states. I will not pursue this deviant thought! In any case, if it is true that the states of the world do not form enough of a society for Rawls to apply his concept of distributive justice to them, it would also seem that human beings in the world at large cannot be regarded as forming enough of a society either.

Nozick would, I presume, attach no meaning to inter-minimal-state distributive justice. But his philosophy leaves room for considering the world distribution, because individuals' entitlements have nothing to do with states. The distribution of world income is unjust, in so far as property was obtained by aggression or fraud in the past. Nozick could thus agree with the claim that aid should be considered as (inadequate) reparations for unjust colonial expropriations and exploitation, this being the USSR line on aid. How this should be assessed, and who exactly should pay, I do not know. Nor is it even clear who should receive. The case of Latin America would, for instance, be peculiar, for most Latin Americans have little Indian blood. Nozick calls this the principle of rectification, but himself raises many more questions as to how just rectification could be carried out than he gives answers. No good theory of justice can, presumably, be as inapplicable as this seems to be.

Nozick also has two particular criticisms of Rawlsian arguments, which may throw a faint glimmer of light on to the international stage. He takes issue with Rawls's claim that the increase in production resulting from social cooperation creates the problem of distributive justice. He imagines ten Robinson Crusoes, some richer than others, whether because they work harder, or are cleverer, or have chanced to land on better islands. They suddenly discover each other. Nozick suggests that the poor might make claims on the rich in the name of justice, although there is, and has been, no social cooperation. A theory of justice would then be needed, Nozick suggests, to show that these claims are without merit. He has furthermore provided such a theory. But it seems to me that Rawls could argue that the claims were without merit on the grounds that the ten Crusoes in no way constituted a society, and that justice presupposes a society. This might be the reason why the claims lacked merit, and not that the Crusoes were entitled to their holdings, and that no one's entitlement can be justly removed.

Rawls also seeks to show that well-endowed people (who are coerced to aid the poor) have no cause for complaint. They need the cooperation of the poor. He writes: 'we can ask for the willing cooperation of everyone only if the terms of the scheme are reasonable. The difference principle, then, seems to be a fair basis on which those better endowed could expect others to collaborate with them . . . ' (p. 15). Nozick correctly remarks that the 'then' in this sentence is mysterious. We can imagine two Crusoes with, respectively, incomes of 10 and 2. Then they are given an amnesia drug, and veils of ignorance. On Rawls's principles, they might proceed to set up a nation state and constitution, which gave the better endowed Crusoe 8 and the worse endowed Crusoe 7 (allowing a 25 per cent gain from the division of labour). Would this be fair? One would have thought that Rawls must answer 'yes', because the new situation has emerged from his veil of ignorance, etc. But he cannot say, as he does, that it is a fair division of the spoils of cooperation, for this is appealing to the outcome of an historical process, as a result of which one lost 2 and the other won 5. What would happen when the effects of the amnesia drug wore off? One of them would be very unhappy that he had not remained a Crusoe.

In principle, these arguments can also be related to aid and the gains from trade. The Crusoes may merely be setting up a trading-cum-aid system, not a state. Rawls's principles would then (in my opinion) result in free trade, and aid on an unimaginable scale. But, again, this could not be represented as a fair division of the gains resulting from the opening up of trade.

It seems clear that distributive justice requires a moral community, in which individuals accept at least some mutual obligations. It would be futile to say that the distribution of wealth between the wholly isolated Crusoes was unjust. Even if they formed a mere system (for the concept of a system, presupposing much less contact and assumption of obligation between members than in a society—see Bull 1977, pp. 9–15), being aware of each other and having some occasional contact, but still not entering into obligations or having any way of settling disputes, etc., it would still be close to futile to talk of distributive justice. If, in such circumstances, one Crusoe made demands in the name of justice, he would be presuming, perhaps hoping to create, a community which did not exist, but which, if it did exist, would perhaps recognize an obligation to aid him. We must therefore ask what sort of community exists in the world—and perhaps what sort is embryonic if not born.

Current claims

It is clear that a society of states exists, and that many claims to interstate justice are both made and recognized. Most of interstate justice is concerned with sovereignty, with the right to conduct wars claimed to be just, with equality of treatment in international organizations and international law, and so on. This is what Professor Tucker refers to as 'the old equality' (Tucker 1977).

But claims of the Third World to transfers of resources, and to special treatment in trade, are made at least partly in the name of *distributive* justice. Nevertheless, there seems to be no doubt that the political leaders of developing countries are primarily demanding justice as between states. Many still lack confidence that their sovereignty is secure, and believe that they are excessively dependent. So they are demanding greater equality of liberties, and equality of respect. They want to be more powerful, and better able to exercise the right to defend themselves. Most of this can come only with an increase in wealth. So greater material equality is closely bound up with the aspiration to be able to play a more significant role in the world political order. This is also no doubt a large part of the reason why so much stress is put on industrialization, and why there is a lingering belief that more people is no bad thing.

We economists (including myself) are too prone to assume that a country's objective function to be maximized is the (weighted) present value of consumption per head. We know really that it is not so, but we still often forget it. Equality of states, not people, is what the NIEO is about. This is implied by the tremendous stress on sovereignty in the various NIEO declarations. For the reasons that follow, it is also implied by the fact that commodity agreements are the most stressed of the desired economic reforms. The aim here is surely to raise commodity prices, and not merely to stabilize them. By now, many Western economists have pointed out that the poorest people in developing countries would be likely to lose by such further cartelization of world commodity trade. But such arguments seem to cut no ice in the tropics. It is true that sometimes developing country spokesmen invoke distributive justice in the name of mankind. But this, I think, has to be regarded as rhetoric if at the same time they insist, as they do, that internal equality is their own affair. One cannot convincingly say at the same time 'you have an obligation to help our poor' and 'our poor are our own concern'.

But none of the reasons produced by political philosophers as to why some should have their liberties restricted in order to benefit others apply to states. With utilitarianism, it is the utility of individuals that is the final arbiter. Utility cannot be enjoyed by states. For non-utilitarians, redistribution is justified by giving the status of a right to adequate access to the means of securing health, etc. Again, it is human beings who are deemed to have such rights. Certainly, states (and other collectives) admit to moral rights and duties by seeking to justify their actions, in terms of both international law and international justice. But Nozick would clearly maintain that no state has the right to incur international obligations which require it to tax its citizens for the benefit of other states (or, indeed, individuals in other states).

Many, including Rawls, would agree that the value of an individual's political and legal rights increases with his wealth. There seems to be a clear analogy in this respect between individuals and states. Formal equality in terms of international law is already granted to states; but substantive equality in the exercise of these rights demands material equality. Substantive equality would require that all states had nuclear weapons, and so were equally capable of fighting a just war. But redistribution between states on such grounds is clearly not accepted as part of international morality, which implies, of course, that the desirability of substantive equality of states in the world order is not admitted either. Not only is it not admitted: the very idea of substantive equality of states is in hopeless conflict with nation-states and the idea of self-determination. The analogy breaks down. There is normally no compelling reason why any one person should not be as wealthy as any other. But divergence of numbers is a compelling reason why the Welsh cannot be equal to the Russians.

The strongest claim I have seen to a community of states among whom distributive justice might be said to apply has been made by Professor Ali Mazrui. To quote:

> The Nuremberg trials helped to redefine aspects of morality and gave coherence to the idea of 'crimes against humanity'. The formation of the United Nations signified that new global institutions were needed. The anti-colonial movement in Asia and Africa heralded new triumphs for the principle of self-determination. And racism based on color all over the world found itself increasingly on the defensive. We were witnessing the birth pangs of a new international moral order. It is partly on the basis of that new moral order that we now hear demands for a new international economic order. Indeed, the latter hardly makes sense without a redefinition of international morality itself. The demand for a new international order is a culmination of a quest for appropriate norms to govern relations among collectivities—a quest that goes back to the Treaty of Augsburg of 1555 and far beyond. (in Bhagwati 1977, pp. 373–4)

It seems to me that this passage confuses two different concepts, a universal humanistic morality and inter-state morality. The Nuremberg trials were based on the concept of humankind. Since only the defeated suffered for their crimes against humanity, the trials have also to be seen as emanating from great power politics; but nevertheless, the morality claimed was humanitarian and universalistic. The issue of racism is similarly based on the idea of human equality. But self-determination is concerned with the creation of nation-states (a nation being, *ex ante*, any community which has claims to be a state; *ex post*, any community whose claims have succeeded). The twentieth-century idea that those particular communities which can be deemed to be nations should be self-governing can certainly be seen as a change in international morality, although, of course, this morality is overlain with the expediencies of power politics, which often determine whether a claim to nationhood is recognized. But in any case, the stress is on nations, not persons. The political rights of persons may (or may not) be better served in a world of nation-states—and this possibility may have supported the change in international morality; but distributive justice seems to have very little to do with the ideal of self-determination. It is thus difficult to see that those parts of the NIEO which are concerned with distributive justice are based even partly on the humanistic foundations cited by Mazrui. If they were, it would not be true (as it is true) that the NIEO 'hardly makes sense without a redefinition of international morality itself'.

This implied or proposed redefinition consists of a set of imperatives obliging richer states within a society of states to help poorer states, without questioning their behaviour towards their own citizens, or towards those of other countries. I can see no moral theory backing up the development of such obligations. Still less can one say that they are now accepted by the richer states. Developed countries have, of course, accepted aid targets, thereby putting themselves in a position in which they can be (rightly) berated for their failure to take their promises seriously. But what sort of obligation have they accepted? Certainly not to give regardless of the recipients' behaviour. The assumed obligation is only to transfer a certain volume of purchasing power to developing countries in general. This is no different from rich men accepting that they ought to give so much to charity, or to charitable organizations whose policies they approve. They are far from accepting any such notion as an international income tax. A state does not tax its own citizens in order to help their enemies. These transfers are essentially political, although helping the poor (or development) can enter (lexicographically?) as another objective. The preservation of peace comes before international justice, or at least has a bigger weight, if there is any conflict between the two. (On order versus justice see especially Bull 1977, ch. IV, and Tucker 1977, ch. III.)

Most Western liberals are treading a different path. Tucker refers to the 'regnant intellectual elites' and calls the movement 'the new political sensibility'. There is a continuous outpouring of books and articles which are essentially trying to arouse the conscience of people in the West towards the appalling poverty of hundreds of millions of people in the developing countries. The appeal of such books and articles is universalistic and in the name of humanity. Many liberals would claim that Western governments have a duty to support basic needs and to reduce inequality in the world. If governments do not accept this, or anyway do not fully accept it, it is because they do not dare to spend much on programmes which have little popular appeal. And that they have little popular appeal is an unfortunate fact. Sympathy depends on knowledge, contact, and familiarity. Many intellectuals, but few of the electorate, travel to developing countries. To this extent, the regnant intellectual elite seems to be appealing to a community which hardly exists. Some of the same elite try desperately to create a sense of community by stressing 'growing interdependence', a phrase that is seldom given a factual content. Some authors have expected that the concept of the welfare state would spread outwards to embrace mankind. If anything, the opposite is happening except possibly in a very few countries. This is not surprising, for egalitarianism at home, implying high taxation, may surely be as easily competitive with as complementary to the idea of helping foreigners.

Humanitarian appeals tend to ignore many difficulties. Most particularly, they tend to ignore the fact that states (or, more strictly, the changing governments of states) come between the donor and the recipient; or else they assume that donors can impose conditions which will ensure that poverty will be reduced. If the appeal is humanitarian, there must be some assurance that the aid reaches the poor to a reasonable extent. This assurance has been undermined in recent years by exaggerated, even false, statements to the effect that the mass of the poor have gained little, or even lost, as a result of the growth of the developing countries.

The international organizations tend to fall into the same category as Western liberals. Thus, the ILO submission to the World Employment Conference is entitled *Employment, Growth and Basic Needs*, with the sub-title *A One-World Problem*. The delegates' accepted declaration of principles speaks of ensuring 'full employment and an adequate income to every inhabitant of this one world in the shortest possible time'. Since this can be read as implicitly going over the heads of nation-states, and carries overtones of interference with the policies of developing countries, it is not altogether surprising that the concept of basic needs has since run into criticism from a number of developing country spokesmen. A further reason is that meeting basic needs might slow down the industrialization which is almost everywhere preferred by leaders in developing countries. Mr Robert Macnamara has also, of course, been vociferous in his appeals to increase aid and to direct it, and development in general, towards the mass of the poor. He has spoken of 'a global compact'. Similarly, the Development Assistance Committee of the OECD has endorsed the idea that basic human needs should be a central purpose of development cooperation. Making aid dependent on human rights (more or less the same basic rights as those, for example, listed by Rawls—see above) gets a still worse reception in developing countries.

Moreover, it is not only political leaders and foreign office spokesmen in developing countries who think this way. Even very westernized and liberal academics from developing countries are usually nationalists first and egalitarians second. This is not, of course, to say that they are usually unconcerned about inequalities and poverty in their own countries; but, not surprisingly, they get irritated when Westerners criticize the elites of developing countries both as self-serving and as far more interested in nationalistic objectives than in the poor. Few, I suspect, would support a compact of increased aid if it went with an effective surveillance of policies to ensure (supposing this were a possibility) that development was wide-spread and human rights respected.

A serious conflict of values has thus become evident. It has often, in the past, been argued by liberals that one of the defects of aid was that Western governments tended to impose their values on developing countries, and thus distort their development plans. The implication was that the values of developing countries should be respected. I never thought myself that this was a very serious argument; the conflict of values was exaggerated, and the fault of donors lay more in such things as aid-tying which had nothing to do with values. But now that 'the development community' is promoting the idea of redistribution, and Mr Carter the idea of human rights, there is a serious conflict. Both equality and liberty are Western ideals; very few developing countries have embraced that of equality, and still fewer, if any, both ideals. If the DAC countries, or the World Bank, proceed very far in the direction of trying to impose redistributive policies, or refusing aid to countries whose policies do not seem to be directly poverty-regarding, conflict will surely be exacerbated.

4. CONCLUSIONS

What I have said and surveyed in the preceding section leads to no obvious conclusions. So I shall jump to a few.

The most serious recent efforts to define an acceptable general theory of justice having failed, one seems to be driven to echo Hedley Bull, who writes: 'justice is a term which can ultimately be given only some kind of private or subjective definition . . . My starting point is simply that there are certain ideas or beliefs as to what justice involves in world politics, and that demands formulated in the name of these ideas play a role in the course of events' (Bull 1977, p. 78). But this does not imply that 'distributive justice' must be treated purely as an emotive term. One can at least discuss the boundaries of its legitimate use—boundaries which are changing as they have certainly changed in the past. Nozick has denied that it can simply be applied to an end distribution. I would agree with this, and always have (cf. Little 1957, pp. 65–6). One cannot judge a distribution without knowing how it arises—what historical deserts and rights it satisfies. But I find it difficult to agree with him that rights cannot be watered down by the state for the sake of alleviating poverty—not all rights, but some. Similar views are expressed in a recent paper by Deepak Lal (1978), which examines the issue of liberty and basic needs, very rightly pointing out that in India, which contains the great majority of the world's poorest people, both ends must be served and that they may conflict.

On the international stage, the meaning and extent of community seems vital. I think the idea of justice requires a moral community. Those who appeal to the community of man seem to be going beyond what exists. One can perhaps see their efforts as trying to further the idea.

This idea, however, conflicts with the thrust of NIEO. The international economic order is an order of states, an order with very many new members. What is being claimed, as a matter of justice, is no interference with the fullest sovereignty, equality of opportunity (e.g. that trade negotiations should in practice be fair to all states), and equal participation in international economic decision-making. But transfers and unequal treatment (e.g. preferences) are also claimed as a matter of distributive justice. The primary desire is to strengthen the nation, and to reduce inequalities of power. (Whether or not this would be conducive to world order is examined by both Bull and Tucker.)

It seems to me that few in the West would yet agree that the poverty of a state gives it a right to receive, regardless of its policies. Some want political strings, and others want to promote redistributive policies. The combination of the NIEO and the new liberal egalitarianism have produced a more serious dilemma for aid than when I wrote about it in the mid-sixties (Little and Clifford 1965).

The difficulty is that strengthening weak states, and aiding poor people, are both respectable aims. My own view is that, in the case of most countries, the poor will benefit from inter-state transfers without trying to exercise major leverage on the governments' policies, and will benefit enough to justify large increases in aid. I would not tell British or German citizens or politicians that poor countries have a right to receive aid. I would tell them that aid does good, despite the unjust behaviour of many developing country governments. I think that donors are entitled to choose their projects, and that they can increase (a little) the impact on the poor this way.

They are also entitled to favour countries whose policies they like, and to refuse aid to some. But I think it is dangerous to try to exert leverage on major thrusts of internal policy. A compact (Alliance for Progress!) in which redistributive policies, or respect for human rights, was promised on one side, and more aid on the other side, would be honoured in the breach, and give rise to recrimination. By attaching strings, it might avoid the complaint that developing countries do not want charity. But I do not set much store by that argument; developing country leaders ask not for alms for themselves, but for international aid in the name of states, or nations, or people. Finally, I would oppose discriminatory trade arrangements; and the increasing political management and cartelization of trade, which increases dependency, as unlikely to help the poor or the poorest states, and possibly disruptive of world order.

References

Barry, B. (1973), *The Liberal Theory of Justice*. Oxford: Clarendon Press.

Bhagwati, J. N. (ed.) (1977), *The New International Economic Order: The North–South Debate*. Cambridge, Mass.: MIT Press.

Bull, H. (1977), *The Anarchical Society*. London: Macmillan.

Lal, D. (1978), 'The Basic Needs Approach and the Third Development Decade'. Mimeo.

Little, I. M. D. (1957), *A Critique of Welfare Economics*, 2nd edn. Oxford: Clarendon Press.

——and Clifford, J. M. (1965), *International Aid*. London: Allen & Unwin.

Nozick, R. (1974), *Anarchy, State and Utopia*. Oxford: Basil Blackwell.
Rawls, J. (1972), *A Theory of Justice*. Oxford: Clarendon Press.
Sen, A. K. (1973), *On Economic Inequality*. Oxford: Clarendon Press.
——(1978), 'Ethical Issues in Income Distribution: National and International', paper presented to the Saltsjöbaden Symposium on 'The Past and Prospects of the Economic World Order', August (mimeo).
Tucker, R. W. (1977), *The Inequality of Nations*. New York: Basic Books.

19

Ethics and International Economic Relations (1992)

It may be useful to start by underlining an important difference between the viewpoint I am going to take and that of many moral philosophers. I do not believe in natural rights, laws, or liberties; by which I mean rights, laws, or liberties that are independent of any community or society. I accept that people may have rights, but these rights are created by, and are nugatory without, a moral community.

My brief is to take a liberal egalitarian point of view. What does this mean? There are two extreme doctrines. One is that there should be no restriction of liberty for the purpose of pursuing end-state equality. The other is that every restriction of liberty is justified that leads to greater equality. By 'equality' I mean economic equality somehow defined, not equality of 'respect or concern'. I take it, as most do, that there may be tension between the two.

I do not know of anyone who subscribes to the latter doctrine. The former has been argued by Nozick.[1] Oddly enough, it is also the view of Rawls, who claimed to make liberty lexically prior to equality.[2] Despite this, of course, he ends up with his famous difference principle, to the effect that inequality is justified only to the extent that it benefits a representative member of the poorest class. I have found his reconciliation of these apparently conflicting doctrines unconvincing.[3] But that need not worry those who take the view that some but not all liberties may be restricted for the sake of equality. I am happy to include myself in this class of persons. This is hardly going out on a limb. I am only ruling out what I regard as extreme views.

There are many possible measures of equality.[4] In taking an egalitarian viewpoint in any degree, one has to assume that there are some measurable changes in wealth distribution that would both indicate greater equality and be regarded

This paper first appeared as a chapter in B. Barry and R. E. Goodin (eds.), *Free Movement* (Harvester Wheatsheaf, Hemel Hempstead, 1992). Permission to reproduce is gratefully acknowledged.

[1] R. Nozick, *Anarchy, State, and Utopia* (New York: Basic Books, 1974; Oxford: Basil Blackwell, 1974).

[2] J. Rawls, *A Theory of Justice* (Cambridge, Mass.: Harvard University Press, 1971).

[3] See I. M. D. Little, 'Distributive Justice and the New International Order', *Issues in International Economics*, ed. P. Oppenheimer (London: Oriel Press, 1980), pp. 37–53.

[4] See e.g. A. K. Sen, *Economic Inequality* (Oxford: Clarendon Press, 1972).

by egalitarians as desirable. An acceptable measure of equality might reflect only the relative position of the poorest.

The view is advanced elsewhere in this volume by Lal that a state has no right to restrict liberty (e.g. the liberty of a person to dispose of his property in any way he wishes) for the sake of achieving more end-state equality; but that it can justly do this to relieve poverty. Poverty relief is distinguished from redistribution on the grounds that the former is a public good, and the very purpose of a state is to provide public goods. I find this argument difficult to accept. To include poverty relief, or a safety net, as a public good, like defence or law and order, seems to be straining the definition of 'public goods'. More important, if the reduction of poverty is a public good, it can be argued on very similar, even identical, grounds that greater equality of wealth is also a public good. I propose to include poverty reduction under the banner of equality.

The questions to be discussed here mostly concern what restrictions on international movements of capital and commodities a state is justified in enforcing. The division of the discussion between migration of people and of goods, services, and capital is rather artificial. Nothing can be said from an ethical viewpoint about either without deciding what obligations a state has to foreigners. If, for instance, it was agreed that the state existed solely for the benefit of its own citizens, or some class of its own citizens, then the value of restrictions to be imposed on international movements (if any) would be a function only of the economic consequences for its own citizens. However, even if some restriction were deemed valuable, it might be unacceptable on grounds of undue denial of liberty.

It may be useful to start with what is, I think, an extreme view. Imagine a Nozickian minimal state established by notional contract for defence, law, and order. It has duties and rights only towards its own citizens. Who are they? The original contractors, and, it must obviously be supposed, their descendants. I can already imagine problems. For instance, what about adopted children? Could I adopt a thousand boat people? Let us side-step such problems by assuming that the original contract somehow defines citizen-worthy descent. Such a state would surely have no right to prevent its citizens dealing with foreigners. But foreigners themselves can have no rights. The state should not stop them, but they would be unlikely to buy land and reside, or make investments, with no protection at all. There would no doubt be some international trade, but perhaps not much, for there could be no international enforcement contracts.

To my very limited knowledge, contract theorists—indeed, moral and political philosophers in general—are very weak on international matters. This is true for instance of Rawls. He does imagine representatives of states meeting behind a veil of ignorance. According to him, they come up with more or less conventional principles to regulate inter-state behaviour, but not with any principles of distributive justice. It is not altogether clear why this should be so. But one can suggest a reason. The existence of states is taken as given, and their representatives are not supposed to be suggesting rules for world government. Unlike the constitution of a state, there is no mechanism for realizing principles of distributive justice. Moreover, if the veiled participants are invited to take states as they are in reality (as the veiled participants in the conference establishing justice within a state are supposed to take human beings as they are), then we have the familiar difficulty that states are unjust, which makes it difficult to justify an international difference principle.

It does not help to suppose that the veiled participants are simply human beings, not representatives of any state. They would then be forming principles for world justice. But how futile if they cannot usefully propose a constitution for the world! It is no use agreeing to a maximin principle if there is to be no constitution under which a set of rules embodying that principle can be enforced. It is also worth remarking that such veiled participants would probably not subscribe to the conventional inter-state principles. For instance, why should it not be just to invade an unjust state, or at least interfere with its internal affairs?

Let us forget about contract theories, and be realistic. States have been constituted by force, and many of them deny their subjects liberties that most people would regard as important (and some as natural or basic). Few show much concern for equality. How do we want a relatively wealthy, democratic and egalitarian state to behave in these circumstances? Do we want it to treat foreigners purely as instruments for the economic welfare of its own people? If so, it would be entitled to regulate migration, trade and capital movements with this end in view, and would be limited only by the requirement that in so doing it must not trespass too much on the liberty of its own citizens.

The last proviso is surely necessary. Without it the state might say that I could invest my money abroad since there is an anticipated return (which it taxes). But I would not be allowed to subscribe to Oxfam.[5] However, even with this proviso, most people who consider themselves as liberal and to some degree egalitarian would surely think that it is going too far for the state to treat foreigners solely as instruments.

However, it must be noticed that, at least in the matter of migration, states treating foreigners solely as instruments comes close to reality. Migrants come in rather freely if they are wealthy and will pay taxes, or are talented and can be expected eventually to contribute more than they cost. All states now prevent, if they can, large numbers of poor migrants. If poor, they would probably make the state's own poor worse off, and if too numerous they would not assimilate, and if allowed to settle would create ethnic or communal problems that can seriously undermine the well-being of existing citizens. (Emigration presents different problems. I deal with this below.) One hardly needs to add that trade and capital movements are regulated in like manner. Governments protect their own industries, especially labour-intensive industries, without thought for their

[5] This could be regarded as a rather extreme case of equality within a state constituting an argument for regulating international transactions, and circumscribing liberty. There are more realistic cases, not involving a diminution of world equality, which I shall discuss below.

employment potential in developing countries, and so on. And where a country does not regulate, that is either because *laissez-faire* is regarded as anyway the best policy from the point of view of its own citizens or because it does not want to restrict liberty too much.

But what of international aid? Is that not an exception? Governments do not generally argue as if it were. Aid is generally justified on grounds of self-interest (usually unconvincingly to my mind). Despite the existence of a small constituency for aid on the utilitarian principle that it is good for the rich to give to the poor (and that some part of the aid will percolate to the relatively poor in most poor countries), governments are probably correct in thinking that such arguments have little general appeal. (They seem to have more appeal in Holland, Denmark, Norway, and Sweden than elsewhere.) Disasters are an exception. The reasons are clear. People are shocked into sympathizing with the victims. To some extent the same seems to apply to migration. The distinction made between political and economic refugees hangs on this.

In general, the governmental behaviour I have described seems to reflect popular thinking. Protests even from intellectuals are usually quite muted. Can we define a core of widely accepted ethical thinking that underlies the manner in which states actually regulate or do not regulate dealings with foreigners?[6]

Clearly, it is not universal utilitarianism. Even if poor states had benevolent and efficient governments with a proper concern for the mass of their peoples, there would be almost no support for the massive transfers which such utilitarianism would seem to imply. Nevertheless, I suggest that a weighted and constrained utilitarianism best fits the case. First, utilitarianism has to be constrained by rights, for people do believe in rights and corresponding duties. To use a familiar philosophical example, it is my duty to save my tiresome mother from fire, rather than the rich visiting philanthropist. Equally, rights (positive rights) have to be constrained by utilitarianism. In accepting a liberal egalitarian stance whereby some rights may be traded against equality, we have already accepted that.

Second, utility has to be weighted by social distance; charity begins at home. There is little doubt that the marginal utility of someone with whom one is acquainted weighs more than that of an unknown Bangladeshi (except sometimes if a flood is vividly reported on television). I do not think this is wholly a matter of special duties, such as the special duty most people think they owe to their

[6] Brian Barry has suggested that this question implies acceptance of the moral possibility of forming a social welfare function from individual values, an idea that I rejected 37 years ago (see I. M. D. Little, 'Social Choice and Individual Values', *Journal of Political Economy*, 50 (Oct. 1952), reprinted in *Rational Man and Irrational Society? An Introduction and Source Book*, ed. B. Barry and R. Hardin (Beverly Hills, Calif.: Sage, 1982). In asking whether there is some widely accepted ethical thinking (on the part of those who would consider themselves both liberal and mildly egalitarian) to which governments are sensitive, I insist that I am not concurring in anything so diabolical as the construction of a social welfare function. To argue that some degree of consensus may exist surely does not commit one to any belief in an objective moral code, or the dictatorship of some metaphysical general will. I have reread and am fully convinced by what I wrote in 1952.

families or their dogs. Furthermore, if duties extend far beyond rather narrow boundaries of kith, kin, and friendship, they seem to require a utilitarian base. Admittedly, duties may sometimes trump utility. Who thinks it wrong for a testator to leave at least some of his estate to his rich son? But what grounds are there for believing that a rich person has a duty to give to poor people who are remote from him? Only that they are poor. Even if we substitute 'lack of basic needs' for poverty, I think that is still utilitarianism.[7] This is not to say that some people may think more in terms of rights than utilities. Thus, in the case of a famine a person might be more moved by the argument from a right to live than by the high marginal utility of a starving person. But rights also suffer from social distance, in the sense that the further removed a person is the more one is inclined to think that there is someone else, or some other organization or state, whose duty it is to help. For myself, I might add, nationality is not a hurdle in assessing effective social distance. I am more likely to give to Oxfam than to a charity whose recipients are equally unknown deprived Britons. But I guess I may be in a minority.

I have thus far concentrated on foreigners. But international movements or transactions may also be regulated for egalitarian reasons, with due regard to liberty, within one's own country. This has been treated only in passing. Protectionism is an obvious example. Another example of great interest to developing countries is emigration and the related control of capital movements. Most liberals probably think it an intolerable affront to personal freedom to prevent a person emigrating. But if he is paid less than his contribution to society in that country, possibly for egalitarian reasons, then the country and perhaps its poorer members may suffer, though they may not. (Remittances have been, since 1974, an important part of the national income of South Asian countries, as well as Turkey and North Africa.) Even so, most liberal egalitarians (certainly myself) think he must be allowed to go. Jagdish Bhagwati has tried to resolve this conflict by suggesting that the host country should put a special tax on these migrants and return it to the country of origin. Ingenious, but a non-starter!

On top of this, should the migrant be allowed to take his fortune with him? There would be more disagreement on this score. Prima facie, if a government has a right to tax his property for redistributive reasons, it should equally have a right to exact an equivalent once-and-for-all tax on exit. In brief, he should be allowed to take a part of his fortune. (The rest should be returned to him if he came back.)

What should I deduce from the actual behaviour of Second and Third World countries? Many regulate and some virtually prohibit emigration. Very few

[7] A weighted utilitarianism can envelop almost any theory. Rawls's theory may even gain by thinking of it as utilitarianism with a weight of 1 for the disadvantaged, and 0 for the others. It can also deal with Sen's objections to utilitarianism—that cripples and Indian peasant women should get more than they would if society's objective were to maximize utility. Furthermore, it is hardly less subjective. There is already room for a good deal of disagreement about relative marginal utilities.

permit more than a token amount of money to be taken. They do not behave in a liberal manner, but this is seldom for egalitarian reasons. Different cultures weigh liberalism and egalitarianism differently. The weight of one or the other may indeed approach zero.

Let me now address myself more specifically to some of the questions that form the subject matter of this book concentrating on movements of merchandise and money. But it is unlikely that any unambiguous answers can be given. The taking of a liberal egalitarian stance rules out only some extreme views. Moreover, the undercurrent of utilitarianism that I have admitted implies that policies must be judged by their consequences. The consequences are for economics. Needless to say, they are usually debatable. But they cannot be usefully debated in a forum composed predominantly of philosophers and political theorists. Where economic consequences are involved, I can give only my own views.

The essential standpoint I am taking is that a government is there to maximize some function of the utility of its citizens, subject to certain rights not being trampled on. But foreigners are not to be treated solely as instruments. There are degrees of foreignness ranging from long-resident aliens to totally unknown inhabitants of distant lands. Some human sympathy is felt by most or all people. So one does not want one's government to put all foreigners beyond the pale; some consideration should be shown to all human beings. Thus, negative rights should always be respected. But positive rights to some standard of living are not recognized, at least in the case of non-residents. However, some very limited aid should be given on utilitarian grounds. (Aid is less than 0.5 per cent of national income for most rich countries, and some even of this can be credited to self-interest.)

Speaking more personally, I would myself like my government to give more aid, despite my knowing that it is very difficult to give aid effectively for the poor and that much is wasted. Of course, there is a minority of liberal egalitarians who would go much further. But if my constituency is to include most people who would think of themselves as liberals, and who agree with some element of redistribution within their own country, then I cannot go much further.

It obviously follows from what has been said that it may be ethically appropriate for any country to restrict capital movements in or out. The circumstances are that such restriction increases the welfare of its citizens.

But should there be no international limitations on the sovereign rights of a state in this or other respects in the name of 'global distributive justice'? To speak of global justice at all requires, I believe, a global moral community. (This follows from my rejection of natural law.) I cannot conceive of justice as between, say, those on Earth and those on some planet in another galaxy (supposing that we on Earth could know of their existence and whether they were rich or poor relative to ourselves, but could never communicate). I admire people who try to develop such a community for this globe, but it hardly exists. Therefore, it hardly makes sense to speak of global justice. But one can, of course, favour a more equal distribution, regardless of nationality, without any belief in global justice.

Some fifteen years ago, the idea of a 'New International Economic Order' (NIEO) was mooted and actively demanded by the 'Group of 77' (which includes nearly all developing countries, numbering many more than 77). But the developing country proponents of the NIEO had greater equality of states in mind, not people. There was a strong emphasis on sovereignty; and they resented the idea that their poor were anyone's concern but their own.

The actual suggested constituents of a NIEO almost all implied more aid, and more international controls. In my opinion the controls would have done the poor of the world no good. The aid component of the proposed measures would probably not have increased total aid. (Donors are not that easily fooled.) Most of the measures proposed paid no attention to the relative poverty of developing countries, and on balance the wealthier would have benefited most (if any benefited). The aid component would have been without strings. But in my opinion aid (grants and concessionary loans) can be justified only if they go predominantly to the poorest countries, and sustained only if the public in the donor countries can be assured that they go to countries with reasonably viable general economic policies that show some concern for the welfare of the mass of the people. Strings are needed. The NIEO concept seems to have faded away.[8]

I have briefly considered aid. Let me finally address some other specific international concerns. I shall do this from the viewpoint already described, but I shall make that viewpoint a little more focused by supposing that as a rich-country citizen I believe that helping the poorest people on Earth has a higher priority than it appears to be accorded by the governments of industrialized countries. What can and should be done in suggesting any institutional reforms still depends both on their practicality, including what can be made acceptable to poor countries, and on the economic consequences. I will illustrate the problems taking only a few examples.

Debt is the hottest current topic. Essentially, the burning question is how much debt, if any, should be forgiven—and whose debt, and who should bear the cost. A longer-run institutional question might be whether international borrowing and lending should be controlled in some way—with such control becoming part of an international economic order. Note that this would be the institution of an order rather than its reform, for the debt arose from disorder.

The background is probably relevant to both questions. In 1974 OPEC created an enormous payments surplus. If a major recession was to be avoided, this had to be offset by other countries creating corresponding deficits through expansionary policies. Inflation was also magnified by the oil price rises, which made the industrialized countries reluctant to expand. Developing countries were less reluctant. So the commercial banks recycled the 'petro-dollars' to some of them

[8] I considered the components of the NIEO in *Economic Development: Theory, Policy and International Relations* (New York: Basic Books, 1982), ch. 17.

(for several years at extremely low real interest rates). All would have been well if enough of this borrowing had been devoted to investments with a return which would at least cover the payment of interest on the debt. In fact, most of it was used for investment, but much of this investment produced little or nothing. Debt was already high, but not impossibly so, when the second oil-price shock hit. Many countries found retrenchment too difficult and continued to borrow at an alarming rate at the now high rates of interest that had come about largely as a result of President Reagan's economic policies, until the crunch came when they ceased to be able to borrow.

The above scenario applies to a good number of countries, but not all. Some countries, e.g. Nigeria, Mexico, and Venezuela, experienced highly favourable external shocks, still borrowed excessively, and are now in deep trouble. In Asia, the scenario applies only to the Philippines, which in many ways resembles Latin American rather than other Asian countries.

Now should the debt, or some of it, be forgiven? The assumed emphasis on poverty suggests not, except in the case of some African countries (where indeed some debt has been forgiven). A famous Indian economist, T. N. Srinivasan, has protested against debt forgiveness.[9] India has little debt and a high proportion of the world's poorest people. Rather than forgive debt to relatively wealthy Latin American countries, aid to India should be increased. If taxpayers are to bear the cost of debt forgiveness, it is likely that it would be competitive with other forms of aid which might therefore be reduced.

Other ethical problems arise. The conceptions of *justice* I have discussed say nothing about deserts (what is deserved, not barren areas). Yet some commentators on the debt problem seem to put this up front. The highly indebted countries were incapable of managing their affairs properly; so it is their fault. Alternatively, the bankers were very foolish and moreover pushed the developing countries into borrowing (but what about *caveat emptor*?). Bank equity holders and senior staff should suffer (but that would not be enough, for not many banks could be allowed to go bankrupt). Yet again, one can argue that the citizens and taxpayers of the rich countries benefited; for if the bankers and their borrowers had not been foolish, there would have been a deeper recession in the 1970s. Finally, arguments from moral hazard are raised.

Personally, I am not much moved by arguments about deserts or moral hazard. Countries and banks are not people and do not learn in the same way. Those countries that repudiated their debts in the 1930s were in the van of the creditworthy in the 1970s; and there will not be another debt crisis for forty years. Personally, and *pace* T. N. Srinivasan, I would favour quite a lot of debt forgiveness, but I am not prompted to this view by any conception of global justice.

Does the debt situation suggest that there should in future be more international control of borrowing and lending to be part of the international order?

[9] W. H. Buiter and T. N. Srinivasan, 'Rewarding the Profligate and Punishing the Prudent and Poor', *World Development*, 15(3).

Bank surveillance and control of foreign borrowing and lending by a country's own banks and other institutions is prima facie a country's own concern. Certainly, developing countries would be, and have been, up-tight about any limit on their freedom to borrow on the Euro-dollar market (which might be required in the interests of a stable international currency). Of course, that does not settle the question. I fear the matter is too complex, and I am not expert enough, to go further into it. But I suspect that a very cumbersome and over-restrictive apparatus might be created to fight the last war.

Let me turn to something easier—*multinational corporations*. Tremendous heat was generated in the 1970s on this subject by some developing country governments and spokesmen and by the 'development establishment'. That multinationals might do economic harm in innumerable ways was hypothesized; but, above all, the fear was that they might undermine a country's independence. Of course, a country has a right to control incoming foreign investment; every country I know of does. They also have a right to make foreign companies fulfil certain conditions of operation; many do. When a country has a highly distorted price mechanism, it is true that some investments by foreigners may do harm (just as it is true that some investments by natives may do harm). This is because the distortions (by definition) thrust a wedge between private and social profitability. Some control could be a second- or third-best solution to this problem. But domestic economic reforms would be better.

The sheer volume of foreign interests—in industrial investment or real estate—either overall or in particular industries or areas could threaten independence. Suppose Germans bought one of the northern Swiss cantons lock, stock, and barrel! But countries are in control, and quite sufficiently xenophobic. So what has this to do with the international order? Or international justice? The furore of the 1970s did result in a small UN institute. I have never heard of it since; the heat has died. Multinationals are now more welcome, and controls have been somewhat reduced (rightly, in my opinion). This is not because of any change in the behaviour of multinationals, or any institutional change. It seems simply to have been because radical opponents of capitalism and nationalist opponents of foreign capitalists shouted too loud and lost their voices.

Lastly, take trade. This is an easy one to end with. There is no doubt that industrial protection on the part of the rich countries harms the poor in the poorest countries.[10] To my mind, the high protection which the governments of poor countries insist on (very gradually this insistence is waning) also harms the poor in almost all countries.[11] I believe it also harms their development in a more general sense.

[10] I have written 'industrial protection', because it is possible to argue that rich-country agricultural protectionism benefits the poor in some food-deficit developing countries. On balance, I think I would argue that it is harmful, but I prefer to side-step the issue.

[11] High protectionism in poor countries has favoured industry and urban areas against agriculture and rural areas where most of the poorest people are. Within industry it favours capital-intensive industry, thus limiting the demand for labour. Creating a high demand for labour is the best way of

There has been a tendency to globalize problems that are not global at all, not even international. But protection is not one of these. There is a strong argument for an international institute. This is because almost every country has a tendency—indeed, seems to feel a compulsion—to use trade restrictions to solve some internal problem. There is, even from the individual country's point of view, almost always a better way of dealing with the problem—but in the short run trade restrictions seem easiest, politically or administratively. In the long run I believe all lose. An international institution that ties countries' hands can do much good. Of course, there is such an institution; in its heyday the GATT did much good. For reasons I need not go into, it is in sad decline. This has been the fault of both rich and poor countries.

If it is desirable to tie countries' hands in the area of trade, why not in other areas? For instance, could not controls over international investment be subject to limitations imposed by an international agreement embodied in a monitoring quasi-judicial institute similar to the GATT? Am I not being inconsistent in seeing trade and not international investment as a global problem? In principle I am; but perhaps not practice. I think a beneficial agreement with teeth would be too difficult to reach.

I believe something rather close to free trade and freedom of international investment is in the interest of all countries. But on top of this, I would regard it as a bonus that the poor of the world would stand to gain most, provided that the economic policies of countries were themselves reasonably neutral and did not bias production in ways that limited the extent to which the masses could benefit. Liberalism and egalitarianism should not here be in any global conflict.

helping the poor. Freer trade is likely to be inegalitarian only in those few countries where the landed interest is rich. Taxation could eliminate this problem. But if for political reasons taxing the pastoralists or latifundians at the front door is ruled out, then industrial protection may be a way of imposing taxation at the back door. This has been given as a reason for protection in Australia.

References

Andrews, P. W. A. (1949), *Manufacturing Business*, London, Macmillan.

Arrow, K. J. (1951), 'Little's Critique of Welfare Economics', *American Economic Review*, 41.

Ayer, A. J. (1936), *Language, Truth, and Logic*, London, Victor Gollanz.

——(1940), *Foundations of Empirical Knowledge*, London, Macmillan.

Balassa, B. (1976), 'The Effects Method of Project Evaluation', *Oxford Bulletin of Economics and Statistics*, 38.

Barry, B. and Goodin, R. E. (eds.) (1992), *Free Movement*, State College, Pa, Pennsylvania State University Press.

Baumol, W. J. (1946/7), 'Community Indifference', *Review of Economic Studies*, 14.

——(1952), *Welfare Economics and the Theory of the State*, London, Bell.

Bergson, A. (1976), 'Social Choice and Welfare Economics under Representative Government', *Journal of Public Economics*, 6.

Bergsman, J. (1970), *Brazil: Industrialization and Trade Policies*, London, Oxford University Press for OECD.

Bhagwati, J. N. and Desai, P. (1970), *India: Planning for Industrialization: Industrialization and Trade Policies since 1951*, London, Oxford University Press for OECD.

Brassey, T. (1873), *On Work and Wages*, London, Bell & Daldy.

Brassey, Lady (1886), *A Voyage in the Sunbeam*, 10th edn., London, Longmans, Green.

Cairncross, A. (ed.) (1989 and 1991), *The Robert Hall Diaries, 1947–53* and *1954–61*, London, Unwin Hyman.

——and Watts, N. (1989), *The Economic Section 1939–1961*, London, Routledge.

Castle, B. (1993), *Fighting All the Way*, London, Macmillan.

Chakravarty, S. (1964), 'The Mathematical Framework of the Third Five Year', in P. N. Rosenstein Rodan (ed.), *Capital Formation and Economic Development*, London, George Allen & Unwin.

Chenery, H. B. and Bruno, M. (1962), 'Development Alternatives in an Open Economy: The Case of Israel', *Economic Journal*, 72.

Dow, J. C. R. and Saville, I. D. (1988), *A Critique of Monetary Policy: Theory and British Experience*, Oxford, Clarendon Press.

Evely, R. and Little, I. M. D. (1960), *Concentration in British Industry*, Cambridge, Cambridge University Press.

Graaff, J. de V. (1956), *Theoretical Welfare Economics*, Cambridge, Cambridge University Press.

Joshi, V. and Little, I. M. D. (1994), *India: Macroeconomics and Political Economy, 1964–1991*, Delhi, World Bank/Oxford University Press.

Kemp, M. C. and Ng, Y.-K. (1976), 'On the Existence of Social Welfare Functions, Social Orderings and Social Decision Functions', *Economica*, 43.

Kennedy, C. M. (1952–3), 'The Economic Welfare Function and Dr Little's Criterion', *Review of Economic Studies*, 20.

Keynes, J. M. (1940), *How to Pay for the War*, London, Macmillan.

King, T. (1970), *Mexico: Industrialization and Trade Policies Since 1940*, London, Oxford University Press for OECD.

Lal, D. (1975), *Appraising Foreign Investment in Developing Countries*, London, Heinemann Educational.

——(1980), *Prices for Planning: Towards the Reform of Indian Planning*, London, Heinemann.

Lewis, S. R. Jr (1970), *Pakistan: Industrialization and Trade Policies*, London, Oxford University Press for OECD.

Little, I. M. D. (1957), 'Classical Growth', *Oxford Economic Papers*, NS 9: 152–77.

——(1957), 'The Economist in Whitehall', *Lloyds Bank Review*, 44 (April): 29–40.

——(1961), 'The Real Cost of Labour and the Choice between Consumption and Investment', *Quarterly Journal of Economics*, 25 (Feb.): 1–15.

——(1962), 'Fiscal Policy', in G. D. N. Worswick and P. H. Ady (eds.), *The British Economy in the 1950s*, Oxford University Press.

——(1964), *Aid to Africa: An appraisal of UK policy for Aid to Africa South of the Sahara*, London, Overseas Development Institute/Pergamon Press.

——(1964), 'Tax Policy and the Third Plan', in P. N. Rosenstein Rodan (ed.), *Pricing and Fiscal Policies*, London, Allen & Unwin, ch. 3.

——(1972), 'On Measuring the Value of Private Direct Overseas Investment', in G. Ranis (ed.), *The Gap between Rich and Poor Nations*, London, Macmillan, ch. 8.

——(1979), 'An Economic Reconnaissance', in W. Galenson (ed.), *Economic Growth and Structural Change in Taiwan*, Ithaca, NY, Cornell University Press, pp. 448–507.

——(1982), *Economic Development: Theory, policy and international relations*, New York, Basic Books.

——and Clifford, J. M. (1965), *International Aid: A discussion of the flow of public resources from rich to poor countries with particular reference to British policy*, London, Allen & Unwin; reprinted Chicago, Aldine, 1967.

——and Mirrlees, J. A. (1969), *Manual of Industrial Project Analysis in Developing Countries*, ii, *Social Cost–Benefit Analysis*, Paris, Development Centre, OECD.

—— and ——(1974), *Project Appraisal and Planning for Developing Countries*, London, Heinemann Educational.

——and Rosenstein Rodan, P. N. (1957), 'Nuclear Power and Italy's Energy Position', Washington, National Planning Association.

——and Scott, M. FG. (eds.) (1976), *Using Shadow Prices*, London, Heinemann Educational.

——and Tipping, D. G. (1972), *A Social Cost–Benefit Analysis of the Kulai Oil Palm Estate West Malaysia*, Paris, Development Centre OECD.

——, Scitovsky, T. and Scott, M. FG. (1970), *Industry and Trade in Some Developing Countries: A comparative study*, Oxford, Oxford Development Centre OECD/Oxford University Press.

——, Cooper, R. N., Corden, W. M., and Rajapatirana, S. (1993), *Boom, Crisis and Adjustment*, New York, World Bank/Oxford University Press.

Lipsey, R. G. and Lancaster, K. (1956–7), 'The General Theory of Second Best', *Review of Economic Studies*, 24.

MacDougall, D. 91987), *Don and Mandarin*, London, John Murray.

Ng, Y.-K. (1979), *Welfare Economics*, London, Macmillan.

Power, J. H., Sicat, G., and Hsing, M.-H. (1970), *The Philippines and Taiwan: Industrialization and Trade Policies*, London, Oxford University Press for OECD.

Robinson, J. (1956), *The Accumulation of Capital*, London, Macmillan.

Rosen, G. (1985), *Western Economists and Eastern Societies*, Delhi, Oxford University Press.

Rosenstein Rodan, P. N. (ed.) (1964), *Capital Formation and Economic Development*, London, George Allen & Unwin.

Samuelson, P. A. (1967*a*), foreword in J. de V Graaff, *Theoretical Welfare Economics*, Cambridge, Cambridge University Press.

——(1967*b*), 'Arrow's Mathematical Politics', in S. Hook (ed.), *Human Values and Economic Policy*, New York, New York University Press.

Scott, M. FG., MacArthur J. D., and Newbery D. M. G. (1976), *Project Appraisel in Practice*, London, Heinemann Educational.

Singh, M. (1964), *India's Export Trends and Prospects for Self-Sustained Growth*, Oxford, Clarendon Press.

Squire, L. and Van der Tak, H. G. (1975), *Economic Analysis of Projects*, Baltimore, Johns Hopkins University Press for the World Bank.

Sugden, R. and Weale, A. (1979), 'A Contractarian Reformulation of Certain Aspects of Welfare Economics', *Economica*, 46.

Suzumura, K. (1980), 'On Distributional Value Judgements and Piecemeal Welfare Criteria', *Economica*, 47.

Collected Works of I. M. D. Little

Books (in order of publication)

A Critique of Welfare Economics (Clarendon Press, Oxford, 1950; 2nd edn. 1957).

The Price of Fuel (Clarendon, Press, Oxford, 1953).

Nuclear Power and Italy's Energy Position, with P. N. Rosenstein Rodan (National Planning Association, Washington, DC, 1957).

Concentration in British Industry: An empirical study of the structure of industrial production 1935–51, with R. Evely (Cambridge University Press, 1960).

Aid to Africa: An appraisal of UK policy for Aid to Africa South of the Sahara (Overseas Development Institute/Pergamon Press, London, 1964).

International Aid: A discussion of the flow of public resources from rich to poor countries with particular reference to British policy, with J. M. Clifford (Allen & Unwin, London, 1965; reprint Aldine, Chicago, 1967).

Higgledy Piggledy Growth Again: An investigation of the predictability of company earnings and dividends in the UK, 1951–61, with A. C. Rayner (Blackwell, Oxford, 1966; reprint Augustus M. Kelley, New York, 1971).

Towards a Strategy for Development Co-operation, with Special Reference to Asia, ed. with H. B. Chenery, F. Baade, J. Kaufmann, L. H. Klaassen, and J. Tinbergen (Rotterdam University Press, 1967, and contributed chapter on 'Aid: Project, programme, and procurement tying').

Manual of Industrial Project Analysis in Developing Countries, ii, *Social Cost–Benefit Analysis*, with J. A. Mirrlees (Development Centre, OECD, Paris, 1969; also French translation).

Industry and Trade in Some Developing Countries: A comparative study, with T. Scitovsky and M. FG. Scott (published for the Development Centre of the OECD by OUP, 1970; also French and Spanish translations).

A Social Cost–Benefit Analysis of the Kulai Oil Palm Estate West Malaysia, with D. G. Tipping (Development Centre Studies Series on Cost–Benefit Analysis, Case Study no. 3, OECD, Paris, 1972).

Estudio Social Del Costo-Beneficio en la Industria de Paises en Desarrollo: Manual de Evaluacion de Proyectos, with J. A. Mirrlees (trans. from *Manual of Industrial Project Analysis*, ii) (Centre de Estudios Monetarios Latinoamer, Mexico City, 1973).

Project Appraisal and Planning for Developing Countries, with J. A. Mirrlees (Heinemann Educational, London, 1974).

Why We Need A Wealth Tax, with J. S. Flemming (Methuen, London, 1974).

Import Controls versus Devaluation and Britain's Economic Prospects, with W. M. Corden and M. FG. Scott (Guest Paper no. 2, Trade Policy Research Centre, London, 1975).

Using Shadow Prices, ed. with M. FG. Scott (Heinemann Educational, London, 1976).

Una Critica dell' Economica del benessene, trans. Guido Tesarum (Instituto Editoriale Internatzionale, Milan, 1976, with new introduction by the author).

The Case against General Import Restrictions, with M. FG. Scott and W. M. Corden (Trade Policy Research, London, 1980).

Economic Development: Theory, policy and international relations (Basic Books, New York, 1982).

Small Manufacturing Enterprises: A comparative study of India and other economies, with D. Mazumdar and J. M. Page, Jr (published for the World Bank by the OUP, 1987).

Boom, Crisis and Adjustment, with R. N. Cooper, W. M. Corden, and S. Rajapatirana (Oxford University Press, New York, for the World Bank, 1993).

Macroeconomic Analysis and the Developing Countries 1970–1990 (International Centre for Economic Growth, San Francisco, 1993).

India: Macroeconomics and political economy 1964–1991, with V. Joshi (World Bank and Oxford University Press, Delhi, 1994).

India's Economic Reforms 1991–2001, with V. Joshi (Clarendon Press, Oxford, and Oxford University Press, Delhi, 1996).

Picking Winners: The East Asian experience (Social Market Foundation, London, 1996).

India's Economic Reforms and Development: Essays for Manmohan Singh, ed. with I. J. Ahluwalia (Oxford University Press, Delhi, 1998).

Contributions to books (in order of publication)

'Fiscal Policy', in G. D. N. Worswick and P. H. Ady (eds.), *The British Economy 1945–50* (Oxford University Press, 1952).

'Sources of Power: the long-term outlook', in A. Shonfield (ed.), *The Chambers of Commerce Award* (London, 1958).

'Direct versus Indirect Taxes', in R. A. Musgrave and C. S. Shoup (eds.), *Readings in the Economics of Taxation* (American Economic Association/Allen & Unwin, London, 1959).

(with R. R. Neild and C. R. Ross) 'The scope and limitations of monetary policy', in *Principal Memoranda of Evidence Submitted to the Committee on the Working of the Monetary System*, iii (HMSO, London, 1960).

'Fiscal Policy', in G. D. N. Worswick and P. H. Ady (eds.), *The British Economy in the 1950s* (Oxford University Press, 1962).

Comment on 'Evaluation of "Social Income": Capital Formation and Wealth by P. Samuelson', in D. C. Hague (ed.), *The Theory of Capital*, conference held by IEA at Corfu (Macmillan, London, 1963).

'Tax Policy and the Third Plan' and 'The Real Cost of Labour and the Choice between Consumption and Investment', in P. N. Rosenstein Rodan (ed.), *Pricing and Fiscal Policies* (Allen & Unwin, London, 1964).

'Executive, Co-ordinating, Supervisory and Evaluation Machinery', in *Overcoming Obstacles to Development: Impressions and papers of the Fourth Cambridge Conference on Development Problems*, 12–25 September 1965 at Jesus College, Cambridge, ed. R. Robinson (Cambridge University Overseas Studies Committee, 18 Petty Cury, Cambridge, undated).

'Direct versus Indirect Taxes', in K. J. Arrow and T. Scitovsky (eds.), *Readings in Welfare Economics* (American Economic Association/Richard D. Irwin, Homewood, Ill., 1969).

'Public Sector Project Selection in Relation to Indian Development', in A. V. Bhuleshkar (ed.), *Indian Economic Thought and Development* (Popular Prakashan, Bombay, 1969).

'Regional International Companies as an Approach to Economic Integration', in P. Robson (ed.), *International Economic Integration* (Penguin Books, Harmondsworth, 1971).

(with J. A. Mirrlees) 'Further Reflections on the OECD Manual of Project Analysis in Developing Countries', in J. Bhagwati and R. S. Eckaus (eds.), *Development and Planning: Essays in honour of Paul Rosenstein-Rodan* (Allen & Unwin, London, 1972).

'On Measuring the Value of Private Direct Overseas Investment', in G. Ranis (ed.), *The Gap Between Rich and Poor Nations*, conference held by IEA at Bled, Yugoslavia (Macmillan, London, 1972).

'Social Choice and Individual Values', in E. S. Phelps (ed.), *Economic Justice* (Penguin Education, Baltimore, 1973).

'A Critical Examination of India's Third Five-Year Plan', in C. D. Wadhva (ed.), *Some Problems of India's Economic Policy* (Tata McGraw-Hill, New Delhi, 1973).

'The Economy of Poor Countries and their Population Stabilization: an introduction', in H. B. Parry (ed.), *Population and its Problems: A plain man's guide* (Oxford University Press, 1974).

(with K. M. McLeod) 'The New Pricing Policy of the British Airports Authority', in G. P. Howard (ed.), *Airport Economic Planning* (MIT Press, Cambridge, Mass., 1974).

'The Use and Abuse of Capital in Developing Countries', in Y. Ramati (ed.), *Economic Growth in Developing Countries—Materials and Human Resources: Proceedings of the Seventh Rehovot Conference* (Praeger, New York, 1975).

'Bretton Woods'; 'Development Economics'; 'Necessary and Sufficient Conditions'; 'Take Off Point'; 'Underdevelopment'; 'Welfare, Welfare Economics', in A. Bullock and O. Stallybrass (eds.), *The Fontana Dictionary of Modern Thought* (Collins, London, 1977).

'Welfare Criteria, Distribution and Cost–Benefit Analysis', in M. J. Boskin (ed.), *Economics and Human Welfare: Essays in honor of Tibor Scitovsky* (Academic Press, New York, 1979).

'An Economic Reconnaissance', in W. Galenson (ed.), *Economic Growth and Structural Change in Taiwan* (Cornell University Press, Ithaca, NY, 1979).

'The Developing Countries and the International Order', in R. C. Amacher, G. Haberler, and T. D. Willett (eds.), *Challenges to a Liberal International Economic Order* (AEI Symposia, Washington, DC, 1979).

'Distributive Justice and the New International Order', in P. Oppenheimer (ed.), *Issues in International Economics* (Oriel Press, London, 1980).

'Comment' on Richard S. Eckaus, 'Strategies of Development and the International Division of Work', in *Conference Internacional Sobre Economia Portuguesa* (Fundacao Calouste Gulbenkian, Liboa, 1980).

'Social Democracy and the International Economy', in D. Lipsey and D. Leonard (eds.), *The Socialist Agenda: Crosland's Legacy* (Jonathan Cape, London, 1981).

'The Experience and Causes of Rapid Labour-Intensive Development in Korea, Taiwan Province, Hong Kong and Singapore and the Possibilities of Emulation', in E. Lee (ed.), *Export-led Industrialization and Development* (ILO, Geneva, 1981).

Comment on S. Kuznets's 'Driving Forces of Economic Growth: What can we learn from history?' in H. Giersch (ed.), *Towards an Explanation of Economic Growth: Symposium 1980* (Institut für Weltwirtschaft an der Universität Kiel, 1981).

'Indian Industrialization before 1945', in M. Gersovitz *et al.* (eds.), *The Theory and Experience of Economic Development: Essays in honour of Sir Arthur Lewis* (Allen & Unwin, London, 1982).

'Import Controls and Exports in Developing Countries', in R. K. Ghosh (ed.), *International Trade and Third World Development* (International Development Resource Books, Westport, Conn., 1984).

'Discussion', in A. P. Thirlwall (ed.), *Keynes and Economic Development* (Macmillan, London, 1987).

'A Comment on Professor Toye's Paper', in L. Emmerij (ed.), *Development Policies and the Crisis of the 1980s* (Development Centre OECD, Paris, 1987).

'Crosland, Anthony', in J. Eatwell, M. Milgate, and P. Newman (eds.), *The New Palgrave: A dictionary of economics* (Macmillan, London, 1987), i. 728.

'Comments on Wolfram Fischer, "Swings between Protection and Free Trade in History"', in H. Giersch (ed.), *Free Trade in the World Economy: Towards an opening of markets* (Institut für Weltwirtschaft an der Universität Kiel, J. C. B. Mohr (Paul Siebeck), Tübingen, 1987).

'Resource Use Efficiency and the Small Scale Enterprise', in K. B. Suri (ed.), *Small Scale Enterprises in Industrial Development: The Indian experience* (Sage, New Delhi, 1988).

'Comment on Professor Findlay's Paper', in G. Ranis and T. P. Schultz (eds.), *The State of Development Economics: Progress and prospects* (Blackwell, Oxford, 1988).

'The Macroeconomic Effects of Foreign Aid: Issues and Evidence—A comment', in C. J. Jepma (ed.), *North–South Co-operation in Retrospect and Prospect* (Routledge, London, 1988).

(with V. Joshi) 'Indian Macroeconomic Policies', in G. Calvo, R. Findlay, P. Kouri, and J. Braga de Macedo (eds.), *Debt, Stabilization and Development: Essays in memory of Carlos Dìaz-Alejandro* (Basil Blackwell, Oxford, 1989).

'Ethics and International Economic Relations', in B. Barry and R. E. Goodin (eds.), *Free Movement* (Harvester Wheatsheaf, Hemel Hempstead, 1992).

(with V. Joshi) 'Future Trade and Exchange Rate Policy for India', in R. Cassen and V. Joshi (eds.), *India: The future of economic reform* (Oxford University Press, Delhi, 1995).

(with V. Joshi) 'Macroeconomic Management in India 1964–94', in V. N. Balasubramanyam and D. Greenaway (eds.), *Trade and Development: Essays in honour of Jagdish Bhagwati* (Macmillan, London, and St Martins Press, New York, 1996).

Articles (in order of publication)

'A Reformulation of the Theory of Consumer's Behaviour', *Oxford Economic Papers*, NS 1 (Jan. 1949).

'The Valuation of Social Income', *Economica*, 16 (Feb. 1949).

'The Foundations of Welfare Economics', *Oxford Economic Papers*, NS 1 (June 1949).

'A Note on the Interpretation of Index Numbers', *Economica*, 16 (Nov. 1949).

'Welfare and Tariffs', *Review of Economic Studies*, 16 (1949).

'The Economist and the State', *Review of Economic Studies*, 17 (1949).

'Economic Behaviour and Welfare', *Mind*, 1 (1949).

'The Theory of Consumer Behavior: A comment', *Oxford Economic Papers*, NS 2 (1950).

'Direct versus Indirect Taxes', *Economic Journal*, 61 (Sept. 1951).

'Electricity Tariffs: A comment', *Economic Journal*, 61 (Dec. 1951).

'Social Choice and Individual Values', *Journal of Political Economy*, 60 (Oct. 1952).

'L'Avantage collectif', *Economie Appliquee* (Paris), 5 (Oct.–Dec. 1952).

'Classical Growth', *Oxford Economic Papers*, NS 9 (Jan. 1957).

'The Economist in Whitehall', *Lloyds' Bank Review*, 44 (Apr. 1957).

'Die Rolle des Nationalokonomen in Whitehall', *Konjunkturpolitik*, Berlin (1957).

'The Aims of Monetary Policy', *Oxford Institute of Economics and Statistics Bulletin*, 19 (Nov. 1957).

'The Role of the Economist in Whitehall', *Administration*, Dublin, 6 (Summer 1958).

'Atomic Bombay?', *Economic and Political Weekly*, Bombay (29 Nov. 1958).

'Some Aspects of the Structure of British Industry, 1935–1951', with R. Evely, *Transactions of the Manchester Statistical Society* (Session 1957–8).

'The Strategy of Indian Development', *National Institute Economic Review*, no. 9 (May 1960).

'The Third Five-Year Plan and the Strategy of Indian Development', *Economic and Political Weekly*, Bombay, 12 (1960).

'The Real Cost of Labour and the Choice between Consumption and Investment', *Quarterly Journal of Economics*, 25 (Feb. 1961).

'A Critical Examination of India's Third Five-Year Plan', *Oxford Economic Papers*, NS 14 (Feb. 1962).

'Welfare Criteria: A comment, a reply', *Economic Journal*, 72 (Mar. 1962).

'Higgledy Piggledy Growth', *Oxford Institute of Economics and Statistics Bulletin*, 24 (Nov. 1962).

'Two Comments', *Economic Journal*, 73 (Dec. 1963).

'Welfare Economics, Ethics and Essentialism: A comment', *Economica*, 32 (May 1965).

'Regional International Companies as an Approach to Economic Integration', *Journal of Common Market Studies*, 5 (1966).

'Direkte Gegen Indirekte Steurn', *Finanztheorie*, Cologne (1969).

'Symposium on Project Appraisal in Lesser Developed Countries', *Journal of Agricultural Economics*, 22 (1971).

'Trade and Public Finance', a memorial lecture for V. K. Ramaswami at the Delhi School of Economics, November 1970, *Indian Economic Review*, NS 6 (1971).

'The New Pricing Policy of the British Airports Authority', with K. M. McLeod, *Journal of Transport Economics and Policy*, 6 (May 1972).

'A Reply to some Criticisms of the OECD Manual', with J. A. Mirrlees, *Oxford Institute of Economics and Statistics Bulletin*, 34 (1972).

'Coping with the Arab Billions', with R. E. Mabro, *Financial Times*, 22 December 1973.

'Economic Relations with the Third World: Old myths and new prospects', *Scottish Journal of Political Economy*, 22 (1975).

'Perspectives for the Second Half of the Second UN Development Decade', *Journal of Development Planning*, no. 9 (1976).

'Import Controls and Exports in Developing Countries', *Finance and Development*, 15/3 (1978).

'Robert Cooter and Peter Rappaport's "Were the Ordinalists Wrong about Welfare Economics?": A comment', *Journal of Economic Literature*, 23 (1985).

'Small Manufacturing Enterprises in Developing Countries', *World Bank Economic Review*, 1 (Jan. 1987).

(with V. R. Joshi) 'Indian Macroeconomics Policies', *Economic and Political Weekly*, Bombay, 28 February 1987.

'Small Manufacturing Enterprises and Employment in Developing Countries', *Asian Development Review*, 6/2 (1988).

(with V. Joshi) 'Les Politiques Macro-Economiques Indiennes', *Revue Tiers Monde*, 30 (Oct.–Dec. 1989).

(with J. A. Mirrlees) 'Project Appraisal and Planning Twenty Years On', *Proceedings of the World Bank Annual Conference on Development Economics* (Washington, World Bank, 1991).

'Trade and Industrialization Revisited', *Pakistan Development Review*, 33 (Winter 1994).

'India's Economic Reforms 1991–96', *Journal of Asian Economics*, 7 (1996).

'Comment on "Review-Debt Adjustment and Recovery"', *The World Economy*, 19 (Sept. 1996).

'Protection and the Industrialization of Developing Countries', lecture given at York University, Toronto, 1968, published in this volume (Paper No. 8).

Reviews (in order of publication)

A la recherche d'une discipline economique by M. Allais, in *Economic Journal* (Sept. 1950).

Income and Wealth, series I, ed. E. Lundberg, in *Journal of Political Economy* (1952).

Welfare and Competition by T. Scitovsky, in *Econometrica* (1952).

Welfare Economics and the Theory of the State by W. J. Baumol, in *Economica* (Feb. 1953).

Principles of Private and Public Planning by W. Keilhau, in *Economic Journal* (Mar. 1953).

The History of Economic Analysis by J. A. Schumpeter, in *Economic History Review* (1955).

An Expenditure Tax by N. Kaldor, in *Economic Journal* (Mar. 1956).

The Role of the Economist as Official Adviser by W. A. Johr and H. W. Singer, trans. J. Degras and S. Frowein, in *Economic Journal* (Mar. 1956).

Theoretical Welfare Economics by J. de V. Graaff, *Economica* (Aug. 1957).

Some Economic Aspects of the Bhakra Nangal Project by K. N. Raj, in *Economic Journal* (June 1961).

Indian Economic Policy and Development by P. T. Bauer, in *Economic Journal* (Dec. 1961).

Equilibrium and Growth in the World Economy by R. Nurkse, in *Economic Journal* (Sept. 1962).

The Development of the Indian Economy by W. B. Reddaway, in *Economic Journal* (Sept. 1962).

The Management of the British Economy by J. C. R. Dow, in *Economic Journal* (Dec. 1964).

Project Selection for National Plans, i, by A. Papandreou and U. Zohar, in *Journal of Economic Literature* (1974).

Economic Growth and Social Equity in Developing Countries by I. Adelman and C. T. Morris; and *Redistribution with Growth* by H. Chenery *et al.*, in *Journal of Development Economics*, 3 (1976).

Pioneers in Development ed. G. M. Meier and D. Seers; and *The Hobbled Giant: Essays on the World Bank* by S. Please, in *Finance and Development*, 22/1 (1985).

The Role of the State in Economic Change ed. H.-J. Chang and R. Rowthorn, in *Journal of Development Economics* (1997).

Index